MW00564300

The Swimmer

Also by Patrick Barkham

The Butterfly Isles
Badgerlands
Coastlines
Islander
Wild Child
The Wild Isles *(editor)*
Wild Green Wonders *(collected journalism)*

The Swimmer

The Wild Life of Roger Deakin

Patrick Barkham

HAMISH HAMILTON
an imprint of
PENGUIN BOOKS

HAMISH HAMILTON

UK | USA | Canada | Ireland | Australia
India | New Zealand | South Africa

Hamish Hamilton is part of the Penguin Random House group of companies
whose addresses can be found at global.penguinrandomhouse.com.

First published 2023
003

Copyright © Patrick Barkham, 2023

The moral right of the author has been asserted

Set in 11.8/14.75pt Fournier MT Pro
Typeset by Jouve (UK), Milton Keynes
Printed and bound in Great Britain by Clays Ltd, Elcograf S.p.A.

The authorized representative in the EEA is Penguin Random House Ireland,
Morrison Chambers, 32 Nassau Street, Dublin D02 YH68

A CIP catalogue record for this book is available from the British Library

ISBN: 978–0–241–47147–0

www.greenpenguin.co.uk

MIX
Paper from
responsible sources
FSC www.fsc.org FSC® C018179

Penguin Random House is committed to a
sustainable future for our business, our readers
and our planet. This book is made from Forest
Stewardship Council® certified paper.

For Roger's friends, who came up 'like weeds,
spontaneous and unstoppable'

Life is not a walk across an open field.
Ken Warpole, friend of Roger, citing a consolatory Russian proverb

Try and see life steadily and see it whole. That's what one of our schoolmasters would say to us.
Ben Barker-Benfield, schoolfriend of Roger

Contents

A BRIEF CHRONOLOGY

Introducing some of Roger's friends and relations

(see back pages for full index of people)

1940s

11 February 1943 Roger Stuart Deakin born in Watford to *Gwen* and *Alvan Deakin*. They are thirty-four and he is their first and only child. He grows up in a two-bedroom semi-detached bungalow in Hatch End, an outer suburb of London.

1950s

September 1953 Roger wins a 'direct grant' paid by his local council so he can attend Haberdashers' Aske's Hampstead School. Here he meets lifelong friends *Tony Axon* and *Tony Weston*, who later, with his wife, *Bundle Weston*, inspires Roger's purchase and restoration of Walnut Tree Farm.

1960s

October 1960 Roger is following the trial of D. H. Lawrence's novel *Lady Chatterley's Lover* in the newspapers when his father, Alvan, dies suddenly of heart failure on the London Underground. He is fifty-one.

1961 Roger obtains a place to study English at Peterhouse College, Cambridge. In his final year, he becomes friends with *Dudley Young*, who later takes an academic post at the University of Essex. Roger looks up to him but Dudley divides opinion among his friends; the pair eventually fall out over *Waterlog*.

1964 Roger graduates from Cambridge and moves to London, renting a ramshackle flat in Bayswater. His first job in advertising is with Colman, Prentice and Varley but he also buys and sells furniture on the Portobello Road. He becomes friends with flatmate *Tony Barrell*, a great wit and rebel, who later moves to Australia.

1967 Takes a copywriting job with Leo Burnett, buys a Morgan sports car and falls in love with *Margot Waddell*, a friend of Dudley in Cambridge. Roger is turned down by Margot but she becomes a trusted friend and confidante.

1968 Meets *Jenny Kember née Hind*; they marry in 1973 and their son, *Rufus Deakin*, is born in 1974. The couple separate in 1977.

1969 House-hunting with Jenny in Suffolk, they find the ruin that becomes Walnut Tree Farm in the village of Mellis.

1970S

1970 Buys Walnut Tree Farm for £2,000; soon after acquires four fields: a total of twelve acres. Begins restoring the old farm, helped by friends and local builders.

1972 Appointed creative director of Interlink advertising agency; commutes between London and Suffolk.

1974–75 Affair with *Jo Southon*, a colleague at Interlink.

1975 Takes a position teaching English at Diss Grammar School.

1978 Leaves Diss Grammar and becomes a freelance consultant for Friends of the Earth, working on campaigns including Save the Whale!

1980S

1980 Meets *Serena Inskip* who becomes his partner until 1990. In 1981, she moves into Walnut Tree Farm with Roger.

1982 Co-founds the charity Common Ground with *Angela King* and *Sue Clifford*.

1982–83 Promoter for Aldeburgh Festival, successfully bringing rock, pop and folk concerts to Suffolk, including American star Carole King.

1990S

1990 Works on *A Beetle Called Derek*, an ITV series for young people about the environment.

1990 Splits from Serena and gets together with his old friend Margot, now an influential psychotherapist at the Tavistock Centre in London.

1991–95 Makes ITV documentaries covering subjects including allotments, the Southend rock-music scene and glass houses.

1995 Separates from Margot. Comes up with an idea for 'The Swimming Book'.

1996 Signs a contract to write 'The Swimming Book' – later *Waterlog* – for Chatto.

1997 Roger's mum, Gwen Deakin, dies on 17 August aged eighty-eight.

1997–98 Relationship with the composer *Errollyn Wallen*. Important male friends alongside his lifelong school 'chums' in the latter part of Roger's life include the writer *Terence Blacker*, art director *Gary Rowland*, and film production designer *Andrew Sanders*.

1999 *Waterlog* is published.

2000s

2000–01 Relationship with *Annette Kobak*, biographer, broadcaster, writer and painter.

2001 Signs a deal to write 'Touching Wood' for Hamish Hamilton, which is published in 2007 as *Wildwood*.

2001–04 Travels widely to research *Wildwood*, including trips to Australia, Kazakhstan, Kyrgyzstan and Ukraine.

2002–06 Relationship with *Alison Hastie*, Roger's partner until his death.

2003 Becomes friends with the writer and academic *Robert Macfarlane*, who later accepts Roger's request to be his literary executor.

2006 Diagnosed with a brain tumour in April. Roger dies at home, at Walnut Tree Farm, on 19 August. He is sixty-three.

Introduction

Here lies One Whose Name was writ in Water
The final lines on the grave of John Keats

The wellspring of Roger Deakin's life can be found in a small village scattered on the arable plains of north Suffolk. A bumpy track parts a common where the grass ripples like an inland lake in midsummer. At its end, hidden by a thicket of sallow and ash, is a low, old house made of oak from the woods and clay from the ground. Beyond is a patchwork of small meadows, dancing with butterflies and thickly hedged by blackthorn, hawthorn and bramble. Field edges are decorated with unexpected items: a disused railway wagon, a decrepit green truck, a shepherd's hut like a little chapel. Several abandoned cars appear to float in a sea of grass.

If, in the early years of this century, you stumbled upon Walnut Tree Farm, you might find Roger bent over a battered desk in the shepherd's hut, writing; or tinkering with the mechanics of an ancient grey tractor in the barn; or stoking a bonfire in the meadow; or wallowing in a claw-footed cast-iron bath set in open air on the sunny south side of the house. If you came on a summer's day, you might encounter only green silence, broken by the splash of the swimmer in the 'moat' hidden behind a curtain of hazel and rosebay willow-herb. Shaded by a tall willow at one end and a field maple at the other, this linear pond, thirty-three yards long, five yards wide and nine feet deep, was the starting point for the swimming journey that made Roger's name. Spring-fed, its water was soft and sweet. Newts hung among the duckweed that trailed like tiny stars into the depths as the swimmer stroked his way from one end to the other.

Sliding into this cool green water was a kind of shamanism for Roger. It gave him a frog's-eye view of the world, which entranced readers of his first book, *Waterlog*. Here he swam out from his moat and around Britain, not along its coastline but really *in* it, via rivers and streams, lakes, lagoons and lidos; beauty spots, secret spots, forbidden places.

It was an obscure idea, written for a modest advance, by a first-time author who was in his fifties, but *Waterlog* took off when it was published in 1999. This travel adventure, social history and memoir was so attentive to plants, animals and place that it became part of the burgeoning genre of nature writing. Readers loved seeing the British countryside in a completely new way, and they loved their guide – a funny, enthusiastic, plucky and poetic hero who wooed us with his stories.

Over time, *Waterlog*'s influence percolated many parts of society. Most prosaically, it frog-kicked a revival in open-water 'wild' swimming in Britain. Outdoor swimming clubs were reinvigorated. The physical and mental benefits of cold water that Roger explored – the 'endolphins' – were widely discussed in the media and further researched by scientists. Books, TV programmes, websites and swimwear manufacturers dived in, while Roger's reputation grew as he entertained crowds at the emerging network of literary festivals in the early 2000s.

And yet Roger never published another book in his lifetime. Barely seven years after *Waterlog* swam into the world, he was dead. For most of those years, he laboured on an ambitious book about humanity's relationship with trees and wood; *Wildwood* could only be brought into being in 2007, a year after he died. It was followed by another posthumous book, *Notes from Walnut Tree Farm*, a collection of beautiful observations drawn from his copious notebooks. The precision of his gaze and the metaphoric dazzle of his writing ensured his status grew in the years after his death when he was championed by fellow writers including his friends Robert Macfarlane and Richard Mabey. Roger came to be feted as a writerly sage and an original thinker, a kind of green god, and yet he was much more elusive and interesting.

Writing was one channel that flowed in a braided life. All generations are fascinating but Roger was one of the most compelling members of perhaps the most distinctive generation that ever lived. You will meet many more of them in these pages. The older members of this generation suffered the misfortune to be born in the midst of a war but by the time they were children there was peace, rebuilding, and eventually an economic boom. Those born in the early 1940s, such as Roger, avoided National Service by a few months and entered adulthood just as sex was invented – between the Lady Chatterley trial and the Beatles' first LP. As Roger himself observed in the sixties, there grew a 'complete chasm' between his generation and his parents'. Never before, and I think never since, has there been such a gulf between one generation and the next. Roger was in the vanguard of a cultural, social and psychological revolution as he and his peers cast off traditional tastes and mores, from notions of duty to a short back and sides. Looking back, this seems easy. His generation were given great gifts – a welfare state, social mobility, plentiful jobs, cheap property and accessible global travel – but they made the most of their opportunities. And their renunciation of decades of ossified ways of being did not come easily; it had to be conceived and struggled into existence. Roger and his friends committed to a lifetime of challenge, exploration and change. Some, in their eighties now, are still adventuring and protesting.

Many new ways of doing things that they forged have become commonplace in contemporary life. Roger cast off the conventions of suburbia, the nuclear family and the nine-to-five. He curated his own 'family', a circle of 'chums'. He was a freelancer with a portfolio career long before such working patterns were widespread and an environmentalist before the word was minted. Alongside such firsts are lasts. He was among the last of an age which is lost to us today – when a child could roam far from home and form their own intimate bonds with animals, plants and places; when life could be improvised and when generalists ruled; when an adult with a certain level of education and a socially acceptable skin colour seemed free to turn their hand to almost anything, without any training, or talk their way in anywhere.

Roger's career riffles like a wild river, full of unexpected meanders as improbable dreams become reality. As a child, he developed a profound curiosity about wild life, wild places and people, wondering how they lived and what was on their mind. He brimmed with enthusiasm for so many things. As a young man, he became an advertising executive in swinging Soho in 1964 but (implausibly) claimed he earned more money buying and selling furniture – recycling and upselling stripped pine – on the Portobello Road. As the sixties ended, he dropped out and headed to the country, raised goats and raised his own house. After restoring this timbered ruin, he became an English teacher. Later he morphed into an environmental activist, playing a key role in the Save the Whale! campaign. In 1982, he co-founded a prescient new charity, Common Ground, which championed 'ordinary' countryside – hedgerows, verges, orchards – via artistic happenings. Somehow, he also found the time to become an impresario, putting on small gigs and then major concerts. Later, he took up film-making, writing, directing and producing some elegiac stories of everything from allotment life to end-of-the-pier shows. Finally, in writing books, he found a single but constantly changing line of work that seemed a perfect fit for his temperament and desires.

These are his career facts but Roger springs to life via incidents such as: in childhood, he made money by collecting and selling bulrushes; as a teenager, he customised his friend's lifeguard badge to gain the plum summer job of lifeguarding at a local pool without any qualifications; as an adult, he kept newly hatched chicks in the basement of his ad agency; travelling home, he talked a train driver into slowing down the London to Norwich express so he could jump on to the footpath beside his house rather than proceed, like an ordinary passenger, to the station five miles to the north.

Roger embodied an age of freedom and rebellion but such declarations give solidity to a life that shimmered with constant movement. Jobs, schemes and relationships came and went but the magical kingdom he created at

Walnut Tree Farm was always there. Like the lines Roger admired by the poet John Donne, the farm and its fields were the fixed foot of a compass while he was the foot that moved around it. 'Thy firmness makes my circle just, / And makes me end, where I begun.' The farm, he declared in a letter to a friend in the 1970s, is 'so much a product of my imagination, that I feel complete there as nowhere else. Indeed the more I'm there the more of myself I leave there when I go away, so I feel less and less me when I go away.' And yet he continued to leave his place in Suffolk, restlessly travelling, adventuring, seeking.

'Complicated' is one of his friends' favourite adjectives for him. Roger was gregarious and he needed to be alone; a countryman who cleaved to the city; a passionate environmentalist who adored fast cars; defiantly modern and worshipping the past; a lover of peace and a loser of his temper. As one partner put it, Roger possessed a compulsion to jump boundaries. Enigmatic, amphibious, watery: whatever he did, slipping through life, the Swimmer was determined to resist the anchor, the mooring, the still water – and the deeps.

*

Here lies One Whose Name was writ in Water. Roger noted down the lines on the gravestone of John Keats when he visited the Romantic poet's resting place in the Cimitero Acattolico in Rome in 1982. Roger's transcription is, literally, watery – his notebook ink blotted by a summer rainstorm. I came to realise the truth of this epitaph for Roger too after I wrote 90,000 words of conventional biography and found they ill-served the fluid spirit of an unconventional man. My first draft had a definitiveness that Roger eschewed. I wanted to shrug off judgements and labels. Besides, Roger wrote more beautifully about his life than I could. So I made him the lead narrator.

Roger was a writer long before he became a published author. His nine-year-old self wrote about his travels. His twenty-five-year-old self penned advertising copy. His fifty-year-old self wrote television documentary scripts for a living. All the while, he scrawled marvellous letters to entertain his friends. And his notebooks were the siblings he never had, to whom he confided his feelings and impressed with stories.

I began mining the shards of memoir he dropped into these notebooks and letters, jottings and journalism, and put them together into a life story that felt true to him. The structure is mine – Roger didn't really do structure – but each story and its style are his. Roger usually wrote many drafts of the same tale and I've tried to create the best version, which wasn't always the last one. I've excavated fragments of memoir that were deemed superfluous to the final version of a book or a feature story but are relevant here. For instance, the original draft of a magazine story he wrote about ice-skating contained vivid childhood memories which were cut from the published version. Throughout, I've added moments of narration, a little extra research and a few factual details in Roger's voice but I have never invented scenes or introduced feelings that he did not express.

To give you an example of my method, one of my favourite Roger stories is the time he was dispatched to Venice to write some advertising copy for the Royal Navy in the summer of '69. This tale opens Chapter 5 and the first paragraph, which sets the scene in a 'biographical' way, was written by me. But the genius of the story which unfolds was almost word-for-word typed up by Roger at the time in a letter to his friend Margot Waddell. He was entertaining and impressing her; the glorious descriptive writing, the pacing, the swearing, the comic scenes and the denouement are all his. I've slipped in a couple of extra details – for instance, '*Bulwark*'s captain, known by the men as "TC", was reputedly famous for a "fastidious wit"' – which Roger might have added were he writing it up as autobiography. The two short paragraphs which conclude this episode by revealing the copy he produced and the fate of his advertising career are mine.

In the final three years of Roger's life, his mind cast back more and more, and he filled his notebooks with vivid recollections from early childhood. He appears to have been inching towards a memoir but he never began one and so the opening chapter is a little more creative: I imagine how Roger might have started this book were he well enough to do so in 2006. Even here, many of the words are his, blended from drafts of *Waterlog* and transcriptions of voice recordings he made on a Dictaphone while driving between Suffolk and London. Later in this biography, when Roger's life – and particularly his love life – is beset by cross-currents, I play it very straight, and only quote directly from what Roger wrote at the time or afterwards.

Throughout this biography, Roger's enraptured view of his world is interspersed with the memories of his friends. Sometimes these are from their letters or published writing but mostly they are from many hours of conversation with me. Their testimonies provide multiple interpretations of the same events, and cast doubt on the idea of life as one simple flow. When the going is good, travelling between Roger's writing and the recollections of his friends feels like a witty conversation. I can picture the warmth between him and his great friend Tony Axon as they trade comic stories of their schooldays. But the exchanges between Roger's viewpoint and those of his lovers provide a more nuanced duet, sometimes harmonious in its mutuality and occasionally discordant, furious or tragic.

My method is not flawless. If history is written by the victors, then survivors have the best opportunity to write biographical history. Roger's partners have the final word on their relationships with him and he, of course, cannot respond. One person's portrait of a past relationship, even in the calm distance of many years on, is likely to be coloured by the way it ended. Marrying Roger's ecstatic 'before' to a lover's cooler 'after' might create the impression that Roger was an impossible man, who was gifted glorious relationships and then threw them away. Was he? I can almost hear his protestations: 'no, no, you misunderstand – it wasn't like that at all'. Lacking his no-doubt-disarming defence, I hope you have enough evidence here to make up your own mind, if this kind of judgement is important to you.

Readers may ponder how I've presented clashing realities. I can only declare that I have tried feverishly hard to be honest and fair, to not load the dice or provide false balance in moments of controversy. Where there is conflict, I've only quoted people who have direct knowledge of a particular event. I've ignored hearsay. Critical voices have not been silenced but nor have they been amplified. If one person is quoted in these pages making a specific point, it has usually been raised by other unquoted people too. I've not included discredited views and I've not included information that I know to be wrong just to discredit someone.

*

I never met Roger Deakin, and it is strange to come to know him so intimately and not know him at all. We shared the same sky. I grew up in rural Norfolk and understand his love of nature and his experience of the uncompromising arable landscape of East Anglia. Even though I was born here, I know how Roger felt as an outsider in a region where farmers and landowners call the shots.

My parents belonged to Roger's generation, and arrived in East Anglia shortly before he did, also buying land and keeping goats. My dad is a month older than Roger, while Roger's son, Rufus, is a month older than me. Like Roger, my dad grew a mass of curly hair, rebelled against the stultifying mores of his parents' generation, and became an environmentalist and an inspirational teacher. Surprisingly, given the small worlds that are environmentalism and East Anglia, they never met either.

Early on, I thought not having encountered Roger would bequeath me a crisp, clear and neutral gaze. What was I thinking? How can a dispassionate method well serve a passionate man? There's a lovely line by Tom Stoppard: *biography is the mesh through which real life escapes*. Despite watching videos of Roger, listening to his voice and reading a million or so of his words, I came to crave his physical presence to engender that innate sympathy we feel for another living being.

As I learned more of Roger's life, I became haunted by the possibility that we had passed each other in the street, or inhabited the same space at the same time. In the early 1990s, my dad moved to a cottage on Church Street in Eye, the small town three miles from Roger's home. I regularly visited Dad there, little knowing that less than fifty yards up the street lived Roger's mum, Gwen, whom Roger visited regularly at the same era. Roger also researched *Waterlog* in the University Library in Cambridge just when I was sat there too, swotting for my finals. When I moved to London in the late nineties, I hung out in the North London pubs and restaurants where Roger also arranged to meet friends. Researching this biography, I discovered he had read my *Guardian* journalism, a distant relative of mine worked with him and, most bizarrely, I bought my first home from one of his neighbours. I hoped a lost memory would pop into my head: suddenly, there was Roger, standing before me. It never arrived.

Finally, early in 2021, Roger materialised, wearing a dark green jumper, in one of my dreams. He was slightly hunched but then he stood up and straightened his shoulders and I saw that he was a formidable person. He was enthusing about something, and punched me lightly on the arm. I saw his energy, and how he took people with him; for the first time, I felt it.

Shortly before I decided to make Roger the narrator, he appeared again in my subconscious. This time, he travelled with me and my family on the train, disembarking at Diss. As the train stopped, he lingered in the carriage by the door and I saw that he was fragile and far more vulnerable than everyone realised. I opened the door for him and held his arm as he stumbled. As he departed, he asked: 'Is there anything else I can help you with?'

I guess it was a leading question.

Can we rely on a great romantic to be an honest biographer of themselves? Can we rely on anyone to be an honest biographer of themselves? Am I the ghost or is Roger the ghost? After thirty months following in his wake, inhabiting his territory, residing in his mind, meeting him in my dreams, listening to him and his friends, and interrogating many versions of his shared history, I'm still not sure.

Would Roger like 'his' biography? Honestly, I think his first reaction would be shock and probably outrage. Every little detail mattered to him. These are his words, but he would have put them together in another way. And my way isn't his, no matter how hard I try. Perhaps, one night, I'll be granted another five minutes with Roger in my dreams where I can explain. I will say, I've done my best to be true to you and to your friends who have lived, loved and sometimes suffered with you. Thank you for helping us see more of the world and its glory. Thank you for seeking freedom, for living so fully, for challenging those around you, and for being true to yourself. Thank you for your generation, who have parented my own and who continue to shape our world, for better and for worse, long after they have ceased sharing our skies.

Patrick Barkham

CHAPTER I

Lucky Dip

No one, least of all me, can evoke Rog better than he himself.
Margot Waddell, memorial service address for Roger, 2007

What we have to decide is whether life is a little, cautious, grasping affair,
or whether it is wonderful.
Roger Deakin, The Whale Declaration, *1979*

It is early 2006, and Roger is distracted.

*

One day almost a decade ago, a summer storm fell on my moat. Water tumbled from the gutters as I shrugged off everything in the kitchen and ran out through the long wet grass. It was warm and somehow safe in the moat. I swam length after length – thirty yards of clear, green water – breaststroke, enjoying the clean incision of my out-thrust hands as if in prayer, out-flung arms as if in exultation. The frog's-eye view of the rain on the water was magnificent. Rain calms water, it freshens it, and sinks all the floating pollen, dead bumblebees and other flotsam. Each raindrop exploded in a momentary bouncing fountain that turned into bubbles and burst. The downpour intensified, and a haze rose off the water, as though the pond itself was rising to meet the lowering sky. Then the storm eased, and the pond was full of tiny dancers; water-sprites springing up like bright pins over the surface. All water was once rain. Swimming through all this I had the curious sensation of being dry, of having found the best shelter of all from the storm; a guest of the pond goddess.

That June deluge became the beginning of my book, *Waterlog*, in which I swam through the British Isles. One idea changed my life and it seems to have changed the lives of others, but for months it was simply one idea among a multitude. My brain felt like those pieces of litter blown about on the side of a motorway, scattered between Suffolk and London and my too-frequent peregrinations. I was a freelance film-maker in midlife, an environmentalist, and a creator of charities, campaigns, schemes and adventures. I had a base but no ties, at the end of a long love, with my son Rufus having reached adulthood and journeyed to Australia. I subsisted, as always, on ideas, which I recorded on a Dictaphone as I drove my ageing Citroën CX GTI, at speed, between homes and friends and meetings.

How about a film about complaining called *Moanin'*? The London International Festival of Whistling on the South Bank? A documentary about the Norfolk freemasonry? A film about Welsh male-voice choirs around the world? A programme on the last pie and mash shops? A film about lawns? Treehouses? What about that great unheralded workhorse of the garden, the wheelbarrow? A series of string-quartet concerts in swimming pools to replace ghastly piped 'muzak'? A short story set in an allotment? Or *Now Listen Here*, a series about contemporary music that would 'open wide the mind's cage-door', as Keats put it?

One idea, 'The Swimming Book', rose above the clamour. Various friends had long badgered me to write a book but there was always a more pressing diversion: a house, a renovation, a relationship, a hay-cut; an object, project, event or campaign. I was fifty-three and I had always resisted the anchor or becoming becalmed in still waters. 'The Swimming Book' demanded to be written. But the act of swimming also turned me into a writer. What you need to write is energy, sexual potency and solitude. Swimming gave me plenty of all three.

I was never a champion swimmer but I have swum since I was a small boy, and usually outdoors. I schemed my way to a job as an unqualified teenage lifeguard and rowed on England's rivers for my school and university college. Throughout my life, I have mucked about in vessels of all descriptions: an aquatic bicycle I invented and built; a canoe called *Cigarette*; a Royal Navy destroyer. Once, at school, I won a breaststroke race, and I stuck with it in adulthood. Gliding through the water, head up, is the naturalist's stroke. You see more, placed on equal terms with the animal world around you: the newt, the moorhen and the grass snake, coiling its way across the surface of the water, head held high as if it does not like to get splashed.

The swimming journey first suggested itself in my moat, a linear pond dug into the clay to the south of my sixteenth-century farmhouse. The yeoman farmer-builder who excavated it found a useful source of clay for the base of the house; it created a barrier of sorts against livestock; and it was a status symbol in this part of Suffolk, where late-medieval moats are commonplace. During the three and a half decades I have lived here, the moat has been a leaf-filled swamp, a boating lake, a dining room – when thickly iced – and my own, spring-fed, plant-cleansed natural pool.

When I began *Waterlog*, I became obsessed with what D. H. Lawrence calls the 'third thing'. For nearly three years, I gave my life over to the elusive element that is water. The writer and the swimmer in me both had an identical aim – to leave our baggage behind and float free. Like all swimming, this was an escape, and it was also stimulation and consolation. Immersion in natural water has always possessed a magical power to cure. I can dive in with a long

face and what feels like a terminal case of depression, and come out a whistling idiot. Swimming was my Keatsian 'taking part in the existence of things'
and it bequeathed a new way of seeing the world. Britain looks very different
from its ponds, streams, rivers, lakes and seas. On land, so much is signed,
interpreted or controlled that reality becomes virtual reality. The watery
realm resists all that. Travelling in water becomes a subversive activity, as I
discovered when I swam the trout-filled riffles of the Itchen and was accosted
by the River Keeper of Winchester College. Crossing the Fowey, in Cornwall, I was chastised by the coastguard for making the swim without the
harbourmaster's permission. I was mistaken for 007 when emerging from a
stately home's ornamental lagoon. I contracted *Frenchman's Creek* swamp
fever, I was panged by the guilt of being a philanderer of rivers, and I experienced the numbing chill and purple knees provided by the swirling brown
North Sea on Christmas Day.

The climax of my aquatic tour of Britain was the discovery of a hidden
canyon, a deep gash in the limestone beyond the top of Wensleydale filled
with white water. My descent into Hell Gill's dim and glistening insides, a
succession of cold baths, was one long primal scream. It was a rebirth and a
rite of passage, like every swim. But there was a greater, cumulative effect
from all these natural swims. Some people pass through holes in trees or walk
over hot coals. It is a response to a simple need to change in the same way as
trees shed their leaves in autumn or grow new ones in spring. I swam in cold
water. The tree has branches lopped off but grows out new shoots. It may
bear more fruit the following year.

To my surprise and delight, *Waterlog*, an obscure idea with a small print
run, has continued to bear fruit since it was published in 1999, an occasion we
marked with music, drinking and swimming at the outdoor council pool
behind Covent Garden. As dog-eared, water-smudged copies are passed
between friends, *Waterlog*'s journey has inspired people to discover or redis-
cover wild water. Clubs that coalesce around ancestral swimming spots on
stretches of river that were once moribund are busy with members once again.
Campaigns to save civic pools gain vigour.

In the six years since, I've splashed through the shallows of celebrity life –
breakfast shows, columns, literary festivals – which is not something I ever
coveted. Meanwhile, I have plunged into the cool depths of researching what
Edward Thomas called 'the fifth element'. I have immersed myself in trees to
write 'Touching Wood', a book about wood as it exists in nature, in our souls
and in our lives. 'A culture is no better than its woods,' wrote Auden and our

woods, like water, have been suppressed by the modern world. They have come to look like the subconscious of the landscape.

I've been telling stories since I could talk, just as in the beginning my mother told stories to me. My first were boyhood fantasies I shared with friends after escaping my tiny bungalow on the edge of London for the spinneys and ponds then found nearby; next came essays at school where my best teachers did not suppress a child's natural inventiveness; letters to chums about interesting travels to boost their spirits; and then stories to make a living and sell products, stories to delight and seduce. All the while, my own tales were electrified by the thousands I read, particularly romantic yarns of adventure and liberation: Blyton, Crompton, Stevenson; Lawrence, Keats, Jefferies.

A year after the beginning of sexual intercourse as identified by Philip Larkin, I graduated and moved to London. Through the sixties, I wrote blurb for Penguin Books – *Rogue Male* and other thrillers by Geoffrey Household – becoming a copywriter and then creative director for advertising agencies in Soho. I sold stories about Coca-Cola, BMW and British Coal. 'Come Home to a Real Fire' was my best-known line, reasserting the pleasure of a real fire in an age of central heating. Its plangent note resounded with the public, until it was recycled and subverted, as all the best lines are, by Welsh Nationalists in their incendiary campaign against second homes owned by the English.

In advertising, I learned the discipline of writing and rewriting, sanding and polishing, labouring over a single sentence for days. But I tired of the stories I was selling and so escaped to the country, where I raised goats and my own house, and taught storytelling to young people at the local grammar school. There is no more intimate way of getting to know your neighbours than by teaching their children. It was the time of the Barsham and Albion fairs in the Waveney Valley, a rural culture built by an extended family of quasi-hippy immigrants to the countryside, based on the values of the *Whole Earth Catalog* and John Seymour's *The Fat of the Land*. Self-conscious self-sufficiency sounds dreary but this was a moment of liberation and celebration. For a brief golden epoch, we built with our hands and imaginations ephemeral, dreamlike, Gypsyish, shanty capitals in fields full of folk. Dancing and music played a big part.

Later, the gigs I arranged for our local heroes led me to host major concerts for transatlantic rock stars. The films I devised with friends became documentaries shown on national television. I also organised street gatherings to save the whale, campaigning for Friends of the Earth to protect disappearing cetaceans and rainforests. As green concern became concentrated on these far horizons, I co-founded the charity Common Ground, collaborating with artists and writers to speak for our near horizon: the quiet, ordinary, local nature of hedgerows and old orchards that surrounded me at Walnut Tree Farm and should still surround us all.

I have always written down stories – dreams, fragments, reflections, moments of great joy and despair and anger – in old school notebooks that line my shelves. I live in a library made up of millions of my own words. Writing stills my mind. In recent years, I've found my thoughts restlessly returning to many minuscule memories from childhood.

My hair has turned from brown to grey and is now frost-white. The crinkles around my eyes and lips are deepening into crevasses. When I cut a branch of fallen elm, the grain seems more resistant to my saw. When I cross the moat on my return from a long adventure, past the ash and the walnut, a pair of guardian trees that watch over the place, I always feel the relief a badger must feel as it eases itself back into the sett after a hard night's foraging. Now, however, it takes me longer at rest to regain my vitality. Strange pain assails me in the night. And yet when I wake the world seems as young as ever on a glittering winter's morning. It is time. At the dawn of 2006, the time has come to share some of my stories.

CHAPTER 2

The Wild Boy

A war baby – reared outdoors – my second home, the Cosy Cabin – the luxury of daydreaming – adventures in the wilds of suburban Hatch End – an unreconstructed hunter-gatherer boy ornithologist – stilt-walking and ice-skating – the romance of travel – my father, Alvan Deakin – my great-uncle, Joseph Deakin, the Walsall anarchist – hook-handed Grandpa Wood and my hero, Uncle Laddie – more about my mother, Gwen, rebel and force to be reckoned with – claustrophobia

The bomb shelter on our street. The cherry tree on the corner. The laurel hedges I raided to fill my butterfly killing jars. Singing lessons with Mrs Gillard, putting her hands on my stomach as I sang. Skating with Ann Wilks. The sound of the bass booming into my pillow on Saturday nights from the dance band at the recreation pavilion. The roller skates bump-bumping over the gaps between paving stones as we sped downhill past the railings through which we fed Mr Stimpson's chickens with bread crusts. Major Cracknell. Mrs Cracknell yelling at Hitler to get off her garden fence. 'You think I can't see you, but I know you're there. Come out of there, you devil!' She would rattle at the fence with her broomstick. We minded our own business.

Britain was at war when I was born but my earliest memories are of peace. I lay gazing at sunshine dappling the leaves of the trees above me, placed in the optimum spot in the garden for growing by my mother, who believed that leaves filtered sunlight, allowing the most beneficial of its rays to pass through and nourish me with vitamin D. I must be as brown as a berry, and so I was parked in my pram under lilacs, hazels and apple trees behind our tiny half-bungalow at the point where London ended and the countryside began.

There was a run of glorious summers in the forties. Looking back, I remember every daylight moment being in the garden with my mother, who was evangelical about the benefits of fresh air. My early childhood was mostly a relationship of two, my mother and I, together in the garden that she cherished. I was the apple of her eye. Like most war babies, I saw less of my father, Alvan. He was serving as a warrant officer in the RAF, controlling the movement of troops. He was at home more than many fathers during the conflict but he was stationed in Germany after the war's end until 1946. And at home, my father rather shrank from view. Mum was the force of nature.

Gwen and Alvan came to parenting late by the standards of the day. They were in their thirties when they married, in Warwick, in September 1940, and were both thirty-four when I was born on 11 February 1943. No more offspring followed so I was an only child: lively, healthy, much admired and perpetually grubby. Tousled hair, grimy hands, dirty feet, filthy clothes. What a mess. Mum would despair. Sometimes, I eschewed clothes altogether, running naked in our back garden, which was much bigger than our two-bedroomed semi-detached home. I was full of energy and conversation and a lust for adventure. On one occasion I fell into the cess pit in the garden; another time, I tried to bring down the enormous elm in the bottom hedge, aiming a hatchet at a minuscule notch over what seemed like several years, barely making an impression, while my parents benignly turned the other way.

No. 6 Randon Close was built on high ground in the suburbs north of Harrow. Behind our garden was Hall's dairy farm, which must have been some of the closest farmland to the city. Standing in the garden with London at my back, I gazed out at what seemed to be the whole of rural England stretching into the distance beyond Hatch End and Pinner Hill. Looking from our front door in the opposite direction were rolling suburbs, houses increasing in density all the way to the city's centre, which could be reached in a three-minute trot to the station at Headstone Lane and a half-an-hour train, or a slower tube on the Bakerloo line. My father was one of the commuters who lined the platform each morning to catch the train to his job with British Railways, based at Euston station. One side country, the other side town; I've kept one foot in each throughout my life.

JOHN MILLS, *older cousin* People used to say, 'He is rather precocious, isn't he?' Highly intelligent but people found him trying at times. He was quite hyperactive. He was into everything as a young boy. He had these crazes – from one thing to another – but was particularly involved with wildlife.

ANDREW CROOK, *cousin* As a child, Roger told you everything he did. He could be rather bolshy and pushy. He was eighteen months older than me and that gave him a huge amount of power. He was quite intimidating on occasions and he used to make comments that I didn't understand.

I longed for some alternative habitat to our cramped kitchen and living room, and my father built it for me at the bottom of the garden. It was a wooden shed, and we called it the Cosy Cabin. We wrote the name on a tin sign above the door. It was my refuge from the trials of family life and school, and I was allowed to sleep there on a camp bed in summer.

I assembled a family of animals to live with me: beetles and woodlice in matchboxes, guinea pigs, rabbits, white mice and other pets I procured from the wild, including pigeons. Some creatures, a toad for instance, would enter as guests and be observed for a while before being set free. I remember the toasty aroma of the animals' straw bedding, fresh hay, the rank hogweed I collected each morning, and the sound of multiplying rodents chewing contentedly. In my bedroom there were grass snakes, lizards, tree frogs, stick insects, fossils, and a praying mantis or two on the curtains. I had a pet crow at one time, which would sit on my shoulder. Gerald Durrell was my favourite author; these creatures were my friends. My parents' indulgence fills me with amazement and gratitude. I didn't know it then but my father was much influenced by Henry David Thoreau and his retreat was a shed complete with nine bean-rows in the bee-loud glade of the local allotments. He was also fond of quoting William Cobbett, who observed how pigeons gave children 'the early habit of fondness for animals'. As an only child, relationships with other animals were hugely important to me.

In the Cosy Cabin, I learned the sheer luxury of daydreaming. It has been my making and my undoing. How many days, weeks, months have I lost to it? Perhaps it isn't lost time at all, but the most valuable thing I could have done.

My nocturnal dream world was a big part of my life too. My lucid, serial dreams are still quite as real to me now as they were then. I had a dream friend, and went to bed each night secure in the certainty that I would continue my serial dream with her. She was slightly older than me, and the relationship was entirely asexual. We went on adventures, we talked, and other dream chums entered our world. I could break off in mid-dream in the morning and resume it that night. This dream world was a happy one, and a consolation from daily life, even though my childhood was far from unhappy. The dream friendship was central to my existence, but so far as I know I spoke of it to no one. My parents never had the slightest trouble in getting me off to bed. Much later, I was reassured to learn from Ronald Blythe that he had a slightly senior female dream friend as well.

ROGER DEAKIN, The Wellingtonian *school magazine, Easter 1953*

My Dreams

My dreams I always dream,
So strange they usually seem,
To trees a furlong high
The birds do backwards fly,
And leopards lurking in the trees
To feast upon my bonny knees.
The dreary morning comes at last,
And all the strangest dreams are past.

*

Like every child of my era, I was soon roaming beyond the confines of my garden. Through the bottom hedge was a large field, two ponds and a brook, still preserved today as they were then in the green belt – we called it London's Corset as teenagers. The green may remain but the range and abundance of species has long gone. In the fifties, I found hares and herons, partridges and plovers. The cuckoo called above the trundle of suburban trains. Occasionally, I might put up a snipe.

My friend David Baldwin and I were kings of this wild frontier. We equipped ourselves with wooden rifles, spud guns and an aluminium Vibro catapult that would shoot out a boy's eye at twenty paces. We obtained Davy Crockett hats made of rabbit skin with tails down the back and sang the song about the King of the Wild Frontier from the Disney movie as we built dens.

Sticks were our weapons of choice. They were useful in woods for thrashing a path through nettles and also provided hours of fun for me and a family of five brothers called Winney when we discovered that the whip in green sticks of ash or hazel could be used to propel balls of moist clay impaled on the tip huge distances from our back gardens over the rooftops. As soon as our parents were out, salvoes of mud shells would rain on to the street on a wing and a prayer that no one was passing by.

From sticks we made arrows and fishing-net handles. You could never hold a stick without reaching for your penknife, which was the beginning of all craft. Sticks taught me the basic anatomy of wood and how it behaves under the blade: how it splits, how it bends, how it breaks, how bark peels to reveal the white sapwood and how, when you whittle it, you come to the pithy centre, or the brown heartwood, or encounter the sudden toughness at the junction of a branch. Hours of whittling with my penknife taught me about the relative resistance of each different wood, the hardest being the seasoned oak lid of my school desk.

We played Robin Hood with Mr Stimpson, the bailiff of the nearby dairy farm, unwittingly cast in the role of the Sheriff of Nottingham. We crept about in the corn, or hid in the fringes of the wood observing Stimpson's movements intently. We learned to recognise the excitement of his poultry when he fed them and knew he would be sufficiently distracted at such moments for us to make a bolt across the green field to the cover of the trees.

This spinney was the closest wood to home. But Bricket Wood was the ultimate destination for our expeditions, combining the mysteries of nature and of sex. When we were thirteen or fourteen, we messed about on track bikes which were not motorbikes (except in our heads) but rudimentary bicycles made from bits of scrap Rudge, Raleigh or Dawes in our back gardens. They had only one gear, a very low one, and gas-piping cow-horn handlebars so wide it was all we could do to stretch out and reach the rubber grips, let alone get them through the garden gate. There were no mudguards and, at most, a single unreliable brake. Instead of inner tubes, we put hosepipe in the tyres, so each time the join came round the bike bucked like a bronco and almost threw us off. The machines were fiendishly uncomfortable and no good for our fertility. Mine was adorned with a squirrel's pelt with its tail flying out rakishly from behind. It gave me the appearance of an escaped character from *The Wind in the Willows*. I have no idea why I thought it might be attractive to girls.

Dismounting after a morning's sport, we would ease ourselves painfully along Hatch End High Street like cowboys in new chaps. If these were pioneering mountain bikes, they differed from their modern counterparts in a far more fundamental respect than sophistication: we did not consume these things, we invented and made them.

For a long time, I was too scared to climb trees. I was the one left standing at the bottom squinting up through the branches asking, 'What can you see from up there?' Letters from chums travelling have always since sounded to me like those shaming accounts of church spires, distant mountain ranges, barrage balloons, fire engines dashing down lanes and (from very tall trees) the sea. Things I could have seen for myself if I'd had the guts to risk breaking a leg.

Perhaps my fear dated from the time we Cubs assembled for our first jamboree on one of the further fields of Hall's Farm. We arrived flushed with the glory of a grand march, complete with brass band and drums, along the high street. Our arms still ached from holding up the banner of the 1st Hatch End Cubs, now lying furled beside us. Cross-legged and expectant, we sat in rows under a hot August sun, leaning forward for a better view. We didn't seem to notice the acute discomfort of the stubble-field assaulting the tender skin of our inner thighs. We waited before a fine old oak in which a gang of Scouts, proud owners of the tree-climbing badge, were going to demonstrate the gentle art to us groundlings.

We were bidden to silence as the first Scout began to scale the tree, swinging himself up like a gibbon through the lower limbs. He went higher, disappearing now and then in the shadow of foliage. He was tall and blonde and he made it look easy. The higher he climbed, the further his socks slipped down to his plimsolls. Then, quite suddenly as he scrambled into the top branches, there was a loud report – a branch cracking – and he came spinning down through the leaves like a shot pigeon.

His falling seemed to happen very slowly, and the sound of his body crashing through branches and leaves lives on in me now. Then came the thud as he hit the ground. It made us all feel sick and frightened. None of us had ever witnessed a human body being so seriously injured. The blonde boy lay there, winded, silent. Then his groaning began. Scoutmasters and Cub mistresses gathered round him and brought blankets. Two St John Ambulance men in black uniforms appeared and knelt down. It seemed ages before an ambulance came bumping over the field. Nobody said anything to us, and nobody dared ask. They carried on with the jamboree, minus the tree-climbing. The ambulance drove off with him, leaving the broken branch behind.

The diving board at Watford baths was another terror. In the pool, I measured myself against my own fear; climbing to the first board, and then the second, and finally the stomach-wrenching top board, where I stepped off into space, as I have done a hundred times since in my dreams. Stepped off for what seemed like a five-minute fall down to the green tiles at the bottom.

Water was always part of my childhood universe. My friends and I dammed the muddy autumn streams in the field-ditch just beyond our garden and raced our pooh sticks down its mighty nine-inch flood, clearing the oak leaves and brambles that impeded their progress as diligently as river engineers. In the middle of the field, behind a veil of willows, was a large pond. Our arrival would send up the heron with a grouchy cry and a slow beating of wings. At the pond's edge, like the heron, we could pounce on exotic European tree frogs, a small, brilliant-green amphibian which must have been introduced there by local hobbyists who, like me, would routinely top up home-made aquariums with whatever wild treasures they could seize.

The day we first discovered the carp in that pond was like finding pieces of eight glinting out of the green depths. Keeping an eye out for Mr Stimpson, we would surreptitiously fish for the carp with the relish of poachers. Elsewhere, there were bomb sites to explore, still abandoned a decade after the Blitz. The wild reasserted itself so fast: fireweed, brambles and buddleia rampaging over the rubble.

I was an unreconstructed hunter-gatherer boy ornithologist, typical of the fifties, when children who loved nature freely collected whatever they could catch. A snail, a pebble, a leaf, a dead beetle, a chrysalis, a bit of sheep's wool on a fence – my pockets were a bird's nest, a microcosm of the local landscape, of habitat and haunts. My finds were of great personal value to me, although my most prized possession was the net I used to catch butterflies, which were plentiful during that run of fine post-war summers. Mine was no home-made bamboo-and-net-curtain affair but a serious professional model with aluminium frame. In the evening, I caught moths by lurking, net poised, beside a bright light run off an extension lead out to the garden. I gathered laurel leaves from the neighbours' hedges and crushed them in a 'killing jar', producing a natural chloroform that rapidly subdued my captives. While the insects' wings were still soft, I spread them in display and pinned them to a cork board to dry. Collections were typically kept in drawers so they wouldn't fade in the sunlight but I stuck mine on my bedroom ceiling so I could lie in bed and gaze up at a firmament of Lepidoptera. Later, I took my net to my penfriend's place in the south of France and captured my first swallowtail and praying mantis which, smuggled home, was the first of many a mantis to live on the kitchen curtains.

When we stayed with my cousins, Andrew and Ian Crook, at their home in Painswick, Gloucestershire, Uncle Frank would take us to hunt for belemnites and devil's toenails, silurian brachiopods, ammonites and an occasional sea urchin at a nearby quarry. Patiently, Frank fostered our passions; flowers and fossils, quarried from the beacon. One morning, we rose early to head out with his poacher's gun and felled a squirrel. I touched the warm, thin fur, as Uncle Frank slotted back the gun into the innocent walking stick. I turned the squirrel into my first piece of taxidermy.

ANDREW CROOK This is a bit of poetic licence. Roger said he wanted to stuff a squirrel. So he talked Father into getting up at dawn, and Father took his twelve-bore shotgun and Roger and I went into the woods and Father shot a squirrel for Roger, which he brought back to the house. He then went to the chemist to get some alum and carried out the role of taxidermist. It never appeared again so perhaps it wasn't as good as it should've been.

IAN CROOK, *cousin* Speaking to my father later in life, I think he found Roger rather ill-disciplined. His parents were far more tolerant and permissive and that grated a bit with Dad. He told me he disciplined Roger on one occasion, and Roger was really angry about it. Roger thrust a stick or bamboo cane through the window of our garage and hooked paint pots off a shelf as a revenge move. Anarchic is a good word. It's also asking for trouble.

At home, my spud guns were eventually replaced by a real airgun. As a child-naturalist I took potshots at birds and rabbits in the fields. 'Consideration' is the word my parents always used. 'Have some consideration' or 'Show some consideration', a slightly different thing, so I was taught to raise the peak of my school cap to neighbours in the street and to give up my seat on the Underground to almost anyone unfortunate enough to be standing. Ladies, certainly, and older people. There was sense in this. Who needs to sit down when they're seven years old and bursting with energy?

This basic idea of consideration is at the heart of all true conservation. You act out of fellow feeling for other living things, and other people. Most of the degradation of our land, air and water is caused by selfishness. Selfishness and consideration are the two opposites that were constantly before me as choices when young. Should I do the selfish thing, fire my airgun through the neighbour's garden fence, perforating it almost to destruction? Or should I do the considerate thing and fire it dutifully at the target pinned to a tree? Or not fire it at all? I confess I enjoyed shooting very much and only gave it up when I had 'worked it out of my system'.

RODNEY JAKEMAN, *friend* I would cycle over to 6 Randon Close early on weekends and we would head out with our airguns. Often the wildlife was totally untroubled and perfectly safe. Occasionally a pigeon would be brought down.

JOHN MILLS Roger had an answer for everything. 'I didn't intend to shoot that squirrel but it happened to be in the line of the gun,' he said when he brought in a dead squirrel, which he took home and skinned. He wasn't very successful. They were always smelly things.

My natural-history adventures were in the company of male friends but there were plenty of female playmates to share the trends of the fifties. After the yo-yo craze, and about a year before the hula-hoop craze, we had a stilt craze. The neighbours, who had been driven half-mad by the sound of roller skates clicking over the gaps between the paving stones and the grinding trundle of steel wheels on concrete, were drawing a collective sigh of relief when the hollow clip-clop of an army of stilts hobbling on the cobbles assailed the net curtains of the neighbourhood.

Stilt-racing had arrived, and my playmates and I discovered the novel experience of greeting the grown-ups in our street with a lofty, condescending 'good morning' from a great height. Suddenly, we could look down on them. We could even have patted them on the head. For short-arses like sickly little Colin Voysey, stilts were the perfect answer. Not only did they achieve parity of height by adjusting their blocks a notch or two higher, but smaller children were more nimble stilt-walkers, being less top-heavy.

Our suburban stamping ground was blissfully free of traffic in those early fifties. Low brick walls separated the front gardens from the pavement along Randon Close, and we made use of them as mounting blocks. My father built me a pair of stilts in his workshop. You moved the blocks up or down by loosening a thumbscrew and inserting it in a different hole in the pine stilt-leg. Beginners started with the blocks close to the ground. The higher you set your blocks, the higher your centre of gravity, and the harder it was to balance. Losing your balance could be unnerving, and beginners tended to make crash-landings. There was soon an outbreak of grazed knees and elbows. Landing safely was always the problem. The simplest solution was to step off the stilts on to a garden wall. Otherwise, you had to fall forward as gently as possible and step off at the last moment using the stilt in the manner of a pole-vaulter. Good stilt-walkers could pole-vault up on the stilts as well and career off along the street in long, confident strides. Beginners shuffled along, wary of lifting their stilts high enough, and often tripped, with disastrous results.

Bicycles offered more mobility. When I was given a BSA too big for me on my tenth birthday, my father said, 'You'll grow into it,' and indeed by the time we were into our teens we had all spent so much of our lives on bikes we were like centaurs. I practically slept astride the crossbar.

A winter pleasure was ice-skating. Skating is one of those words that triggers a flood of memories, not least the glee that came from the postponement of ordinary life during snow and severe cold. As soon as winter clamped down with a big frost, a small gang of us would get up while it was still dark and trudge across a silver field to skate on the pond where we fished for carp in the summer. We launched ourselves across the shallow rim of the pond where it was ribbed by frozen flurries of snow and our skates rattled over the ice. Each of us wrote our own signature on the blank sheet of ice in bold swirling graffiti that soon resembled the doodles on the pad beside my home phone. The girls, in white skating boots, wrote in elegant italic script. We boys skated mostly in straight lines or zigzags, crossing out the girls' graceful calligraphy. The music of skates was a rhythmic 'swish' as the blades sliced through the virgin surface of black ice; a great contrast between the static, frozen world of ice and the explosion of energy that is skating.

The great source of the magic was that we were walking on water. Then, as we acquired some skill in the art, it was the thrill of flying across the ice. The intense experience of skating stayed with you: the frosty wind rushing up your nostrils; the shouts of joy or alarm; wrapping up, padding up; the elaborate lacing of boots. I remember the freedom more than the chilblained toes or bruised sacral vertebrae.

Sometimes we would pause, polish a window in the ice and lie on our bellies searching the black depths for the wily carp, buried snugly out of sight in the mud. Then the distant jangle of a school handbell from across the fields, wielded by my mother, would summon us back to wolf a hasty boiled egg, and set off for school, where there would be bitter, frozen milk at break-time and more steely ice in the playground: a lethal slide like a Roman arena, flanked by baying boys urging on a queue of kamikaze flyers.

*

My childhood unfolded during an era of austerity. Our home was tiny and money was a constant worry for my parents. Meat, cheese, fats, sugar, tea and sweets were still on the ration in 1950. But I had my Cosy Cabin, stilts, roller skates, ice skates, an unlimited supply of pets, and a forest of early books and radio serials that fed my hunger for fantasy and adventure. *The Famous Five*, *Just William*, *Swallows and Amazons*, *Treasure Island*, *The Land of Counterpane*, *Parlicoot's House*, and the BBC's *Norman and Henry Bones*, *The Boy Detectives*. Choosing books in the public library, it was lines like 'he reverted to a feral state' or 'he obeyed the call of the wild' that gripped my imagination. I also studied Scouting books: the 'On the Riverbank' section showed a camp, how to drive in stakes and make a clothes horse, a stick-tripod for cooking over a fire, a wood and rope bridge across a river; how to tickle trout, trap minnows, gather rosehips for syrup and blackberries for jam. There were the *Observer* field guides to identify the birds, flowers and fossils. And my child's aptitude for close observation was encouraged by the *News Chronicle*'s *I-Spy* series. These pocket-sized books, starting with *I-Spy at the Seaside* and followed by *I-Spy Birds* and *I-Spy in the Country*, contained fifty pages of pen drawings, with points awarded for each spot. I kept the books in a secret dossier made from a cigar box and labelled 'Private and Confidential – I-Spy Tribe'.

It is interesting to note how rare or common things were perceived to be in the fifties, compared to our present-day perceptions. In *I-Spy in the Country*, a grass snake scored a surprisingly low twelve, not much more than a frog, toad or scarecrow at ten, and less than the fifteen for a cattle grid. An otter scored a mere twenty, at the same level as a road sign saying, DANGER THIS ROAD IS SUBJECT TO FLOODING, and only marginally more than a thatched pigsty at fifteen. (I have searched high and low for a thatched pigsty and I still haven't seen one.) One of the highest-scoring sightings in *I-Spy at the Seaside* was, in fact, the porpoise or dolphin. Both scored a princely forty, and it was time to open the Tizer if you saw one. I saw my first porpoise swimming in a school off Portrush on 20/4/54. I spotted my first lugworm on 17/9/53 at Eastbourne.

We were a family who read books in the living room in the evening but we were also among the first to buy a television set. In 1947, 4.3 per cent of the adult population had the fool's lantern in their homes. Ours was an expensive Bakelite Bush with a ten-inch screen. There was one, fuzzy black-and-white channel, the programmes didn't start until 8 p.m. and the live broadcasts via the transmission tower at nearby 'Ally Pally' frequently failed, to be replaced by an image of a potter's wheel. In the early days, most of the country couldn't receive any pictures at all. For our cousins, visiting from the Midlands, watching our television was a highlight of their trip to London.

JOHN MILLS He was a bit indulged rather because he was an only child. He never went without, I'm sure of that. Whatever his latest craze was, they bought whatever kit it was. I remember an awful lot of stuff at their house.

In the days before they pruned its last syllable along with the branch lines, my father worked for British Railways and we were always travelling on the cheap or free tickets that went with the job. Rather grandly, they called them 'Privilege Tickets'. In a modern sense, we were model citizens: we had no family car and travelled only on foot, bike, bus or train. At weekends we went walking in the Chilterns equipped with my butterfly net, binoculars, a Sauternes-bottle minnow trap, saucepans for blackberries or rosehips, and my *I-Spy* books. On holidays we went further, first to Jaywick Sands, then Cromer, Cornwall, Scotland, France, Italy, and always by rail.

ROGER, *diary, 1 September 1952* We crossed a bridge over the Rhône which was the first time I had seen it. Beyond the bridge was a village where we went in the church. We then proceeded to climb the mountain. When we were half-way up daddy took a photograph of me. When we were almost at the top mummy thought it was too dangerous so we had to turn back. When we were down the mountain we saw some Swiss gypsies. When we got back to the hotel we had five different kinds of meat and chicken and cabbage soaked in vinegar and chips.

I spent more time than most boys in the trance of the train's rhythm, gazing out of railway-carriage windows at glimpses of other lives. There were women hanging out washing in Welwyn Garden City, barges on the Grand Union Canal, trainspotters at Crewe, hens spilling out of their arks in fields beside the Ovaltine factory on the way to Coventry. Such glimpses tantalised me: I began to imagine these lives and places for myself.

My father's side of the family were all railway people and, in an era of steam engines, the romance of the railways equalled the romance of the Navy. Steam locomotives were organic, crafted, living, coughing, panting things. Railwaymen were fiercely loyal to their trade and tribe; a strong camaraderie existed between them wherever we went. Occasionally, as my father's son, I would get an unofficial ride on the footplate of an engine on a quiet branch line, be lifted up to reach the handle, and sound the whistle. I never collected mere abstract train numbers, but loved the plumed beauty of the steam locomotives, and would run with my playmates to the end of our street in the evenings to watch the Flying Scotsman go by, beginning its night journey to Glasgow. This time my glimpse of another world was from the outside in: waiters laying the tables for dinner; lights in the portholes of the mail coach, with its lacrosse-stick contraption to catch the mailbags hung out on gibbets along the line; passengers glancing absently out as we stood waving.

We took the train from London to Cromer. Cotton-wool clouds were swept from the sky by the sea as we reached the coast, the church tower puncturing the skyline. The houses had big chimneys of brick and flint, gabled roofs, balconies and even Gothic turret rooms where maidens sat at their sewing machines. Down in town, Rovers and MGs, Wolseleys, Austins, Morris Oxfords and Humber Super Snipe lined up in the car parks.

We rented a flat near the cobbled lifeboat slipway and would be half-woken early each morning by the throaty chugging of ancient tractors on the beach, hauling wooden crabbing boats into the water. I would watch them bring the crabs in at breakfast time, silently impressed by the fishermen's casual ability to handle the waving crustacean monkey-wrenches, and marvelling that none had less than a full deck of fingers and thumbs.

I took my big ex-RAF box kite, mustard yellow and standard issue to pilots in case they ditched in the sea. Grounded and struggling like a wild beast on the sand, it was almost taller than me, but it would shrink to the size of a skylark as it rose so powerfully on its curving string that by the end of the day I had blisters from clutching the unravelling spool of skin-polished hazelwood, half-hoping for lift-off. It must have been wizard, I imagined, adrift in the North Sea in a rubber dinghy flying a box kite all day and living on Horlicks tablets while you waited for the spotter plane. In a moment of enterprise,

I painted twin 'O's on the yellow sails and my mother helped me arrange ribbons into an 'X' on the aluminium frame between them. I wrote a letter to the OXO company with the good news that I was advertising their product over Cromer beach and wondering how much they would be prepared to pay for my services. I never received a reply. As an only child, I became unusually close to my kite and dreamed each night I was flying too, high over the pier.

*

We converted the bungalow's attic to become my room and den – a whole floor to myself, accessed via my own ladder. We had crystal radio sets and mine was housed in a plywood box next to my bed. The signal was so weak you could only listen in with headphones which meant hours of pleasure after lights out with Radio Luxembourg and, later on, Radio Caroline. Connie Francis, Eddie Calvert's golden trumpet, Danny Kaye, and 'Magic Moments' with Perry Como arrived, loud and clear, in my hibernaculum beneath the blankets. More importantly, so did 'Tammy': Debbie Reynolds sang about the whis'prin' of the cotton trees, and I was entranced. What exactly cotton trees were, I had no idea, but Debbie could sing no wrong and Tammy was in love, and I was with Tammy, whoever she was. This was a landscape we could only imagine, and therefore a landscape we happily located in our own woods, with ourselves as heroes. Later came *The Goon Show* and Eccles's eternal lament that 'You can't get the wood, you know. You just can't get the wood.' What wood? Why? No matter, it sent us into paroxysms of helpless laughter.

*

I am a woodlander; I have sap in my veins. Alvan Marshall Greenwood Deakin – it never occurred to me to ask my father where any of his top-heavy cargo of names came from, or to take much notice of the fact that my mother's maiden name was Wood. And it was years before I ever gave a thought to any possible connection between these names and my own love of all things wooden.

I was suckled on sap. Things get under other people's skin. They get under my bark. I am much drawn to people who make things – stonemasons, sculptors, woodcarvers, joiners, builders. The Woods were woodmen. But on my father's side, there were the anarchists. Woods have always been the traditional home of the outlaws – of those who love freedom – and there is a strong part of the Walsall anarchist in me too.

Alvan, Al to his friends, was born on 16 January 1909 in Walsall. His parents, Jane Read and Charles Deakin, married thirteen years earlier and had their first child, Charles, in 1905, followed by Jennie in 1907. When my father arrived, Charles senior, a railway clerk, was forty-four and Jane, a teacher, was thirty-nine. In earlier generations, the Deakins were farmers, labourers and blacksmiths but also excise officers and accountants, mostly across the Midlands. The Deakins and its variants, Deakins, Deacon and Dakin, were ultimately descended from the Norman family of De Akeny, Dakeny or De Acquigny, from Acquigny near Louviers, who fought along-side William the Conqueror in 1066.

My father's respectable, lower-middle-class parents were defined by their socialism. Charles spent his life in the service of the railways, working his way up from a provincial booking clerk to a rather more important traffic clerk at Curzon Street station in Birmingham. He joined the Railway Clerks' Associ-ation, and played a major part in establishing the Labour and Co-operative movements in his home town of Walsall. My father followed his father into the railways, becoming a booking clerk with the London, Midland and Scot-tish Railway at Lichfield station when he left school at seventeen. In 1935, he moved to London with the railways. When war broke out, he entered the RAF, emerging to marry my mother in September 1940. After the war, he returned to his safe, steady railway work.

As a Deakin, my father grew up under the shadow of scandal: his uncle was an anarchist and so-called terrorist. It was only towards the end of his life that I discovered the exciting and hitherto carefully concealed truth that my great-uncle, Joseph Deakin, was one of the Walsall Anarchists.

Six years older than my grandfather, Charles, Joseph Deakin was described as 'dreamy and poetic' and resembled the young poet Shelley when he emerged as the unofficial leader of the socialist movement in his home town. He joined the railways aged fifteen and his workmates at Wednesbury Goods Station presented him with a copy of the works of Victorian economist Thor-old Rogers 'in appreciation of his geniality and uniform kindness'.

Joe co-founded the Walsall Socialist Club when he was twenty-nine, his sincere speeches were well received, and he travelled to the Socialist Inter-national Congress in Paris in 1889 and Brussels in 1891, where he met Karl Marx and Pyotr Kropotkin, the Russian socialist and anarchist thinker. Unfor-tunately, that year Joe Deakin also encountered a charismatic Belgium-born 'Frenchman' called Auguste Coulon.

The mysterious Coulon claimed to be a professor of languages with connections to progressive parties in Dublin and France, but he lived in an expensive house in Bloomsbury without a visible source of income. As the new director of the Anarchist School, founded by the renowned French anarchist Louise Michel, Coulon advocated the violent overthrow of society in speeches at Hyde Park Corner and in radical magazines such as *Commonweal*.

On Joe's way home from the 1891 congress, he visited the Autonomie Club in Soho. Here, Coulon asked after a mutual friend, Frederick Charles, who had joined Joe's Socialist Club in Walsall. Deakin told him Charles had found work in an iron foundry. 'Oh, he will do to make bombs for us,' Coulon is said to have cried.

That autumn, a strange letter arrived in Walsall for a French political refugee, Victor Cailes. Signed 'Degnai', it enclosed a sketch of a bomb and asked if it could be made in Walsall. It was written on Coulon's instructions by a neighbour. Cailes wrote back to Coulon, who assured him that the letter was genuine.

Joe Deakin could not read French, so his Socialist Club comrades Cailes and Charles reassured him that the bombs were not for Britain but would assist the revolution in Russia. The men agreed to help the revolutionary effort. A wooden 'pattern' of the bombs was built by another club member, William Ditchfield, while a different friend produced some iron versions. These were sent to a foundryman asking for a quote for three dozen castings of the pattern. The foundryman didn't want the job and quoted a high price, 20 shillings per hundredweight. To his surprise, it was accepted but the labourer who was to manufacture the cast concluded that the patterns were so poorly made it was impossible to use them.

As Coulon's bomb plot inched forward without much conviction, the anarchist agitator did not keep a low profile. 'No voice speaks so loud as dynamite,' he publicly proclaimed, recruiting a student who was given nitric acid and glycerine to make dynamite. He also wrote to the Walsall men to 'hurry them up' with their bomb-making.

Joe Deakin was then asked by Cailes to take a bottle of chloroform to London. As he walked towards the Autonomie Club, he was arrested by detectives from Scotland Yard. Charles and Cailes were picked up the next day and a week later Ditchfield and two other associates were apprehended.

The six members of the 'Walsall Anarchist Plot' appeared at Stafford Assizes on 30 March 1892 charged under the Explosives Act. Anarchist bombs had been detonated in France and Spain and the arrival of allegedly violent terrorism in Britain caused a sensation. Press reports fed this hysteria. This plot was 'one of the most dastardly and wicked crimes it is possible to conceive', thundered *The Times*. 'Like treason it is aimed at the very heart of the State.'

Cailes was described as 'a stocky, heavy-browed Frenchman' but Joe Deakin, 'an inoffensive little railway clerk', was painted as an innocent-looking stooge. After his arrest, Joe was interrogated by Inspector Melville of Scotland Yard. The detective manipulated the accused railway clerk into 'a highly emotional condition' before allowing him to overhear a conversation, apparently between Charles and Ditchfield, confessing their role in the conspiracy. Joe was tricked into making a detailed confession, outlining his part in events.

Charles, Cailes and their associate Battola were found guilty and sentenced to ten years. Joe Deakin was found guilty and sentenced to five years. Ditchfield, who was illiterate, and another club member, John Westley, were acquitted. Detectives later denied an allegation that Ditchfield gave evidence only after being given whisky and cigars.

The trial judge failed to interrogate the biggest mystery of all, however. Why was Auguste Coulon never even questioned by the police when there was strong evidence that he was the ringleader? The judge ruled that Inspector Melville of Scotland Yard, who oversaw the police operation and was chief witness for the prosecution, need not answer defence questions about the nature of his relationship with Coulon. The Belgian's income from the Anarchist School was tiny and yet he lived in a lavish home. When the arrests were made, Coulon disappeared while his wife seemed to be under police protection. Coulon was eventually traced to a comfortable flat in Brixton. Testimony from Coulon's brother suggested that Coulon was a police spy. Subsequent research revealed he had been paid by Melville for two years before the arrests. 'Spy' was putting it mildly: Coulon was an agent provocateur.

Coulon vanished and his paymaster, William Melville, was rewarded with a key role in the government surveillance agency that became MI5. Following the convictions of the Walsall men, there were rallies and a Trades Union Congress resolution calling for their release. But the Home Secretary of the day refused to re-examine this miscarriage of justice. The jailing of the terrorists was useful publicity for Lord Salisbury's minority Conservative government ahead of a general election.

Joe Deakin served his sentence in Parkhurst, where he became the prison librarian, continuing his self-education with the help of William Morris,

George Bernard Shaw, Sidney and Beatrice Webb and other early socialists. On his release, he returned to his former home, becoming a major influence on the Labour movement in Walsall and a source of guidance for many councillors as they pushed for improvements to housing, sanitation and working conditions.

JOHN JAMES MCSHANE, *former Labour MP for Walsall*, Walsall Observer, *11 September 1937* By hundreds in this town he was spoken of in darked and awed whispers as 'the anarchist Deakin'. Joe Deakin was one of the shyest and most sensitive creatures I have ever known. To those who intimately knew the man, to myself particularly, who had often in the midnight hours listened to his shy and delicate confidences, and had marvelled at the extraordinary sweep with which he took in, as it were, all the departments of knowledge, whether of literature or economics, science or history, painting or drama – to us, I say, he was one of nature's miracles. In my fairly wide experience in Parliament and elsewhere, I have met many informed and capable men. But I can say, without a trace of exaggeration, that I have never met another comparable with 'Joe' Deakin, in range of knowledge, in ability, and in tenderness of feeling.

Joseph Deakin was a true defender of the greenwood spirit of democratic freedom; I think of him belonging to the outlaw tradition of Robin Hood. More than a century after his prison sentence, the wrongly imprisoned Birmingham Six and Guildford Four were eventually exonerated thanks to investigations by the *Panorama* programme. Had there been television in 1892, so would the Walsall Anarchists have been freed, their names cleared, and their lives not blighted.

*

My father was a committed union man. He served ten years as Correspondence Secretary to Euston No. 2 Branch of the Railway Clerks' Association, an 'important and onerous position' according to the union. For one humble clerk among 688,000 employees in the nationalised behemoth founded in 1948 by Clement Attlee's post-war Labour government, the bureaucratic ladder stretched a long way up. But he was praised for his hard work and modesty by his peers, and was eventually promoted to chairman of a committee that instructed staff about newly electrified rail lines. Supper was on the table when he returned every evening. If Mum went away to visit her sisters, my father would cook tomatoes on toast, for breakfast and dinner too.

Union colleagues admired my father's 'loyalty and integrity'. But friends enjoyed his sense of humour: one, David Fell, said Alvan had a 'gift' for 'seeing the funny side of things'.

P. ROBSON, *Correspondence Secretary of the union* He had, with all his reserve and reticence, a genius for affection.

MARGARET WOOD, *sister-in-law* He was such a dear, so soft-hearted and kind and full of go, always ready to do anything for anyone. Alvan was one of nature's gentlemen.

GORDON WOOD, *brother-in-law* I always admired his sincerity and complete lack of malice – he appreciated the good points and ignored the bad ones.

ANDREW CROOK, *nephew* Uncle Alvin was a smashing man. He was placid but pleasant and honourable; very self-contained, which was made up for by Gwen.

TONY AXON, *Roger's oldest friend* He was a very quiet sort of chap who, without putting too fine a point on it, was rather hen-pecked.

My father loved his adopted city of London. He would visit the public gallery of the House of Commons to listen to the big speeches of the day, enthralled by the great socialist orators: Nye Bevan, Ernest Bevin and the up-and-coming Michael Foot. He showed the sights to his sisters-in-law and other relatives from the Midlands. I came to know London through him as well.

*

The adventures of my mother's family, the Woods, all nine of them, were the stuff of my bedtime stories. I was raised in an oral tradition of home-grown folklore narrated by my mother and peopled almost entirely by her siblings – two dashing uncles and four aunts. My grandparents, Welsh Grandma Jones and silver-haired Grandpa Wood, with his one left hand and a steel hook for his right, had upheld our sylvan traditions by christening two of them Ivy Wood and Violet Wood.

My mother's older brother, Sidney, was known to the family as Laddie. To my mother, and to me, Laddie was nothing short of a hero, the original bachelor uncle, straight from the pages of the *Boy's Own* annual. Laddie was outgoing and funny but also enigmatic. At Kenilworth, where he still lived in the family home when we were children, he parked his open-topped MG TF in the drive.

JOHN MILLS He was quite a character. He was a cyclist of considerable note and then he went into the air force. He was thirty-five and didn't have to go in. He was sent to Iraq and he was very brave. He was also a good swimmer. He was a confirmed bachelor. There was never any question of marriage. He smoked a lot and had a heart attack in his late fifties. He drove several MG sports cars. Grandfather called them 'pneumonia wagons'.

When a tractor and trailer loaded with bombs started to roll away down a hill in Iraq during the Second World War, Laddie gave chase, and leapt on to the bombs. Because they were smooth and rounded, he slid off. So he gave chase again, jumped on to the trailer, climbed on to the tractor and eventually brought it to a halt, averting a crash and a potentially disastrous explosion. Laddie was a swimmer and a cyclist and a champion at both. How the crowd at the amateur cycle races at Coventry stadium roared when Laddie, hanging strategically behind the pack until the last lap, would suddenly stand on his pedals and power past the opposition to win. He also had his own key to the open-air swimming pool.

I swam with my cousins in the Avon at Stratford, in the Chess near Chorleywood, and in the Thames at Lechlade. But my earliest memory of serious swimming is of being woken very early on holiday mornings with my parents in Kenilworth by a sudden rain of pebbles at my bedroom window. They were aimed by Uncle Laddie. My cousins and I were reared on mythic tales of his exploits – in races, on high boards, or swimming far out to sea – so it felt an honour to swim with him. Long before the lifeguards arrived, we would unlock the wooden gate and set the straight, black, refracted lines on the bottom of the green pool snaking and shimmying. It was usually icy, but the magic of being first in is what I remember. 'We had the place to ourselves,' we would say with satisfaction afterwards over breakfast. Our communion with the water was all the more delightful for being free of charge. It was my first taste of unofficial swimming.

ANDREW CROOK Roger was more romantically enchanted by the stories than any of us. He was very close to Laddie and they used to do crazy things together. At the wedding of our cousin John, Roger and Laddie thought it would be a jolly jape to put tins and cans on John's car. They knew it was a Mini, and they were mortified when the vicar got in his car and drove away. He also had a Mini.

*

Gwendoline Wood was born on 27 September 1908 in Cannock, the third of seven children. When her parents, Sidney and Adelaide, were courting, Sidney, a young miner, lost his right hand. He was cleaning a traction engine and someone turned it on. 'You can't possibly marry me now I'm a cripple,' he wrote to Adelaide in a letter, but she did. He was also illegitimate, and carved opportunity from disability: rather than a life of manual labour, Sidney was raised up from the mine into a white-collar world, becoming a time-keeping and wages clerk at the Cannock and Rugeley Colliery. He attended night school and passed his exams to join the civil service. He moved posts and houses, working for the national census and as a public health inspector, living in Truro before settling in the Warwickshire town of Kenilworth, where he and his wife and their seven children lived in style, assisted by a housemaid. Sidney was well read, wrote left-handed verse, and his one-handedness did not prevent him driving both a motorbike and a car, clipping his hook into a peg device on the steering wheel so he could hold the wheel with his hook while changing gear with his left hand.

The silver-haired 'Grandpa Wood' slicing the air with his silver hook was a formidable sight in my early childhood but so was Adelaide, a forceful mother of seven: Laddie, Gordon, and five daughters. Dorothy, known as Doris, was the eldest, followed by Gwen, Ivy, Violet and Margaret. The Wood sisters were sporty and adventurous. Gwen was a ballroom dancer, who played tennis and swam. Margaret played cricket for Warwickshire's women's team; her nose was broken on several occasions for interesting reasons, from being smacked in the face with a cricket bat to falling off a sledge head first. The sisters remained close, and were always talking, trading stories and opinions.

When I was small, neither my mother nor her sister, Margaret, ever lost an opportunity to dress me and my cousin Adrian as girls, even regularly putting grips in our hair before bedtime. Adrian, we used to joke, later became an enthusiastic member of the Cheltenham & District Cross-dressing Association. He was a complete Peter Pan. He never had children because he was one himself; the idea of being forever young was very prevalent in our family.

ANDREW CROOK, *son of Ivy* There was an air of confidence about the Wood family, particularly the women. Unless you were incredibly brave and had armour on you wouldn't argue with them. The sisters considered themselves a dynasty. It wasn't something that carried in our branch of the family because my father and mother were very level-headed.

JOHN MILLS   The Wood sisters were all very strong characters, all strong personalities. They had a good sense of humour but they also argued a lot amongst themselves.

My mother was stylish, determined and a superb natural gardener, achieving prodigious blooms wherever she went. Gardening is part of the gift of nurture she gave me and I learned about plants at her knee. I watched how she saved seeds, the papery purses of honesty, and scattered them at random in unpromising corners. Mum liked the happenstance of self-seeded wild flowers but her catholic gardening style encompassed suburban favourites too: lilac bushes and the shocking-pink exhibitionism of mallows. When I won a sixth-form biology competition to bring in and identify the most spring flowers, I was happy to admit that my mother helped me, and got me going.

My mother and I were always at our happiest indulging the outlaw side of our family nature. It was a time of rapid suburban development close to our home. When a grand house in Hatch End was scheduled for demolition to make way for blocks of flats, we stole in and made off with the stone urn that stood outside the kitchen door. Many years later, we drove in her open-topped car to the gardens of Holkham Hall on the Norfolk coast. Here we found espalier fruit trees, laden with plums, pears and apples that the estate didn't seem to harvest, so we leaned innocently against the wall feasting on ripe plums, and scrumped a few pounds into our ample pockets. 'It's a shame to see good fruit going to waste,' we agreed on the way home.

ROGER DEAKIN, *school essay, 1956*   On the whole I believe I have been brought up quite well by my parents. The only major mistake they made was having me, I am told.

TOBY KIDD, *great-nephew*   Gwen seemed to be quite sparky. She was always described as the fun, slightly rebellious sister in the gang.

GRAHAM 'BEN' BARKER-BENFIELD, *schoolfriend of Roger*   She was an independent, impressive sort of woman. She drove a Triumph Herald in an era when there weren't many women driving sports cars. She had get-up-and-go, an adventurous streak that Roger definitely shared.

BUNDLE WESTON, *friend of Roger*   She really was the perfect mother for Rog. She let him have so much leash but was always there for him. She had warmth and a sense of humour and such kindness, but nothing soft about her. A good edge.

TONY AXON Gwen told you what you were going to do. She was a force to be reckoned with but so was Rog. When I was invited over for Sunday lunch, Gwen treated me as if I was a grown-up. I was fourteen and she'd say to me, 'Would you like a glass of sherry, Anthony? Roger's having orange juice.' It was really embarrassing but very funny. I liked her.

ANDREW CROOK If you spent a day in the house you needed to spend a day out of it. Gwen was a powerful personality. She was quite dominant.

JENNY KEMBER, *Roger's wife* Roger came from this very small bungalow in Hatch End. It was really tiny. His mum was a delight, a lovely woman, but the situation was tricky. He was an only child, she had wanted more children but Roger's father wouldn't let her and said they couldn't afford more. It was all quite claustrophobic. She was quite genteel in a slightly suburban way and couldn't have been nicer, but Roger always felt a bit suffocated by her.

SERENA INSKIP, *partner of Roger* He was intrinsically a very wild boy and he was constantly stopped in his tracks by his mum. 'You mustn't do that, Roger.' His mother was an anxious person and it was really scary for her to have a son. I think she wanted a daughter, and he had a lot of spirit.

JULES CASHFORD, *friend of Roger* If you have a dominant mother, there is a point when you're frightened to be yourself.

CHAPTER 3

The Schoolboy

Glimpses of prep school – fear and loathing and uniform – my triumphant chairmanship of the Lower School Natural History Society – the stuffed rat that thought it was a wombat – early entrepreneurship selling bulrushes – Tony Axon, brilliant wit, consoling presence and lifelong friend – spearing octopi in Spain, performing theatre in Germany and inspiration in English literature – swimming, rowing and further adventures in France – loitering with The Gang – Buddy Holly on the Dansette – inventing the aquabike – first kiss, first paid employment – the New Forest camps – D. H. Lawrence and the death of my father – scraping into Cambridge

Our school bus was Toby, a red open-topped Wolseley with a golden retriever on its front seat called Duke, the school being Wellington, a prep school in Hatch End. The school playground was an orchard, with a patch of concrete at its centre. In summer it was full of the birdsong of small boys, punctuated by toots from the narrow-gauge steam railway that threaded its way between the trees and was the headmaster's passion. Boys were expected to keep the line free of windfalls, and there was a resident black Manx cat who thought sleepers were for sleeping on. Its favourite game was to leap clear at the last possible moment, causing speculation about its absent tail. That was my first experience of the orchard: as a place to dream about in lessons, a haven from toil; a playground.

There were music lessons in the assembly hall, Dr White at the upright piano, singing 'Early One Morning', 'My Bonnie Lies Over the Ocean', 'Loch Lomond's Braes are Burning', 'Cherry Ripe' ('Ripe, I-ee, cryee'), and in lessons I first learned to write in pencil, with an India rubber to hand and a sycamore pencil-box with a sliding lid and hinged upper chamber that cunningly swung out to reveal an inner container. The pencil-box was also my first tool-box, and it was beautifully crafted, its cavities hollowed and grooved to a perfect fit. I have still not outgrown pencils. They are my first, most spontaneous means of expression.

Wellington Prep School; little, local and long gone; where nail-biting was regulated by the painting on of bitter aloes. Then there was stuttering and dreading my turn to read in class. As it came round to me, I would be searching ahead in the prose for the hurdles, which stood out as if in orange highlighter.

ROGER DEAKIN, 'A Visit to the Nuffield Motor Works', The Wellingtonian magazine, summer 1953 On Wednesday the 6th May at 10 a.m. the Scholarship Class, Upper and Lower Remove boarded the coach which was to take us to Oxford. We had a very enjoyable journey on which I saw a pair of partridges, a pied wagtail, a mallard drake, and a mute swan on her nest. When we arrived at Cowley, the first department we visited was the tyre fitting department, where the men were fitting tyres on to the rims. These men can fit as many as three hundred and twenty tyres in one day ... After this we went into the upholstery stockroom where carpets and other articles of upholstery were stored. As leather is scarce real leather is only used in the front seats of Morris Minors and Morris Oxfords, but in the front and back seats of the Wolseley. Vynide (made by the ICI) is used for the back seats of Morris Minors and Morris Oxfords.

*

When I was ten, a sudden change. Schoolboys, disinfectant and, shortly after eleven o'clock, upper notes of boiled cabbage from the kitchen: the scent of schooldays at Westbere Road, Cricklewood.

I lived near the Kodak works in Harrow and everyone for miles around was woken at 7 a.m. by the factory hooter, and tipped out of the house to work at seven forty-five by another hooter, with reminders at five to eight and a final emphatic blast at eight o'clock. It was the same in every mill and mining town further north. The arrogance of industry literally ruling the roost, or disturbing the peace. When the five-to-eight hooter went, I would seize my satchel in panic, and belt up the hill to the station to catch the 8.04 train from Headstone Lane to Kilburn High Road. When the 8 a.m. hooter went, people walking briskly on the streets would break into a run, bounding down the steel-tipped wooden steps of the station bridge on to the platform, some jumping on to moving trains, poised on the running board with an open door for agonising seconds as the train accelerated before they flopped into smoke-filled carriages like netted trout. Mornings in Harrow were a mass crescendo of panic, orchestrated by Kodak and British Railways.

Wearing starched grey shorts and a dark blue blazer bearing the motto 'Serve and Obey', I took the train and then a bus up Shoot Up Hill before crossing the railway bridge to Haberdashers'. It called itself Haberdashers' Aske's Hampstead School, so we got our apostrophes right. My curly hair had been subdued, cut short, tugged straight and parted beneath my peaked cap. I have loathed neatness ever since – and uniform and collars and ties. And haircuts.

In this big, noisy red-brick school of nearly a thousand boys, my education was paid for by the state for I won a 'Middlesex County Award'. About a third of the school were 'direct grant' boys like me, who came from families who couldn't afford the fees but had taken entrance examinations and were deemed worthy of a Haberdashers' education.

NIGEL BROWN, *friend* The Middlesex County Awards were the mechanism by which bright eleven-year-old boys could get their fees paid if they were selected to a school like Habs. I don't remember sweating about the exam paper and interview. They were really rather keen to have these scholarship boys.

The school's results were good and the schoolmasters set our sights high: about forty pupils went to the universities of Oxford and Cambridge each year. We never discussed it at the time but around 40 per cent of the boys were

33

Jewish, and the names on the honours boards in the corridors were predominantly Jewish. In the years above me were the future Conservative politician and European Commissioner Leon Brittan, and Peter Oppenheimer and Michael Lipton, boys who would become eminent economists. The vintage year after mine featured advertising legend Martin Sorrell; David Elstein, who later became the boss of Channel 5; and the future historian Simon Schama.

Another television personality to-be sought me out in the queue by the tuckshop wall. The wall was dotted with penny-sized pits gouged out by generations of boys clutching their pence, twirling them into the brick declivities and screw-drivering out the brick dust. Here I was unjustly accused of pushing in by the school bully, Michael Bukht, who later became known as Michael Barry; 'the Crafty Cook' on television in the 1990s. I was a little first-former. He was a big third-former with a reputation for boxing clever and he upended me in the dustbin in front of everyone and a chorus of cowardly simpering cheers.

KEVIN TIERNEY, *classmate* Roger was an agreeable boy, with an unruffled manner and a sense of humour. He was also pretty enough to be cast as a girl in our all-male school plays.

BARRY BINGHAM, *classmate* He had an open, friendly, if somewhat shy appearance.

MICHAEL HOLLINGTON, *friend* He was a leader, a person with masses of ideas and projects. It was astonishing how confident he was, coming to a place where I didn't feel confident at all to start with. It's almost as if he knew what he wanted to do already. Roger could be described as what I would then have called a 'naughty boy' and that was one of the attractions of him.

BRIAN PERMAN, *friend* He was very earnest. A group of us had all sorts of scrapes. Roger was not totally approving. He wasn't bolshy at school.

NIGEL BROWN He wasn't a conformist – he was an enthusiastic and strong-minded 'independent'.

School report, 1958 Rarely uses ability in full. Relies too much on charm.

I was Deakin, or Deaky, Deak, Dicky and Freaky; and Rog to my friends. That first term, I joined the fifty members of the Lower School Natural History Society and gave a talk on fossils. My friend Ben Barker-Benfield gave one on 'Cavies'. The next year, elevated to chairman, I opened our sessions with a talk on 'Tortoises and Terrapins' and founded the Taxidermy Section. We caught rats in traps at school and brought trophies from home: squirrels, moles and rabbits. From these carcasses we fashioned stuffed rodents, squirrel pelts, moleskins and various rabbit skins, cured in saltpetre to make Davy Crockett hats. In *The Sword in the Stone*, Wart's heart is transformed by magic into the skins of a series of animals: a fish, a badger, an oak, so that he can understand the world from inside. It is about a different kind of education and a way of learning about nature from the inside instead of from the outside, as on nature TV.

TONY AXON We were hopeless at stuffing them. A rat ended up looking like a wombat.

J. F. 'JEFF' COOPER, *biology master and head of the Lower School*, Skylark, *the school magazine, 1955* Special mention should be made of the Taxidermy Section organised by R. S. Deakin, a group small in number but large in enthusiasm, who gained useful experience in skinning, stuffing and mounting specimens. Several creditable examples of their work were on show at the Natural History exhibition on Commendation Day. Deakin's keenness in collecting enabled him to bring home from Yugoslavia a large green lizard, two smaller ones, two praying mantises, and a stick insect – all alive.

MICHAEL HOLLINGTON He founded the Lower School Taxidermy Society, and I joined the minuscule team that met in 'Jeff' Cooper's room by special permission of the head of the Lower School. Roger was incredibly inventive. And that fell into his writing and his later persona in *Waterlog*, because he was dramatising himself. I tended to follow him, and on one occasion we were both kept in detention after throwing library books on to the tops of the book-cases containing them, inciting the wrath of the librarian on duty. One Christmas, probably 1954, Roger invited me to stay with him at his home so we could earn money by singing carols as a duo – an instance of the element of enterprise that went with his iconoclasm. He was an entrepreneur, you might say.

J. F. 'JEFF' COOPER, Skylark, *1954* R. S. Deakin, the 3S collector, deserves special mention for raising – on his own initiative – £2 10s by collecting and selling bulrushes in the summer holidays and by singing carols at Christmas.

*

14 January A grand snowball fight. Lower School won.

24 January I came 36th in the cross-country race.

25 January A talk at the Natural History Society on The Ring-Necked Pheasant.

30 January My terrapin dead. And a sandpiper on the pond.

Roger's Lower School reports

J. F. COOPER, *autumn 1954* Should now know his weaknesses (maths in particular).

J. F. COOPER, *spring 1955* He must make up his mind to work seriously throughout next term.

J. F. COOPER, *summer 1955* He has not applied himself consistently to his work. Hence a rather disappointing report.

J. F. COOPER, *autumn 1955* Well below average.

In Class 1A, aged ten, I met Tony Axon. He became a consoling presence through life and a great mentor in the telling of comic stories, a truly original and brilliant wit. The key to Tony is that he is an only child, and loyalty and constancy are his great virtues. He has given me years of laughter, gusts of honest laughter. Tony's mother and father, Hilda and Frank, were models of a loving relationship, and the foundation for all the love in their family. We, his friends, were all Tony's family; all his brothers; the siblings he never had as a child.

Tony is one of life's great adventurers, a Don Quixote with a gift for self-mockery and a natural affinity with Jacques Tati. A pioneer and a natural, fearless voyager, Tony led the way – as champion backstroker in the school team; as captain and No. 7 in the rowing eight, setting the rhythm and pace; always embarking on endless hitch-hiking marathons, always travelling in hope.

BEN BARKER-BENFIELD Tony Axon and Rog, they were like brothers.

TONY AXON I always imagined it was a bit like having a brother. We could go quite long periods without phoning each other and then seeing each other every day for a few weeks. There was no need to stay attached because we grew up having some sort of bond.

JOHN HUGGINS, *friend* He and Tony Axon were quite hilarious. They were a double act. I remember almost crying with laughter.

CAROLINE CLIFTON-MOGG, *friend* Tony Axon is honestly one of the best people in the world. He's a joy.

With our pale knees, khaki shorts and chronic sunburn, on one school trip we were pioneers to Blanes, a fishing village on the Costa Brava. We munched Errol Flynns, Spanish churros, which were oily and liberally coated in sugar and purchased from the side of a brightly illuminated silver van. There was a fairground atmosphere along the seafront, which was dotted with shooting stalls with bent air rifles and prizes of miniature bottles of Spanish champagne and Martini. Tony Axon won several.

Among the rock pools we speared an octopus with a toasting fork, bashing the poor creature's ink out against the sea wall, and parading it back to our hotel triumphantly a-dangle from the toasting-fork harpoon, and persuaded the chef to cook it. I don't remember eating it, though. I took my butterfly net with me and cheerfully caught and chloroformed a swallowtail or two.

Tony and I swam across the bay to the port jetty. It seemed a long way, and perhaps it was. We fancied we saw a shark approaching, but this was pure fantasy, and we eventually made it to the other side and sauntered back along the beach in a leisurely sort of way. Halfway along, we encountered an ashen-faced search party led by 'Jeff' Cooper, head of the Lower School, combing the shallows for bodies. They looked at us as if they had seen a pair of ghosts and we got a telling-off from the poor man. These days it might have been the end of his career.

TONY AXON My memories of swimming across Blanes Bay are pretty vivid. Whatever it was that we encountered halfway across was pretty scary, and I don't think it was 'fantasy' at all. 'Jeff' Cooper was probably ashen-faced.

ROGER DEAKIN, *essay, 'Spain and Its People', 1956* The standard of living in Spain is very low and there is really no middle class, the majority of the people being poor and a few very rich . . . There are few good roads, most of them being narrow rough tracks, dusty in summer and muddy and almost impassable in the winter. The main form of transport is the mule and cart . . . All Spaniards are cruel to animals, thinking that animals were put on the Earth for their use. This is shown by the fact that two of the national sports are bullfighting and cock-fighting.

TEACHER 16/20 Vivid and interesting, paragraphing weak.

*

JOHN HUGGINS We were taken to Shakespeare plays and the school was very strong on languages. Haberdashers' taught Russian, which was pretty unusual at the time. It was quite progressive. Prefects were allowed to beat boys with a cane. That was one of the less progressive parts of Habs.

TONY AXON In those days, Haberdashers' was a very bolshy school. We thought the headmaster, Dr Taylor, was a bit of a bourgeois twerp but we came to realise that he was an innovator, who recruited impressive teachers. Bill Nicholas wrote a strip cartoon for the *Daily Sketch* and taught English. He was a brilliant wit and dressed incredibly nattily – yellow socks, cavalry twill trousers, which in those days were considered cool – and we emulated him as far as possible. If boys got all giggly about certain words, Nick would say, 'When I use the word "sensual", for your information, I am not equating it with the word "sexual".' Then Peter Doughty arrived to teach English and he was a huge inspiration for Rog and for me. I was pretty lost in my first year at A level but Doughty lifted the veil – teaching me simply how to get a handle on what poems and plays were about – and it all became terribly clear. The two of them were exceptionally good teachers.

NIGEL BROWN Both Bill Nicholas and Doughty were interested in teaching contemporary literature, living literature rather than the academic syllabus. Nicholas was dapper and he had a way with words. We thought that was the kind of person we'd like to be.

TONY AXON Dr Taylor had some strange but valuable ideas, such as taking the school play on tour in Germany barely ten years after the war. We journeyed by rail with our own scenery which travelled in a wagon of its own, being hitched on to the end of the trains we took. We stayed with German families and this was very formative because we grew up thinking the Germans were baddies, and we moved from Heidelberg to Karlsruhe, performing in professional theatres. In Pforzheim, Rog and I found a shop selling stink bombs. We inadvertently let one off in the town's Stadttheater, to the consternation of the mayor. I'm sure Rog found it as formative as we all did.

BEN BARKER-BENFIELD The thing about staying with German families was to get a family with a girl, because we went to an all-boys' school. Haberdashers' was a great place for humour. The culture among the boys was enormously fertile and creative. It was founded upon jokes. Dirty jokes if possible. Roger joined in. We hung around in little cliques where you'd try and outdo each other and listened to *The Goon Show* on a crystal set. I wouldn't underestimate its subversive impact on young brains. You have to cut into history somewhere. There is always something that precedes what you're looking at. In Roger's case, what preceded him was the war. Young people went off, saw terrible things, and came back to this fucking class-ridden place. All this stuff about duty to King and Country – you stay in your box and die. And it's all crap.

*

Military service was still commonplace in most fee-paying schools and Haberdashers' required its boys to join the Combined Cadet Force in the fifth form. This, supposedly, was to prepare us for National Service, which still loomed in the late fifties before being scrapped in 1960. 'If you don't join the Combined Cadet Force, what's going to happen when you have to do National Service?' masters would threaten.

I was a miserable little army cadet on a school field-camp when I discovered a swimming hole on the Little Ouse, a bay of sand so fine and clean it could have been from the seaside. We had been billeted to the Norfolk Breckland, it was high summer, and the rough, woollen, khaki uniforms were prickling us all crazy in the heat. So were the thick socks and heavy boots. Someone must have taken pity on us because we were piled into the back of a truck and bumped along endless sandy tracks until we reached this mirage of a river, stripped off, and felt its welcome embrace like all our mothers soothing and kissing us cool. I felt the caress of long tresses of viridian water crowfoot swaying and trembling in the current. The water was crystalline and sparkling, with the sun's brightness reflected back off the fine, chalky, gravelly bed and fish skidding in and out of the weed sheafs.

Haberdashers' own swimming pool was not so alluring: 17.6 yards of heavily chlorinated water in a crepuscular basement. One hundred lengths were a mile. In my last year at prep school, I swam more than a mile in the Watford baths and it provided me with a slender straw of self-confidence to which I clung during my daunting early days at secondary school. I beat a boy called Smith who was school champion at everything else and had tried so hard not to be beaten that he spent the following week in bed, to my deep satisfaction.

At Haberdashers', the top board was close enough to the roof to reach up and grasp the iron rafters, slippery with condensation, and go out swinging hand over hand, then let go. As first-formers we watched our swimming heroes do this; big boys with names like Leal, Sluice, and the most stylish swimmer in the school, Lester Clark. Leal was the finest diver, executing magnificent swallow dives off the high board in the Seymour Hall pool in Marylebone in front of the restless galleries at the annual gala. He would even fox his opponents by swimming halfway up the pool underwater in the hundred-yard breaststroke. At the 1954 gala, I won the breaststroke race but I didn't make the school swimming team, unlike Tony, a champion backstroker.

TONY AXON We used to hang out together on holiday and both of us loved messing around on boats. In winter, we went to Regent's Park Lake and went sculling; in summer, we'd be on the Serpentine. Rog was good at rowing. He was in his element in boats. I'm not sure how he became interested in swimming. I got a job on Hampstead Heath as a lifeguard in the lido. In summer, we were seconded to the mixed pond. It was lovely but not many people used it in those days. I'd take my sandwiches and a book and spend all day there and a number of times nobody came at all. Rog visited and was swimming away. Then he said, 'Can I borrow your lifesaving badge?' He'd applied for a lifeguard job at Harrow swimming pool but didn't have any qualifications. My name was stamped on the back so he put boot polish over it and rubbed it smooth and in the end you couldn't see any indentations, and I think that was the beginnings of it all.

When Tony broke his foot and couldn't play rugby, he gave rowing a go and soon I joined him. Cricklewood was miles from the river and it was a slow traipse on buses and trains to reach the Thames. But we were excused the last period of school every Tuesday and Thursday, and again during Wednesday afternoon games. Training was not glamorous. Our coach, Mr Percy, would tear along the towpath on a bike, shouting at unwary pedestrians to clear the way. We were boathouse orphans, lacking a base of our own, and endured a peripatetic existence, moving between borrowed lodgings. First was Tom Green's boathouse, a rat-plagued shed festooned with a hundred years of accumulated river detritus. 'Ma' Green cooked on a bottled-gas stove while Tom was known to disappear for several days on drinking binges. 'Green's boathouse provides for "homeless" tradesmen, artisans and women who like the river,' reported a newspaper from that era. Next we rowed from a boathouse on Eel Pie Island, which could only be reached by a chain-link ferry and would soon become a nursery for the Rolling Stones and Pink Floyd.

TONY AXON It was a rather magical spot, and the magic extended to the river itself.

Later we graduated to the Ibis boathouse in Chiswick, which for the first time provided hot showers and changing rooms. It also had a bar and Mr Percy and our other coach, Mr Browning, would turn a blind eye if the underage crew wanted to refresh themselves with a half of mild.

JOHN HUGGINS The rowing was quite a privileged thing to do. We got away from school, were able to have a beer and nobody would tell. We never wore anything other than a T-shirt even during the winter. A bit like wild swimming, it prevents you getting things.

When the London bus strike of 1958 made it even more arduous to reach the river, Tony and I discovered a new mode of travel: hitch-hiking. Why spend hours on a bus or train when you could put up your thumb and be chauffeured around the North Circular Road? It was cheaper, quicker, more fun, and the start of many a hitch-hiking adventure together. Hitch-hiking meets the need for casual contact with strangers. The car is strangely intimate, yet doesn't threaten anyone with eye contact; a kind of confessional. In this vanished world of innocence, we talked to strangers and developed a number of routines. 'Just how fast can this car go?' was a favourite. Or we would turn tour guides and inform the driver of the passing scenery. 'Those houses are listed, you know.'

TONY AXON We thought this to be very amusing. The 'we' didn't normally extend to the drivers.

*

Each year of my early teens, I rode the Blue Train from Victoria station to the south of France to visit my penfriend, Jean-François, in Menton. I suppose both of us must have had travelling in our blood because our fathers worked for the railways; our exchange was arranged through the British and French rail unions.

The Channel crossing on the ferry, slipstreamed by seagulls, and the sight of the mailbags being hoisted ashore in huge nets by the Calais cranes, the dockside alive with blue dungarees and stevedores, already conferred the status of rite of passage on that first journey. For an English adolescent the Train Bleu provided the full range of initiation rites: the customs, the crossing of Paris by Métro from the Gare du Nord to the Gare du Lyon, the need to utter the first halting words of classroom French. At the Gare du Lyon, I walked up the platform admiring the high blue carriages of the Compagnie Internationale des Wagons-Lits and the enthalling roster of the Blue Train's itinerary: Paris – Dijon – Lyon – Valence – Avignon – Marseille – Toulon – St Tropez – St Raphael – Cannes – Nice – Monte Carlo – Menton – Ventimiglia. I travelled almost to the end of the line.

During the night, I drifted out of sleep to hear the insistent ghostly voices of the station announcers: 'Dijon! Dijon!' and later still 'Lyon!' At breakfast time I was woken by stewards clattering along the corridors, peeped under the blind and saw the Mediterranean on fire as we steamed along the coast past the empty beaches of Fréjus and St Raphael. Everything was so much brighter and clearer than in my cool native suburb. The sky was a deep bold blue I had never seen before. Shadows were inky black and had sharp edges.

In Menton, the French of my textbooks came deliciously alive. *Café, croissant, pain au chocolat, la mer, le soleil, la table*: all took on a brilliance like a revelation. Along the rocks towards Cap-Martin, men in bright blue denim trousers twitched silver-backed olive leaves bound on sticks to lure the wily octopi from their lairs. When we bathed in Menton, shoals of small fish skidding across the harbour's clear water like shadows, I felt I was being baptised into a new life.

I had lucked out, of course, in landing a penfriend with a place in Menton. The Villa L'Hermine was on a steep hillside behind the town, surrounded by orange orchards, olives and prickly pears. At night, geckos strolled upside down across the ceiling as we dined, serenaded by choirs of crickets and tree frogs. Jean-François and I would creep up in the dark to the concrete irrigation tanks that served as the frogs' echo chambers and catch in our torch-beam rows of vivid green males with their bubblegum larynxes comically inflated. We glimpsed others in the shadows apparently in flagrante, still singing lustily in their passion. In the mornings, the cicadas took up the song in the Corsican pines, cranking up like old gramophones as the sun rose higher.

*

ROGER DEAKIN, *essay, 'Reactions to Life in Suburbia', c.1957* I live just on the outside of London's corset, the Green Belt, and should therefore be able to claim that I live in a semi-rural area or rural suburbia. My reactions are, first, one of almost complete contentment . . . I'm never bored. If there is no school work to do, there is the Church Youth Club, the church, shops and plenty of friends to be found locally. There are also some swimming baths nearby as well as plenty of material for painting and sketching. My main interest, however (besides girls), is wildlife, and this can be pursued behind my back garden, where there is a farm, and a large field backing on to my garden, in which are to be found hares, partridge, ducks, herons, occasionally snipe, plovers, weasels, foxes, crows, carp in the pond and green tree frogs.

*

For some reason, the cast-iron metallic ring of a crow's call reminds me of Watford, and Benskin's Brewery at Croxley Green, and the viaduct the train passed over on the way to my violin lessons on Saturday mornings with Mr Piper. It makes me think of the old Albion lorries the brewery used for its deliveries of Benskin's brown ale, and the sound of their starter motors. That could be it: the special quality of sound of a starter motor that hasn't quite engaged the under-note; the elusive quality in the abrasive call is haunting precisely because it is so hard to pin down, so defiant of description.

I never wanted to be at those violin lessons. I wanted to be with my friends gathered on bicycles outside Giles record shop in the middle of Hatch End. There was Ricky Wright, who later became Pink Floyd's keyboardist, Puss Pratt, Brian Perman, Douglas Catterell and half a dozen camp followers. We modestly styled ourselves as 'The Gang' and would loiter in the listening booths all Saturday morning and come away with the 45s of Elvis, the Everly Brothers and Lonnie Donegan. Riding back to Ricky's three-storey house in The Avenue, we would pile upstairs past his good-humoured parents and play our singles over and over again on the Dansette. I can remember the real thrill and conviction of going up to the counter at Giles and buying Buddy Holly's 45 with 'Peggy Sue' on one side and 'Everyday' on the other in the autumn of 1957.

TONY AXON He put me on to Buddy Holly. He had the EP of 'Peggy Sue'. As soon as I got back to Golders Green I bought a copy myself.

SUE CARR-HILL, *former wife of John Huggins* Roger borrowed John's Dansette record player and never gave it back. John and I and my friend Sue went round and played records in Roger's den. I can see Roger sitting at the kitchen table eating the breakfast that he'd made. A cold fried egg on a plate, Roger dipping bread and butter into this cold egg. I remember thinking, how revolting. My mother was a good cook. She would've never let me eat a cold egg. He always had a scheme going, Roger, because he was very, very clever. I wouldn't say he was out for himself, he was a lovely guy, very friendly, but he was in touch with you when it suited him.

The Saturday parties with The Gang at the youth club in Hatch End were an adolescent torture. I would arrive attired in a rust-coloured chunky-knit crew-neck pullover and matching brown shirt, bottle-green corduroys, brown suede shoes, yellow paisley cravat, and yellow-and-brown socks. We would endlessly map out the sequence of words and movements that would lead to a kiss at the goodnight gate. Then there would be that final, disastrous lunge at the girl, desperate, ill-timed and badly aimed. The first time I missed completely, and kissed a yew tree.

ROGER, *poem for Patricia Houlihan, undated*

> Funny how running water
> makes us piss.
> Could insectivorous plants
> make us kiss?

*

KEVIN TIERNEY, *classmate* At school the principal manifestation of radicalism was the Campaign for Nuclear Disarmament, not domestic socialism. Nevertheless, we all knew that we would soon enter a society in which – if we were not careful – we might become 'wage slaves', and an aversion to this fate permeated the sixth form. Roger aimed for an independence which excluded 'wage slavery'. He was not alone in this; another school contemporary, Tony Weston, had the same ideal and in due course he too renovated an old house. Both Roger and Tony were in revolt against their suburban backgrounds, although Tony was also against Blake's dark Satanic mills whereas Roger, while disliking them, accepted them as a necessary evil.

TONY AXON We had a handicrafts master at Haberdashers' who was very nice. He was gay, and he taught us things like weaving, which I really enjoyed and Rog did as well, and Tony Weston became a really competent potter. Tony was a classmate who lived in Kenton, quite close to Roger. He was a poet and a very interesting man who never went to university. Neither Rog nor I quite understood why. Rog was in awe of Tony who had a slightly wry sense of humour and was the inspiration for Rog getting into handicraft, woodwork and, later, building his own house.

BUNDLE WESTON Tony Weston was a year older than Axon and Rog, and they both rather venerated him. The three of them were in the same rowing eight and they were into poetry. Tony was a bit of a mystic wonder – he clearly had this something that Roger really wanted into. It was all a bit grown up – Tony had a girlfriend who was actually three years older than he was! We got engaged before Tony even left school. And then Tony and I went straight out into the country and bought two derelict seventeenth-century cottages, and proceeded to do them up.

Tony Weston was a tree-climber and when he landed up in the Stanmore back hospital, he found himself on the same ward as the Battle of Britain Spitfire pilots who had fallen out of the sky in their planes and suffered similar injuries: fellow high-flyers, swingers of birches, members of the Icarus Club. Pilots are people who show us the way. Both bone and tree are grained and living, and naturally hollowed for strength.

One summer, Tony Axon and I built a hydrocycle, or aquabike (we could never decide which sounded better), from old bits of bicycle into a kind of rickety pedalo. We planned in all seriousness to cross the Channel. Tony supplied a length of bike chain and we attached a wooden frame to old petrol cans for buoyancy, and then fixed a bicycle frame to the wooden frame. The chain powered a paddle wheel at the rear. We found a light and filched a lifebelt from the ponds at Hampstead Heath, where Tony was lifeguard, painted *Eccles* on the lifebelt after the *Goon Show* character, and mounted it on the front of the bicycle. It was very wide so we borrowed a cart from the Scouts to trundle it several miles from Headstone Lane to the Grand Union Canal at Watford. Our parents attended a special ceremony at Cassiobury Park. My mother launched it by trying and failing to smash against its bows a miniature bottle of Martini won by Tony on the shooting stall in Spain. *Eccles* floated, and even progressed in a stately, wonky way from side to side of the canal but was promptly vandalised a week later, the lifebelt stolen and the light smashed up.

*

I began work in the last days of the horse and cart, with the clop of hooves and the sound of wheels on the road ringing in my ears. Like many boys of my generation, my first job, unpaid yet richly rewarding in terms of street status, was as a milkman's assistant. I was five or six when I first tasted the daily pleasure of riding shotgun on the milk float's wooden bench beside Sheperth the milkman and behind Daisy the horse. Sheperth wore a striped blue-and-white apron with a big leather money pouch slung diagonally across his shoulder. It shone with the accumulated grime of pennies and two-bob bits. On Saturdays, when we collected the milk money, Sheperth raised one knee at the doorstep to support his satchel as he rummaged for change, shaking it to rearrange the coins for the women in dressing gowns at the door. Even if there wasn't a handy doorstep, he still lifted his knee, dangling one foot in mid-air and balancing on the other, delving in and doling out, sometimes leaning back against a sideways fence to steady himself as he scribbled in his ledger with a pencil he produced from behind his ear.

These were the days of tits pecking holes in the gold-top bottles to steal the cream. Frost would freeze the clot of cream in the neck of the bottle, its expansion forcing up the shiny top, exposing it seductively. I collected the empties, sliding my fingers into their icy necks to clutch several at once and rattle them into the metal crates. Sheperth wore woollen mittens with cut-off fingers and flicked the reins to start Daisy ambling on down the road, her breath steaming the morning air. She wore big leather blinkers and peered out from inside them like a creature in a cave. It was always a moment or two after we moved off that the luxuriant tail would rise up and arch itself into a plume, a canopy into which the rank odour of horse exploded and billowed in our faces three feet away, perched on our folded blanket on the cart's wooden bench. Sheperth never said a word. I would look back to see the householders with little shovels and buckets emerging in our wake like seagulls in a furrow, scooping up the golden nuggets of dung, which also steamed. Riding home, the milk float was stacked to its roof with crates of empties and jingled like a tambourine to the rhythm of the trotting horse.

I had a paper round for a few years after that. The newsagent paid me 10 shillings a week and I didn't enjoy it much. I worked for Fourboys, and our competitors from Smith's always made a point of beating us up whenever we met on the pavement. The canvas bag of newspapers came in useful as a shield. *Reveille* or *Tit-Bits* always had to be folded discreetly inside the *Mail* or *Express*.

Tony Axon pioneered truly original jobs, as a pool lifeguard and blanket-packing at Harrods, where we made off with a nude mannequin on the bus and were exposed when her brown paper wrapping came off. Later we became stagehands at the Windmill Theatre in Soho under cigar-smoking John Gale, Britain's Leading Stage Manager (self-styled) and Stammering Cyril with the red nose. 'Get those ff-f-fucking t-tttabs shut, boys!' We ate salt-beef sandwiches in the Nosh Bar opposite the theatre.

TONY AXON It was term-time and we were both prefects but we got a job for ten days at Harrods during the Harrods sale. The school never noticed that we weren't there. We were packers in the linen department and there was a board in the packing room with all these labels on it – 'By Express Train', 'Fragile', 'This Way Up', 'Not To Be Delivered Before Christmas Day', 'To Be Delivered Before Christmas Day'. Harrods had been bought by Hugh Fraser of House of Fraser, and he had a flat in Hans Crescent, twenty yards from the store. One day he bought some handkerchiefs and sent them through to be delivered by van, across the road. So we did pass the parcel, wrapping it in ten layers so it grew bigger and bigger. Then we plastered the package with all the labels and threw it into a chute which swept down to these lovely, stately electric vans, which would glide away to deliver goods. If it took ten seconds to go down, the head of the linen department who came storming up only took five. 'Who the fuck's done that? Don't you know who he is?' That was a bit of a black mark.

Then I happened to walk across the floor to go to the loo. We weren't supposed to be seen by the public but I spotted Katharine Worsley, who was engaged to Prince Edward, Duke of Kent. As I sauntered back, I saw that there was a packet being made up of her purchases which would come our way. When it arrived, there was an envelope attached. We thought it probably revealed the cost of her shopping spree, and the *Daily Mirror* might be interested, and we could earn a tenner for the tip. There was a kettle permanently on the boil in the packing room for endless cups of tea, so we steamed the envelope open. Unfortunately we were bent over the envelope steaming it when in walked the head of the linen department. We were fired. Rather surprisingly, we were paid for the five days we had worked there.

The following summer holidays, with another Haberdasher, I decided to get a job in the theatre. We traipsed around stage doors asking for work. After about four of them had said, 'Are you in the union?' we asked if there was a theatre that didn't require union membership. There's only one, they said, and that's the Windmill. It was a Soho striptease club, famed for being the only theatre in London never to close during the Second World War because the shows were considered good for squaddies' morale. It was run by Sheila van Damm, a rally driver who set a new speed record at the Monte Carlo rally of 1953 in her Sunbeam Alpine.

47

Rog was green with envy but I got him in there at Christmas. It was great fun and bloody hard work. There were six shows a day, and we would start at nine in the morning with rehearsals and finish at ten thirty at night. We had to get the stage ready for the next act. There was a glass floor and we laid out the tap mat, a floor cover made of wooden slats joined with wire, so the tap dancers wouldn't shatter the glass. It was heavy and took two of us to roll it out. By the sixth show, we were knackered. One evening I was working with our fellow stagehand, Andy Flack, a female impersonator who introduced us to salt beef, and we were getting slower and slower. The band wanted to go home early and so did the stage manager. They opened the curtains and we were still rolling up the mat before the fan dance. Andy suddenly stopped and leaned on the mat and said, 'Look, Tone, we're in the fan dance, dear.' The audience burst out laughing.

*

During the Easter holidays of 1959, and again later that summer and the following year, botany and zoology sixth-formers took the train from Waterloo to Beaulieu Road in the New Forest for a week-long field trip run by our biology teacher, Barry Goater. A formidable lepidopterist, ornithologist and all-round naturalist, Barry infected us all with his wild enthusiasm.

ROGER DEAKIN, *notebooks, 1959* List to bring: Clothes: jeans and belt, green and fawn jerseys, shirts check, navy blue, brown, green check, cravat, beret, socks, plimsolls, old shoes, pyjamas, tracksuit tops. Camping equipment: safari bed, kitbag and rucksack, Primus, meths and paraffin, jack knife, breadknife, mug and plate, knife, fork, spoon, soap, facecloth, toothpaste, towels, handkerchiefs, soap powder, matches, torch, mirror, teacloths, lavatory paper, porridge bowl, groundsheet. Biological equipment: specimen tubs and corks, tins, butterfly net, some muslin, cage trap and bait, *Observer* books, notebook, tape measure, bell jar, ethyl acetate, cotton wool, string, trowel. Food: bacon, porridge, sardines (2 tins), peas (tin), loaf of bread, biscuits, cooking jar, tin of pineapple, marmalade, coffee (tin), flour, pearl barley, tea.

BARRY GOATER, *assistant biology master* The boys were intelligent and enthusiastic. They were backed by intelligent and enthusiastic parents. They were golden years.

GEORGE PETERKEN, *fellow student; later a renowned ecologist* Roger had an omnibus-enquiry style of natural history – all, of everything, in every way.

IAN BAKER, *friend* Education is what you remember after you've forgotten everything you were taught. That's true of Haberdashers'.

Although he would modestly deny it, Barry Goater was the instigator of an extraordinary educational experiment. In a quiet corner of the New Forest, he established a camp for the detailed study and mapping of the natural history of a stretch of woodland, bog and heath surrounding Beaulieu Road by his biology sixth-form. The camps became an institution at our school in the relatively treeless Cricklewood, each generation of sixth-form naturalists tasting the intoxication of discovering the wild for ourselves. Each of us had a particular project, literally a field of enquiry, and the work we were doing was genuinely original. We learned the scientific disciplines of botany, zoology, ecology, and we kept our eyes open as all-round naturalists. What we found was particular to the place and, best of all, it belonged to us.

Beaulieu Road was our America, we were pioneers, and the map we jointly drew and refined through gradual accretions of personal observation represented not only the complex natural ecology of the place but also an ambitious cooperation between generations of the sixth-form botanists and zoologists. Through our cumulative endeavours we charted the relationship between plants and animals. The records we kept were a testament to our own human relationships as well. We were learning how exploration and scholarship can progress in time through the free exchange of ideas. Small wonder that the experience influenced so many of our lives so profoundly.

BARRY GOATER We camped, two per tent, beside the railway cutting, had the use of the lavatory on Beaulieu Road station, and were supplied with bread and milk by the Beaulieu Road Hotel. All other supplies were brought by the boys and myself. We used to go for a week in the spring holidays and another in the summer, with occasional visits by one or two at other times of year. Several Old Habs, including George Peterken, came after they had left school.

Just as in *Swallows and Amazons*, Richard Jefferies's *Bevis* or any explorer's journal, we enthusiastically set about naming all the topographical features of our three miles by two of wild haunts at Beaulieu Road on a handmade map. We naturally adapted the old names where they existed, and made up our own where they didn't. We drew our water in green canvas buckets from a pure spring under the railway embankment known simply as The Spring, or Campsite Spring. Beyond it, in a gentle valley across Black Down, lay the source of the Beaulieu River at a confluence of its wooded headwaters.

Over by Station Heath lay the boggy Gentian Valley with its marsh gentians, and First Bog, snowed with the fluffy tops of cotton grass. On the other side of the railway through Botrychium Bridge (named after the moonwort that grew on the bank nearby) was found the mysterious Great Bog, where the snipe lay so close they could go off like landmines from under your boot. The bridge, christened after the ferns that grew on it, would have been Moonwort Bridge had it not been for our mentor's preference for Linnaean accuracy over poetry. Barry Goater insisted we use the scientific names drawn from Latin and Greek for each species. If poetry is about making connections, then Barry taught me poetry. That's what the poetry of Earth is. Those first names were like the names of first girlfriends. They were emotionally charged with all the potency of an early revelation. As a naturalist you hope never to lose your virginity, always to be looking with wonder, to remain innocent, wide-eyed.

Barry was unfailing in his insistence that close observation, often involving hours of patient counting and recording, was the foundation of all good science and truly original discovery. He was insatiably curious about everything, climbing trees to inspect bird's nests, getting up at daybreak to check the Tilley-lamp moth trap, or leading night patrols across the heather armed with torches and nets to sweep it for moths and caterpillars.

BARRY GOATER I don't recall Roger specialising in anything in particular but he was very enthusiastic about everything we did. Attendance was entirely voluntary and the whole thing was built upon a sense of trust and camaraderie between us. In the evening, I took those who wished to come mothing. The others went to the pub, had a game of darts and behaved impeccably. There was no question of discipline. We just did things together.

We made a point of camping inconspicuously and leaving the place a little bit tidier than it was. That was an important part of education. It wasn't teaching but it was camping for the first time, sharing a tent with a colleague and cooking up your own breakfast. I thought that was important. Some of my colleagues thought it was trivial. I thoroughly enjoyed it.

IAN BAKER Something took Roger's fancy and he got on with it. He was a generalist; a serious enthusiast, a serious eccentric and very good company. We would run downhill with our lightweight canvas camp beds held high above our heads and jump in an attempt at flight. On another occasion, Roger stepped on to some sphagnum moss, began to sink but, rather than panic, he was curious to know how deep he would go. The summer of 1959 was a really hot summer and evenings at the Beaulieu Road Hotel were controlled underage drinking. Nobody got out of hand or anything like that. It was well done. One day we were working near a pool we called Crater Pond. Roger said, 'I fancy a swim. Do you?' No way. He jumped in as if he'd been doing it forever.

Over the course of a total of twenty-four camps from April 1955 to the spring of 1961, everything any of us discovered was logged in two volumes known as the Beaulieu Tomes. Some of our projects read almost like Swift's accounts of the scientists' experiments on Laputa in *Gulliver's Travels*: 'He had been eight years upon a project for extracting sun-beams out of cucumbers, which were to be put into vials hermetically sealed, and let out to warm the air in raw inclement summers.'

Tucked away in the botanical tome is a survey of the algae of Beaulieu by my friend Ian Baker and me in which we took samples in phials from forty-seven different watery locations and laboured over microscopes to identify seventeen different genera of algae. We were sixteen. In that same August week, under 'Other interesting records' is one of the many footnotes: 'A young nightjar was found by R. Deakin amongst the heather in a stony place opposite the campsite on the east side of the railway.' The well-oiled, liquid churring of these oddly moth-like birds was a continuous background to our summer evenings and nights in the camp, like taxis waiting with engines ticking over.

Later, some of my Beaulieu-inspired poetry appeared in the school magazine, including a Wordsworthian effort occasioned by my first encounter with a marsh gentian in the eponymous valley. I felt that poetry was somehow subversive of the scientific approach Barry Goater encouraged us to adopt. Yet he was always so full of passion for nature he could never hide his own strong emotional attachment to the New Forest. Not one of us was immune to the poetry of the place. It was only much later that, by teaching me to make connections, the Beaulieu camps revealed the intimate kinship of ecology and poetry.

This kingdom taught us how rewarding it can be to look closely at things. Well over half a dozen of the Beaulieu Road regulars became full-time botanists or zoologists, and others, like me, came away with a far deeper understanding of natural history, its pleasures and endless possibilities. Now, at a time when most children have never been more alienated from nature, it looks to me like the most radical, imaginative and promising direction for education to take in the future.

THE TIMES, *21 October 1960, a newspaper cutting kept by Roger* D. H. Lawrence's novel *Lady Chatterley's Lover* was described by prosecuting counsel at the Central Criminal Court in London yesterday as a book which 'sets on a pedestal promiscuous intercourse, commends sensuality almost as a virtue, and encourages and even advocates coarseness and vulgarity of thought and language'.

On Wednesday 26 October 1960, a policeman came to our door and told me my father was dead. Well, actually what happened was that my father didn't come home on his usual train and my mother was already worried, pacing the kitchen, filling the house with foreboding.

There was a knock. I answered the door and there were two policemen there, for solidarity, I suppose, on a difficult mission.

The first policeman said, 'May I come in?'

My mother knew what they had to say straight away. It was the moment she had been dreading.

'It's bad news, I'm afraid, madam.'

It was just like *Dixon of Dock Green.*

My father had been found, dead, that afternoon on a tube train at Great Portland Street. He'd had a heart attack. He died less than a mile from where my Great-Uncle Joe was arrested in Tottenham Court Road in 1892. Both policemen took off their helmets and turned them round and round by the brim as they spoke. Their overwhelming dark blue bulk filled the sitting room of our tiny bungalow, displacing something, making my mother and I feel very small and insignificant.

I was seventeen and, the next day, I was sent to identify the body at the small, modern coroner's office across the churchyard of St Pancras Old Church behind the station. I have a vivid recollection of the churchyard: Thomas Hardy's ash tree rising, growing out of a rubble of gravestones like stacked books in a bookshop. A tree rising out of the dead – Yggdrasil, the world tree, a great symbol of life in the face of developers who have been criticised for expunging this place ever since Dickens wrote about the coming of the railway in *Dombey and Son.*

When I got to the office, the kindly coroner's assistant spared me the experience, so I never saw my father dead. He just went out that morning and disappeared out of my life. It felt odd, as well as sad. After ten days at home making awkward efforts to support my mother, I returned to school still wearing a black armband as people did in 1960, and my embarrassed friends avoided my eye. It was almost as though I myself had died, so ghostly, so invisible did I feel. Thus did I acquire my sense of loss, of expulsion from paradise. A deep-seated feeling that has followed me around all my life and I've never shaken off.

TONY AXON Rog didn't turn up for school on a particular day but he'd given a note addressed to me to a boy who was at Haberdashers' who lived up the road. I thought, what on earth is this? He wrote, 'My dad died yesterday,' and at the end, in a flourish, 'burn this'. Which was rather theatrical.

Letter of condolence to Gwen Deakin from a neighbour His health must have been an anxiety for some years now and we have admired the way in which you have borne your anxiety.

SALLY, *work colleague of Alvan, Euston House* Roger I hear has been a great help and comfort to you, Gwen, as I knew he would be, and it was very pleasing to me to see what a fine fellow he has made.

The office at 222 Marylebone Road I do hope you will find compensation in your son, who I know was a great satisfaction to his father.

DR TOM TAYLOR, *Haberdashers' headmaster, letter to Gwen the day after Alvan's death* If there is anything I can do to help Roger when he comes back I do hope he will come and see me.

MARGARET WOOD, *Gwen's sister, letter* I am so glad Alvan had his holiday this year, he did so love travel, and you must console yourself with the thought that he crammed into his short life more than most people do in eighty years.

TONY AXON It was the first funeral I ever went to and the service was followed by a cremation. I went with my mum, who had got to know Gwen at various school functions. Rog had a strong relationship with his mum but I don't think he had a very strong relationship with his father.

SERENA INSKIP Roger often spoke of his mother telling him, 'You've got to be a good boy. If you're a naughty boy you'll upset your father and then he'll die.' And then he did die. For a child, that's absolutely terrifying.

MARGARET WOOD, *letter to Gwen, 1 November 1960* I must write and say how marvellous I thought you were yesterday. Alvan would have been, and in fact is, very proud of you and your son, you both showed great courage. However, for both of your sakes I do hope you will now let go the bonds and really let your emotions have their way, it is nature's safety valve and it is not a crime to have a good old cry. I, for one, would feel much better if I thought you would or have done so, particularly Roger. He is so young, and yet he conducted himself like a man of forty or more. I remember Joan Sochett was like that and would not cry, and she was quite ill afterwards, so <u>please</u> if he has not done so help him. Alvan would understand, I am sure, and no one would think him a baby.

TONY AXON I doubt that Margaret's suggestion that Gwen have a 'good old cry' fell on fertile ground. Gwen wasn't the crying kind – she was quite a tough nut, and quite different from my mum to whom tears came very easily.

THE TIMES, *3 November 1960, newspaper cutting kept by Roger* The novel *Lady Chatterley's Lover*, by D. H. Lawrence, was adjudged not to be obscene yesterday by a jury at the Central Criminal Court. The jury was absent for three hours considering their verdict. There was an outburst of clapping, instantly silenced by the usher . . .

THE TIMES, *editorial, also kept by Roger* The more reverently such an act is regarded the less it is talked about. A decent reticence has been the practice in all classes of society and much will be lost by the destruction of it . . . A great shift in what is permissible legally has been made. But not morally. Yesterday's verdict is a challenge to society to resist the changes in its manners and conduct that may flow from it. It should not be taken as an invitation to succumb.

*

SCHOOL REPORT, *autumn term 1960* Mature member of the form.

SCHOOL REPORT, *spring 1961* Excellent contribution to life of school. House Vice-Capt.

SCHOOL REPORT, *summer 1961* Expect distinguished Cambridge career.

TONY AXON Rog wouldn't mind being called a late flowerer and I certainly was. Our O level performance was pathetic. In lots of schools we would've been slung out. But they persevered and then we sailed through A levels. Rog was going to do biology, chemistry and physics but the physics teacher said, 'Look, I think you ought to read English,' so that's what happened. He did English and a couple of sciences. All our friends got into universities hither and thither but Rog and I were high and dry. Then the headmaster told Roger that he'd organised an interview at Peterhouse and he told me I'd got an interview at Trinity in Cambridge.

We both got offered places, which was even more surprising. In March 1961, the letter from Trinity accepting me coincided with a rejection from Hull. To get into Cambridge you had to have Latin O level, which neither of us had. Again, our headmaster came to the rescue. Two teachers gave up their free lessons to teach us Latin in eight weeks, before we sat the O level exam in June. We had to go to Cambridge to take it because we were too late for the exam board used by Haberdashers'. When we went up to Cambridge in October, Rog and his mum didn't have a car so my parents drove across to Headstone Lane and put his stuff in the car and he came with us.

My father's death meant my mother had to go out to work all day to keep me at school. I offered to leave and get a job but there was really never much question of it because I was supposed to go to university. So I tried hard to get to Cambridge where for three years I affected the young gentleman during term-time and worked on building sites frantically hard in the vacations to pay my mother for my keep, and pay my own way. Result: a second strand in my life – a practical, working-with-hands one.

CHAPTER 4

The Student

Learning to think with Kingsley Amis – a star-fucker, a fashion icon and the proud first student owner of Bob Dylan's LP – my first love Gloria – Tony Axon's old jeep – Cambridge ices up – 'Bit of a devil for the women, old Rog' – dancing – up and off and do with Erica – boiling up pigs' trotters for a real treat – friendship with Dudley Young – a night out at the notorious Tickell Arms – Rog and Dud

Six of us arrived at Peterhouse in October 1961 to read English with Kingsley Amis as our supervisor: Richard Handford, Richard Eyre, Tony Ryan, Nick Squire, Derek Frampton and me. On our first night in the college we all met in someone's room and nervously exchanged notes. Eyre and I had both jumped ship as sixth-form scientists to do English. Handford, later an executive producer of TV series such as *The Bill* and *Casualty*, was quite clear that he was going to make films. Almost all of us were going to make films, we reckoned, and three of us did, in the end. Frampton became a schoolmaster. The foppish, gangling Squire failed his exams, dropped out, and was replaced by a convert from the classics, Graham Cadwallader. Ryan, a Gothic figure who always dressed in black, even black gloves, seemed especially close to Amis. Ryan's father had the rambling, Irish, Tavistock Hotel near Westbourne Park tube station in London, and 'The Tavvy' soon became a favourite London rendezvous with Amis, who spent a good deal of time in the city. Ryan could write brilliant, iconoclastic essays, but he was also an extravagant toper famous for his reckless benders. On one occasion he strode straight into the River Cam in winter and was lucky to be rescued. He never got the first people said he might achieve, and I know nothing of the rest of his life.

The University Library became one of my favourite places in the world. Sir Giles Gilbert Scott's heavy-duty design for the outside of the building was not universally admired but it was impossible not to be enthralled once you stepped inside and began to wander about its labyrinths like Charlie in the chocolate factory. I'd walk and climb for miles in there, up and down its austere corridors and steep staircases, following esoteric clues scribbled on scraps of paper in the librarians' special code. I loved the questing spirit of the place. Even better was the serendipity of searching the shelves for the book you thought you needed and discovering an even more interesting volume perched cheek by jowl beside it.

Like us, Kingsley Amis was new in Cambridge, and took his teaching seriously. I was nervous about meeting him.

TONY AXON Roger kind of worshipped Kingsley Amis. A few months before Rog went up to Cambridge, Amis was on *Desert Island Discs* and so Rog was hunched over the radio writing down quotes and all of Amis's preferences. He learned it all by heart – the fondness for the poetry of Robert Graves; his favourite song, 'Shim-Me-Sha-Wabble' by Bud Freeman and His Famous Chicagoans – and managed to slip references into their conversation. I'm sure that was helpful in impressing Amis.

The college gave Amis a modest, elegant first-floor room that bridged across one end of the Old Court to the chapel like something in Venice. Halfway through our first supervision, he surprised me by observing it was already half past ten and time for a glass of Madeira. There was the hawkish hooded eye, the sudden sharp, piercing glance, the bad teeth, and the stunning mimicry, often of figures like Leavis, Eliot or Auden. He would burst into his clownish one-man shows for an audience of anything from one to half a dozen of us.

As a teacher, Amis blended precisely the right levels of the formal and informal. He addressed us as 'Mr Handford', or 'Mr Deakin', and invariably treated us with great respect and a refreshing directness. Early on, I somehow revealed in an essay about Milton's 'Lycidas' my difficulty with the word 'winds' in the lines:

> We drove a field, and both together heard
> What time the Gray-fly winds her sultry horn.

Amis gently invited me to read this out to him, and, sure enough, I mispronounced 'winds' to rhyme with 'finds'. 'How exactly would you wind a horn?' he asked, putting me on the spot until I worked it out for myself.

RICHARD HANDFORD, *friend* Kingsley Amis and Roger and I started at the same time so we were his guinea pigs. I don't think anybody had read English at Peterhouse before us. We wrote a weekly essay for Kingsley. My early experience was terrifying because my English teacher at school said it wasn't for us to have original thoughts. During my first supervision, Kingsley said, 'I don't want to know what Theodore Redpath said about John Donne and I don't want to know what T. S. Eliot had to say about John Donne, I want to know what you think.' I thought, my God, I never expected to have to say what I thought. He was quite challenging. After the first tutorial, he said, 'Why don't we meet in the Little Rose next time,' which was the pub across the road from Peterhouse, and we had supervisions there for the rest of the year. I would have a half and Kingsley would have a pint and then go on to something stronger. And eventually I did learn to express my own thoughts.

KINGSLEY AMIS, *note to Roger, 10 May 1962* Hearty apologies, but Friday afternoon is no good either. Could you make it Monday at 10 or 12? and – to keep you occupied – read more of Spenser – including minor poems. Yours, Kingsley Amis.

If it was anywhere near lunchtime, you would often be invited to join him in the Little Rose. Grown-up drinking, as well as poetry, featured strongly in our education with Amis.

MAY LING CADWALLADER, *wife of Graham Cadwallader* The great man would always make them sit down and have an alcoholic beverage. One day he said, portentously, 'Today I want you to listen to something that's very important. These people are very important,' and he put on a record, and it was the first time Graham ever heard the Beatles.

Amis didn't much enjoy Cambridge and made no secret of it. He must have thought the place stuck-up, toffee-nosed, time-warped. He lived in a big house on the Madingley Road and would invite us round now and then, and we suburban boys would get a glimpse of a more relaxed, peopled, bohemian way of life.

KINGSLEY AMIS, Memoirs *(1991)* There could be something faintly, now and then not so faintly, disreputable about the kind of open house Hilly and I kept in Madingley Road.

Invitation to Roger to attend cocktails with Kingsley Amis at 9 Madingley Road, 13 June 1962 Up to one female companion welcome.

RICHARD HANDFORD I remember going to one party at Kingsley's at the end of our first summer term in 1962. It was a pretty alcoholic occasion. It was a glorious summer evening and we were in the garden. We were all offered liberal quantities of an innocuous-looking 'cup' which Kingsley had clearly laced with vodka. It was probably a test to see which of us could hold our drink. Two or three ended up collapsed in the flower beds, while the few of us still standing eventually adjourned with Kingsley to a pub off Trumpington Street to attempt drinking a yard of ale. Needless to say we all failed.

There was a donkey on the wide lawn at Madingley Road. It wandered freely in and out of the house, and Hilly dispensed sandwiches to us pimply undergraduates. We all liked Hilly. Plenty of dons kept pets at that time. Dr Mark Pryor, the senior tutor of Trinity, kept an army of guinea pigs to mow the lawn of his house in Chaucer Road.

Amis never seemed to have much truck with the other Peterhouse College fellows, Denis Mack Smith, Maurice Cowling, or Watson, the unraveller of DNA. You never saw him in a gown, or dining at the high table. He was at home in the Little Rose, or his house on Madingley Road. He seemed to slip in and out of the college quietly, reading and marking essays diligently, occasionally writing Larkinesque comments in the margin – 'Ouch!' or 'Argggghh' – and getting on with his supervisions. He didn't give lectures and clearly wasn't much liked in certain quarters of the university hierarchy. I once caught up with F. R. Leavis in the street to ask him about something after his lecture and he enquired who supervised me. When I told him, he said, 'Now that IS a serious disadvantage,' as though it were a known fact.

*

We were naturally interested in clothes, and our supervisor, we noted, was never less than dapper. He would often wear the multicoloured barred silk ties that were sold in Primavera, an arty shop opposite King's. There were brown suede Hush Puppies, pink socks, and pale grey Prince of Wales check trousers and some sort of grey-and-black dogtooth jacket. Richard Eyre, with his sawn-off gown, the snappiest dresser in the college, busy playing Bongo Herbert, the prototype pop singer in Wolf Mankowitz's *Expresso Bongo*, easily outdid us all, even Amis, whose style and elegance somehow went with his love of Byron, whom he in no way resembled, but taught me to admire.

CHRISTOPHER MEYER, *friend* I was in this very small group of nerdy history scholars. There were about four of us and we were deeply unfashionable. Then I learned, through somebody I knew in Jesus who was always up with the latest fashions and listened to the right music, about this guy called Roger Deakin. 'You should meet.' We did all meet. This was when Carnaby Street was the height of fashion and Roger had the very first album I had ever seen by Bob Dylan, a mark of his super-fashionability. Roger always knew exactly what kind of shirt to wear, and music to listen to. In college terms, I was a bit of a star-fucker and Roger was a star and I thought I must tuck into his slipstream.

We would sit in his rooms, listening to Dylan, and he set up a poker school one evening. He had a very open side to him and a very secret side to him. He was very hail-fellow-well-met, incredibly affable, always smiling and joking. You felt comfortable in his company. He had a long-term girlfriend lurking around the place but I was never quite clear what the relationship was and if you pried or poked a little bit he then clammed up immediately.

DUDLEY YOUNG, *friend* We used to chasten Roger when he got a little bit out of line. We'd say, 'Trendy, trendy, Rog.'

ERICA BURT, *girlfriend* He was charming, absolutely charming. But restless. And not necessarily at ease with himself.

CHARLES ANSON, *friend* Roger was a great man of the moment. He was, as the French say, *bien dans sa peau*, he was very comfortable in his skin, and for that reason was a very popular friend. One of his really attractive characteristics as a person was he was such a free spirit. You'd think, get a pint of Pimm's and go out on a punt at six in the evening, and be conventional, but Roger was always up for taking a punt out at four in the morning and seeing the dawn break on the Cam.

One summer night at dusk, a dozen of us took punts the two and a quarter miles upstream from the weir above Silver Street bridge to the mill pool by the village of Granchester for a moonlit swim. Here we swam, on and on into the night.

RICHARD HANDFORD I wasn't the enthusiast for swimming in the Cam that Roger was but we all swam, naked, in the dark. Only then did it occur to most of the females that the very bits that they felt they ought to be covering up were the bits that showed most of all because they were white. Whereas the rest of the bodies weren't as white as that.

MARGOT WADDELL, *friend and later partner in the 1990s* Punting was something that really attracted me to him in the first place – that he really loved it. He was keen on getting on to the river and being part of the water. That was lovely and it was very unusual. He'd see a punt and think, that one looks a bit ropey, I can fix that up. It was his own thing. I'd never encountered someone who could fix punts and to whom that was so important. He was a one-off in that respect. In so many respects.

GWEN DEAKIN, *letter to Roger, February 1962* Dear Roger, You have not let me know whether you have received your shirts or the parcel from Jean-François. I would like to know because if you have not received them I must act quickly . . . Would you like me to come up and see the play or would you rather I did not? Drop me a line if it is only a card. I know you are busy, but I shall be pleased to know whether you have received the parcels . . . lots of love Mum.

PS. I was fined £1 on Monday last. The cheek of it is they have fined me for 'stopping on ped X'. This is their terminology. If I was on a crossing why all the fuss about the time and not allowing carmen to load there. Apparently it is not a prohibited parking area. I should be interested to go back and see the crossing.

ELSPETH, A *young woman wooed by Roger, letter, April 1962* Dear Roger, Thanks for your very interesting, amusing and unexpected letter together with the enclosed stamp. Please don't expect me to reply in the same vein, for one thing I've only had coffee to drink, and secondly I couldn't anyway! If the book you are writing – which I'd love to read – is anything like your letters, then I'm sure it will be published.

*

My first car, an old Triumph Gloria with running boards and headlights on stalks, would always have to be parked on a slope, so it could be bump-started by eco-friendly gravity. Its windscreen wipers worked perfectly at all times except during rain.

TONY AXON I had a jeep for a term at Cambridge, which I bought for £25 from a friend. It was left-hand drive, bloody uncomfortable and freezing cold, although Rog and I once drove to a party in Oxford. Another time, I drove Rog and a girlfriend to a party and the happy couple disappeared under a travelling rug in the back of the jeep for the whole journey. I was like a chauffeur but that's what friendship is for, I suppose.

One evening, Rog and I were negotiating the snaking bends in the village of Harston on the A10, south of Cambridge, when we looked in the mirror and a motorbike started to overtake us. Rog was in the suicide seat and took exception to this manoeuvre, leaning out, waving and shouting, 'Way-hay, Geoff Duke!' – after the motorcycle-racing superstar of the 1950s. The motorcyclist stuck out a hand and flagged us down. He was a police officer.

'Has this car been ten-year tested?' the officer asked.

This was the new MOT certificate, and the jeep didn't have one. So I took it to Marshall's, the only garage in Cambridge which did the test, and they told me they couldn't produce one because it didn't have brakes on the wheels. They were only on the propeller shaft. Eventually they gave it a pass but I got in terrible trouble, not with the police but with my college. Students weren't allowed cars in Cambridge and I was fined 6 shillings and 8*d*.

Later, Rog kept a Triumph Gloria in Cambridge, a 1930s car with a Coventry Climax engine. He sold it to me for £15 and I drove it down to Spain.

*

The exceptionally cold winter of 1963 was the winter of the death of Sylvia Plath. It was endlessly grey. Had it not been for the perpetual clouds, it would have been even colder. All through January and February we crouched around our gas fires and awoke beside stone-cold hot-water bottles. The Cam and Granta rivers were frozen solid.

I used to hasten down Mill Street each morning and sit lacing up my skates by the Granta amongst dozens of others busy declaring their shared passion for the ice. The atmosphere was memorably festive and good-humoured, even anarchic, like a Brueghel painting. The ice drew us all to it, and the river became the main thoroughfare. People skated, strolled, made slides, played ice hockey, pulled sledges, rode bicycles, even motorbikes. The cardboard boxes of old skates that had languished in the corner of every junk shop in the city suddenly walked. A gang of us skated to Grantchester and back, the professionals whizzing past us streamlined in body-stockings and balaclavas, heads down, hands clasped behind their backs, like high-speed penguins. Older skaters pushed brooms before them to steady themselves. I showed off my trick of throwing Jelly Babies into the air and catching them in my mouth like a performing seal while skating at full speed. The river was full of shouts and the swish of skates, the ice engraved and criss-crossed in sugared lines. Someone even drove a Mini along the frozen Ouse from Ely to Littleport.

The miracle was in the spontaneity of the occasion: the sudden transformation of the landscape and the physical laws of nature that enabled us to walk on water. Reincarnated by the frost, the fen people, normally sedentary and earth-bound, toiling in their potato fields or allotments, mysteriously emerged like swallowtails or dragonflies from their larvae, skimming about the frozen fens with all the urgency of Cinderella at the ball.

TONY AXON Someone drove an Austin 7 to Granchester on the ice. Someone else put an Austin 7 on the roof of the Senate House. Nobody found out how they did it but it took ages to get it down again. It was rusting on the roof. The mains gas pipe cracked in Trinity Street and we had a fortnight without any gas heating. So we got electrical heaters which fused the lights.

ERICA BURT It was amazing because it was a hoar frost, it wasn't snowy, and it didn't go from the trees for at least a month. The college flooded the hockey pitch in Homerton so we could skate on it. And the rooms were so cold. I had a friend from Trinidad and he became ill and a hot-water bottle that he put in his bed froze solid. It was horrendous. We put our feet right in front of the gas fire but it was the first year I didn't get chilblains. The world was turned on its head for a bit because we could walk into a college and stay overnight and no one knew. We didn't have to go through the porters' lodge; we could walk out the back and across the river. We could cycle on the Cam. So there was quite a lot of that going on.

*

VARSITY HANDBOOK, 1962–63 The Male to Female ratio in the University is about 8:1. Cut out those men who are not prepared to stick the pace, and it falls to 7:1. Cut out those who have steady girl friends at home and it falls to 6:1. Include Addenbrooke's Nurses (Telephone 56361) 5:1, Homerton (475471) 4:1 and foreign girls 3:1. A reasonable enough figure for any man. With careful management, a man can run three girls: one in Cambridge, one at home, and one in London.

VARSITY HANDBOOK, Women's Page Don't let success go to your head. Remember, there are ten men to every woman, but brains aren't everything – especially where well-paid secretaries and well-groomed Bell School girls provide strong competition; not to mention the week-end influx from London. If you have long hair, wash it and brush it; if you bicycle, avoid very straight or very full skirts; they can be equally embarrassing. About entertaining: it is important to repay hospitality . . . For most men the long trek to a women's college is an event.

ANNE, Homerton College, 16 May 1962, note to Roger Don't forget that you and two friends are coming here to Hall on Monday 21st May at 6.30 p.m. Please be on your best behaviour and bring your 2/6 along with you! Love, Anne.

ANNE, Homerton College, 24 May 1962 Was it you, Andrew or Rory who did not pay 2/6 for your meal? I wonder if you could inform the offender that I am damned if I am going to finance him for free meals!

JOHN HUGGINS, letter to Roger, May 1962 Bit of a devil for the women, old Rog!

DUDLEY YOUNG You know that line of Larkin's. It began then, because of the pill. Before it began, we were all a bit sexually shy. Because we were of that previous world. And Beatles are very good on shy. They wrote some lovely, acute lyrics. The Beatles were new and the sixties were being lit up.

TONY AXON Rog had quite a number of girlfriends at Cambridge and relationships of various degrees of seriousness. On one occasion we were at Golders Green station and we bumped into Tony May who had been at Haberdashers' and he had these two really nice women with him, so we all went to the pub. They were sisters called Sarah and Charlotte. We said, 'If you're ever in Cambridge . . .' and quite amazingly we later received a letter saying, 'We're coming to Cambridge.' Wow. They had rented a hotel room, I think they were quite wealthy, and we had a great evening. We taught these girls a dance called the Madison, which was really big in France and Spain. One of the steps was 'De Gaulle' and there were all these gestures and it was great fun. Charlotte rather swept Rog off his feet. The elder sister, Sarah, was tragically killed in a car crash not long after that and her sister, Charlotte, family name Rampling, went on to a dazzling acting career. We never saw them again.

CHARLOTTE RAMPLING ON ROGER Unforgettable.

DUDLEY YOUNG All of a sudden there were the Beatles, so we did start dancing and Roger was good at it and loved to dance.

ERICA BURT Dancing? No, that wasn't his scene.

TONY AXON Was he a good dancer? Not really, no. He enjoyed it very much but he wasn't very natural. Invitations to parties were delivered on cards that were known as stiffies, and one summer both Rog and I received a terribly grand invite for a party in the top of a turret in Trinity Great Court being hosted by the Honourable somebody or other. The invitation said, 'Bring a bottle of champagne.' We sprogged along with our Marks & Spencer's champagne and there was a butler who poured us a glass of champagne when we entered. It was a sunny evening but all the curtains were drawn and there was music and people dancing and, when our eyes adjusted, we saw it was all men dancing together. We backed out rather quickly, and said to the butler, 'I think we'll, you know . . .'
    'I quite understand sir,' he said.
    'Would it be all right if we recovered our champagne?'
    'Of course, sir. Which bottle is it?'
    Rog immediately said, 'Mine was the Moët.'
    'And, um, mine was the Taittinger,' I said.
    Rather ostentatiously, we opened one bottle and sat drinking it on the steps by my digs above the Barclays Bank on Sidney Street. We sat there and these

two Spanish girls walked by. I said, 'I think they are speaking Spanish.' Rog said, 'Ask them if they want to come to a party.'

'Would you like to go to the smartest party in Cambridge tonight?' I said in Spanish.

And one of the girls, Teresa, said, 'We're already going.'

'I don't think you are,' I said pompously. 'Let me see your invitation.'

She produced an invitation which said, 'David Frost and Friends invite . . .' And I said, 'Well, what a coincidence, we're going there too,' and off we all went to David Frost's party.

TERESA AXON Me and my sister had been invited to go to a party by a man who was a drummer and was going to play at the party. We were speaking in Spanish and these two men spoke to us in Spanish. 'Excuse me, would you like to come to a party with us?' We said, 'No, we are already invited to a party. If you want, you can come with us.' We had no clue who David Frost was but Tony said this was the best party in town. We had a table, we were dancing, and we were friends from then on.

I was an au pair and studied at a language school on Station Road. We called our flat Alaska. We would make a mould of a shilling in the freezer, put it in the gas meter, and it would work, and there was a hole and the water drained out the bottom. We thought Cambridge was a monkish place. There was nothing open after 9 p.m. Everything was closed. I thought, I will never live here, and then I married and came here for fifty-five years. After that first party, me and my sister went with Roger to the museum because Tony had the flu. I thought Roger might be my man but Roger was looking for somebody with a name like Rockefeller. Being friends was lovely.

TONY AXON In the summer, I became involved with Amnesty International and got roped into delivering food parcels for Spanish political prisoners. Teresa had given me her phone number so I visited her home in the seaside village of Llafranc. I got to know her better and kept in touch but her father said she couldn't come and live with me in England unless we got married. So we got married and Roger was best man.

TERESA AXON Roger was our only friend to come from England for our wedding, and he wrote and read a poem in Spanish: *Yo traigo flores / de muchos colores, / deseándote felicidad / para una eternidad* [I bring you flowers / of many colours, / wishing you happiness / for an eternity].

*

ERICA BURT I came to Homerton in 1962 to train to be a teacher. I was seeing a guy at Peterhouse and that finished but I'd also met Roger there and he got in touch and we had quite a lot in common – we had both been to school in North London and I'd studied botany and zoology like Roger. He was unpredictable. Suddenly he'd say, 'Let's do this,' and off you'd go, because you knew it was going to be good fun. He was nothing like anybody else I'd ever known or have known since, really.

We would go to Kinema, the little arts cinema out beyond the city centre on Mill Road, and watch the latest French or Italian releases. I went with Rog and Richard Handford to watch *Jules et Jim*, which was released in 1962, and we danced down the street afterwards, singing, and discussed it for hours. Rog loved French and Spanish food and took me out for meals down Mill Road. I had moussaka for the first time at a Greek taverna. He would smuggle me into his rooms afterwards but was more scared of being discovered than I was. It was ever so funny. 'Don't talk,' he would whisper.

BRIAN SHUTES, *student neighbour of Roger in Peterhouse* We had to behave, as two Nobel Laureates, Professor Max Perutz OM and Professor Sir John Kendrew, occupied rooms on the floor above us.

ERICA BURT It was always up and off and do with Rog. He was never in a place long enough for me to reflect on our relationship. It wasn't straightforward in the way that my friends would know when they were going to see their boyfriends. I never knew. He didn't phone me up to arrange to see me the following Thursday at seven. He only came out to Homerton on perhaps two occasions. But I never said no to seeing him, I'd drop everything because you knew it was going to be great. It was on his terms but when you were with him, you'd have his attention.

He was a bit like quicksilver. He was a very transparent person; he wasn't secretive or holding anything back. But friends were important to him, perhaps too important. If there was an upset, he couldn't understand why, whereas most people would just let it go. So I think relationships have always been quite tricky. It's easy to say of an only child but he never quite understood give and take – 'forget it, it's not that important' – and he could hurt very easily.

VARSITY HANDBOOK, 1962–63 May Week – usually the first fortnight in June – is the grand climax to the social year. Essential are chicks and cheques, girls and Granchester, late nights and lolly, popsies, parties, and punts. Warn your bank manager or try taking his daughter.

ERICA BURT Roger and I both made things. There was a Swedish shop in Cambridge which sold these wonderful fabrics and me and my girl friends made our ball dresses out of them. I created my dress for the Trinity May Ball, to which Roger invited me in 1963. He was at his most charming and we partied all night and punted down the river to Granchester at dawn for breakfast. Later, he took a Canadian girl to a May Ball. Richard Handford was really sweet and said, 'He doesn't know what he's missing.' Richard was much more grounded. Roger wasn't grounded. That's not a criticism. I sensed he was rather lost. When this Canadian girl had gone, I was company for Roger again.

*

ANNETTE KOBAK, *contemporary of Roger at Cambridge; later partner* The Cam froze over in '63, we heard the news about Kennedy and Sylvia Plath took her own life that year. It was very intense but, more than that, it was a crucible of change. What we were born into, the fifties, was excruciatingly dull. It was so normative. Everybody was keeping their heads down, unsurprisingly after the Second World War. Particularly in the suburbs, if you had a dull home to come back to, there was no particular excitement, except France. For a lot of people, France was an escape route; I had a penfriend in France and ended up reading French and German at university. Roger, too, took journeys to the south of France.

JOHN HUGGINS We hitch-hiked to the south of France in the summer of '63 when 'l'affaire Profumo' was all over the French papers. Roger had a penpal who had a holiday home there. Those were the days when if you put a Union Jack on your rucksack people thought that was a good thing. We got this amazing lift from a grocer from near Fontainebleau well into the south. En route, the driver, our patron, insisted that we stop at various vineyards and sample the local wines, which he wouldn't take a franc for. He continued driving, after glass after glass. After lunch, with more wine, we were put in the back of the van on loose metal chairs, on the metal-bottomed van. We slid on each corner and only just avoided sliding out of the van's sliding doors. We slept out under the stars then spent a week at the villa. Roger was adventurous at that time, much more than me.

*

SUNDAY TIMES, *Atticus, February 1963, cutting kept by Roger* When Amis resigns his post at Peterhouse College, Cambridge, he is retiring to Majorca – 'just for

69

a year'. The brave man proposes to take the family's pet donkey Debby with him, customs difficulties notwithstanding.

We had no inkling Amis was going to leave at the close of our second year in the summer of '63, although towards the end he would sometimes rearrange supervision appointments by having the college porters deliver formal hand-written cards to our pigeonholes. We all liked and respected him, and missed him when he was gone. We rather limped through our final year with a succession of makeshift supervisors, none of whom had the slightest chance of matching the style, let alone the wit, of their predecessor.

RICHARD HANDFORD In the third year, we volunteered to share rooms and were given a large, oak-panelled room on the ground floor of Great Court at Peterhouse, off which we each had a minute bedroom and a gyp, which was the kitchen. Roger liked to invent new recipes that would stink the place out. He bought a whole load of pigs' trotters which he proceeded to boil up and our rooms smelled like a tannery. Which was typical of Roger. He was always after a good bargain and pigs' trotters were nearly free.

DUDLEY YOUNG We made friends at Cambridge. I read philosophy as an undergraduate in the States, started a BA in English at Peterhouse in '63. After a term I was allowed to give up my BA and switch to a PhD on Yeats. I thought that was a feather in my cap. I had this huge scholarship, which meant I was very intelligent. It said in the fine print. I was two years older than Roger and for a long time I was the elder brother, I suppose.

RICHARD HANDFORD Roger admired Dudley tremendously, both his intellect and also his other abilities.

TONY AXON Dudley had rather an impressive bod.

VICKY MINET, *girlfriend of Dudley and friend of Roger* Dudley always had a fan club around him. He was naturally outdoorsy and he seemed to be very successful with women. He was always incredibly rebellious, he appeared to be a wild man, and all the young men thought he was the most marvellous role model.

SARAH DICKINSON, *girlfriend of Roger* Dudley was very impressive. Big man. Big voice. He had an Oscar Wilde swagger to him; there was a virtual cane in his hand, in a pompous sense. He was that sort of man.

GILBERT REID, *friend* Dudley had a dog called Heidegger.

MARGOT WADDELL He was a one-off, Dudley. And I think Roger always wanted to be a one-off.

DUDLEY YOUNG In those early days, I didn't threaten him at Cambridge. I was this weird Canadian coming in, I wasn't running to be the big man on campus; Rog and Richard were the big men in the college.

RICHARD HANDFORD I suppose Roger and I were active in the life of the college but I don't think we did anything terribly distinguished. I very rarely went to lectures, and I don't think Roger went to that many either, so we would tend to sit up half the night, putting the world to rights. Roger was a great philosopher. He always had deep thoughts which he would run past me, some of which were great and some of which were not quite so great.

CHARLES ANSON I remember going with Roger on expeditions to the more idiosyncratic pubs like the Tickell Arms outside Cambridge. It was run by an absolute eccentric, Kim Tickell. There was always Wagner playing and good food and a fascinating, unusual atmosphere which was quite fun for an undergraduate.

GILBERT REID The Tickell Arms was a rogueish and famous place. Kim Tickell was gay and pretended to be extremely misogynist. Perhaps he really was. It was part of his schtick. He had a German-Austrian boyfriend and they pretended to adore the German army and used to play the funeral march of von Hindenburg to annoy the farmers when they came in for their early pint before the chic crowd arrived. Behind the bar, Kim would ask very provocative questions of young ladies which today would probably land him in jail; then, it was an initiation rite for the ladies and their companions. You had to duel a bit with Kim Tickell. You could eat game there and there was buckshot in the game, and Roger was part of that caper. It was very amusing.

I was fresh from the Continent, I'd worked in Paris, so I was an abstract thinker, an existentialist. Roger had the Anglo-Saxon allergy to that sort of generalising discourse. I remember a conversation, I think it was in the Tickell Arms, where I was pushing the existentialist line: people are free to change their conditions and to do this and that. Roger said, 'No, people aren't free,' and he mentioned a relative who had TB and died young and he argued very doggedly, and I retreated. I felt rather ashamed of my puerile Sartrian belief in total liberty.

I was very impressed by Roger, he was charismatic but low-key, whereas Dudley was intellectual Barnum and Bailey. Dudley was extraordinarily charismatic. Conversation was the dialectical dance. You learned about Hegel and Heidegger and Greek theatre and he was exceptionally persuasive and he also played on the idea of being a bit diabolical. Dudley hypnotised a lot of people and he was a Mephistopheles for some. And he knew everybody – Robert Lowell, the American poet, a lot of really swishy Rothschild bankers, intellectuals, psychoanalysts – and Roger did look up to Dudley. But Dudley could really rub people the wrong way. He was a provocateur: western civilisation on its death throes; the spiritual apocalypse; men have been castrated. There was a misogynist side which maybe clashed with Roger's gallant side.

DUDLEY YOUNG I was mildly charismatic. There was a period when people actually did think I had something to say. 'Authority' was a big one for my generation. It was still around when I was at Cambridge. But I had some authority. Or I was given some. I was on a very rich scholarship and then I went out and bought a car. A Morgan. In the second year, I moved out of Cambridge to the village of Whittlesford. I said, 'Fucking hell, we're in England, we should ride a horse.' So I bought this clapped-out racehorse called Ferughi-bear. It's a wonder she didn't kill me. I'd take her down to Duxford aerodrome and open up the throttle and I'd come off because this horse would go crazy. Roger and Tony Weston came out and built me a very good lean-to stable for my horse. He and Tony were in charge. They knew about how to do it. And I was a gopher, I would bring them a cup of tea. It's a comic moment in which Roger didn't even have to compete; he streaked right past me.

BUNDLE WESTON Dudley wasn't very nice.

SOPHIE WESTON, *Bundle and Tony's daughter* You can be a nice rogue but he was a bit of a shit, wasn't he?

BUNDLE WESTON People could say that Rog was a bit of a rogue but he was so nice, and so vulnerable. And Dudley probably was a rogue. He liked to humiliate people.

CAROLINE CLIFTON-MOGG Dudley was the cool one, having women coming out of every pocket, and Roger rather thought that was terrific but they were such chalk and cheese. Roger gentle, very clever, very creative, and Dudley thought he was all those things but wasn't. And whereas everybody was drawn to Roger, Dudley tended to repel.

JULES CASHFORD Dudley rented a cottage in Whittlesford which was beautiful. Organised everything financially. Spoke across everyone. Roger idolised him. Soon after I first met Roger at the cottage, I got up to go next door to make some coffee. And Roger rose and opened the door for me, which was totally unnecessary and wonderfully strange but he was ridiculed for it by Dudley, which was nasty. There was a bite in it. I don't think it did anyone any good; certainly not Rog. But he was overawed. If you are a small boy in some place in your feelings, and you saw Dudley who had the freedom to do what he wanted, say what he liked, get away with it and pay for it – or not – then I think you would be vulnerable to over-endorsing that. And you shouldn't have wanted that because, if you were Roger, you were much better the way you were. And once he got out of Cambridge and away from those kind of influences, he really came much more into himself.

CHAPTER 5

The Ad Man

Rebellion in Venice in the summer of '69 — finding the Queen's Gardens
flat in London — writing blurb for Penguin and copywriting for CPV — living with
a pencil behind my ear — making a killing with the clocks on Portobello — a straight
aspiring to be one of the heads — Margot and a thwarted proposal — driving in the snow
with Celia — falling in love with Jenny — the gamekeeper's cottage — the jeep,
Champ — island bliss at the sixties' end

DUDLEY YOUNG We never thought we were having the sixties. We were just growing up.

I joined the Royal Navy in 1969. For our generation, growing our hair, listening to *Tommy* on double vinyl or watching the Rolling Stones release hundreds of large white butterflies in memoriam for Brian Jones in Hyde Park, there was probably never a less attractive time to fight for Queen and Country. Which was why I flew to Venice with a photographer and art director for my advertising agency, Vernon's. To turn military service into an irresistible proposition for young pacifists, I was to rendezvous with 800 Royal Marines on HMS *Bulwark*, the third biggest ship in the Royal Navy, for a week on manoeuvres off Malta.

Venice. A violet sea in the early morning, blue rising into paler blue, edged with spires, roofs, domes. There was no boat to meet us at the aerodrome so we hired a gondola and took lunch in St Mark's Square. Sitting well back in a cane chair before iced glasses of Campari, I watched the aerobatic pigeons, a thousand wingbeats purring into the pale blue. As the church bells boomed, these pigeon Red Devils soared and wheeled and pirouetted in mid-air, falling on the paving stones like a grey blanket shaken in the wind.

We proceeded in our gondola to glide up to the biggest ship ever to drop anchor in the sound between San Giorgio and San Marco. Earlier in the year, *Bulwark*, fondly nicknamed 'The Rusty B', had received television documentary-makers on board as part of a drive for positive publicity while in the Mediterranean. So I was taken aback when the captain, J. A. Templeton-Cotill, on top of giving us the coolest welcome ever, sent the Officer of the Day to ask me to get my hair cut. *Bulwark*'s captain, known by the men as 'TC', was reputedly famous for a 'fastidious wit'. Off duty, he may have matched cravats with silk shirts in shades of pink, lime green and yellow, but he drew the line at my mane. To the captain, I was from a different tribe. Not his tribe, and therefore dangerous. The look of puzzled fear was fascinating. I dispatched the Officer of the Day back to the captain with the message to fuck off. No more was said that day.

The next morning, curls still flying, I persuaded a pilot to take me up in a Sioux helicopter for a scenic tour of Venice and the lagoon, and another excellent lunch in St Mark's Square. When we returned, and I climbed out in my flying suit, the captain happened to be on deck entertaining the Italian Admiral of the Fleet. Apparently the admiral thought I was one of the crew. Again the captain sent orders that I should cut my hair. I became furious and roared off to see him and ask him what he thought he was at. The outcome was a three-quarter-hour row in front of a number of Templeton-Cotill's brothers in which I gave him a long lecture on Hospitality, Good Manners, the Role of the Gentleman, the Human Rights He Was Meant to Be There to Protect, Prejudice, and Why He Was a Stupid Cunt.

The captain banned me from the wardroom and from eating with the officers, which of course I welcomed. By this time we had set sail for the Adriatic. The rumour about what happened went around the ship before we had even finished our little interview and I promptly became the hero of the lower decks, where I took up residence in the Petty Officers' Mess, learned a few hundred dirty jokes, enjoyed a great deal of rum, and took my leisure under a pleasant sunshine in a lifeboat with a book.

The moment we arrived in Malta, I hired a convertible Chevrolet, drove to the far end of the island and took up residence in an extremely expensive hotel for a few days' waterskiing, swimming and reading. When I got back to Vernon's, they amazed me by being deeply sympathetic and sent off a strongly worded protest to the Admiralty. To my even greater amazement, the Admiralty were most apologetic. It turned out that this bastard Templeton-Cotill was reputedly the richest man in the Navy and therefore was heartily loathed by most of the other aspiring Sea Lords in the Admiralty.

I wrote plenty of copy for the Navy. My favourite words were placed alongside an image of a naval ship coming through the mist on a choppy sea, sailors stood bravely on the bridge: 'All the good guys are still riding white horses.'

The Navy didn't like it but I was not much bothered. I really found out what it was like to be different – to be an outcast – on that ship. And it was time to cast off. I had already handed in my notice at Vernon's and would leave at August's end. The sixties were drawing to a close and I was possessed by a new desire to get out of the nine-to-five and the grime and clamour of London. The warm fields of Suffolk were calling.

*

Five years earlier, in the summer of 1964, I drove the Triumph Gloria from Cambridge to London for the final time. Before leaving the university, I had taken a small walk-on part in *Nothing But the Best*. Alan Bates was an amoral young estate agent tutored in the art of social climbing by Denholm Elliott. I was a dinner-jacketed student, entering a stately home for a summer ball. My friends and I were in love with the glamour of film but new priorities were more pressing: find a place to live and earn a decent wage.

Plenty of Cambridge graduates were heading for well-paid jobs in the City, Christopher Meyer and Charles Anson were off to the Foreign Office, but Richard Handford, Tony Axon and I tried the BBC. Their general traineeship was the pathway to radio, television, travel, excitement, and the BBC of that day looked kindly upon entrants from Oxbridge. We took an exam and an interview and flew through both. Then we had to appear before the final board. None of us got the job. Hundreds of graduates had applied for a handful of positions. By the mid-sixties, the BBC traineeship was the grand prize for ambitious graduates, and successful applicants were those who demonstrated the kind of preternatural commitment to journalism that would turn them into legends of the industry, from Melvyn Bragg to my former schoolmate David Elstein.

We rejects were offered a chance to work our way up from a more lowly position but I didn't fancy the grind of studio manager. Nor did Tony, although Richard took it up. Tony landed a job at *The Economist* and I began writing blurb for Oliver Caldecott, a South African anti-apartheid campaigner who became the principal fiction editor for Penguin Books. Caldecott championed Penguin Modern Classics and gradually introduced 'new age' books including the Carlos Castaneda series. I wrote the words on the covers of the Geoffrey Household thrillers *Rogue Male*, *Rough Shoot* and *Watcher in the Shadows*. *Rogue Male* became a seminal text for me and my friend Tony Barrell.

TONY BARRELL, *memoirs (unpublished)*, 2007 Roger Deakin and I spent a couple of years devouring Household as a necessary antidote to J. R. R. Tolkien's elaborate pantheon of invented monsters and heroes which was very big at the time. The rogue male was a metaphor for what we were doing: hiding in the country, in my case on a part-time basis. For Roger, it was a life's work. But hiding from what?

Barrell, as we all knew him, derived the verb 'to quive' from Geoffrey Household's Major Quive Smith, the gentlemanly villain of the piece, to describe wriggling along a leafy ditch-bottom, flat on your chest in pursuit of, or flight from, whatever or whoever you didn't want to see you. *Rogue Male* may be said to be one long quive from beginning to end. Barrell had black hair, black eyebrows and wore dark polo necks and navy corduroy.

BOB MARSHALL-ANDREWS, *friend and flatmate* Barrell was left-wing, off-the-wall, very funny, very rude.

JANE NORRIS, *Tony Barrell's wife* Tony put an exhausting amount of energy into being clever and funny. He was never at a loss for a smart remark or a quip. He could be witty and he could also be vicious.

GILBERT REID He was a rambunctious, dominating presence. And he was always projecting ideas – pop cultural ideas.

JENNY KEMBER Tony Barrell was quite aggressive and quite mouthy. I learned to love him later but initially he was quite scary.

TONY BARRELL, *memoirs* Three years as a student wandering between the semi-genteel outer ring and boho enclaves of Liverpool convinced me I never wanted to live in a suburb.

Barrell and Tony Chapman, a copywriter who became my colleague and friend, came to live with me in my greatest find of the sixties: the flat at No. 23 Queen's Gardens.

All over London, graceful, crumbling terraces were being pulled down. Those that remained were empty or crammed with new immigrant populations exploited by greedy landlords. Inner London's population almost halved in the fifty years from 1939 but we were a counter-current: well-educated young artists, architects, actors, writers, musicians, hippy émigrés from suburbia who would fill these unloved terraces with life and laughter. We would eye derelict buildings with interest. Could we squat this or that?

Queen's Gardens was an elegant, tatty stucco terrace built in the early years of Queen Victoria. The second-floor flat at No. 23 was better than a squat because it came with the peace of mind granted when your landlord is the Church Commissioners, the organisation that administers the Church of England's estate. Behind the wide front door set between Doric pillars was a sweeping staircase. The flat began with a long corridor, off which were bedrooms, a bathroom, box room, a kitchen containing a huge old-fashioned range cooker, and a high-ceilinged living room with large windows on to the narrow strip of tree-filled communal garden. It was available for a peppercorn rent so I took it, and installed my chums.

RICHARD HANDFORD I was exceedingly annoyed. How had he managed to get this when my father was a vicar and therefore I had more entitlement for a charity flat from the Church Commissioners than he did?

CAROLINE CLIFTON-MOGG Queen's Gardens is a very narrow square. It was never smart or beautiful because the proportions of the buildings versus the square are wrong. The bit in the middle is too close to the houses. It was also too close to Paddington, which was always slightly dirty and sleazy.

TONY BARRELL, *memoirs* Hundreds of these palatial mansions decorated the streets around Hyde Park and most had been converted into flats or budget hotels. Ours ran across two frontages, and stairwells, on a level that was probably built for the children of the great family. Above us were the servants, below the dining and 'reception' rooms, and in the basement the scullery and coal stores. An old man called Mr Jackson used to live down there belowstairs, where he stoked the coke boilers which provided our hot water (but not central heating). He let us know he was alive with a penetrating hacking cough. The long hallway that linked the original buildings was carpeted in crimson cord and, according to whoever was counting, there were five or six bedrooms. Roger decided it wasn't enough, and added another by building a large head-high shelf, like a mezzanine floor, in a little room accessed by a short staircase opposite the kitchen.

BOB MARSHALL-ANDREWS It was a wonderful flat, years ahead of its time. It was painted in bizarre colours – dark mauves, reds, yellows, blues.

CAROLINE CLIFTON-MOGG It was a post-university pad – a word that nobody has used for fifty years – and it was just vile. Those were the days when everybody had dark-coloured sheets – maroon everything. And of course, all those boys had dark-coloured sheets and towels so that you wouldn't see how dirty they got. And there was me like Mrs Tittlemouse scurrying about trying to keep the lavatory clean and saying things like, 'Would you mind putting the seat down?'

SARAH DICKINSON It was noisy, there was a lot of stripped pine, and circular paper lampshades hung from the ceiling.

MARGOT WADDELL The flat was full of life and music, fast filling up with stripped-pine furniture and Spanish earthenware long before such things became fashionable. In fact, it was filling up with every conceivable type of object, natural and otherwise, eccentric forebears of the squashed dried frogs that later lined the kitchen windowsill at Mellis.

JANE NORRIS Roger would surround himself with dried flowers and pebbles and odd bits of antique this and that which he'd found, and everything would be arranged. It gave it a beautiful feel. It was a very inviting place, part of the whole charm, and very much created by Roger. He really wasn't tyrannical but even in Queen's Gardens you knew you couldn't mess with Roger's things. Pebbles that must not be moved was quite neurotic for someone who was a generous spirit. Over the years, I realised it was an intrinsic part of Roger's being – collecting things, arranging them, and then they became sacred.

BUNDLE WESTON The flat was absolutely that of a rampant entrepreneur. Who but Rog would get a lovely place in Queen's Gardens, determine the rent of his mates who would fill it, and leave himself to pay a fraction of the bills? They were all upwardly thrusting and 'we don't need to live with Mummy any more' so no one cleaned the lavatory. It was hideous, and you can imagine the kitchen. Roger's bedroom was very much like a teenager's bedroom – plates and crumbs over the floor and yet he was able to say to one girl who lived there, 'You mustn't treat this place like a hotel, you need to be in some evenings.'

CAROLINE CLIFTON-MOGG When I came back from America in the summer of 1967, Rog said, 'Come and live here for a while.' He liked to have chums' nights; I wanted to go out and meet some nice men. And so he'd say, 'I thought we'd have a chums' night tonight.' 'But I've been asked out on a date, Rog, I need to go on dates!' 'But the butcher gave me these bones and they're really nutritious and I've made bones stew and other chums are coming round to eat it.' He wanted his little, trusted group. It was about loyalty and when I'd say I was going out with some new amazing man, I was being disloyal, although I was just living in the flat. Those ideas of loyalty and trust go with his romanticism.

DUDLEY YOUNG There was always room for guests. It was very alive and busy and populated for years, very much Roger's signature place. They were sassy, and they were satirical. The repartee was very quick. These guys were very good at it. And they were making money too.

*

Tony Chapman was earning good money putting words in a persuasive order and so I joined him at Colman, Prentice and Varley, a stuffy but expanding advertising agency with expensively located offices in Mayfair, a ten-minute walk from the flat. By 1965, CPV was 'a long way from the sort of agency where copywriters would bring lion cubs into the office and a new account was celebrated with champagne', wrote John Pearson and Graham Turner in *The Persuasion Industry*. It was considered a 'second-tier' operation and yet it still employed an in-house sommelier to make the most of a cellar full of fine wines.

I wrote campaigns for Cadbury's chocolate and the catchphrase 'So dark it's almost wicked' was on television commercials at the time. When I joined chums in the Leinster Arms for a pint, they would greet me with 'Here comes Roger, so dark he's almost wicked.'

For one campaign, we devised a competition for Coca-Cola which asked readers of a popular newspaper to complete the following sentence: 'I always keep Coca-Cola in the house because . . .' Our clear winner was: '. . . because I can't stand drinking it in the garage.' We had to run it past our client the day before announcing the winner and Coca-Cola went crazy. We were compelled to choose a more anodyne answer which didn't stick in anyone's memory.

ANDREW CRACKNELL, *friend in advertising* It was one of the first industries where you didn't have to wear a shirt and a tie. You didn't have to wear shoes if you didn't want to. All first-name terms. It is difficult to imagine how stultifying it was working in an office in the sixties if you weren't in a business like journalism or advertising or showbiz adjuncts of the record industry. It was an atmosphere that suited people like Roger with a fairly relaxed mien and a slightly renegade attitude. It was fun, and I used to work quite hard. I imagine he did too.

*

ROGER DEAKIN, *quoted in* Adweek, *1974* When I first started at CPV I was making more money flogging Spanish earthenware and First World War cavalry bandoliers down the Portobello Road than I did at the agency . . . I like wheeling and dealing – I'm a rampant entrepreneur.

*

I was becoming an unusual mixture of advertising executive and furniture salesman, making half my living from tables and chairs during the very early days of stripped pine. I like pine much better in its material form as timber than in its vegetable life as a tree. Pine left bare and simply oiled with linseed or walnut takes on the patina of its daily use. It absorbs the grime and sebaceous oil of the hands and elbows that rest on it deep in thought. It glows and grows golden in the sunshine that slants in through the window.

I was stripping pine in my mother's backyard in Headstone Lane during university and I continued at Queen's Gardens. My schoolfriend Tony Weston introduced to me the junkmen in places that seemed the end of the world, like Molehill Green in Essex, somewhere the far side of Bishop's Stortford, or Mr Carr at Swordingford, near Audley End, an emporium of chaises longues, Windsor chairs, smoker's bows, corner cupboards, chests of drawers with white porcelain handles, Welsh dressers, blanket chests.

The junkmen never looked happy. They were hunched and wrapped up in pullovers and overcoats, or jackets with leather patches on their elbows. The pained expressions they wore were professional, discontented about what they were offered by hopeful bargainers or the escalating prices at the auctions.

At university, I made coffee tables from hefty planks of wood with a long edge untrimmed, so one side of the table possessed the natural curve of a tree trunk. The wood came from the timber dock at Surrey Quays, which would be closed by the decade's end. I also acquired sheets of wood from paintbrush manufacturers Harris for a song because they were disfigured by woodworm. This was treated, or cut out, and the tops were sanded, polished, and four screw-in legs were fitted beneath. I once made a table out of part of a derelict ash springboard brought back to Cambridge as a souvenir of a swimming expedition to an Oxford college. But its legs were too thin so even in retirement it retained its spring, and everything you put on it spilled.

For years I lived with a pencil behind my ear, first for carpentry, marking the positions of the saw-cuts or mortices to be chiselled out, then when reading to mark a passage of special note in my book. After moving to Queen's Gardens, I spotted an opening at Portobello Road market, which filled the narrow Notting Hill street with bustle on a weekend. The antique dealers arrived at dawn and finished their wheeling and dealing by midday. They didn't want the trippers who drifted down the road in the afternoon. But my friends and I could take over their stalls at lunchtime and sell all afternoon to the groovy types who had just climbed out of bed.

Tony and Bundle Weston were living in two seventeenth-century cottages on the border of Essex and Hertfordshire for which they paid £1,000 in 1962. Between doing up the houses, Tony wrote poetry and made pots.

On Portobello, Tony found an antiques dealer who was only too happy to promise his stall to them. The market inspector was content too because he could pocket double rent. So every weekend, Tony and Bundle filled their Mini van with Tony's pots and drove to London, parking around the corner on Elgin Crescent and selling their wares on the market. I shared their stall and bought a Mini van too.

Between copywriting, I cruised auction houses, targeting sales of unwanted items from British Rail, army surplus and the Post Office. At one sale, I discovered 200 large clocks from the GPO. Some were in wooden cases with a short pendulum that was broken but many were in perfect working order. A few were as big as coffee tables. Bidders had to tender for the whole lot; I offered a pathetic amount, some 10 shillings per clock, and, to my surprise, won. Tony figured out how to mend the broken pendulums with a simple repair involving half a razor blade and I sold them on the stall. Harrods bought about two dozen from me for a window display for twenty times what I paid for them. We had a good party on that.

GILBERT REID Physical objects and manipulating the physical world were very important to Roger and that links to the earthiness of D. H. Lawrence. Perhaps Roger, with his extreme sensitivity to things, had a strong feminine side, which Lawrence had too, I think, in dialectic with his very masculine side.

Farmhouse chairs were always cheap at auction and, as breweries moved from wooden barrels to metal ones, I picked up a load for almost nothing. I cut many in half and sold them as garden planters, a few years before the garden centres caught on. Other barrels I broke up so I could attach their curved metal staves to farmhouse chairs, converting them into rocking chairs. Bob Marshall-Andrews, who had moved into the box room at Queen's Gardens, was my assistant. When we sat in our first chair and began to rock, we fell off backwards. We had placed the staves equidistant on the chair, not realising that a rocking chair has more rocker at the back than the front. After tweaking our design, we made a lot of money selling the rockers on Portobello Road.

CELIA, *girlfriend, 1967–68* He made the rocking chairs. He said to me, if I sold seven I could have one. And I did find seven buyers and he gave me one and my twin sister has still got it. But he wouldn't give me one until I sold seven. I sold quite a few.

ROGER, *notebooks, 1968* Sold to Christian Aid on 12th March: 2 rush seat Rockers £12, 1 smokerbow Rocker £8, 1 corner cupboard £8 10 shillings, 1 Dresser £16. ORDERS: Judi Dench, Phil Wigley, C's friend.

In summer, my friends and I would drive through France to see Tony Axon at Tere's family home in Llafranc. On the way home, I stopped in La Bisbal, a small town which would later become renowned for its pottery market. Beautiful traditional folk pottery – ceramics glazed dark brown and streaked with metallic greens and blues – could be bought for a few peseta. After filling the van, I drove home through the night, not stopping, and shouting 'keep me awake' to my girlfriend. This, too, was sold on Portobello for a healthy margin.

*

CHARLES ANSON He was the most successful, spectacular meteor of our generation. He was earning good money and he was in a topical area. Advertising and the media were part of the emerging sixties.

RICHARD HANDFORD There were two sides to Roger. One was the romantic. The other was to be the man about town, dressing smartly, with the sports car. It seemed to be Roger. Actually, in retrospect it wasn't, but he was trying that role out.

ERICA BURT There was always this look to the high life.

ANNE CRAWFORD, *girlfriend* He said to me fairly early on in our relationship – 'I'm doing advertising to make a load of money to buy two things. One is a Morgan car, and the other is a place in the country.'

ANDREW 'ROON' HUTTON, *friend and neighbour* Roger was straight but wanted to be one of the heads. Tony Barrell was my songwriting partner and we called ourselves Mushroon. Barrell asked me one day, 'I don't want a job – how do I stop?' I said, 'Do what I do. Watch.' And so he did. And he stopped, and he learned very quickly that you can do that. He and I wrote music to ads. Little jobs floated in. All of this was closely observed by Roger. He was intrigued by the songwriting partnership. He basically really wanted in. Meanwhile, he was waiting to get his Morgan sports car. It seemed to me such a strange thing. You had to wait years to get one. They were handmade. I always felt this relationship with his fucking car was a midlife crisis in his twenties. He got his Morgan, and drove it round with much pride and pleasure and I found it ridiculous and risible.

CAROLINE CLIFTON-MOGG The Morgan is about as hokey a sports car as you could get and yet it's got this aura. Anyway, it's jolly uncomfortable to drive to Cornwall in it.

ROON HUTTON In 23 Queen's Gardens Roger was by far the best writer amongst the three of them but he wasn't cool and he knew it. One day he gave me this piece of paper. Now Barrell could give me words on a piece of paper and instantly, like Bernie Taupin and Elton John, the music would come, boom, but Roger gave me this thing and I thought, it's a very lovely little poem but it's not rock 'n' roll, mate. I was embarrassed. And I said, 'Roger, it's a lovely thing, thank you, but I've got to go,' and it never happened.

ROGER DEAKIN, *poem*

Pigeon

The pigeons perching in this tree
Seem oblivious of me
Perhaps because they understand
I hold no weapon in my hand

Pigeons fly
High high
Pie in the sky

And my best moments are compiled
Of getting close to something wild
For if I watch with covetous eyes
Seeing so many flying pies
They'd have gone away long ago
Like a shy girl I used to know
Shy girl
Shy

*

We could walk out of one job and into another in the sixties, and a move was the best way to obtain a pay rise. I trebled my salary in July 1967 by joining

Leo Burnett, a big, international agency. We wore corduroy in those days. Barrell wore navy, Chapman wore black, I wore dark brown. I also went in for brown herringbone-tweed jackets or overcoats. The jacket was very expensive, bought from Jaeger after working with Ken Russell on an advertising campaign for the brand. Ken wore the full works: brown herringbone trousers, jacket and matching cap. I couldn't even afford the jacket, but bought one anyway. I now realise that all these English-country-gentleman outfits were designed to make you look as much like a ploughed field as possible.

ROGER, *notebooks, 1967*

Definitive products of our age
1. The Desert Boot
2. The Donkey Jacket
3. The Jean
4. The Corduroy Trouser
5. The Anglepoise Lamp
6. The Pentel
7. The Morgan Motor Car
8. The Y-front
9. Instant Coffee

BOB MARSHALL-ANDREWS Sartorially in the 1960s Rog was the Thing.

GILBERT REID Roger was an extraordinarily handsome guy. Sort of Hugh Grant type but more solid, not so ephemeral as Hugh.

SARAH DICKINSON Roger was very egalitarian. Maybe that's what I found so attractive, apart from his romanticism, that he didn't treat me as a chattel. He was wonderfully curious and he listened well, and he looked different from all the others. He had that curly hair and he had very beautiful soft eyes and I remember his voice. He had this wonderful voice.

JENNY KEMBER He was very different from other people. He had this mass of curly hair, a moustache, he was quite eccentric and he definitely had charisma.

CAROLINE CLIFTON-MOGG Roger liked Cool. But in some ways Roger was very uncool, and that was his charm. He was always the eager puppy but he was never super-cool. Although probably later in his life, people would have thought he was.

JANE NORRIS Their infallible seduction technique at Queen's Gardens was Sunday lunches. They were wonderful, because both Roger and Tony Barrell could actually cook at a time when men didn't necessarily cook. They used to roast this huge piece of beef with Yorkshire pudding and roasted vegetables. They would have quantities of very cheap nasty Spanish red wine. The kitchen was quite small, you'd be crammed around the pine table, and they would be young British men being terribly clever and funny. Everyone around would laugh, especially the girls attending.

SARAH DICKINSON We drank a lot of very cheap red wine from huge glass goblets on a pine table. There was a lot of cooking, Rog loved that, but it was the scraps you probably wouldn't give to a dog.

ANNE CRAWFORD I walked in the door and I can still see it now. Roger was sitting with his back to the window. I looked straight at him and there was obviously a connection right at the start. He was never ever, ever a boring person. But he decided I was getting too keen. I was in love with Rog. He did not want to be tied down and that was that.

SARAH DICKINSON He pursued me in the most glorious way. One weekend, there was a knock on the door and this box arrived covered in black shiny paper and his very distinctive handwriting. And inside this box was one single red rose and a poem. I was only twenty-one and this was the most romantic thing that had ever happened to me. So I was completely hooked and then this was enhanced by his curiosity and his passion and his romanticism and his lovely pale blue Morgan. We became an item. During our 'hot' period, he once turned up with a gift of a huge antique copper samovar (including lid).

TONY AXON Rog was going out for a while with a very nice girl called Sarah Dickinson. Then he met this other girl who had a glamorous job in television. We had lunch one day and he said, 'Oh this Pamela or whoever is absolutely fantastic.' So I said, 'What about Sarah?' He said, 'I'm having lunch with Sarah tomorrow and I've got to tell her. How do I handle it?' I came out with all the clichés. The script could've been written by a machine – remaining good friends and all that. Roger wrote it down. He was having dinner with the new girl in the evening. So it was a busy day. I didn't hear from him until Monday morning. He said, 'Those suggestions that you gave me – did you get those from a book?' I said, 'No, it's just things I've heard people say, why?' 'Because I had a ghastly lunch with Sarah who burst into tears and everyone in the restaurant was looking over and I felt so sorry for her, and then I went to dinner and almost word for word I got the same message back.' He laughed, wryly. But his ego was a bit deflated.

As the sixties unfolded, I sought out the countryside. Visiting my friends Dudley Young, Phil Wigley and Gilbert Reid at their rented cottage in the village of Whittlesford outside Cambridge, I met Margot Waddell.

GILBERT REID Margot was extremely striking; ethereal; Bloomsbury incarnate. She tended to wear big, flowery drifty things, and give the idea that she was the Earth Mother. She had a way of rounding her lips when she was going to say something significant, almost in the form of a Cupid's bow, and she had these very sincere eyes. She had a radical side too – a sixties revolt against the system; I think a Black Panther was staying in her basement at one point.

DUDLEY YOUNG Margot was extremely spiritual in the 1960s when I first knew her. I tutored her for the Tragedy paper on which she got a first. She was wonderfully rich, in her conversation and her intelligence.

MARGOT WADDELL In those early days, Roger was simply one of the most unusual and glamorous people I'd ever met. He already had a way with words; he was already an expert scavenger of useful and useless objects; he charmed with his Tiggerish intensity; he was already mixing with many of those who were to become lifelong friends – 'the chums' as he put it. For he had, in particular, a powerful sense of loyalty, so clear in these enduring friendships, and he had a capacity, too, for generosity. He was both convivial and a loner, and there was always a touch of sadness and anxiety beneath his energy and humour.

He was endlessly creative, selling furniture in Portobello market, which I thought was exotic beyond belief, and he was also very literary. He knew a lot more about English literature than I did. And then he suddenly decided he wanted to be in the country, and I was a big part of his life in terms of tooling around in his Morgan, trying to find somewhere to live. It was incredibly exciting looking for a house through the eyes of someone who had a knack for spotting the unobvious. He really wanted to be my friend, and my friend was Dudley Young who was Roger's friend from Peterhouse. That was difficult because Roger felt that he was somehow second best to Dudley.

Margot joined me in the Morgan as we drove, mostly in first gear, through the lesser-known lanes of Norfolk, Suffolk and Cambridgeshire. By now, Tony and Bundle Weston had moved to their next renovation project, a cavernous derelict barn and farmhouse on the Hertfordshire–Cambridgeshire border. Once again, Tony was doing it up all by himself, and I had determined to do the same. I wanted a ruin, which I could rebuild myself, reuniting my mind and body with my hands, wood, stone and soil.

BUNDLE WESTON We were away and Roger stayed with Margot at our barn. It was in what became our daughter Sophie's bedroom that Roger first proposed to Margot. But Margot was after one of her tutors, Bob Young, who she got, and Roger was turned down.

ROGER, *notebooks, 1967* Margot and I sort of pass objects back and forth to one another. I lend her *Games People Play*. She sends it back via Gilbert. I give her a red mug. Think about writing too. Maybe she does. Funny how when you agree with a girl to be good friends, you end up hardly ever seeing each other. Yet Margot is such a fine image for me that I keep seeing her everywhere. On pages of magazines. In the play *Women in Uniform*. She is like a principal boy. Holding her shoulders up straight and gazing far ahead, looming up everywhere in my life. That joyful expression you get when you meet her: that really gets me.

What would have become of that had I <u>really</u> persevered? Take that night at the theatre. I was so scared I could hardly get my breath. Blushing like a baboon's arse. Yet she was delighted to see me. It was sort of poignant, and even triumphant, when she finally said hello, and I got the famous Joyful Smile. Christ, that was worth sweating for. Oh Margot, you fascinate me. That's your trouble; you're fascinating. It distracts the eye.

*

JANE NORRIS That little spot around Queen's Gardens at that time was very neighbourly. Tony had serious friends dotted about. It was very companionable, sustaining and fun; lots of jokes; lots of good times. But Roger did not partake in any of that. He didn't go to the pub with the blokes at the end of the working day which is odd because he always would've been welcome. He didn't come across like a loner. His social style was gregarious and humorous and clever, and he had all that energy. Was he that much of a loner? There was something about Roger that held back.

GILBERT REID In those days, there was the illusion that you could float in this undefined world for a very long time. It was just after the sexual revolution and it was before AIDS. Women's liberation was coming up but it was before women had figured out the full implications of sexual liberation, which meant that guys could stay Peter Pan for a long time because, to put it brutally, they could have sex, and wonderful companionship, and they didn't have to necessarily get married. And of course, the pill from 1961 had changed the underlying equation. Oh my God, didn't we just have it our own way?

ROGER, *notebooks, September 1967* What am I up to with Celia? I always knew from the day I first saw her she was a prickteaser. Those skirts, just a little too short. Talking on the phone just a little too much. Yet she's not. Celia is incredibly great and gentle and good. Beautiful in a lot more than the one obvious way. And in time, quite a short time probably, she really would sleep with me. So what am I playing at trying to rush her? Trying to upset her? Deliberately playing the wounded, peevish, child-lover, deprived and impatient. Mostly I think tonight it was those familiar intimations of 'wasting some of my precious time'.

CELIA, *girlfriend 1967–68* I came to London at nineteen and I was working as a secretary to Jay Levinson, the art director who worked with Roger at Leo Burnett. You went up in a lift, there was a very smart girl on reception and a bowl of fruit from which you could take a piece every morning. I used to do dictation for Roger and go and sit in his office. One day he asked me out for a drink after work and it just snowballed from there. I was flipped with him from day one. He reminded me of Donovan with all that dark curly hair. I just loved going to work because he was there. I'd stay over at his place the night before and we'd go to work together, although it was a bit embarrassing working with him and then being together.

ROGER, *notebooks, October 1967* We went first with Celia to the Loose Box for a drink of Anjou rosé (very good). It was full of awful Knightsbridge types. We collected a bottle of the same rosé and went to the flat (me dressed up in suit still) where we cooked good ole sausage and egg + beans, drank rosé and had a delightful time. Much better than any restaurant. That girl really does make me feel at home. It's great. She stayed the night too. Magical bed scenes. Really incredible. I was so excited I lay wide awake quivering all night. I was very glad about what happened. So was she. She's on the pill now too. The greatest invention of modern science – along with penicillin!

ROGER, *notebooks, November 1967* What a strange weekend. Margot and Celia. The ideal and the reality meeting. Ow! I went nearly hysterical with the appalling confrontation of it all. What the hell am I up to <u>ever</u>? I waded into the situation fully aware that they would meet. Margot knew too, but presumably didn't care. But did she? What am I to do? I must not exhaust myself with too many friends and loves and sudden passions if I can manage it. Do things very deliberately, invest in the future a year hence, and let no opportunity slide even an inch or a half-day. And stay close to the friends I already have whom I love and who love me, and get into no more misman-aged situations than may occur by accident. This is my great failing – the desire to be all things all the time to all people. It just doesn't work. Worse than that, it brings much misunderstanding and much difficulty. Simply to be one thing to one person at a time is what I must try to do, and I suppose I'm doing quite well with C. at the moment. It's something I simply have to con-centrate on before I cause some big disaster, to someone else, or myself, or both of us.

ROGER, *notebooks, December 1967* Wrote C. a little thing, Three Words – If I could see you / Ten seconds a day, / Can you guess / What I'd say? – and some stuff about love nearly setting my hair on fire. And it's like that too! Exciting as hell. Then in the evening I got all my gear ready for Cornwall and we went to Sarah's party. Great! Terrific time, with C. looking unbelievably good in a brown velvet dress with white lace Prince Charlie ruff collar and cuffs. Lovely! We danced with our heads touching the ceiling, and talked for hours.

CELIA We used to go to lovely places in London – little dinners and pubs – and he introduced me to Rachmaninov and we went to see *The Magic Flute*. He was great fun. We'd go and stay in Cambridge a lot with Dudley, who was like a hero to Roger.

I loved his Morgan – the little blue machine that obeyed us two. I drove it too and had to double-declutch. I was so confident in those days, I could drive anything. There wasn't much traffic on the roads either. We would chase the sun. It might be cloudy in London but we'd drive down to Cornwall and see the sun in the distance down near Fowey and we would literally chase the sun and find it and stop the car and have a picnic. I remember going down to Cornwall in the snow and we had the roof off. I don't think he ever shut that roof.

ROGER, *notebooks, December 1967* The snow and the cold fantastic. We started out at ten to seven the next morning – the roads freezing, water freezing on the windscreen and the journey looking grim. Everyone had said we'd never get there! But we stopped for breakfast in Andover at about nine, and suddenly we were in Wiltshire in bright sunshine and packed snow all shining on the road. The Morgan purring along, muted by the soft snow, and everything unbelievably beautiful! Somewhere near Honiton, I pulled off the road to stop, and buried the Morgan in a snowdrift. It was bitterly cold, and my hands nearly froze off trying to scratch snow away from the wheels. Then a lorry towed us out. We arrived at Hatt House at about 3.30 p.m. What a place! Tom Jones living at its best! Celia's little ten-year-old stepsister is lovely, very bright as kids of oldish fathers often are. I wrote her a nonsense poem for her autograph book:

Roger and Celia came all the way
From London to Hatt one cold snowy day.
They rode on a sledge painted six shades of blue
Drawn by six purple reindeer, whose noses were too.
'Well, how about that!'
Said the black cat at Hatt.

Sir Douglas Marshall – C's stepfather. Huge fat Churchillian character, obviously consciously modelled on 'Winston'. All old Tory MPs seem to be the same! Full of stories, anecdotes, reminiscences. But a very kind old boy – always ready with a noggin before, during and after meals. But, my God – what a huge difference between our two generations – complete chasm! All the time it was C. I was thinking of, touching her foot under the table – more exciting than I could ever have imagined. Every touch like a hot poker! We retired early to bed, quite exhausted.

Sunday 10 December We got up early – nine or so – to brilliant sunshine on the snow and went on a long walk round the rolling fields that surround Hatt. What a place! White doves billowing, muscovies flapping, pheasants – ornamental Reeves's, a cock Lady Amherst's pheasant, ferrets – bright golden rushing creatures, soft and affectionate with long delicate claws like Chinese fingernails. And the dogs! An old retriever called Brownie, and an even softer little King Charles called Charlie. Then there are two magnificent gun dogs – a black and a golden Labrador – called Bess and Amber.

Sleek bullets of dogs who torpedo you from across the lawn and paw you lovingly.

One unforgettable moment that morning – standing in a little lane on the shining snow kissing with the sun streaming on us, and the hum of electrical wires and birds singing! What sweet kissing – we're absolute champions, maestros, geniuses!

Sunday afternoon. We took the roof off the Morgan and drove headlong through the snowy lanes to the coast between Saltash and Looe. The sea was completely calm, the tide lapping gently out, and the sun beginning to drop. Almost no one on the beach. We wandered for two miles up the beach eastwards, then touched a big rock and turned round past some oystercatchers. As the sea-birds on the foreshore piped, we stood for ages kissing out there on the beach as the sun went down. We watched a solitary little boat slip out from Looe and across the red burning wake of the sun, seeming to catch fire as it crossed.

What a scene! The kind of Total Romantic Experience one has once or twice (if one is me) in a lifetime – which have no relation to time, seem to have lasted forever; and do last forever because you remember every detail. How we talked about the sea and the country and the town and held hands all the time! Then we climbed back into the car and switched the radio on to a French station – which came in so clear across the sea – and seemed just right for this evening – we were, after all, in another country. Next day it all seemed like a dream. But we know it wasn't.

CELIA I had no idea he was so smitten with me. I suppose he was just private. He didn't express his emotions to me, really.

ROGER, *notebooks, December 1967* The Burnett Christmas party in the evening. V. boring to begin with. C. looking magnificent – so pretty in velvet again. We did a good deal of the old looking across the room at one another. She said her heart nearly dropped out when I arrived! Dancing together was great – but I suppose everyone must have realised! Perhaps not. John Rowland got very concerned about me getting unhappy about C. dancing with Jay. I really do get ridiculously jealous: I nearly left while he was dancing with her! I had loads of gin.

CELIA The office party was something you looked forward to the whole year – when you could see people not in a work environment, just letting their hair down. They were fabulous parties with the dancing and the music. It was wild and it was fun.

ROGER, *notebooks, 27 December 1967* Work awful, Bob and Jay studiously ignoring me. Christ, what a bad scene!

ROGER, *notebooks, 29 December 1967* In the afternoon, I got fired by Bob. Ugh! I was furious with the cunts. The cold little fascist plainly never liked me, or resented me and my kind of free-ranging 'fun' work. Celia came in halfway through our little interview and noted my pale, furious face. When I left, she was almost in tears – she knew what had happened. I simply went out of Bob's office, collected my coat, my chequebook and my book, and left, asking her to come straight to the flat. I collected a bottle of champagne and went home and listened to Rachmaninov. Celia arrived, very concerned, but I soon put her at ease, and we celebrated in great style, and drank a good deal.

Rotten old Leo Burnett, the intellectual whorehouse.

ROGER, *notebooks, January 1968* I nearly went mad sitting in a tube train in a tunnel outside Gloucester Road. I was about to either break down crying and weeping and grovelling, or run about the carriage, shouting insanely and tearing the newspapers from the silent people's eyes. 'You're all imprisoned in here. Do you hear? Imprisoned! These doors may never open. And there's nothing, nothing you can do about it. You sit here silent – how can you when you've no idea what the hell's going on out there? Why has this train stopped? Why? Go on, shout it out, you'll feel better: W H Y?' But then the train started and I leapt out of Gloucester Road station as though I'd just robbed a bank.

ROGER, *notebooks, February 1968* Celia and Mel's 21st birthday party at Hatt. The party was full of debby girls from round about but great as soon as the awful atmosphere of formality had broken down and I'd had enough champagne to unwind myself and C. We got very tense to begin with simply because we hadn't seen each other all day . . . She looked great in a long white dress, very simple, with a red velvet bow down its front. We danced in the big room for ages and all we wanted to do was go up to the big bed with the dimming light and go to sleep together.

CELIA The party at Hatt was a little bit stilted probably because my parents invited the Cornish set but my twin sister and I had a flower party in our flat in London which was much more fun. We were decked out in flower-power stuff – I wore flowers and probably not much else.

ROGER, *notebooks, 1968* C. suddenly very depressed and tearful – straight physiological depression mostly, I think – but she was hard to cheer up. Perhaps it was one of those moments when she realised how much she was in love with me, yet how separated our lives and friends are – how much older I am in every way. At those moments, she panics, imagining that I'll surely run off quite soon, leaving her hopelessly in love with me for the rest of her life. Her eyes fill with tears and she says she wishes she'd never met me. 'You must have broken so many poor girls' hearts,' she once said – which I thought at the time would make a good pop song. She's right, though, which isn't so funny. Evil by default rather than intention would be my plea for defence. The last thing I want in the world is to break anyone's heart – but the only way not to, as far as I can see, is to go into cold storage.

ROGER, *notebooks, summer 1968* Barrell has said definitely that he's returning to the bachelor fold. So have I.

There is no further mention of Celia in any of Roger's notebooks or diaries.

CELIA I remember distinctly going over to his flat and he said, 'I want to be free.' No explanation, there was no other woman, and I couldn't believe it. It was 100 per cent one day and the next that was it. There was no cooling off. But at that age it was just fun – young love, in London. We didn't expect it to last forever. After I bust up with Roger at the end of '68 I thought, I want to get out of London, so I went to the Channel Island of Herm and worked there for two summers selling ice creams on Shell Beach. That's where I met my future husband. I never had any contact with Roger again.

*

ROGER, *notebooks, December 1968* Well, this girl has upset me. Definitely got inside my body to work havoc with my appetite, my mind, my sleep. What a situation, lying awake, feeling ill, upset, missing her one moment, rebuking myself for giving in to emotional pressure the next and refusing to play any games, then making fantastic plans to impress her, thinking of ways I might have pleased her better, hoping for days to fill with her company, then plunging into the deepest gloom at the thought that she is enjoying at this very moment my fondest, most ambitious, romantic dream – a farmhouse in the

Dordogne. Why continue? What higher peak could I ever take her up? What brighter sun could I ever dream of sharing with her?

JENNY KEMBER I was living in the King's Road and in late '68 I went to have tea with Caroline Clifton-Mogg who was living in Queen's Gardens. I met Roger and we got chatting. He was very proud of his Morgan car and said, 'I'm going to this party, girls, would you like to come too?' So we all piled into the car. I was just twenty-one, a naive ex-boarding-school girl, and I was slightly in awe of this rather wild Cambridge graduate who was five and a half years older.

CAROLINE CLIFTON-MOGG Jenny was the right person at that time because she was a very well-brought-up hippy, really. She was always a gentle person, very laid-back, and she had this calm way. So Roger would come up with the next idea and whereas his friends would go, 'Oh for God's sake, really? That's not going to happen,' Jenny would go, 'Oh, all right, then, fine.'

GILBERT REID She was a very elegant girl but more traditional than Roger felt himself to be.

JANE NORRIS Jenny was a nice girl – warm, smiling, amiable, approachable, with that voice and those upper-class connections.

LESLEY WARD, *Jenny's friend* She was such a gentle soul and so friendly. She wasn't 'cute', more sort of classical. She was a natural girl, didn't wear make-up, wasn't fussed about clothes. She had an air of confidence, though I guess it can't have always felt like that for her inside. She was calm and very clever, far cleverer than me, always had a good vocabulary and read things carefully. If she had gone to university, she would have been more than a match for young Roger but that wasn't what floated her boat. Roger was an intellectual. I came from a working-class family so I inherited some kind of deference to him. I was invited for supper and he was sprawled on the floor, animated and passionate about Joni Mitchell, and it felt like a teenage thing to me. Alas, I had never gone overboard so completely for music in that passionate way.

ROGER, *notebooks, 22 December 1968* The sun shines and my poetic soul is burgeoning. My first run across the Kensington Gardens to Prince of Wales Terrace and back in twenty minutes. Jenny: I like my body when it is with your body.

ROGER, *notebooks, Christmas Eve* Drive up to Cambridge with Jenny. All a bit of a hurry. But we're close. I felt close all day. Wanted to hold her. But no time! Tea with Simon Schama. Peterhouse porters wonderful. They looked after Jenny for me.

ROGER, *notebooks, January 1969* We're made to give straight, with open hands, wholeheartedly. Less is a compromise. Dilution. Waste of precious time. Mockery of ourselves. For love is something very simple. No power game. (That's something neurotic, pathological almost; something designed to avoid pure personal contact.) All I believe is that we have something, you and I. Jenny and Rog. That thing. Something that won't bear playing with. Something that is either whole or nothing. Something above male pride. Above compromise. Above tactics or melodrama or impatience. A moral certainty. A simple knot of two hands. And if we act against a moral certainty, we alter ourselves forever. We are less whole. Act for it (however hard that is to do), and we make ourselves more whole together.

*

At weekends, Jenny would join the chums at a gamekeeper's cottage on the edge of the Waveney Valley in Suffolk. The place was sequestered in the woods far from any public road and was generally reached by train from London to Beccles. In the station car park, we kept an Austin Champ, an American military jeep from the fifties that did about four miles to the gallon. We just left it there, with the keys in the ignition. When we collected it, we drove as far as the Little David petrol station at Stockton, then turned off along a muddy track across the brown fields and through the woods. There were so many different browns, in fact, that you could say some were dull, some bright, and some dazzling.

ROGER, *notebooks, 1969* There's only one way to reach the cottage apart from on foot or by bulldozer, and that is by Champ. Champ is as tough as a prize-fighting conker soaked in vinegar. Champ is also more rounded and friendly than Land Rover, and looks like a lorry next to little Jeep. It has chewing-gum tyres, ten gears, four-wheel drive, and iron cushions on all seats. If Champ throws you from the driving seat, or rather chair, Champ bowls on alone through fence, ditch and forest. That's the kind of sonovagun this Mother is. Champ is powered by an overpowering Rolls-Royce unit with about 600 cylinders and a radiator you can fill a nice hot bath with when you arrive. At 60 mph, the only thing you can hear is the 600 cylinders.

We seemed to spend a great deal of our time servicing the cottage. The rule was that we saved up and collected at least as much firewood as we burned. There was no electricity, so fires, candles and paraffin were all the more vital. Each lamp had a personality and each made a special noise. One guttering lamp sounded like a fishing smack pop-popping across a bay. Another hiccupped. A third was like a lightship in fog. There was a stove in the kitchen over which we spent much time huddled. It took ages to get into its stride and was usually going nicely when it was time to leave.

There were beds everywhere, upstairs and down, and several layers of the rags and carpets we could pick up for next to nothing at auctions (bare feet being one of the orders of the day). The informal proximity of beds, the modest scale of the cottage, the numbers of us, and copious intoxicants created a dormitory atmosphere, and there was much talking after lights-out. Barrell invented an organic breakfast cereal to be called 'Dobbin'. I think it was dried cowpats, flaked, and mixed with a few raisins. Now and again there were mushrooms.

JENNY KEMBER It was all oil lamps and woodburners and very romantic.

TONY BARRELL, *memoirs* With a lot of knowledge, craft and effort, old remote cottages could be made comfortable, and we had a lot of indoor fun, but if we went out into the fields around us, we'd stare at the ploughed earth with its specks of chalk and flint, glistening under the mist, the dead grass, the empty hedgerows, the leafless trees, beaded with motionless dew that never seemed even to drip, let alone evaporate, waiting for the next frost, with only the choked croak of a pampered pheasant to break the silence, knowing in our hearts that anything of any interest was dormant, as it should be, hibernating; which was what we were doing in a way.

Stockton Woods were well supplied with pheasants, and we all learned to appreciate them as individual characters. Our affection for them probably led to their downfall, by making them far too trusting. The boy at the Little David garage kept tame magpies and jays in an aviary. They were very clever, and no doubt well fed, but we felt sorry for them all the same. There were good second-hand bookshops all over Suffolk then, and we rarely returned to London empty-handed.

One of our main preoccupations was photography. Barrell, in particular, took it very seriously and toted a Pentax or a Nikon around the woods and hedgerows. We made weekly expeditions to the fish café in Bungay for lunch and some covert portraiture with the telephoto lens. In that era there were still plenty of authentic Suffolk bumpkins to be met, or seen stumping about.

TONY BARRELL, *memoirs* Once when Roon and I were chopping logs from a diseased and broken elm, a pair of round-bodied, well-sweatered, ruddy-faced men, with blue eyes and wispy fair hair tucked under caps and beanies, emerged from a thicket, and without a crackle underfoot or a word, and only the barest look our way, disappeared into another part of the wood. It was like being close to wild animals, as if we'd sighted a couple of badgers. 'Hobbits,' whispered Roon (an aspirant elf).

ROGER, *notebooks, 1969* The working out of a prose style is one of the things you begin to get to in the vale of the mid-twenties. And besides that (or along with it) the working up for a moral framework. No, not framework – river – centre of the Earth. That one's friends are one's conscience.

We wrote at the cottage. It had a tower, which was reached from a spiral staircase that ran up from the garden. At the top was a small room with bare walls, furnished only with a table and chair, so the occupant sat looking out into the woods – or stared out of the window, sharpened pencils etc. – and wrote. Or at least, that was the idea. Various aspiring writers had made contributions to an informal anthology of graffiti, inspiring or depressing. 'Getting and spending we lay waste our lives' was one. A Robert Graves poem about the young bird-catcher on his way through the woods was another.

*

In September 1969, I took a long holiday in Formentera, a windy, spindly island, full of weather and very close to the sky. Copywriting for a holiday company produced a free villa and I travelled there with Jenny. Bob Marshall-Andrews and his girlfriend Gill joined us. Margot didn't take up my invitation to join the tribe for she was working in Africa.

Formentera was long and narrow, shaped like balalaika, with no cars and many hippies. It was such a small island, nine miles long and barely twenty yards wide in places, that we were terribly exposed to the weather, to a new and freshly beautiful world. Everywhere we went was an adventure, an experience closer to childhood. Despite the ongoing oppression of Franco's Spain, here was a vision of freedom and love.

HANK WANGFORD, *singer and friend* It was the end of the road of the hippy trail. Lots of my friends had taken a VW camper across Iran and Afghanistan and filled the van with dope and driven back. It was safe and easy to do. They'd do maybe two runs and they'd all buy big fincas on Formentera and were made for life. It was an idyllic place.

BOB MARSHALL-ANDREWS It was wonderful. Totally sybaritic. Basically we were a lot of very middle-class hippies. It was international, the whole of young Europe was there, and if you could find those hundreds of hippies now you'd find the most successful people in Europe.

JENNY KEMBER We did a lot of bicycling, we did a lot of swimming, we cooked wonderful meals on wood fires. It was quite a wild holiday and it was very romantic.

BOB MARSHALL-ANDREWS Roger absolutely adored Jenny, and she him.

This was my new kingdom and I was very proud of it. Formentera was an island of shooting stars, cliffs, dunes, ancient volcanoes, driftwood, pine, cactus, palm, flowering rosemary and swallowtails. Our villa was on its own among pines and rosemary bushes, and we could climb on to the roof like going up on to the bridge of a ship, and watch the sea 200 yards away. Outside our kitchen door was a tree laden with figs and red-and-yellow rebel finches. To keep the hawks happy, and the flies agile, there were more lizards than I had ever seen. They came in a range of autumn shades from aquamarine through grass green to brown, but the brown ones yielded right of way to the grass-green ones, who in turn tended to stop in their tracks and steal wistful glances at the aquamarine ones. They were incredibly cunning and intelligent. On the beach, they gathered round you like sparrows, and took bread from your hand, disdainfully with their long bony noses in the air. Something like D. H. Lawrence must have experienced in his poem 'Snake'. It was my first contact with the reptile world since my tortoise had a miscarriage by sitting, exhausted, on the egg it had spent two hours laying on the garden lawn.

Our water came from a well, we ate thousands of eggs and chickens, and fell in love with a new dog each day. They were mostly hounds – long foxy ears, long pointed faces, long thin bodies and even longer tails and legs – but they were unbelievably playful and friendly, and underfed. When a storm struck while we were out riding, we were soaked to the skin within seconds and took shelter in a stone barn. There we found one of these dogs, a young bitch, tied up guarding a wooden plough, but very willing to make friends in exchange for a pat on the back. Only when we left could we hear her barking, and we could still hear the plaintive barking a mile away.

In the evenings, hoopoes were silhouetted with plume helmets and long beaks against the sunset, like a puppet show. The sunsets were so precipitous it felt like if we all stood on the sand with our backs to the land and yelled 'Encore!' loud enough it might pop back up again for the benefit of all those still fumbling with their cameras.

Near the villa was a long spit of lagoons, coral sands, and dunes stretching two miles to another tiny island, Espalmador, which was virtually uninhabited. Most days, we cycled along a glittering white, perfectly smooth road of pure sea salt, leading across a network of salt lakes. Then we abandoned our bikes and walked out along this wondrous limb of crushed shells, pulped polyps, and stone volcanic valves. Our little camp was on the perfect curve of a purely calm atoll. We removed our clothes and imagined we were stranded on a desert island, and could only use what we were able to find on the beach. I listed the projects we could make.

ROGER, *notebooks, 1969*

Things to make
Love
A kite – from two split bamboo sticks & some material or newspaper & string
A boat – from cork & paper & sticks ✓
A wood castle – from driftwood on the beach
A tepee – from bamboo or driftwood and blankets or bedspreads wrapped around
A house – on the beach, from stones, driftwood and bamboo
A wood buttermould: carved from driftwood
A fish trap from bottles
A lizard trap
Lampshade – bamboo cylinder ✓
A raft ✓
A sand clock ✓

First was an elaborate sand clock, with bamboo sticks to cast a moving shadow for the hours and every five minutes marked off in shells. It ended up very decorated, like a municipal flower clock, but accurate. Then we made a fish trap: a row of stakes leading into a dead-end sand pool we drove fish into, and a very effective net out of bent bamboo and sacking. There was an unimaginable quantity of driftwood on one side of the spit: bamboo from Tunis, wooden masts from Alicante, rope from Tripoli. And huge oil drums, so we made a raft. The raft was called *Hesperus* (prophetically) and handled like a dream, if a lethargic one, until it capsized and we had to watch it drift away south. We built a little house out of rocks and wood and bamboo, and Jenny and I then got to work on building a beach chess set and a kite.

After the sun set, we cooked over a fire outdoors and then rode our bicycles to the island's two bars in San Fernando, where we drank 301 Spanish brandy. Bottles of excellent *vino tinto selecto* cost 1s 6d (8p). Everybody was reading, smoking and drinking or playing guitars. I read Vladimir Nabokov's *The Eye*, Jean-Paul Sartre's *Nausea*, F. Scott Fitzgerald's *Stories Volume Two*, and Arthur Koestler's *Dialogue with Death*, about his experiences in the Spanish Civil War. The authorities still banned such literature. It was a bit scary reading Koestler in Spain where I seemed liable to run into trouble with the Guardia if not for a minor motoring misdeed, then for wearing shorts in town. One evening, we brushed shoulders with Jimi Hendrix. He was staying over the fields, almost always alone and most spectacular, living very simply, obviously in retreat, and accepted there as probably nowhere else. In a year, he would be dead.

We had a free flight home but we decided to stay on for another week. This was our beach, our own desert island, and we couldn't quite leave.

*

Eventually, we had to return to London and I took another copywriting job. In those days, there were two parts of me – warring when I was not happy, and creating a dialectic which was the powerhouse of my personality. The first part was more central: the teacher. It was what I wanted to be all the time at school when my heroes were my English masters, Nick and Doughty. The second part was the copywriter whose father died when he was seventeen, whose home was never very well off, and who felt terrific guilt about his widowed mother going out to work while he affected the young gentleman at Cambridge. So instead of becoming a schoolmaster I chose the glamorous path to riches (which my guilt-instilling middle-class upbringing taught me to regard as ill-gotten gains) in order to prove my worth and compensate for all the years of leisured study. Having taken this road, I was determined to know the trade or craft I had set out to learn, do some good ads, and reach an arbitrary target figure of earning £2,000 per annum, which I soon hit. Now I'd done all that, and worked most of the guilt out of my system, I was free to move on to my original aim, which was to be a teacher of English. The only snag was that teaching was so appallingly badly paid, and I had acquired expensive tastes: a sports car, a fine flat and a fondness for travel. Still, in 1969 I vowed I must do it, although I told myself that the longer I waited the better, because I would be better educated myself, and subject to fewer internal battles over my own soul.

BOB MARSHALL-ANDREWS Although he made a lot of money, I don't think he terribly liked copywriting. He was very good at it. He had some wonderful ideas.

BULLUS HUTTON, *friend* Amongst the cognoscenti, prostituting your talents as a commercial writer was infra dig. In his defence, he was conscious of the fact he was selling out to the establishment. Nobody could chastise him for it because he chastised himself.

In Bayswater, Barrell and I continued to make 23 Queen's Gardens even more incredible, adding beds and more colour.

TONY BARRELL, *memoirs* Before he moved himself to the country full-time, as a rehearsal for rural reality, Roger tried to move as much of the country as he could into our second-floor flat in Queen's Gardens. He filled his room with debris (not always organic): driftwood, dried flowers, long-stemmed blonde grasses, shiny brown pots from Catalonia, enamel roadside advertising signs for Camp Coffee or Mobil Oil, defunct but not-to-be-buried Remington typewriters, and Bakelite phones. I once nearly chucked out some 'dead' fronds and was told, wisely but firmly, that nothing was ever really dead, and anyway there was another way of seeing them now they no longer had the burden of growing.

The tenantry at No. 23 Queen's Gardens was eclectic: often, Roger the creative director would be away in the country, so all kinds of semi-approved strangers would park in his room for a weekend, a month, even years: female hitch-hikers from Frankfurt, Jesús from Spain, Marie-Aude and Jean-Paul from Paris, and Jasper Parrott who, for a while, ran a business from our biggest room, acting as an agent for famous musicians, singers and conductors. I once got a call from a very distinguished performer:

'Is Jasper there?'

''Fraid not.'

'Tell him it's André Previn [pause] . . . is he in now?'

'No, still not in. Try again later, André.'

Or did I say, 'Mr Previn?'

I spent most of my spare time seeking that place in the country. That summer, I found what I was searching for. Now I had to make good my escape from the world of advertising.

CHAPTER 6

The Builder

Finding Walnut Tree Farm — moving to Mellis — 'A man could get severely damaged if he's caught under a load of falling thatch' — in love with the place as a ruin — creative director at Interlink — coming home to a real fire — the trouble with advertising

HANK WANGFORD The sixties went from about 1963 to 1975. The hippies moved from London up into Suffolk and Norfolk. It's that classic hippy thing: oh man, I'm going to go to the country to get my head together.

DUDLEY YOUNG We had that lovely song, 'The Day the Music Died'. Like the song, I was saying bye bye to all that. 'I'm off to the countryside to trade in part of my brain which I had purchased at the price of my hands. I want my hands back.' I'd lost them. And it was a bad trade. And Roger had wonderful hands. He was a wonderful carpenter.

RONALD BLYTHE, Akenfield *(1969)* The present abandonment of the farms is on the same scale as that of the decade 1871–81, when 200,000 labourers fled their villages for Australia and Canada. Between 1962 and '67 men have left the land at a rate of 20,000 a year and the figure is now approaching 30,000.

ALDOUS HUXLEY *on D. H. Lawrence, quoted by Roger in his notebooks in 2001*
He could cook, he could sew, he could darn a stocking and milk a cow, he was an efficient woodcutter and a good hand at embroidery, fires always burned when he had laid them and a floor after he had scrubbed it was thoroughly clean.

RICHARD MABEY, *friend* It was his kingdom. He built it virtually from scratch. It was an extension of his hair – all his character, his life and beliefs were expressed in the landscape and iconography of Walnut Tree Farm.

*

I pored over maps of Norfolk and Suffolk, deliberately seeking the least-frequented corners, hoping for a ruin drowned in trees a long way down a bumpy track, and that's what I found. The house was falling down when I first saw it in 1969, a chimney rising above the treetops of a spinney of ash, maple, hazel, blackthorn, ivy and bramble, and what was left of a cottage orchard of walnut, greengage and apple. Like everyone else in the village, old Arthur Cousins, the owner, clearly thought the house had crept away to hide itself and discreetly die, like an old cat. He lived across the fields at Cow-pasture Farm with his daughters Beryl and Precious. The abandoned house's roof was a patchwork of flapping corrugated iron and the remaining damp, composting thatch was so verdant with grass and moss, it could have been turf. I love ruins because they are always doing what everything really wants to do all the time: returning themselves to the earth, melting back into the landscape. And long since I moved in, nature has refused to relinquish all kinds of ancient rights of way through the place.

JENNY KEMBER We were driving in the Morgan, as always, which was the most bloody uncomfortable car – your bum is practically on the road it's so low. We used to wear old army-surplus clothes from Laurence Corner – Biggles helmets – because it was so freezing. We drove down Mellis Common and spotted chimneys above the treeline. We got quite good at spotting obviously abandoned houses by this time because we'd been doing it for quite a while. There was no track then, so we walked across the common and it was all slightly barricaded, and we crawled through a very thick hedge and we found it, and it was in a state of some decrepitude. They'd kept pigs downstairs and chickens upstairs and it belonged to the adjacent farm which was owned by Mr Cousins.

ROGER DEAKIN, *letter to Margot, August 1969* I've been mostly in Norfolk, driving about 800 miles in ten days mostly in first gear, looking for the house. Found lots – farmhouses, Elizabethan halls, cottages – but the top of the list is still the Suffolk cottage, whose owner I finally tracked down and spoke with. Now I'm trying to persuade him to sell it. Several other great places in mind, though. I need you to help me decide on which house (I must get one now before I spend my money).

MARGOT WADDELL He found this house and said, 'I want you to come and see. I think I've found the place.' It wasn't called Walnut Tree Farm, it was divided into three separate cottages, Rose Cottage and Walnut Tree Cottages, so we both went up there and it was just lovely.

For several weeks, I paid court to Arthur at Cowpasture Farm, and eventually he consented to sell me the house and twelve acres. We went on to become the best of friends, even sharing Heather, a big-eyed Guernsey housecow, whom we took turns to milk. Arthur was one of the last generation of old Suffolk horse men. For most of his life he had been an independent timber-hauler with his own gang of heavy horses and carts, plying the roads between Norwich and Ipswich hauling timber from the woods to the sawmills, timber yards and shippers. He worked hard, saved up, and bought his farm before the war, when land was cheap. He still hung hagstones, Suffolk's flint version of the evil eye, in his stables and cowsheds to ward off the night mare who might disturb his animals as they slept in their stalls. He was my tutor in husbandry, animal lore, and village politics.

*

ROGER DEAKIN, *essay, 'Reactions to Life in Suburbia', c.1957* My only wish, regarding environmental circumstances, [is] to have a large house with a stream running through the garden.

> JENNY KEMBER Roger had come from this very small suburban bungalow in Hatch End and always wanted to break out and do something completely different. We'd looked at some massive, crumbling houses, almost the size of old stately homes, but the scale of Walnut Tree Farm appealed to him because he could see what he could do with it, and it was achievable and he liked the fact that it had some land around it. The setting grabbed him because it was off Mellis Common, the largest grazing common in Suffolk, and it had the moat which appealed to him and became quite important. He certainly fell in love with it and once he got into it there was no stopping him.

ROGER, *notebooks, 1969* I want my home to be a microcosm of the society I'm looking for; peaceful, loving and cooperative, where everyone has plenty of time for everyone else.

> BUNDLE WESTON When Rog and Axon were in Cambridge they visited us in our ramshackle cottages. Tony worked like lightning and he did it all himself and Roger looked up to him for that. We bought the cottages for just over £1,000, which was my annual salary as a teacher. What can £30,000 buy you now? It simply isn't fair. In 1967 we made our big move, selling the cottages for £5,000 and buying a great shambling place further into Hertfordshire for £5,000: a farmhouse, a field, a spinney, a barn that was falling down, and lovely open cow byres.

*

I have always liked the word 'feral'. I shall never forget the first time I saw François Truffaut's *L'Enfant sauvage* in Paris in 1970, and the deep impression the story of Victor, the wild boy of the Aveyron, made on me. He was captured by hunters in the woods, having apparently been reared by wolves from infancy, near the French town of Saint-Affrique in 1799. The film chronicles the attempts of the anthropologist Jean Itard, played by Truffaut, to 'educate' Victor and teach him to speak. There is a magical moment when, at the full moon, the wolf in the boy obeys the call of the wild, and he throws off his clothes and escapes. 'He had reverted to the feral state,' says Itard in the book he wrote about Victor on which the film is based. To me, this is a thrilling moment. When I first saw this scene, a longing came over me that I should be able to do the same myself. Later that same year, I did set off into the wild in a way. I gave up my job as a copywriter and lived mostly out of doors for eighteen months while I rebuilt the timber-framed house myself, from the ground up. I had never before lived so close to nature, or so simply, and mostly it suited me very well, even the endless hard work and weariness. Looking back, I can see that I had reverted to the feral state in which I spent an important, formative part of my childhood. But I wonder too if my strong desire to find and buy a ruined house, and to repair it and bring it back to life, was a way of bringing my father back to life.

ROGER, *diary, 1970*

16 September Drove to Mellis – slept in van in churchyard.
17 September Moved furniture into garden. Shovelled shit out of end room, swept out the ceiling and walls. Slept in house.
18 September Patched up and washed the windows, all covered in green mildew and cobwebs – spiders – curtains over the doors – mice at night – brick floors. Began scything down the nettles, brambles etc. outside. Clearing the moat, dragging out huge roots of dead old willows. Arranged water – big can of it from farm. And cooked over open fire in the garden. (No fires in grates until chimneys swept.)

Slowly, I stripped the house to its skeleton of oak, chestnut and ash, repairing it with oak timbers gleaned from a barn demolished by a local farmer. I lived in the back of a Volkswagen van for a while, then slept beside the big central fireplace with two cats for company. In spring, I moved upstairs into what felt like a treehouse, sleeping under the stars as I repaired the open rafters in a perch with a canvas roof and walls rigged to an iron bedstead. Soon, the wood pigeons roosting in the ash tree at eye level grew used to me. The tree felt then, as it does now, like a guardian of the house, arching up over the roof in a kind of embrace, and I fought the council building inspector tooth and nail to retain it.

As soon as you begin building or repairing a house, the state walks in and you find yourself under surveillance by a powerful person: the building inspector. I invited him over to the site when I was drawing up the plans because I thought it would be diplomatic and useful. The inspector took one look at the place and said:

'Pull it down and build a bungalow.'

'But this is a beautiful old house.'

'I know,' he said. 'Otherwise I would be condemning it and having it demolished.'

I turned down a substantial grant towards the building costs because it would have meant yet more highly unsympathetic inspections by the officer. One condition of the grant money was to fell the ash tree. I came to dread his visits, and regarded him and his philistine view of domestic architecture with deep repugnance. He wanted me to plaster over the perfectly good Tudor bricks in the hearth, or the 'inglenook', as he insisted on calling it. 'Inglenook' may once have been a perfectly good word but it has been done to death by a folksy exploitation much beloved of estate agents. Today it is of a piece with 'farmhouse kitchen' and 'a wealth of exposed timbers'.

ROGER, *diary, 12 October 1970* Grant approved by council. Bullus. Shifting bales. Building haystack. Old bottles out of moat. Shit out of downstairs off old brick floor.

EDDIE LANCHESTER, *pig farmer and local resident, who helped Roger's renovations* Before Roger bought it they kept chickens in it. He paid £2,000 for it – we could've bought a brand-new bungalow for £3,000. That was a rum place, I tell you, when he bought it. He obviously knew what he was doing.

CHRISTINE LANCHESTER, *Eddie's wife* I don't know that he did. He learned as he went along.

JENNY KEMBER, *quoted in a magazine article about the restoration, 1973* There was five inches of chicken guano on all the floors – all concrete hard. There were rats everywhere you looked or walked. Once, when I was woken in the night, I lit a candle and saw a rat dancing on a chest of drawers. Another day, we were pulling down an old ceiling of plaster in the sitting room and discovered to our delight what we thought was an ancient medieval purse in the floor gap. In fact it turned out to be a most medieval shrivelled rat.

JENNY KEMBER We used to go up there at weekends and camp in the house. Lots of people came and helped carry things around. All the thatch was pulled off and eventually the whole thing was stripped out to a skeleton.

BULLUS HUTTON We were thick as thieves at one time. We'd bomb up to Mellis for the weekend and build his house – me and Marta, he and Jenny. We both liked to work strenuously in our weekday jobs and then get away from it all.

It had a huge thatched roof.

'I don't know how we're going to get that off,' said Roger.

'It shouldn't be too hard to pull off.'

'Do you know anything about thatch?' Roger asked me.

'You have to be from medieval times to know anything about thatch!'

So Roger got the local con man in, who came to take a look, and gazed up at the roof, shaking his head.

'It's a tricky job. It's a dangerous job.'

'How is it dangerous?'

'Getting it off. A man could get severely damaged if he's caught under a load of falling thatch.'

He really didn't know what to do with it. He said he'd come back with one of his workmen.

I said, 'I'm sure we could pull that off.'

'I don't know.' Roger looked doubtful. And then we laughed. 'A man could get severely damaged if he's caught under a load of falling thatch.'

We started to pull off the roof in great chunks. It was like dandruff, falling off, and we were screaming with laughter. 'A man could get severely damaged if he's caught under a load of falling thatch!'

In the afternoon it was all down to the studs. We burned it in a huge pyre in the back field. The con man came back that afternoon.

'Where's the thatch?'

'We took it off.'

'Just the two of you?'

'It took us about half an hour.'

And then we started laughing hysterically. 'A man could get severely damaged if he's caught under a load of falling thatch!'

Everybody loved that sky-blue Morgan and he absolutely bashed the crap out of that thing. We used it as a truck. He took the roof off and we'd go foraging for pantiles. There were always fallen-down houses with great piles of pantiles. We'd either filch them or pay the farmer £20 and we'd fill every available space in the Morgan with pantiles and I'd sit on top of them and Roger drove home on these tracks. It's a wonder the suspension didn't collapse. It was like using a racehorse to pull a plough. We must've looked a comical pair of pretend workmen, workies who weren't really workies. We did attract a fair bit of attention from the local population. Gentleman workies, besotted with our notion of manly labour; the camaraderie of hard work and survival and eating primitively.

ROGER, *diary, 31 October 1970* Found the barn at Stradbroke. Started collecting tiles from it in the van. Three van-loads = 350 tiles. Slow and expensive on petrol. Also found tiles at Willow Farm sale. 500 for £5.

My inky notebooks of the time are smudged with brick dust and thumbed with grimy hands, bogeys, fingernails. They record drawings of roof trusses, lengths of nails, calculations of moments of force: all the stuff I wish I had paid attention to in physics. The engineering I needed to learn. A crash course, if that's the word, in engineering.

BULLUS HUTTON A census man came toiling up the path one day.
'I've come to count you. Do you mind telling me your name?' he asked Roger.
'Roger Stuart Deakin.'
He wrote it all down on his clipboard.
'So you live here and this is your primary residence?'
'Yes.'
'Have you got hot and cold running water?'
'Oh no, nothing like that.'
'Toilet?'
'No.'
'Well where do you go?'
'I do it out the back.'
'Good lord, but you're an intelligent man. What grade of education did you get to?'
'I got a degree from Cambridge.'
The census man looked at him askance. 'A gentleman with a Cambridge degree doesn't even have running water?'

JENNY KEMBER I kept working in London but Roger gave up his advertising job in the second half of 1971 and he rebuilt the house with this wonderful man called Brian McGuinness who was a local cowboy builder, and Eddie Lanchester. It was a long, protracted process.

DUDLEY YOUNG Roger couldn't have done it without Brian McGuinness.

RUFUS DEAKIN, *Roger's son* Brian was a hell of a character and he helped Dad no end in the building of the house. He used to go poaching with Brian McGuinness. He was a proper wild man with loads of children and he was notorious for shagging out the back of the Railway Tavern.

ROGER, *letter, 1976* I watched the film of *Akenfield* this week. I thought the boy/son was very good. He conveyed the hopeless, inevitable way these Suffolk people have – the sense in which they are almost born beaten men. So the men who aren't beaten, like Brian McGuinness and Arthur Cousins, make a terrific point of letting you know they aren't beaten – they feel they have something to be very proud of, so great are the beating-down forces.

EDDIE LANCHESTER I used to labour for Roger, plus have a laugh and a joke with him along the way. It was never really a serious day's work. He'd sort of scheme things more. Roger had an old standard Major Fordson tractor and he wanted to get that going one day. I was with Brian and we said, 'All right, Roger, we'll get it going.' I borrowed a tractor and towed this old Major off to get it started and we parked it next to the house. Roger was desperate to drive it. 'Let me have a go,' he said. Well, he didn't know how to drive it and it went backwards and hit the pinion of the house and came to a standstill. I tell you, it was lucky he was still alive. If it had kept going, that big bit of wood would've taken his head off. But that was Roger, he had to have a go at things. Then he said, 'I'll go forward with it,' and he nearly went into the moat.

BULLUS HUTTON Roger lived totally primitively. He would cook one pot of stew that would last all week. It was always bubbling on the hob and he would chase chickens out of the door.

EDDIE LANCHESTER Roger would say, 'I'll cook you a meal,' and he'd go to the butcher's and get some sausages. He'd be cooking in the house and all of a sudden this bloody chicken jumped on the table and pinched one of his sausages. The cats roamed about and sat on the kitchen table. That was Roger.

JENNY KEMBER I cooked spaghetti bolognese on an open fire. It didn't make much difference what I cooked on the fire, the predominant taste was always smoke.

BULLUS HUTTON Me and Marta would sleep in a big brass four-poster bed in the middle of a cow pasture and we had a roll of industrial polythene under the bed which we'd cover ourselves with when it rained. We'd wake up with the sun shining on the bed and cows licking our faces.

JENNY KEMBER We had a bed with a plastic sheet over the top in the garden because the house was completely wrecked.

EDDIE LANCHESTER We used to go round there and we'd see no one about, and then we'd see this bit of polythene move in the garden. Roger had this double bed out there that was covered up with polythene. Me and Brian thought, what the hell is he doing with it? And then three of them got out of the bed just like we did in the morning. They didn't bat an eyelid. We couldn't believe it. It was a damp old night. I suppose the polythene was keeping the dew off.

TITUS ROWLANDSON, *current owner of Walnut Tree Farm* The three-in-a-bed story went round the village!

*

I found myself then, as I still do deep down, in love with the place as a ruin and therefore partly at odds with myself as its healer. I liked the way the wattle-and-daub walls, baked by the sun to a biscuit, were cratered all over by nesting mason bees or solitary wasps like the peepholes of a Yemeni city. I appreciated the inquisitive tendrils of ivy that poked their heads in through the cracks in the rotted windows, fogged green with algae, patterned by questing snails. I welcomed the sparrows and starlings fidgeting in the thatch and the bats that later flitted through the tented open rafters as I lay dozing in bed, limbs aching sweetly from a long day's labour. I wanted to repair the walls, but at the same time I wanted to foster the passepartout menagerie that refused to recognise them. Somehow, through the sum of minor inefficiencies in a handmade wood-framed house, I succeeded.

ROGER, *notebooks, early 1970s* Tonight two bats, harbingers of death, came fluttering round my head as I lay in bed. With the softest sound, never knocking on the windows, they flew round and round, up and down, seeking escape. I too wanted death to go away from me, but there was no way out, no escape for me either.

DUDLEY YOUNG I would be gopher. I had no skills but I was keen and I'd hold the other end and chop wood. Tony Barrell was the same; he didn't know anything. We were sleeping inside this great open palace of oak beams. The wind went through it and it was very, very beautiful, and I said, 'Rog, you don't want to put walls on this, you want to leave it open,' and Barrell agreed with me. Closing in the walls was a death. And we mourned it properly.

*

Having personally shaped or repaired every single one, I have ended up on terms of the greatest intimacy with every beam, post and pegged joint in the place. I have perhaps also earned some kinship with the people who originally built the house, and probably dug out the moat, twenty years or so before Shakespeare was born. Uncovering the carpenters' coded inscriptions on the rafters and floor-beams was like finding a lost manuscript. They were carved when the oak or sweet chestnut was still green and the house under prefabricated construction at the carpenters' shop, ready to be carted to the site and raised, whole walls at a time, by the combined muscle of dozens of villagers. The proportions of everything, measured in feet and inches, impressed on me the organic nature of the entire structure. The proportion of each room, and of the house as a whole, was predicated on the natural proportions of the trees available.

We tend to idealise builders of timber-framed houses because they were medieval or Tudor but they were no different from any other builders down the ages: they looked for the easiest way to do things. So they went for the least labour-intensive way of cutting timber to size and length. Suffolk houses like mine tend to be about eighteen feet wide because that is the average limit of the straight run of the trunk of a youngish oak suitable in girth for making a major crossbeam of eight inches by seven. The bigger barns tend to be twenty-one feet wide, with slightly bigger timbers. Uprights, too, are of tree height, the idea being to select trees or coppice poles of about the right cross section, so they could be squared with an adze with the minimum of work.

Many of the timbers in my house still have their bark and sapwood in places. The timber was always worked in its green, unseasoned condition, when it is easiest to cut, drill, or shape into joints. Once assembled into the hardwood frame, the timbers would gradually season *in situ*, often twisting or curving as they did so and creating the graceful undulations so characteristic of old houses. One of the saddest things to witness in Suffolk today is the number of fine old timber houses that have been straightened out by builders. The last generation of Suffolk builders understood the old houses well, approaching them as structures that are engineered as much as built. Evolved rather than designed, the timber frame is intended to sit lightly on the sea of shifting Suffolk clay like an upturned boat and ride the earth's constant movement. Foundations were never more than skin deep for this very reason. Now, council building inspectors who should know better insist on absurdly deep, expensive foundations that are entirely wrong for the houses.

*

EDDIE LANCHESTER You could have a laugh with Roger. He used to come down the Tavern, not a lot, but Brian would bring him down there. He never used to drink that much. No one knew him when he arrived from London but he'd make an appointment to meet his neighbours and talk to them and learn about this, that and the other.

I fixed my house and chums came to stay, and we had long conversations, walks and bike rides and swims in the river or the sea together. Most of my friends lived a hundred miles away in London, and large parts of Suffolk were almost off the map. Walberswick and Southwold were on the rim of the known world then, relatively quiet little places, where parking a car was not something you ever thought much about, let alone traffic jams on sunny days.

We were on the margins, we were *les marginaux*, and we identified with the Gypsies in a romantic, starry-eyed way. 'Off the beaten track' and 'unspoilt' were the watchwords. The treks on holiday to find an unspoilt beach. The mad scrambles down to remote coves, simply to get away from other people, to be sequestered, to escape 'the masses', and yet we were socialists.

JENNY KEMBER Roger didn't want a one-on-one set-up with me; he liked the extended group, the community, and that continued from Queen's Gardens to Mellis. He always considered it his house even though we'd found it together and we spent a lot of time there together doing work on it. On one occasion, I invited a friend of mine to stay for the weekend and the house was still not really finished. There was one bedroom that was particularly nice and I thought, I'll make it up with the clean sheets and she can sleep there, and we'll sleep somewhere else. And Roger threw an absolute hissy fit. He was furious with me for taking the initiative and allowing this girl to have this particular room without his permission.

Magazine article on Roger and Jenny's restoration, 1973 Now after all the years of work, the bulk of the house is finished. The walls, floors and ceilings are in place, and the greatest joy of all – the plumbing is installed and functions. All the decorating still has to be done, but with the advent of constant hot water, Roger and Jenny are taking a deserved rest and say, 'All we do now is lie around, eat, have hot baths and wash our hair every other day . . .'

ROGER, *notebooks, 1970* Idea. Mellis – build garage out of scrap cars.

MARGOT WADDELL There were plans for anything and everything – some materialising into a wonderful barn or outside dunny, others remaining in Roger's vivid dream-time: the conservatory he was always going to build, his second barn, to be a games room for the many children who foregathered here. Nothing was quite as random as it seemed; though all was assembled with that ramshackle, just-so-ness that expressed his eye for the unexpected and the curious, and also that touch of obsessionality about where things did or didn't go, despite the apparent chaos.

*

ROGER, *notebooks, early 1970s*

October Poem

I sit here hogging a whole house,
cupboard-loved by four cats
watching my aimless movements
like a moth's on the windowpane.

Outside, a black October night;
here, a cherry log on the fire for company.
Two more elms blew down last night,
donkeys got out again,
there's grass growing round the truck's flat tyre.

The house-ribs ache with emptiness.
Outside the wind heaves like an iron lung.
The cherry log's brandy in the house's gut,

The clock ticks in the kitchen,
a bluebottle zigzags round a bulb,
a cat purrs, and the paper
whispers under the pen.
Doors open every summer night
are shut tight.
Twigs scamper past the walls.
In the morning, I shall carry in more logs.

I really did want people to come home to a real fire. A nation without flames in the hearth and birds singing outside the open window has lost its soul. To have an ancient carboniferous forest brought to life at the centre of your home, its flames budding and shooting up like young trees, is a work of magic.

After taking a break from advertising to restore Walnut Tree Farm, Roger returned to a lucrative job in London, fleeing to Mellis for weekends, and whenever he could.

CAMPAIGN MAGAZINE, *December 1972* Lopex is merging its Central Advertising Service with the 24-year-old Interlink agency, under the Interlink name. Central directors Michael Sayers and John Hankin join the new Interlink board, as does Roger Deakin who becomes creative director.

ADVERTISERS WEEKLY, *May 1973* Interlink is leading a £1 million national advertising campaign for the Solid Fuel Advisory Service, set up in February, to promote solid fuel. A £350,000 press campaign next week will be followed by a £400,000 autumn–winter TV campaign on a 'Come Home to a Real Fire' theme.

ROGER DEAKIN, *quoted in* Advertisers Weekly, *May 1973* Open fires have become fashionable and streamlined appliances such as those designed by architect Jon Bannenberg will make open fires even more popular.

'*Come Home to a Real Fire*', *scrolling text on the TV advert* Great minds such as Mozart, Lenin and Buster Keaton found inspiration in the depths of a coal fire . . . A doctor in Worcester believes that couples with real fires are likely to have a warmer relationship.

GARY ROWLAND, *friend and freelance advertising colleague* The whole premise was that the TV has replaced the fire in the centre of the living room. So he filmed a fire burning, filled the TV screen with it, and there you were sitting in front of the fire like you used to do in the old days. Good old British Coal. It cuts through all that jargon and rubbish, and there's nothing involved other than sticking a camera in front of a fire.

JO SOUTHON, *Interlink colleague* For Roger, 'Come Home to a Real Fire' was about authenticity. He also wanted to support the miners: his grandfather had started life as a miner. We made a two-minute cinema commercial for the campaign, where the screen was filled with the giant close-up of a burning fire for two whole minutes. What could be heard were extracts of miners' choirs and brass bands we had travelled the length of the country to record. Roger was saying, these are remarkable people. We made another commercial in Yorkshire where a mother was waiting for a vintage school bus and a child gets off and they go back to a cottage in a valley behind a stone wall, to come home to a real fire. It was about the countryside and coming home to a real fire, which Roger had at Mellis.

GAIL AMBER, Advertisers Weekly, *October 1973* The new batch of commercials were convincingly simple and direct. Any man with a real fire can forget about the expensive restaurant and dancing till dawn – anytime. But how many men are there around, these days, who can boast a real burning fire? Maybe Interlink's latest campaign will change all that. If for no other reason, I'm hoping it will be a blazing success.

CAMPAIGN MAGAZINE, *October 1973* What makes women seem more beautiful and conversations sound more interesting? I'm sorry, you're wrong – it turns out to be a real coal fire, and the people at the Solid Fuel Advisory Service think it's time you came home to one. The ads are annoying because the solid-fuel people have something that's worth promoting, and this campaign is as soporific as . . . a real coal fire.

TONY AXON As I recall, the campaign was scrapped following a *Private Eye* cover that positioned the slogan below an image of a burnt-out second home in Wales. At the time the Welsh Nationalists were very active.

*

ANDREW CRACKNELL, *friend and then creative director at KMP* Interlink was a fairly small and insignificant advertising agency which didn't do particularly notable work.

RICHARD COOK, *Interlink colleague and friend* Interlink was very, very undistinguished. Unfashionable. Old-fashioned. It employed some nice people but most of them were not very good. It was on St Martin's Lane in Covent Garden but the offices were tacky, a bit run-down and not particularly well organised. If Roger had been serious about advertising he wouldn't have been there.

JO SOUTHON It was a bit of a shabby, old-fashioned agency with rather doddery people. They got Roger in to zip things up. He then employed his own people in the creative department, which was on a separate floor and was like a separate world within the agency. An art director would sit at a big table in the same room as a copywriter and come up with ideas. Each pair was assigned to different clients. Roger had a room down the end of a corridor with a rather beautiful desk. Roger wore a pair of jeans and a denim shirt and sometimes a waistcoat. I never saw him wear a tie. There was a relaxed, friendly atmosphere but the staff on the other floors were besuited advertising chaps from a different era and they were a little bit alarmed by us because we were very different.

JOHN BAYLEY, *Interlink colleague* Roger was the wrong sort of person to be in advertising but advertising had a tendency in those days to hire people who were crazy. On the copy side there was a mix of strange frustrated novelists and poets and journalists. He was completely unsuitable, really, except he was very charismatic. He could sell an ad for clients very well. He was such a charming man too. He had this way of talking to people and convincing them of things. He would have grandiose schemes all the time and sheer personality would get him through it.

*

ROGER, *notebooks, early 1970s* The only problems I'm interested in are insoluble. Which is pretty fucking stupid considering I'm a copywriter. Copywriters are kind of modern troubadours to the court of Coca-Cola. We're here to explain everything and anything in simpleton terms to all of you, regardless of whether you're simpletons or not.

ADVERTISERS WEEKLY, *'Top 50 Agencies of 1973' (Interlink at joint 32)* It was an outstanding year for the creative department. The agency won five Clio awards, more than any other British agency.

JO SOUTHON Roger was fun, he was enthusiastic, he was encouraging to people as a manager. I didn't ever see him being negative to people. He was also going off to Mellis quite a lot when he probably should've been at work.

JOHN BAYLEY As long as you turned the work out from time to time, he was happy. I worked for fifteen creative directors. He was easily the most charming. A lovely man. We were under his wing very much and very fond of him.

RICHARD COOK He was the creative director of the agency. To say he had a very light touch is not really to represent it; he didn't really have a touch at all. He was less like a boss than anybody else I've worked with. I did an Interlink campaign for a company who made very posh cast-iron baths. They produced them in very beautiful colours – dark reds, dark blues, greens – and we did a very characteristic ad of the time which was like a colour chart with baths. Roger said, 'Oh no. What you ought to do is put these baths in a bathroom which is like a jungle – making the bathroom exotic.' He simply said that. It illustrates the difference between Roger's approach and that of somebody doing advertising. What Roger wanted was a bath and the bathroom that he would like, as he was doing at Mellis – turning it into a living place which was specific to himself. The adverts I did were all reason; the adverts Roger did were all feeling.

'Farmer Deakin's Country Diary', Badweek, *a spoof magazine put together by Interlink's creatives, December 1973* Hello there, chums. I expect you're having a rotten time down there in smelly old London, working like merry hell in your stuffy little offices. Up here, in the old countryside, I'm mucking out the cowshed and filling my lungs with good, healthy country air. URG! I must tell old Jackie to get me some air freshener for here . . . Next time I pop down for a quick visit old Bob Gilbert will swallow his pipe when I park the old tractor round the back. I'm afraid the old Moggy finally packed in. I was just driving back from the builders' yard with old Jenny and nine tons of ready-mixed concrete when the bloody thing just fell apart. I'm going to get old Jackie to complain to Morgan about the standard of workmanship on their cars. Anyway, cheerio for now. I won't be seeing you this week as I'm up to my neck in it at the moment.

JO SOUTHON Roger was a rebel. He liked japes and fun. So he got all the copywriters writing rude things about the agency and probably charmed one of the typists to type it all up.

'Deakin expects stiff reprisals', Badweek, *December 1973* Roger 'Farmer' Deakin, head of Interlink's award-winning creative team, said today that he was expecting 'some jolly stiff reprisals' after the publication of the new agency organ, *Badweek*. He had earlier denied that his department had anything to do with the paper. 'My chaps are far too busy to spend their time writing this schoolboy rubbish,' he told us this morning. However, recent evidence suggests that some kind of creative involvement is 'fairly likely'.

JOHN BAYLEY My copywriting partner Ken Dampier and I wrote the whole thing. We took the piss out of all the people in Interlink and everyone thought it was very funny.

'Pool for Interlink?', Badweek, *December 1973* Westminster City Council refuses to comment on rumours that Brooks, Pitcairn, Gillbert and Carr (Construction Division) Ltd has applied for permission to convert the Interlink basement into a swimming pool.

JO SOUTHON In the bowels of the Interlink building was a cinema for showing adverts to clients. They employed a full-time projectionist who sat down there with nothing to do. Eventually he was fired for putting in false receipts. After he was sacked, Roger asked me to look after some newly hatched chicks in the basement. He was off on a trip somewhere and I had to keep these chicks alive, in a cardboard box. He was a difficult person to say no to. In a sense, he was doing what the projectionist had been doing – seeing how far he could go. He knew he could do what he wanted at Interlink whereas if he was at one of the sharper places, a big agency such as Leo Burnett, he couldn't have got away with having his chickens in the basement.

JOHN BAYLEY We were all gobsmacked when he brought those ducks into the agency and just left them for the day. Because he was Roger, and had this twinkle in his eye and this marvellous ability to charm people, he got away with it.

*

RICHARD COOK Roger wore the same clothes and was the same person at Interlink as when I stayed with him at Mellis. He was out of place in advertising, and clearly in place in Mellis, but he was nonchalant enough not to mind. The first time I went up, there was just the bare timber frame of the house. There was no question of advertising coming into the conversation. I can remember a walk. It was a winter dusk and very cold. We strolled through the graveyard of the church and then carried on through the countryside. When we looked back, the biggest, reddest moon I'd ever seen was sitting on the horizon. It was incredibly primitive. If I had been living there 5,000 years ago and seen that moon I would have done whatever I could to propitiate it and keep it on my side. It confirmed that this was a place with ancient connections, as different from St Martin's Lane as any place could be. It was certainly living with nature, and that was the thing that mattered to Roger.

ROGER, *letter, 1975* Advertising's no good because I don't believe in it, so it compounds my guilt. Mellis can only be a very partial solution because it is (a) hugely introspective – doesn't give much to anyone else, and (b) ambivalent about its ultimate aims because the place itself is ambivalent.

JENNY KEMBER It was a bit of a shock when he decided to completely give up advertising and base himself at Mellis. It was a fairly unilateral decision. Although I was there, and was involved, I wasn't really consulted about those kind of decisions. That was how it went.

'Creative director leaves Interlink', Advertisers Weekly, *2 August 1974* Roger Deakin, creative director at Interlink, is leaving the agency, but will continue to work on key assignments for several of the agency's major clients. Deakin, thirty-one, has been responsible for much of Interlink's creative success over the last couple of years and the parting is said to be totally amicable. Deakin intends to work on his own – 'What will I call myself? Roger Deakin. It's my name.'

CHAPTER 7

The Husband

A new rural culture: the Barsham Fairs, the Waveney Clarion *and my extended family of quasi-hippies – marrying Jenny – a trip to check on the donkeys as Jenny goes into labour – Rufus is born – letters to Jo – crashing the Morgan, buying the DS Safari – agonies over love – 'My promised land, a product of my imagination, I feel complete there as nowhere else' – in search of the White Goddess*

Why have I stayed so long on the edge of the great grazing common in Mellis? Not because I was born here or have Suffolk roots, but because of all the hard work, and the accumulated history. I mean my own, mixed up with the people I love. There were the Barsham Fairs and the *Waveney Clarion*, the community newspaper of the Waveney Valley, which I helped write, plan and distribute, as a whole extended family of us quasi-hippies did, from Diss to Bungay to Beccles to Lowestoft. The rural culture we constructed together during the 1970s and early 1980s, based firmly on the values of the *Whole Earth Catalog*, Friends of the Earth, Cobbett's *Cottage Economy* and John Seymour's *The Fat of the Land*, flushed out the pioneer immigrants busy settling in Suffolk – rough carpenters, dirt farmers, musicians, poets, ditch-diggers and drivers of timber-framed Morris Minor estate cars – and put us all to work building what for a golden moment became a new tradition of Suffolk fairs.

It was work – creative, bold, imaginative, but at the same time hard, manual and physical – that drew us together. A shared experience of risk too: you never knew what the weather would do or if anyone would turn up at the gate and pay for it all. Dancing and music played a big part. We had our own local heroes, our own Suffolk Bob Dylans and Willie Nelsons, and any number of ceilidh bands sawing away in village halls on Friday nights. There were whole stages full of fairies at Barsham and there was even a highly successful Rabbit Opera. The modest entrance fee was halved if you wore medieval clothes, so there were plenty of itinerant soothsayers, magicians, wizards and incubae too.

The Thatcher years were a lean time for these fairs. The idea of doing something essentially entrepreneurial and speculative like mounting a fair on an empty field purely for the fun of it and not at all for profit came to be regarded with the deepest suspicion. Why would anybody want to do all that work for nothing? As if to confound the Thatcherites utterly, Barsham Fair closed down precisely because it was growing too successful. Eventually, too many people were rolling up at the gates, some 50,000 of them at the last fair in 1976, so the organisers, the East Anglian Arts Trust, calmly reaffirmed that small was beautiful and shut up shop. The fair had done its job, reawakening the collective imagination of the Waveney Valley folk, and it was now up to others to take up the baton, as they did, enthusiastically spawning a series of smaller-scale fairs that recaptured the intimacy and excitement of the early Barsham gatherings in fields all over Suffolk. There was the Wildream Fair at Valley Farm, Bramfield; the Folly Fair; and the magnificent series of

Huntingfield Fairs amongst the gnarled old oaks on a hillside overlooking Hevingham Hall.

The wild, good-natured hippy fairs were forerunners of Glastonbury or Womad, but without the showbiz or the profit motive, television rights, catering franchises, security companies and tall steel fences. It was a moment of high idealism in some ways, and hard work too, often far removed from the hedonism the fair-makers were sometimes accused of indulging.

PETER SMITH, *friend of Roger* We would now be described as hippies but we never called ourselves that. Counterculture is a bit academic. The core of people doing the fairs had left London, were still quite young and wanted to do something. The fairs lit up the right sort of thing – it was creative, it was artistic and it was also communal. That was incredibly important.

KEITH PAYNE, *in* The Sun in the East: Norfolk & Suffolk Fairs *by Richard Barnes (1983)* Suddenly the possibility of craft as an existence was being reborn, both of the necessity of country living and using the medieval concepts of barter and exchange. The craft thing was important, and like a breath of fresh air – a new approach on how to look after yourself. You could have a garden, an old car, a good time, somewhere to sell your work *and* a feeling that you were a part of something that was new and growing.

Letter, Diss Express, *September 1976* May I heartily endorse everything your splendid Mr Ward said about Barsham Faire last week. Medieval Faire indeed! More like a downright annual rendezvous for hippies and layabouts, I should say. I too was saddened to see so many of today's youth gathered together for what amounted to nothing better than a blatant display of exhibitionism and immaturity. Let us all hope Mr Ward is right, and that this really was the last Barsham Faire!

Yours sincerely, Gen. Sir T. G. 'Tug' Scuffard, Walnut Tree Farm, Mellis, Suffolk.

MEG AMSDEN, *friend of Roger* I moved from London to a seventeenth-century farmhouse in Suffolk with my first husband in 1973. A lot of people moved out of the city and were doing up houses like we were. I saw posters for this thing called Barsham Fair and said, 'We must go, we must go!' So we turned up in August and it was, 'Ahhhhh! Who are all these people? It's amazing!'

Roger was interested in the *Waveney Clarion* because he was interested in writing, so he was part of that group. I loved talking to him. He'd say, 'So what are you working on?' 'I'm doing puppet shows. I've got this idea,' and he'd say one sentence and all my jumbly ideas would suddenly go ker-dunk, ker-dunk, ker-dunk: ah, wonderful. He was very good at seeing into things and seeing the structure of things. It was part of the conversation; you never got any feeling that he was trying to tell you what to do.

VICKY MINET, *friend of Roger* The fairs were magical. They were nicer than Glastonbury because they weren't overrun – they were quite Suffolky, very intimate, local musicians played and there were lots of stalls. Roger was not a key organiser of the fairs, not at all. He wanted a piece of it like he wanted a piece of anything that he was interested in. He fell in love with what the fairs were; I mean, why wouldn't you? Roger began putting on ceilidhs and I went up with Dudley Young. I hardly knew what a ceilidh was. This most beautiful man got up and sang 'The Blackbird' and his beautiful girlfriend played an instrument, and they had children, even though they were quite young. There were lots of children running around. And they all seemed unbelievably romantic and wonderful.

EMMA BERNARD, *friend and daughter of Roger's friend Oliver Bernard* Going through the gate into a completely different world – staying up all night, eating pancakes at three in the morning, people running around naked painted purple – was an amazing liberation at sixteen years old. Roger was always bouncing up going, 'Oh, you've got to come and see this really good band or beautiful woman' or whatever it was. He was a consumer and a cheerleader of the fairs – 'You must come and meet my chum Richard Branson, or my chum Hank Wangford' or whoever it might be. He was always friends with the people who were important, in a shameless way. They were always round his house or doing something with him. His bounce at those fairs was about networking, being friends with everyone, and saying, 'Oh, you'll really like so-and-so.' That was a lovely quality of his.

VICKY MINET The fairs were very good for Roger in that they anchored him in Suffolk; they made him feel part of the landscape.

*

LESLEY WARD, *friend of Jenny Kember* There seemed a cloud of uncertainty about Jenny's relationship with Roger which I never really questioned. Intermittently, Jenny would leak a little dissatisfaction. She wanted to get married or firm up the relationship. He didn't 'spoil' her; there weren't little gifts that said 'saw this and thought of you'. I can't remember seeing him with his arm round her.

We went to Italy with the Open Space Theatre to perform Georg Büchner's *Woyzeck*. I had a small part and Jenny was thrown in as the administrator. Jenny had said that Roger wasn't persistently interested in the physical, and when some male actor took a shine to her, she flowered under the flattery. I remember thinking how sparkly and green her eyes were; I hadn't seen them so lovely. How Roger became suspicious I don't know, but when Jenny returned from Italy he seemed jealous and invited me to lunch, to cross-question me. I valiantly stood my ground. But the result was when she returned, he decided to ask her to get married. She was thrilled.

JENNY KEMBER It was rather weird. He always said he was not ready to commit himself; he liked to be a free spirit. We were still pretty young but I desperately wanted to get married and desperately wanted to have children and had done from quite a young age, partly because I'd been at boarding school and hadn't had much of a family life as a child. I went off on a tour of Italy with the Open Space Theatre and had a whale of a time, we behaved terribly badly and got very drunk and Roger had his hackles up when I came back because I was obviously quite glowing and he hadn't been involved. After that he suddenly got rather earnest and said, 'Well, let's get married then.' And I said, 'Do you really mean that?' and he said yes, so we did.

We got married on my twenty-sixth birthday, 31 August 1973. He didn't want a big church wedding and nor did I because I'm not a religious person. He didn't want a big do, he wanted to do it quietly, a warning sign which I didn't pick up at the time. We got married at Caxton Hall which was then the main London registry office and he only wanted very few people, so there was my mother, my aunt, my sister, and his mum and Tony and Bundle Weston, and Terry Wordingham who was another guy who lived in Queen's Gardens at one point. Then we went for a lunch which my grandmother paid for in Mr Chow's which was a rather trendy Chinese restaurant in Knightsbridge, and that was it. He didn't want a big party.

I felt really happy on the day. In retrospect, I thought he was slightly embarrassed to be getting married because he'd always made a big thing about 'I'm not ready to get married, I'm not ready to commit myself, I'm not ready to put down roots.' Almost as if he felt slightly trapped by it.

JO SOUTHON The day before Roger's wedding, Dudley Young gave him a copy of Joni Mitchell's *Blue*. Dudley had scored across all the tracks apart from

'My Old Man' which had a line about not needing a piece of paper from the authorities to keep us tied and true. This was Dudley expressing his disapproval. It was not very kind when a bloke is about to get married. At the time, Roger thought he was being told some sort of truth by Dudley.

JENNY KEMBER We didn't really have a honeymoon in the sense of us going off somewhere exotic on our own – we took the Morgan to Llafranc to see Tony and Tere Axon and stayed with another ex-Cambridge friend in France on the way. It was all including other people, which wasn't quite the same.

ROGER, *notebooks, 1970s, quoting George Bernard Shaw* What do you call married life? Real married life is the life of the youth and the maiden who pluck a flower and bring down an avalanche on their shoulders.

BOB MARSHALL-ANDREWS There was a lot of Conrad about Roger. He was a man with an ideal conception of himself. The ideal conception of yourself, once it gets hold, is a very dangerous thing. Conrad knew it was a dangerous thing. He wasn't all good, Rog. There was a lot of selfishness about him. Because that's what he wanted his life to be.

JULIA BLACKBURN, *friend* He was attracted to terribly powerful, intensely energetic, often quite classy ladies, and then horrified by them – 'You're nothing but a posh bitch' – but at the same time he chose the posh bitches; the funny this-way and that-wayness of him.

BUNDLE WESTON Later, Rog used to say he was pressured into marriage a lot. Jenny was very delighted to get married to him, and he was not, really. For Jenny, the conditions at Mellis were godawful, they really were. She had a baby, she had no washing machine, she had nothing.

LESLEY WARD When Jenny got pregnant her dream was coming true, but I felt that Roger was a bit squeamish about it, perhaps not really wanting that responsibility.

JENNY KEMBER He and I were still living in Queen's Gardens but he was spending a lot more time at Mellis. I was due to give birth in London and Rufus was five days overdue, and the day before I went into labour Roger decided to go to Mellis to check on the donkeys. And when I went into labour, I was on my own in the flat. Luckily Terry Wordingham came back rather pissed from a night out with a girlfriend and he gallantly got back in his Mini and drove me to Queen Charlotte's Hospital, with me puking into a plastic bag as we went.

Rufus was born at three in the afternoon the next day, 7 December 1974, and Roger did appear just before Ru was born, but only just.

RUFUS DEAKIN Dad drove down from Mellis to Hammersmith in the Morgan, pretty rapidly. He wanted to call me Dylan Dangerfield Deakin but Mum was working with the Open Space Theatre and there was a character in a play called Le Petit Rufus.

JENNY KEMBER I was obviously distracted looking after Ru and not quite so attentive towards Roger, perhaps because I couldn't be. Roger found that difficult. He liked to have a muse sitting at his feet, hanging on his every word.

JO SOUTHON I was rather a precocious girl and when I finished A levels, I went to live with my older boyfriend in London and began working as a receptionist for an advertising company called The Television Department. Luckily, I couldn't type well so I became a producer's assistant. Roger came to them because he wanted to make a commercial for the British Coal Board. We got on very well and at some point I said to Roger, 'If your company employed me you'd save money,' so I got a job at Interlink. I had got married in 1972, when I was nineteen, and then my husband was travelling away with work a lot. Eventually Roger and I started an affair.

ROGER, *letter to Jo from an advertising work trip to Istanbul, October 1974* Dear, beautiful Jo, Well, I don't know, what a peculiar place this is. I've only been here about four hours, but already seen enough to tell you about for at least twelve over a rather long lunch. I'm sitting on a wooden bench on the Galata Bridge, which crosses the narrow bit of (I think) the Sea of Marmara, linking the old city on the Golden Horn with the new city. Next to me and opposite me are a lot of old men sitting outside a sort of café, all smoking hookahs. I'm not sure what it is they're smoking, but I must say it looks and smells like something very strong indeed . . .

The blue shoes look like being a mistake. First of all because this town is so dirty; and even after an afternoon walk (admittedly about six miles) through the city, they're getting noticeably grimy. D'you think we can clean them up next week, Jo? And the second reason is that these Turks seem to share a foot, or at least shoe, fetish. One common symptom of this are the shoe-polish boys (average age about ten) who all seem to keep very busy shining up the tattered remains of the 1950s Dolcis-style slip-on casuals they wear here. Anyway, being so keen on shoes, every time I sit down anywhere and expose my shoes, I get foreigners coming up to me and pointing at them. When I was on that bench, a group of two or three youths discussed the aesthetics of my boots for a full five minutes while I looked out to sea and pretended to ignore them.

The bread I'm eating is pale brown, not salted I think, and contains the occasional bit of grit, to judge by the sounds transmitted by my molars and jawbone. It's good, though, with Doruk, the local wine, at the latter stage of what's turned out to be a most satisfactory dinner floating on a mixture of the Black Sea and the Mediterranean. Satisfactory mainly by virtue of this little notebook by my side which, for this evening, is Jo. Writing to you, or for you, is so much easier and so much better than any other kind . . . I love you Jo, and think of you in everything I do.

ROGER, *telegram to Jo, January 1975* YOUR PHONE IS FRUSTRATING BUT HELLO ANYWAY WILL TRY AGAIN SUNDAY NIGHT LATE LOVE = R+

JO SOUTHON At first, I was undemanding. I was not a powerful person. I hadn't gone to university at that stage and he wanted to educate me. He wrote a book list for me.

ROGER, *Jo's Desert Island Library*

Man Meets Dog by Konrad Lorenz
The Letters of Scott Fitzgerald
Tender is the Night
To the Lighthouse
Little Big Man, Thomas Berger
The White Goddess, Robert Graves
Poetry: John Donne songs and sonnets, *The Penguin Book of English Verse*, Robert Graves, *Man Does, Women Is*, Robert Frost (of course), Ted Hughes, 'The Hawk in the Rain', R. S. Thomas, *Song at the Year's Turning*, *The Stones of the Field*

JO SOUTHON We used to make each other things. I've got an oak chest that he carved out of the beams of one of the barns. Carving oak was like trying to get through concrete so it was a labour of love. I made him patchwork quilts. Roger took me to Holkham Bay once and we camped, and we went together on the train to Cornwall because he had a work trip there. I was at Mellis with him at some point when there was still masking tape around the windows, and I was doing the washing-up. He said that wine glasses shouldn't be put in the washing-up liquid; they should just be rinsed. So the wine glasses were covered in grease because the Fairy Liquid had never been allowed near them. This was bizarre but he had very clear ideas of how things should be done. Then my husband found out about the affair, we separated and I rented a flat in Earls Court. Obviously I was hoping, you could say naively, for something more to come out of my relationship with Roger.

ROGER, *letter to Jo, undated* Darling Jo, Cock crowing, squeaking pen, tap dripping, pink plaster, rugs, floorboards, in bed at one in the morning writing to you, just to be with you. Earlier tonight, a bird in the dark blue night sky doing a haunting whirring display flight, soaring then diving with a vibration of the wings to produce a hollow whirring over and over again above my head. A snipe perhaps, or a lapwing. Me breaking off more willow twigs and planting them along the causeway in the still warm night.

ROGER, *letter to Jo, January 1975* Yesterday there were gales of incredible ferocity, and I sat in here alone through the worst of it, the house literally trembling and shuddering under me and around me, like a captain in his ship. A dozen tiles came flying off the roof, and the top blew off a plum tree into the moat. It was good getting the ladders out and swarming aloft high on the roof clinging on against the gale under a clear, clear blue sky, to fix new tiles back on before the wind could get a hold under the gaps and lift even more tiles off in its next really big gust. Up there on the roof doesn't look very high up from the ground, but when you're there you can see for miles, and everywhere is so wet the fields glisten like sea. *Zen and the Art of Motorcycle Maintenance* too. Feeling at one with, caring for, the house . . .

Wind is so good, making the horses across the common mad and galloping, blowing everything away to a clear cold blue vision of you.

You are like a wind, blowing and gusting in me, making me climb roofs, showing me visions of fields I've never seen before, stretching into the clear blue distance. I love you, Jo.

ROGER, *letter to Jo, 1975* I feel so knocked out by this asthma – sort of incredibly weakened and can't sleep or breathe properly. Sorry to sound so depressing but it will go away in a week or so I expect. God knows what's going on – I don't feel very much in control just now. Jenny's in London and having trouble getting flights to Italy, so she's talking about going to Nassau instead.

ROGER, *letter to Jo, 1975* Spent the whole of today writing a Coal Board ad, which I found fantastically difficult, so low is my motivation.

> RUFUS DEAKIN Dad was crashed into by a motorbike on a back road from Diss to Thrandeston. The bike went straight over the passenger side of the Morgan. It was lucky no one was in the passenger seat. The wooden frame of the car cracked and it sat at Mellis for many years.

ROGER, *letter to Jo, June 1975* There really are virtues to having no car. Gives you a beautiful feeling of being quite cut off. So cut off I've been out working in the garden quite naked all day; a great feeling.

Bicycling to the Pub After a Motor Accident

Third party, fire and theft
Come, do your worst;
I'm on a bike,
And working up a thirst.

*

JENNY KEMBER There was a horrible New Year's Eve party when Ru was still tiny and it was very obvious that something was happening. I confronted Roger and said, 'There's something going on.' I knew it. And I had met her. But being Roger, he said, 'I still love you and I'm in love with her and I have to see it through. I have to let it run, work itself out.' There was no concession to my feelings at all. So that was pretty painful. Very difficult. We were based in Mellis by then and I used to run off to London a lot because it was all too difficult, and he would go away as well.

ROGER, *letter to Jo, June 1975* Darling Jo, Sometimes I feel like a country ravaged by a war. I feel that it isn't any longer a question of me doing any fighting, but of me being fought over, and that if the fighting gets savage, or prolonged, the country is in the end not a country any more, but a ruined battlefield . . .

I don't believe either one of us should ever be obligated towards the other in any way. So long as I can still know you, I can continue to love you, even though you may not love me. In fact the last thing I want is to possess you, because it is by definition impossible both to want and to possess something. But if I lost you, I'd like to lose you to yourself, and not to someone else – and that's emotion, not logic, I should think.

I don't care what anyone says, I like fantasy, I like mystery, I like soft outlines and not hard, I prefer ruins to homes, I like my cars ramshackle and a little dented, I like holes in my clothes, I like snatched conversations that are hard to have.

ROGER, *letter to Jo, August 1975* I've been swimming in the moat a lot. I filled it right up with a hose, and the water's really quite clean. Perhaps a diving board next? . . . I bought the Citroën Safari. Wait till you see it; a really beautiful machine, in fantastic condition. Almost the exact opposite of the Morgan in some senses – high technology as opposed to the simple brutality of the Morgan. But a really impressive machine and similar to the Morgan in that its design is seventeen years old yet looks better than anything else on the road I know, and in that it's a really workmanlike, practical car, built to take a lot of punishment safely and fast.

ROGER, *letter to Jo, August 1975* Panic, choice, loss, they paralyse me . . . The last week, a nightmare of that big loud band of an outer world of mine marching along, drowning out the gentle voice of the inner world. My mother staying, and a running sentimental commentary of appalling unconscious irony on all the apparent idyll that is here. Jenny and I locked in crisis, you so distant yet so present, Rufus and my mother, two innocents on the lawn, sensing something but not able or not daring to enquire.

Hardly had I arrived but I escaped to Cambridge in a car that felt suddenly like your flat must feel, bought enough books to hide in like a monastery for a year, and sat by the river behind Trinity and wrote to Margot because I dared not write to you but desperately wanted you to know what you already knew; that I was suffering with you.

ROGER, *letter to Margot, August 1975* I feel I've never loved anyone so hard and so long, and I've certainly never been loved so hard, so honestly, and with so much understanding. I've always thought of love as some sort of art which, if you got a couple of really original and like-minded artists working on it, would transcend everything. The problem's always been that given a fair degree of originality, like-mindedness proved elusive. At our best, Jo and I really do transcend. But by God there's an awful lot to transcend, and you can't go on living from one Great Moment to the next without quite a bit of medium-to-good stuff in between, as every dramatist knows. And as you know, my reference to drama is not flippant. With us, things do tend to be idyllic and memorable, or unforgettably awful. What goes wrong? Well, just that we both get wildly keyed up in different ways about meeting and that whereas Jo confronts and deals with her private anguishes in private, leaving herself free to concentrate on being together when we are, I tend to confront mine when we actually are together. I sweat and tremble with guilt and fear. They distract me, and we eye each other across the wall of uncatalogued problems. My speciality is bravado. Just when things get difficult and I really ought to stay ashore and wait for calmer days, I put out in the hopes of proving the storm isn't there. Jo has to come to the rescue with patience, wisdom, understanding, love . . .

I've felt so weird and disorientated and scared coming to London in unfamiliar forms of transport (bike, train and taxi in one case; unreliable tortoise of a truck in another) that by the time I've reached Jo I've been a nervous wreck.

A big part of the fear I get is the fear of not being at Mellis when I should be (i.e. when Jenny thinks I am). I really do fear the gods setting fire to it, or setting all the donkeys free on the road, and when I return down the common I really do half expect it to have burned down. And of course most of all I fear the dreadful scenes with Jenny, unbelieving at my cruelty and, as she sees it, weakness. She refuses to understand that I could be in love with Jo because she refuses to acknowledge any of the qualities I find in Jo. She simply sees me as the well-known egotist, flattered by the admiration of a plain and immature and highly unsympathetic girl . . . And then when crises do happen, and Jenny gets appallingly, helplessly upset, there is more and more the question of an increasingly aware Rufus. When there's tenseness between me and Jenny, it really begins to tell on Rufus. Most of all what I fear is Jenny being simply so much less effective as a mother without me. That tells directly on Rufus. She is visibly affected. Jenny is utterly committed to the idea of Rufus having a continuous mother–father household relationship to bring him up. The fact that her own father disappeared out of her life when she was about four makes her all the more determined. So she says that if I go, she would want another man to act as his father. I don't get the feeling I'd have much chance to see him. And the idea of a vindictive scene centring around a kid fills me with horror . . .

And then there's Mellis. Jo and I had a conversation about the power of love between two people transcending the power of attraction of any object or place. Jo fears I'll ultimately live (like Dudley perhaps) without love, choosing to place objects and places – maybe animals too – above love between a man and a woman such as we know. In a way, it's the hardest one of all. I don't know if I could ever leave Mellis. It's so much my promised land, so much a product of my imagination, that I feel complete there as nowhere else. Indeed the more I'm there the more of myself I leave there when I go away, so I feel less and less me when I go away.

I don't want always to be going away to see Jo. I want her to be able to come and see me. I don't know whether I want us to share a home together, we've hardly had a chance to find out what it might be like. I know for certain, though, that we can live and work together, inspiring one another like no two people on the whole fucking Earth.

When we're free.

I admit that I'm sensitive to other people's ideas of good and bad. But eventually I want to be my own idea of a good man. As that's the same thing as a strong man, maybe the teaching will help. I just want to be one who works and loves all the hours on God's Earth and is too busy to torment me, or Jo or Jenny because he's wise and strong enough to know <u>exactly</u> what he wants.

I'm talking about someone very like Jo.

Tell her I never see her more clearly than through tears.

With all my ragged love, Rog

ROGER, *letter to Jo, August 1975* In one way you are right to see the school teaching as a threat to you and me. It means that I'll be here all the time except holidays, weekends and, at a pinch, evenings. Ironically, I didn't see it consciously that way at all. I saw it as a direct putting into action of what we came to call the Dudley Theory of Guilt; that only by gaining the <u>inner</u> strength through guilt-combative work such as teaching could I gain the strength and sense of identity I need to make whatever is the right decision about my relationships.

ROGER, *letter to Jo, May 1976* Animals have a way, when they meet unexpectedly on wild, neutral territory, of subtly showing themselves to one another before any actual approach, so as not to cause any sudden alarm. Now I've at last begun to write to you, the words are going down like a soft turf over which I tread carefully towards you. It was so hard to begin.

I love you.

You mistook my inability to cope for lack of love. When you rang, needing so much to see me, I felt threatened somehow. I reacted as I so often do to crisis; I rolled myself tightly into a ball like a hedgehog and waited for it to go away. (Like the hedgehog, too, I feel I can't get close to anyone without causing them pain.)

A. S. Neill says that hate is only thwarted love. I know I felt you hated me both times we spoke on that awful telephone. I know I felt you thought I was self-satisfied and arrogant and thoughtless and selfish, when in fact I just felt I was overworked, overcommitted, disorganised, indecisive, deliberately (self-protectingly) vague. Living the only way I felt I could cope, from day to day, and scared to death of anything that would upset the precarious equilibrium that enabled me to keep so many emotional balls in the air at once.

. . . You said you resented being part of my fantasy. If that's what thinking about you a lot of the time, every day is, I'm sorry, but you aren't here, and I don't even know if I'll see you again, but I do want to, and I do think about you, and wonder very much what you are doing, and what you are thinking, and how you are.

JO SOUTHON I contacted Margot in desperation. I think I wanted her to tell me what to do. We met, spoke, and I liked her. When it became obvious that nothing would happen between Roger and I – there would be long silences and then a passionate letter and the odd meeting – I thought, I've got to get on with my life. The people I made friends with in the advertising world were all ones who didn't fit and wouldn't play the game. In 1976, I moved to Cambridge and took a teaching degree at Homerton and became an English teacher.

When I read about Robert Graves's life and dysfunctional relationships, it seemed like a more extreme version of Roger's. For Roger, a woman was powerful, remote. The remoteness was important to him. He was more comfortable with a remote relationship than a real one, actually. Robert Graves's idea of the White Goddess. It's not flesh and blood and real. The relationships with me and with Jenny were expending a hell of a lot of energy for Roger. To write a book, he would have to reach a still, calm place, and a place of his own, and a place where he wasn't searching for more, thinking, I've got to find these amazing White Goddess women. By the time he wrote *Waterlog*, I think he'd realised the White Goddess didn't exist.

CHAPTER 8

The Teacher

Enter a new kind of teacher: 'My name's Roger, Roger Deakin' — Diss Grammar School, September 1975 — Byronic flamboyance and Joni Mitchell in the classroom — the new school magazine — parents' evening — 'an immoral person and an obvious Communist' — clashes with Mr Norfolk — Freaky Deaky not Creepy Deaky — Howards End and escape to the wych elm — as lonely as a cloud in the Lakes — 'Freaky's gone' — Mr Deakin gets his pupils' goat

SARAH CRAWFORD, *pupil* I loved the smell of polish and sweat, the bizarre ritual, the extraordinary characters, the serendipity of the odd lesson which came alive. But nothing *truly* came alive until 1975, when Roger joined the English staff.

BILL SEAMAN, *pupil* It was a tsunami of passion and intellect washing over us. We were a very sleepy rural grammar school. And he woke us up.

CLAIRE MORTIMER, *pupil* He was like a creature from another planet.

EMMA BERNARD, *pupil* Most of the teachers were wearing gowns. A tweed jacket was considered really casual. And Roger arrived in this brown corduroy flared suit, with his hair all massive.

JOHN BLAGDEN, *teacher* When Roger arrived he made an immediate impression. Some said a breath of fresh air. Others felt it to be a rather unwelcome draught.

I was surprised how cool I felt the afternoon before, as I collected the books I would need and piled them into the Citroën. At six forty-five precisely the next morning, I was all ready, in my smart green shirt, silk tie from Italy, Olof Daughters boots, and Village Gate brown cord suit. On the drive to Diss, I checked my moustache in the rear-view mirror and imagined one side was shorter than the other. Too late to do anything about that now.

In Diss, I swung my big, shining Safari into the drive of the red-brick grammar school and parked beside the lawn amongst a hotchpotch of Dormobiles, Morris Marinas, and a Triumph Spitfire, which I guessed was driven by the PT master. Then I took the plunge, passing beneath the school's crest and motto *initium sapientiae timor Domini* – the Fear of the Lord is the Beginning of Wisdom – striding along the corridor and entering the male staffroom.

No one seemed to take any notice at all. A couple of faint words; it was very subdued in there. I sat down, hoping I was not making some appalling gaff like pinching the maths master's personal favourite chair, and I instantly felt conspicuously smart. They were all, to a man, dressed appallingly. Dacron trousers, cavalry twill, green tweed jackets, and a tracksuit in one corner. The games master picked up an envelope addressed to me and examined it, turning it over several times, with apparent hostility. I let him do this then, after a pause, opened the envelope myself. It was a letter from the County Education

Office, saying that the staff would do everything to help me settle in. On first impressions, their powers of hospitality seemed limited. None of them appeared very interested in each other either.

We then filed down the corridor in ones and twos, ones in my case, to a classroom where the headmaster addressed us. We all hunched over the children's small desks, with ashtrays provided. The atmosphere reminded me of the first day I went to my school. There was a strong feeling of embattlement. My instincts were all towards the women; they seemed warmer, more dedicated, more intelligent and alive to what we're here to do. Amongst the men, there was an incredible apathy stabbed through with a surprising degree of bitterness for this sleepy country market town. We elected a head boy and head girl for the year, with the headmaster kindly, intelligently and firmly putting everything to the vote, and running things with wit and fairness. There followed a wrangle about discipline, with the teachers debating whether to allow children into classrooms during breaks. The head couldn't see what harm it would do, but some of the male teachers got very hot under the collar about it all. As discussions about discipline continued, I examined the desk where I was sat, decorated with generations of carvings and graffiti. How much better it looked than a boring, plain, varnished desk. And I wondered how I could possibly tell anyone not to play cards in school with a straight face.

MARY TODD, *pupil* I remember the day he walked in; I'm sure everybody does. We were in a school where teachers wore their gowns. Terribly formal, terribly stuffy. And Roger waltzed into the classroom, with his mad hair and brown corduroy trousers and jacket with patches on the sleeves, and said, 'Hello, my name is Roger. Roger Deakin.' No teacher had ever told us their first name before. So we all went, 'What?'

SARAH CRAWFORD I remember the slight shock of seeing him heading down the parquet-floored corridor with his characteristic loping stride. He cut a strange figure for pupils used to be-gowned elderly ladies. Corduroy jacket and trousers, thick-soled brogues, a long knitted scarf wrapped carelessly around his neck like Doctor Who, with a Frank Zappa moustache and wild Byronic curls. He managed to convey both intellectual gravity and dangerous rebellion at the same time.

JO ROLFE, *pupil, diary, September 1975* New teacher, Mr Deakin. Very nice.

A week later He's not good at keeping order.

JO ROLFE But that changed. He soon got the measure of these slightly switched-off, bored pupils. He treated us as young people and he wasn't cynical; I don't think he ever became cynical about education. A few weeks after he began, he took us out of the classroom and we ended up in the hall, acting out Arnold Wesker's *Chips with Everything*.

JO ROLFE, *diary, 1975* It was a brilliant lesson.

JO ROLFE There's nothing like that in my diaries about other teachers.

*

SARAH CRAWFORD In 1975, Diss Grammar School was a small country school, selective only in that it took those gaining the top third of the marks at eleven-plus from surrounding village primaries. Lessons in the lower school were so unchanging that my brother, sister and I passed through first-form English with not only identical textbooks but identical entries in our exercise books. In the fourth year, we were taught geography by the PE teacher who would draw a map on the board in chalk with the numbers 1 to 25 and we had to find out the locations. The French teacher once threw a compass and it stuck into the cork board at the back of the classroom. The school would have been unrecognisable for an alumnus of Manchester Grammar and the quality of education offered was, for the most part, archaic and abysmal. I suspect it was not what Roger expected.

TRACY SHARP, *pupil* Diss Grammar was stuck in the fifties. The girls all did domestic science; the boys all did woodwork. There were male and female staffrooms. There were even male and female careers teachers. The female careers teacher's brief was to get girls into Norwich Union, nursing and teaching – that was the palette of what was expected of you as a woman. And Roger came in with a massive vitality and he was interested in you as a person – finding out what drove you, what you felt passionate about – and he believed in that and believed in the power of that to take you to important places in your life. And nobody else did.

LUCY THWAITE, *pupil* When my parents complained that there didn't appear to be any discussion in English lessons, it was just dictated notes, the elderly English teacher, Mrs Wynne-Jones, told my dad, 'This is Norfolk, these are Norfolk children. They don't need discussion.'

EMMA BERNARD God, there were some scary teachers. There was still the cane and it was still perfectly all right to throw board rubbers at kids in class.

The teacher would also come up behind you and whack you round the back of the head.

BILL SEAMAN I was in the upper sixth when Roger arrived. He spoke about education being *educari*, to lead out. That's what he was doing. He was leading us out. And the rest of the school wasn't necessarily leading us out. Previously we read Thomas Hardy round the class for weeks and then had notes dictated on him. Roger came along with the Romantic poets and said, 'Come on, guys, this is about you, it's about passion, it's about life, it's connecting viscerally with your existence. Can you feel the blood pumping in their veins while they wrote?' Suddenly, the scales fell from our eyes.

CLAIRE MORTIMER I was a bit younger, and in his form, 3Z. He had an extraordinary amount of energy and creativity and he gave you glimpses of another world. He would tell us stories, such as how when he was a student at Cambridge they cut each other's hair, and he read us stories and poems in our tutor time, when he didn't need to, such as 'The Happy Prince' by Oscar Wilde. We studied *Rogue Male* and he asked us to do really interesting things, like drawing the hero's hideout. He made everything magical.

TRACY SHARP Roger was fascinated by words, fascinated by metaphor, and fascinated by the idea of words exploding your understanding into a new way of seeing the world.

EMMA BERNARD He would come in and say, 'Right, today we're going to go to Gaze's auction in Diss,' so we would go out of school and go to the auction to find some object to write a story about. It was such a great thing to do; a real liberation.

BILL SEAMAN There he was, in his Byronic flamboyance, before us young people with raging hormones. For a creative poetry lesson, he chose 'The Good Morrow' by John Donne and Andrew Marvell's 'To His Coy Mistress'. I didn't think dead poets could have anything to say to us, other than it being a technical exercise in looking at language. But Roger was saying, 'No, he's talking to you, and he's saying life is short, seize time.' He'd deliberately chosen all this stuff which is full of raging-hot passion. Week after week in those lessons, you could feel connections in your brain, whole rooms you didn't know were there, lighting up.

Keats was on the curriculum. I'd missed a lesson for some reason and I bumped into Roger in the corridor, and he said, 'Oh, Bill, you weren't at the last lesson,' and I said, 'No, I'm sorry,' and he said, 'Well, let's do it now.' He didn't have to; I'd missed the lesson, it was my problem. He took me to an empty classroom and gave me a one-to-one lesson on Keats. Sitting with him dead opposite me, it was like a furnace door swinging open, and a blast of heat coming at you, in terms of his passion and intellect, engaging me with those big eyes and saying, 'Yes, so what does that mean?' and 'Wasn't that bit great?' It would have been enough to fill a room of people and it was focused in on me alone.

SARAH CRAWFORD His heart lay with the Romantic poets and most particularly with John Clare who I'd never heard of before. Roger's deep emotional engagement with this poetry, undisguised and astonishing for me at seventeen, reflected his own distress at the destruction of natural habitats and his delight in the physical enjoyment of nature. Clare resonated closely with Roger's ecological concerns, which no one else was voicing at the time.

*

ROGER, *notebooks, 2004* D. H. Lawrence detested self-consciousness as something that de-educates children and militates against spontaneous creativity.

Mr Deakin's nicknames Freaky Deaky. Freaky. Trendy Rog. Coustics [as in, acoustic guitar]. Doo-waaah Deakin.

EMMA BERNARD My brother told this story about how Roger once came into the classroom and sat on his desk and started strumming his guitar, quite badly, and singing 'doo-waaah', as if they were going to join in and make a song with him. 'Doo-waaah'. For ages he was called Doo-waaah Deakin. They thought it was the most absurd, hilarious and kind of brilliant thing to do – having a jam session with these fifteen-year-old boys.

CLAIRE MORTIMER The boys used to jump up and down on his car to make it bounce. He had this huge, weird and wonderful Citroën which was parked in a very prominent position. It was like a hovercraft – it went up slightly in the air. It was all part of the persona of Mr Deakin.

JO ROLFE He made everything so exciting. One day, somehow, the subject of ceilidhs came up, and someone didn't know what they were. 'You don't know what a ceilidh is!' exclaimed Roger. 'Right, tomorrow, class, you move the chairs and tables back, and I'll bring a record player.' We did, and we had a ceilidh.

ROGER, *notebook, 1970s* Today being the last lesson of the term, we go to my car and hump out the hi-fi gear, set it up in the classroom, and listen to the Chieftains, after a brief discussion on folk music and its role in society, the invention of the radio etc. The class soon develops into a ceilidh dance, with the desks pushed back against the wall, and all of us whirling round the classroom. Between us, we work out the sequence of steps for a couple of complete dances, and decide we'll try them out on the third form, who have their party in the school hall (organised by the sixth form) this afternoon.

MARY TODD He gave us photocopied purple sheets from the old Banda machine of lyrics to Joni Mitchell and Bob Dylan songs and explained they were poetry, and that was how we started our poetry lessons. And he used to play these songs on a record player for us to listen to, and walk up and down. It was a chalk-and-talk school so we weren't used to it. And it was wonderful.

He was both incredibly creative but also incredibly literal. If we didn't know or understand something, then we needed to discover it directly. When we were studying T. S. Eliot's *Four Quartets*, we listened to Vivaldi's *The Four Seasons*. He liked to see it as relating to your place in the universe. But he was also very challenging because he would suddenly get frustrated that our horizons weren't where he thought they should be.

He was very sensitive about how he was putting across ideas and he really wanted you to make connections and think for yourself, and if you weren't able to do that, he would look at other ways of linking things together for you. But Roger sometimes didn't take other people's perspectives into account because once he was on a roll with something you couldn't get him away from it – he'd be off on his unstoppable riff of enthusiasm, and he couldn't see that it might make you feel uncomfortable, or it might not be something you're interested in. Once Roger was getting excited about a conversation he couldn't see anything outside of it.

*

BILL SEAMAN My parents taught at the secondary modern school in Diss and it had a brass band, metalworking, music, plays. We didn't have anything extracurricular. Roger introduced all sorts of things such as the school magazine. *Cosa Nostra* was pushing on an open door because there were a lot of kids with masses of things to say and no vehicle to say it.

LUCY THWAITE *Cosa Nostra* was 'Our Thing' in Italian. He wanted it to be ours; actually, it was his thing, really. It didn't come from the roots of the kids but maybe it did get us moving.

COSA NOSTRA, Number One, Christmas 1975 An interviewer once asked Bob Dylan what his songs are about. 'Oh,' said Dylan. 'Some are about four minutes, some are about five minutes.' *Cosa Nostra* is about eight inches by twelve. Whatever else it's about is entirely up to you, because it's your magazine, a mirror held up to you. We hope you like what you see.

SIMON POULTER, *pupil Cosa Nostra* was the legit school magazine, which the sixth-form students did. My friend and I started a school indie-zine, which was called *Paranoia*. Roger not only encouraged us to put it together but he helped us learn to do paste-up with cow gum and he paid for the copying. So we made fifty copies. Roger would encourage creativity in everybody. It was pretty crap writing but we were seeing what we could get away with. Roger loved that; he wanted to promote that.

*

JO ROLFE, *report card, autumn term 1975*
French B. Good all-round progress.
German C. Making reasonable progress.
English Language and English Literature A. [Roger's comments] Excellent all round; articulate and well-read, and particularly promising imaginative writer with a natural 'feel' for poetry. RSD.

TRACY SHARP It took ages to read what he said about an essay, but it was full of everything that he loved about it and where you could go with it, and how you could improve it.

EMMA BERNARD He used to write really beautiful comments in brown ink on your essays. It always looked like a friendly note. He was very effusive in his praise and he was very encouraging, particularly if you were writing anything that sounded a bit revolutionary.

At my first parents' evening, I was put in the Medical Inspection Room; the short straw, as usual. I felt like a doctor or a psychoanalyst, waiting for his patients. It was an out-of-the-way, rather forbidding little room, so most parents bypassed me and saw other teachers first. I pondered whether there was a small flask of brandy hidden away somewhere amongst the couches and hot-water bottles, medicine chests and sinks. In the small yard outside the window, a shadowy no man's land at the centre of the school accessible only to birds, a pair of wagtails darted like butterflies in and out of a forest of purple-and-green buddleia that had grown up in there, despite being imprisoned, the erect, purple flowers pressing up almost rudely against the windows. The birds looked as out of place as I felt inside.

Here we were, a large group of people gathering to talk about another group of individuals – the schoolchildren – who knew we were talking about them, but were not there, and would never know quite what was said about them; even though most of it was no more than a string of clichés, platitudes, abstractions. Surely all this would have been more natural and helpful if the children had been here too? Then we could have discussed actual work with the people whom it concerned the most: the children.

At the end of my first term, I was summoned to the head's study and read two angry letters from parents complaining about my fifth-form social studies teaching and withdrawing their girls from my classes – on the grounds that I was an immoral person and an obvious Communist who had obviously only come to the school to politically subvert tender young minds. They also complained that my approach was basically frivolous because I played pop music in class. There were even complaints about the title of the school magazine, *Cosa Nostra*. I told the head it was absurd redneck talk, and made no concessions, but it was obvious that he was 'worried' about me. I felt altogether different after the strange experience that was my first term of teaching. I felt glad I did it, but it didn't really feel as though it was me who did it.

ROGER, *letter to Jo Southon, December 1975* I went to Anthony Thwaite's house to see a play produced by one of his daughters (Lucy) and met him. We landed up talking all evening over about three bottles of wine. He's really amazing. It was really wonderful (word used deliberately) to meet somebody new who was that exciting to be with. His wife's on the school governors and we discussed the possibilities of manoeuvring me into part-time teaching of some kind. They think it's possible provided I don't antagonise the head, which is of course going to require tact.

ANN THWAITE We all liked Roger and admired the way that he had turned his back on the glitzy advertising world in London to live in the country and become a rather ineffective teacher of French [as well as English]. I was a governor of the grammar school at the time but, as a parent, I certainly had little idea what went on. He wanted his pupils to see how different he was from his colleagues.

*

BILL SEAMAN There was a staff versus school hockey match. The conventional male staff turned up with Brylcreemed hair, Stanley Matthews shorts, and leather, hobnailed football boots from the forties or fifties. And then Roger turned up in skin-tight lederhosen, wild Byronesque curls, a Zapata moustache, and an untucked shirt flowing around. There was more contrast between him and other members of staff than there was between the staff and the pupils. We were in the seventies and finally witnessing this huge shift that had taken place in the sixties in terms of sloughing off Victorian and Edwardian attitudes and culture, and he was an absolute emblem of that.

JOHN BLAGDEN I taught maths at Diss Grammar for thirty-four years and the staff were very stable. Most had been there for twenty years or so. Roger's rather different approach to the pupils created the biggest impression. Some of the staff saw it as a threat to good order and discipline.

BILL SEAMAN The staff were right to be wary of him, because he was calling time on a particular way of teaching.

JOHN BLAGDEN He was more often to be found in the ladies' staffroom but most of the English Department were female so it did not seem that surprising. I feel that some of the suspicions about Roger's activities were because he had so little rapport with the rest of the predominately male staff.

ROSEMARY PALMER, *teacher* I don't think Roger always saw eye to eye with the headmaster. The headmaster was a bit old-fashioned. It could even have been about the length of his hair.

DEBBIE BARTLETT, *pupil* The headmaster swept around in his gown with his hands in his pocket, and he would jingle his change.

JOHN BLAGDEN Tony Norfolk was appointed Head Designate in the spring of 1960. When he interviewed me that year he said, 'I believe being effective in the classroom depends upon being accepted and known in the local community. I shall expect you to live in Diss and be seen going about your daily business by the pupils and their parents. You will know them when you meet them in the street and be willing to talk to them.' Mr Norfolk was rarely seen outside of his study – and his secretary made it difficult to see him in it! – but he insisted on teaching English to two groups a year. He was very active in the local shooting community.

JOE GIBBS, *pupil* The headmaster, A. C. Norfolk, did not start teaching until he was thirty-one; Roger started at Diss when he was thirty-two. So that's the first similarity; or rather the fourth, since both men attended private schools, studied English at Cambridge and had successful careers in the outside world (Roger in advertising, Norfolk in the army; rank of major). Norfolk was a product of the Empire when leadership was considered a main quality and essential for the continuation of the Empire. Leadership rested on character, and could be developed through appropriate education. The grammar schools had the task of producing pupils with the appropriate traits of character to serve in the middle ranks of the economy. Honesty, reliability and punctuality were among the qualities needed for people at this level. That was the pedagogical framework in which Norfolk's generation worked; but it was one which was not only rejected as unfit for purpose, but also mocked relentlessly by the best of Roger's generation.

In the spring term of 1976, four sixth-formers were gathered idly in 'the officers' mess' as Roger had called the wooden wartime-era building that had been converted into a sixth-form common room. Enter Antony Norfolk. 'Shouldn't there be an English lesson this morning?' he asked. 'It's been cancelled,' replied one of the pupils. 'Mr Deakin couldn't make it in to school this morning.' Norfolk was completely stuck for words. It was the only time Roger missed a lesson but in the eyes of Norfolk this was enough. A short while afterwards, Roger mentioned in class that the headmaster has asked him if he would mind teaching first-year French in the following year. Roger said he would be happy to do so, as twelve-year-olds have a freshness and willingness to learn. But in fact, this was the first step in Norfolk's demotion of Roger.

DI BARRELL, *wife of teacher Ken Barrell* At one stage, the Head of English left and Roger rang up to speak to Ken. Roger didn't think he would get the Head of English job and that was a real shame because he was excellent. Roger told me, 'Oh well, I think I'm going to give up teaching because I'm getting my only positivity from the children.'

KEN BARRELL, *teacher* He had problems with Mr Norfolk's philosophy and knew he wasn't going to get far. He was thinking of applying for the job of

Head of English but he wouldn't have stood a chance, I'm afraid. He was too unconventional.

*

ROGER, *letter to Jo Southon, May 1976* The effect of the school work on me really is huge. During those two weeks' Easter holiday so much of me came flooding back that I forget about, sort of unconsciously hold aloof, during the term. When I'm teaching, I hold myself in, poised, unrelaxed, wound up in the work. It's almost like being in a monastery.

SARAH CRAWFORD Roger became friends with pupils who tended to come from reasonably outgoing, middle-class families. The ones that had their eye on the utopias that he felt could be achieved.

LUCY THWAITE Roger insisted that we call him Roger and he wanted to be our chum. He was always talking about chums. He wanted to be mates with all of us and we thought that was embarrassing and slightly pathetic, and that's sad because he was a really good thing for us at school.

TRACY SHARP There was quite a lot of resistance to him within the group. Pupils would put up their hands and say, 'Is this on the syllabus, Mr Deakin?' So it wasn't straightforward. There were a lot of people who didn't want to be talking about these wider things. They wanted ways of passing their exams.

LUCY THWAITE He was my French teacher for several years. We spent the entire time getting him off the subject of French. We were supposed to translate the lyrics of *The Dark Side of the Moon* into French but we would just listen to the music and not do a great deal of work. Roger had a romantic idea of being a teacher – that he would open the eyes of pupils most of whom had led very limited lives in the Norfolk countryside – but part of me felt quite cross. He didn't have any of the other teachers' sense of getting pupils through their exams.

*

ROGER, *notebooks, undated* Did I meet any wild children when I was teaching? Yes – some of the teenage girls were incredibly sexy and drove me crazy with desire, crossing and uncrossing their legs under short skirts, or flicking their red hair over mascara eyelashes. 'Get thee behind me, Satan,' I would hiss to myself between clenched teeth as I drove home in the Citroën DS.

JOHN BLAGDEN Roger's arrival caused quite a flutter among the older girls and the uptake of A level English as a subject increased among them. He was willing to, and perhaps even insisted on, discussing subjects that would have been unmentionable prior to his arrival, and his blurring of the boundary of pupil–teacher relationships caused concern among the senior staff. I can say, with absolute certainty, that one mother 'expressed concern' about his relationship with her daughter in the sixth form. Later, she told me she had written to the school about his activities with the girls, but had stopped short of complaining; she thought the relationship was upsetting but no more than that.

SARAH CRAWFORD He was Freaky Deaky. He wasn't Creepy Deaky.

BILL SEAMAN Of course there were girls who were in love with Roger. Why wouldn't they have been? He was in his early thirties. He was absolutely in his prime. Full of confidence and passion with a hairy chest and a bristling full moustache, unlike the weedy little things that we were trying to grow.

SIMON POULTER In 1977, I got on the school bus from Brockdish to Diss and a copy of *Never Mind the Bollocks* by the Sex Pistols went round the bus. We all took it home for a few days. Joe Bernard knew how to play three chords so he was this guitar virus man who showed everybody else how to play the three chords. We started playing guitars and writing songs in Portakabin classrooms during break and Roger would breeze by every now and again and find out how we were doing. We were called The Subversive Elements and he helped us get gigs. He became an ersatz punk-band manager. We thought, OK, great, he's helping us, in that way young people take things for granted. He introduced us to a band called Ronnie and the Roofers and then we got gigs with them at different village halls around south Norfolk. Not only did Roger get us the gigs and help us hump all the gear there, he came and danced with his partner to the – pretty terrible – music. He gave you permission to do things that otherwise you wouldn't have done. And that was critical for me as a young person. He said, 'Why don't you go to art school because then you can be in punk bands and do nothing?' And that's what I did and I've been practising as an artist ever since.

JO ROLFE, *diary, October 1976* Went to see Hank Wangford at Flash in the Pan. Roger and Jenny there. I don't think I've seen Mr Deakin in a tie before except at speech day.

JO ROLFE Roger stopped once and asked if I wanted a lift back home to Palgrave because it was on his drive home and he started talking about goats.

I milked goats every evening, and he ended up buying some and I got roped into milking those. So I ended up being round at Walnut Tree Farm quite a lot. It was very exciting, with all these friends from London, and occasionally famous people.

*

ROGER, *notebooks, 1977* Start the week with my too-well-behaved third form. Saunter in and take the register (Christ – I forgot to hand it in at the school office on Friday!) then send someone to borrow the school Sellotape reel to stick a 'Happy Christmas' speech bubble Colin's made on to a six-foot coypu the class put together and stuck on the wall last week. Then a quick check on the dinner numbers (another note to the school office) and the first bell of the week tingles the ear.

Roger's set texts for his A level English class, 1977–78 Howards End, *The Rainbow,* Four Quartets, *Julius Caesar* or *Macbeth*, the verse of Philip Larkin and Robert Lowell.

TRACY SHARP For our first English literature A level lesson, he opened E. M. Forster's *Howards End* which begins with the epitaph 'Only connect' and spent the first hour exploring with us what this phrase might mean. He then explained that a central character was the wych elm at Howards End. He looked up and asked if we all knew what a wych elm was. Despite being brought up in the country, most of us rather sheepishly admitted we'd no idea. He closed the novel suddenly and said, 'Well, we can't start reading *Howards End* until you've all stood underneath a wych elm. There's a beautiful one at a farm in Wortham, I'll give them a call and we'll pop out in the minibus and give it a look.' All aboard, we were heading for the school gates when Mr Norfolk came rushing out in his black gown shouting, 'Mr Deakin, Mr Deakin, have you got parental consent forms for this?' Roger waved and smiled and shouted not to worry and we'd be back before lunch as we sailed out of the school gates.

JO ROLFE He found a thorn apple growing underneath the wych elm. 'That's thorn apple! That's hallucinogenic!' And he pointed us towards Carlos Castaneda and we ended up reading *The Teachings of Don Juan*.

TRACY SHARP As we all wandered into the dome of interlocking branches and leaves of this old wych elm, we did not really know why we were there but we were struck by being made to stop still and actually look and sense.

DEBBIE BARTLETT That level of spontaneity was such fun and so different from anything else.

TRACY SHARP Literature was not a 'subject' to be 'studied' in order to pass exams for Roger; he revealed to us how reading books might be a vital part of being more fully alive. While he clearly saw any syllabus as a hugely limiting structure that needed to be broken open, he was ferociously ambitious for us all. He knew that exam results were going to be the key to our liberation from the low expectations that the school seemed to have for us.

*

My friend Ken Barrell used to take a hiking party of fifth- and sixth-formers to the Lake District every Easter, and I went with him several times. He was a superb hill-walker, always fit, highly experienced and he knew the mountains and the lakes backwards. We would always climb Helvellyn, Great Gable, Scafell, run the scree at Wastwater and bike up Borrowdale.

KEN BARRELL We never biked up Borrowdale – that was poetic licence, although he would have loved to do that – and he only joined us once, in April 1978. Each Easter, we took a bus up to the Lakes. I would book various hostels and we would walk from one to another, over the highest mountains. I used to really push the kids. Sometimes they hated the first day or two but they really loved it after they got their mountain legs. On the first day, we were dropped off at Haweswater and walked to Patterdale. Roger was extraordinary. He was dressed like a lost First World War pilot, with his goggles on and a leather jacket and protection from the mud with a pair of gaiters. He looked quite eccentric. But it was great that he came. He loved the Lake District and the Lakeland poets.

TRACY SHARP Roger would be reading Wordsworth up on the hillside while Ken would pray as we faced a particularly difficult stretch in proper fog with the darkness coming in.

KEN BARRELL In the evening he'd chat to the kids about Wordsworth or Coleridge. On another day, Roger wanted to climb some more mountains and we went up Crinkle Crags from Eskdale. We walked through the mist and entered another world: blue sky and sunshine with the odd peak jutting above the mist. He absolutely loved it.

WIZARD WHEEZES, *unofficial school magazine, 1978* There was a horribly dangerous and totally un-nice climb up Scafell and a return down 180 degrees out of our way. The nicest day was Sunday when we spent a day in Keswick doing any nice things except walking.

KEN BARRELL It was a very wet week, probably the wettest that I had ever taken, but everyone was very cheerful. On the final day of the week, we only had the morning for walking and he asked me if he could take those who were interested down to Lake Coniston to chat about the Lakeland poets. I was struck by Roger's graciousness, asking my permission. He made the right decision. I took a party up Coniston Fell but we were in the cloud all the time. He was in sunshine down at the lake.

*

ROGER DEAKIN, *cover of a school notebook, 1970s* Name: R. S. Deakin. Form: Day to Day. Subject: Deep depression and the occasional high.

MARY TODD, *diary, 26 May 1978* Mr Deakin has resigned . . .

SIMON POULTER I remember one of the kids saying, 'Oh, Freaky's gone.' It was quite a big thing in school that he was going.

MARY TODD I was completely devastated when he left. We were halfway through our English A levels and we felt like, how the hell do we get through this? And we were all angry with the school.

TRACY SHARP He was always very professional. He never bad-mouthed any teachers but we sensed he must be having a tough time. I thought that he was moving on because he wanted to do other things – environmental activism, film-making. It was like different liquids: institutional life and Roger didn't really go together. I'm amazed he stayed for three years.

SARAH CRAWFORD He was a shock and an irritant to the school hierarchy. I think he thought he was going to this grammar school and would have a wonderful time conveying the delights of literature. For some children, his teaching was an absolute breath of fresh air. Others thought it was stupid and they just wanted to get their O levels and leave. Possibly, he became disillusioned.

JO ROLFE The only time he got angry was when he took our sixth-form group out on to the field after he announced that he was leaving. It was a lovely sunny day and he sat us down. We were supposed to talk about our hopes and aspirations beyond sixth form.

MARY TODD He asked us about what our dreams were and we all just sat there. Not quite sure. And he said, 'You cannot do this! You can't just sit here like a load of contented cows.' And it was like, wow. He was trying to say, if you don't have some sort of dream, you can't move towards it. He taught us many things but that was a really big thing.

TRACY SHARP He had a rant at us. 'What do you mean, you don't have any dreams for the future? If you don't have dreams when you are seventeen, what the hell are your lives gonna be like? Get dreaming.'

MARY TODD, *diary, 30 May 1978* Go to Cambridge. Leave 9 a.m. from Mr Deakin's place. Had fabulous day. Visited all the colleges. Went punting. Great fun! Got back late so stayed with Tracy. Best day since Keswick. If it kills me I'm going to go there. I've fallen in love with it now I've seen it.

DEBBIE BARTLETT We went in his hilarious car that used to almost take off before you drove off. It was a really hot day. This was exam season, and he marched into his old college, arriving at what I subsequently knew was the porters' lodge. The porters objected, and Roger said, 'It's fine, we know our way,' and he went to his old room, knocked, and this poor undergraduate came to the door. Roger said, 'This is my room. Isn't it lovely?' and showed it off to six seventeen-year-old girls.

BILL SEAMAN It wouldn't have occurred to him that going off in a car with pubescent girls was anything untoward because there was no agenda other than a passion and honest enthusiasm for the subject in hand.

MARY TODD Leaving Cambridge that day, I thought, I'd give anything to go to university there. Then the head called us in at the end of the year to ask us about our plans and I said, 'I really want to go to Cambridge.' And he said, 'Well, for-get it, because you ain't gonna get there.' Mr Norfolk had been to Cambridge and he'd look at you and go, 'Huh, I don't think so.' Whereas Roger looked at you and said, 'Yeah, of course you can; if I can do it, other people can do it.'

SARAH CRAWFORD In June 1978, I took my S levels to get into Cambridge alone in the Nissen hut which was grandly titled the Sixth Form Centre. I sat at a table and Roger, the invigilator, sat feet up on the teacher's desk at the front of the room, book in hand. He had some chocolate digestive biscuits beside him and, halfway through a three-hour marathon, he stretched, yawned and rose, offering me the packet. I looked up from my furious scribble, asking, 'Am I allowed?' Roger wheeled and threw his hands in the air, groaning, 'For fuck's sake.' I feel this reveals a great deal of what Roger felt about me personally and his natural frustration with my anxious conventionality. It pains me now to think that, despite my intense engagement with his teaching, I was not, at the time, sufficiently self-confident to learn more of the things he had to impart beyond the classroom.

*

ROSEMARY PALMER, *deputy head* Mr Norfolk had a heart attack and this precipitated his leaving. I had to think of some kind of leaving present. Roger came up with the idea of getting a special edition of F. R. Leavis because Mr Norfolk had studied under him at Cambridge.

MARY TODD There was a final assembly for Mr Norfolk and for Roger. The head teacher had been there for a very long time; Roger had been there a couple of years. After a very formal speech for Norfolk it was Roger's turn and, suddenly, every class that he'd taken came up with these extraordinary gifts. Children bought him Bob Dylan records, books of poetry and the goat.

JO ROLFE The goat was 'presented' in the corridor by the class who were Roger's form when he left. Julian Buck organised it all because his parents kept goats, and had the goat hidden away in his car till that moment.

'Pupils give goat to teacher,' Norfolk & Suffolk Journal, *4 August 1978* Mr Roger Deakin, a teacher who has now left Diss Grammar School after three years, found on his last day that the pupils had really got his goat! However, it was not a case of being driven out by infuriated pupils. On his last session with his own form, 3Z, the very popular Mr Deakin found an addition to his class. It was a three-month-old British Toggenburg nanny goat which came as a leaving gift from the glass. 'They want me to call her Dylan,' said Mr Deakin, 'although she was actually called Nerissa by her previous owner.'

MARY TODD This was a stuffy school that didn't do this kind of gift-giving. It was the power of the young person actually saying, 'We value this.' Roger would give you anything. If you'd liked a book, he'd say, 'Have it' or 'You mentioned this book, look, here it is.' And everybody wanted to reciprocate, express that back to him in ways that were meaningful.

MARY TODD, *diary, 26 July 1978* Break up school. What a dismal day. RD left, very, very sad . . . I cried. It's going to be awful next year without him, he's such a brilliant teacher.

MARY TODD People cried because we'd glimpsed something different. We used to have two hours of double history watching somebody write on a board and say nothing. So to actually have a really meaningful discussion, every single English lesson, was extraordinary.

I became a teacher and Roger was always there in the forefront of my mind in terms of the type of teacher that you'd want to be – the type of teacher who doesn't believe that children have limitations, who looks to make creative connections, who looks to open things up for them.

ROGER, *draft of a letter to his class, August 1978* Now the moon is a bright pupil in the clear eye of the night sky and my mind is clear, now I can write and say thank you for these three years of passion, and pain, and bright eyes and boredom, and desperation, inspiration and discovery, and the love affair of our lessons, sometimes indifferent, sometimes flat and dead, sometimes intense and brilliant, where our combined intelligence hung like a ball of fire in the bare classroom and we resounded, jubilant in its light and warmth – our light and warmth.

It is now three weeks since I left you and until today I've been in the deepest possible gloom. I'm going to miss you really badly.

JULES CASHFORD The joy of writing exactly what he felt I think he got from Keats but his teaching was the main thing that freed him. If you like your students, you have to teach with your own voice. It changes you from the way you think you're supposed to be thinking. Teaching, which he did with 100 per cent commitment, helped him find his voice, and freed him from authority. And therefore made *Waterlog* possible.

CHAPTER 9

The Green Man

Split from Jenny – being a dad – a new lover – the Diss Grammar School Dead Poets Society – a dawn ride to Holkham – the Save the Whale! campaign – the fight to save Cowpasture Lane – why we need Common Ground – 'wide-eyed but contriving' – my first nature writing

There have been certain things I have wanted to do in life with a kind of compulsion – some would call it obsession. I wanted to build a house, I wanted to teach English, in a school, not in a university, because I still think adolescence is a far more interesting time in a person's life and development, and to read poetry at that age can be a revelation that stays with you forever. Then I wanted to do something practical to stand up for nature in the face of the unprecedented onslaught of pollution and casual degradation of the world. We know it is the story of our times but somehow refuse to address it.

JENNY KEMBER We had a group of friends up for New Year's Eve 1976. There was Andrew Cracknell, my friend Debbie McWilliams, and Joe Kember [Jenny's future husband] and his partner Susannah Roper. We'd been to an early-evening party at the house of the poet Anthony Thwaite. Because Roger was rather in awe of him he was on his best behaviour and wanted me to be on my best behaviour, and because it was New Year's Eve we were all a bit drunk. We behaved a bit badly, we weren't terribly reverential to Anthony Thwaite and some of us went to a Hank Wangford gig in Norwich. We left Roger at the Thwaites', and he was absolutely furious because he felt we'd let the side down in front of Anthony. When we eventually went back to Walnut Tree Farm, it all got a bit hairy. There was an awful moment when Roger got quite angry and said, 'I want you to come outside, I want to talk to you.' I think he was getting a bit jealous because I was having a nice time with other people. And it was perishing cold, there was snow on the ground, and he said, 'I want you to come and see the donkeys with me,' and he got quite aggressive and Andy Cracknell stepped in and said, 'Rog, leave her alone, don't be silly, what are you doing?'

ANDREW CRACKNELL Jenny said to Roger, 'All you ever think about is Anthony Thwaite, Anthony Thwaite, Anthony Thwaite.' It was almost like a bit of jealousy. Maybe Roger had been humiliated in some way in front of Anthony Thwaite, I really don't remember the detail. I just remember the fight. Roger and Jenny had a physical fight in front of about ten people that New Year's Eve. It flared up over the fact that he wanted her to come out with him and feed the donkeys and she didn't want to do it because they'd obviously had a row about something earlier, and so they were shouting, 'You will feed the donkeys!' and 'I'm not gonna feed the donkeys!' It was fucking stupid. I said to my partner, I don't think the relationship can survive that because it was so public and so embarrassing.

JENNY KEMBER That was the catalyst moment. I thought: enough. I'm not saying that he beat me up but he got a bit physically aggressive and manhandled me. I left the next day with Rufus and my friend Debbie, and drove back to London. I had put up with the situation for more than two years and I wasn't very happy and felt isolated in Mellis. It struck me quite suddenly that there was more to life than this. Roger felt that because by the time I actually left his affair had fizzled out I was to blame but it had been a long hard road by then. Having your first child was something I'd wanted for quite a long time and the affair sort of ruined it, not between me and Ru, but it was painful. I never wanted to separate Ru from his dad but at the same time the situation was pretty intolerable.

*

ROGER, *notebooks, 2004* For a man to lose his father is bad enough, but to lose his son as well is almost too much to bear. This is what I felt was happening to me when Jenny left, taking Rufus with her and proceeded to do her best to let me see as little as possible of my son. The wound heals, but is like a long scar left in a tree trunk.

RUFUS DEAKIN For the most part, he was a great dad. My relationship with him when I was young was so uncomplicated. We used to make potions for fairies and little people that lived in the woods. There was a postbox by the front moat, outside Walnut Tree Farm, and he wrote miniature notes on tiny pieces of paper with a fine-tipped pen as if they had come from the elves and the fairies – 'thanks for the potion'. He had a great imagination. He read to me all the time – Roald Dahl in particular. He had a good voice and I used to like that a lot. There wasn't a TV at Mellis for years, we'd always do stuff, and he always wanted to make me everything. If I wanted a football, he'd be, 'Look, let's make it,' and he would hunt around for material. Or he'd want to make a bike, when I just wanted a Raleigh Burner.

PETE BERGLUND, *former pupil and friend* This toddler Rufus was running about and Roger was so cool with him. That was still in the day when parents would clip you around the ear, and there was none of that. It was the first time I'd ever seen somebody give a child freedom.

CAROLINE CLIFTON-MOGG Roger was very good with children. He had a very warm side. You can always tell people who really like children because they'll talk to the child, they won't talk above the child about them. It's a very attractive trait.

EMMA BERNARD Being the child of a not-very-grown-up man myself, I can understand how not-very-grown-up men are really loved by everyone. But it's quite tough for their kids. Because actually you want your dad to be a grown-up.

TRACY SHARP I remember spending time with Rufus, enjoying following his play, engraving our initials in a tree with him and loving spending time with this fascinating little child.

ROGER, *letter to Tracy Sharp, May 1980* Rufus asks after you often, and talks to the tiny doll which lives in a niche in the centre beam of the kitchen wall nearest the stairs, and which represents you to him (your effigy, in fact). He is extremely well and happy and last weekend we had an idyllic time together; a beach party on Saturday night at Covehithe, near Southwold, and swimming in the river at Hoxne on Sunday. He was totally cool about swimming in sixteen feet of water!

ROGER, *poem, undated*

For Rufus

When
Roo-and-i
go glinting up the road
in winter wellies
spanking new
this tarmac
every puddle's
a puzzle
you
flash fire
from every one
I know the sun
beams on your
little chapped face
and you shine on me
my son.

JENNY KEMBER When I left, Ru was two and I had no job and no money although I did have the Queen's Gardens flat to go back to. Rufus went to nursery and I did some part-time pieces of work but it wasn't easy and I went for the first and only time in my life to the job centre and said, 'What benefits can I possibly claim?' and they said, 'Well, where's your husband?' And I said, 'He's in Mellis.' 'Why isn't he giving you any money?' 'You'd better ask him.' I think some plodding bureaucrat went stomping up the path to Mellis and knocked on his door and Roger was absolutely furious because in his eyes I had left and why should he support me? Which technically I had, but obviously he should support his son so I got something like £16 a month for the next God knows how many years. It was the absolute bare minimum. He was not known for financial generosity, I should say.

RUFUS DEAKIN For him, the divorce took away his power as a father because I lived with my mum in London most of the time. When I was younger, I only saw him every third weekend and he didn't have control of a lot of things that went on in my life which was difficult for somebody who in today's parlance we'd call a bit of a control freak. He obviously felt that the limited time we spent together was so precious that he tried to cram so much in, which when we were on an adventure was great but when it was focused on schoolwork was stifling. Because he had been a school teacher, he was very drill sergeanty about homework. He wanted to read over everything I was doing. 'Oh, let's do a rewrite on that.' When you're twelve or thirteen or fourteen, it's 'I want to go out on my BMX and fuck around with my friends. I don't want to go over this essay.' So that sort of stuff was difficult.

JENNY KEMBER He wasn't really around much when Ru was very small, and then later – I don't want to be vitriolic about this, I want to be honest – he wanted Rufus to be almost a clone of himself. And Rufus is a very different character and a very different personality. Although he's very bright, he wasn't very academic and he didn't want to be an academic. Roger wanted him to go to Cambridge and read English because he'd done it, and that wasn't in Ru's sights. He was a really judgemental father and that was quite hard for Ru. I can remember Ru saying to me when he was starting to be a chef that he didn't think Roger was proud of him, and that's horrible to feel.

ROB PARFITT, *friend of Roger and Rufus's school teacher when he was eight*
Roger was quite hard on Rufus. As a teacher, I wasn't worried about Rufus, he was rather popular at school and I didn't think he was in any danger,

but I did see that there were some very high expectations that he couldn't match.

JANE NORRIS Roger had very high expectations of Rufus; cruelly high, I think.

JAYNE IVIMEY, *friend* He was intolerant of Rufus. Jenny obviously gave Rufus a lovely family life, because he seemed to be quite a balanced, happy boy, but he was thrown into this sense of inadequacy whenever he went to Mellis.

MARGOT WADDELL Roger was a very difficult dad to Rufus. Roger couldn't take in Ru for what he was. For instance, Ru would watch the motor racing at Silverstone which Roger had contempt for, and Ru was excited by. I wish Roger had lasted long enough to pick up a bit more of who Ru actually was.

BUNDLE WESTON Roger wanted to walk around his acres with his boy quoting poetry and discussing books, and that wasn't Rufus.

ROGER DEAKIN, *letter to Tony Barrell, December 1990* Rufus is about to be sixteen this Friday, and is v. tall – also very nice, and uncannily free of the classic adolescent stroppiness, oikishness etc.

RUFUS DEAKIN Aged sixteen, I was interested in smoking weed, DJing and hopefully getting a girlfriend. I wasn't that interested in school. I did quite well in my GCSEs with zero effort but I was found out at A level when I didn't get anything. I used to bunk off all the time. Parents' evenings were excruciating because Dad would interview the teachers. You could see out of the corner of your eye other parents waiting to get to the desk and he was banging on about, 'Why aren't you teaching this? Why aren't you doing that?' I remember the English teacher in my first year of A level saying, 'Ah, er, Rufus has a 20 per cent attendance record. So I'm not quite sure who Rufus is but he is part of my class,' and Dad turned puce.

I should've never done English as an A level but he was very invested, and it was smothering. When someone pushes and pushes, your reaction is to go, fuck off, I'm not interested. To be blunt, he wasn't proud of me being a chef. He wanted me to be a writer. He would always bang on about me doing a creative writing course at UEA or 'Maybe I could talk to somebody and get you a postgrad thing at Cambridge.' I didn't even get any fucking A levels! But I loved being a chef and I was pretty successful at it; I made a reasonable living, bought a house and travelled around the world. Cooking beautiful food for a couple of hundred people when everything was flowing was a thrilling rush like few others. I love my dad deeply. He was overbearing and annoying, particularly for me as a teenager, but a lot of father–son relationships are pretty fucking complicated, especially in a separated household. So it was a real mixed bag. In general, he was a good dad – supportive and loving – but as a person he could be arrogant, a bit overwhelming and very moody, and I think some of his friends might attest to that as well.

*

ROSIE JACKSON, *lover* We were definitely close by early 1977. I remember meeting Rufus one weekend and it was still very raw for Roger at that time. The way he explained it to me was that Jenny wanted to stay in London and he hadn't; I don't remember him sounding off about Jenny; he was very honouring of her even though he was upset, he wished it had been otherwise and he was very upset not to see more of Rufus. It tugged at his heart. He didn't talk about it a lot, but it was always there, as mine was; it was something we had in common, and we shared that loss, missing our sons.

ROSIE JACKSON, The Glass Mother *(2016)*. The main love of his life was Walnut Tree Farm, a large Elizabethan farmhouse he'd bought in Suffolk in 1969, which he was single-handedly restoring – *not*, he stressed, *renovating*. He talked about beams, wood and trees, about ducks and water, and invited me down to visit . . . the whole place [was] so full of timber beams, it was more like living in a tree than a house. It was cold, the bedrooms especially were freezing, but it didn't matter. When I stood at one of the open windows upstairs, looking out along the limbs of a tree, I felt I'd been returned to the untamed, wild creature I really was . . .

Roger was a man unfettered, as deeply inside his lean, active body as he was inside the rural world. He shocked me by being so in touch with natural rhythms. He was the only lover I've ever known who wasn't put off by a woman's menstruation, but welcomed it as a chance to be more in touch with her natural cycles. The physical contact between us was easy, satisfying, unneurotic. But I wasn't used to this way of being, nor to this kind of man, civilised and cultured, yet profoundly male, free, with an unabashed link to nature I had until then associated with solitude and the feminine.

'Do you think you could get me some work at UEA?' Roger asked on one of our walks, as we ducked under a canopy of berries. 'Some teaching?'

I looked at him, this man of the woods, tried to visualise him enduring the drawn-out minutiae of a board meeting. 'You wouldn't want it, Roger. It wouldn't suit you.'

'I need some money for all the projects I want to do here.'

'I'll ask. But I really don't have that kind of power. I'm too new.'

But I didn't ask. I wanted Roger's world to stay separate, to be uncontaminated by the sterility I was beginning to experience at UEA . . .

Roger and I were lovers, but not in love. We never argued, there was no agony, no animosity. We simply drifted apart as he pursued his work in London and on the farm, and I started house-hunting in Norwich and picked up the threads of my unfinished doctorate.

*

ANDREW CRACKNELL We must talk about Roger and what I called the Diss Grammar School Dead Poets Society. Venue: the kitchen, Walnut Tree Farm, Attendees: five sixth-formers, all female, draped languidly around the room dressed in Laura Ashley, slender fingers thoughtfully running through long silky hair. Robin Williams was played by Roger in a dark flowing coat and a long scarf. It was all perfectly innocent, I'm sure. A lot of Byron and shining eyes, leaning forward, parted lips. But as I said to him later, 'Roger, all these girls are farmers' daughters. They have older brothers who all have their eyes too close together, they all have shotguns, they don't like Keats and anyway, as Seamus Heaney said, "no poem ever stopped a tank". Be careful!' I'd imagine that the soul and spirit of a halfway curious and sensitive teenage girl in south Norfolk in the seventies was pretty undernourished. I'm certain he was terrific with them.

TRACY SHARP After he left Diss Grammar, he said to his A level English class, 'I feel so bad that I have effectively abandoned you in your final year that I will run a series of lessons at Walnut Tree Farm on Wednesday afternoons.'

JO ROLFE He felt really bad about leaving us in our final A level year and so he organised these lessons. We had games on Wednesday afternoons after lunch, so we were less accountable, and we went round then. The lessons would continue into evening sometimes, particularly if Roger had organised a writer–poet to talk to us. The deal was that we provided tea and biscuits or cake. Some pupils' parents wouldn't let them but my parents were so used to him coming round our house – he'd drop me off after school – that it was fine.

TRACY SHARP We were a bit like the Brodie set and we went there, ate honey on toast and drank pots and pots of tea, and had probably the most intellectually exciting conversations that I've ever had. University was frankly a bit of a disappointment after that.

DEBBIE BARTLETT He had a huge, lovely wooden farmhouse table. We used to sit around there and drink tea and carry on where we left off. It was fantastic, intense study time. It wasn't socialising, it was powerful stuff. Larkin was particularly amazing. I wish my supervisions at Cambridge had been as good as Roger's teaching.

JO ROLFE I'm sure some of us were attracted to him but in an inaccessible way. Everybody knew that was ridiculous. He pre-empted all of that by being very available, as a teacher figure and a confidant. His boundaries with education were very open but with us, personally, his boundaries were very, very clear. He hated anything to do with inappropriate behaviour. He never presented himself sexually in any way to any of us. We felt utterly safe with him. There were also usually partners around, and it was a relaxed, open house. If he had kept himself more aloof maybe these crushes would've happened because people would have been more intrigued but he was so open.

KEN BARRELL We used to have kids round our home including the group that Roger had around his, and Roger once called in too. We would have – soirées is a rather grand word, but local people from the community talking to them on an informal basis. The sixth-formers would cook themselves a meal at our house and have a discussion afterwards. What Roger was doing was more than that but it wasn't completely out of the context of the time.

MARY TODD, *diary, 13 December 1978* Went to Roger's tonight – really good Lowell lesson. Had hot roast chestnuts in front of the fire.

MARY TODD Interestingly that was the first time I referred to him as Roger, which shows he was good at drawing lines. It is only as we have got older that we think, wow, that did look odd. But it didn't feel odd. We went over to his house to have weekly lessons and then you'd often see him again at another point in the week – he gave me the *Waveney Clarion* to distribute, and we'd see each other when the Tannahill Weavers played down the pub. There wasn't anything odd about it. We were young and probably naive in many ways but we knew when a man was sleezy, inappropriate or creepy. Believe me, there were other teachers who were some of those things, but certainly not Roger.

JO ROLFE He was the best careers adviser you could ever have. My dad died when I was nineteen and Roger was wonderful through that, and he was there when I had boy troubles. 'If you need a Friar Tuck, use me,' he wrote in a letter. Big bear hugs and lots of discussion. He would quote, 'All of our steps are taken in the dark but it's better to take them than stand still.' Then he discovered I could sew. So we'd do a lot of bartering. I'd patch his jeans, mend his bedspreads; he would take us to places and let us use Walnut Tree Farm. Roger was always in London so a friend and I would move into Walnut Tree Farm and look after the animals. It was a bit of a hideout. We sometimes babysat for Ru. Once, on a very hot day, I arrived at the house and found Roger and Rufus standing in an old wooden water butt. Ru was bobbing around, saying, 'Jo, Jo, get in!' and I remember me and Roger thinking, no, that's not a good idea. Another time, he made a solar water heater with wine bottles and hosepipe. There was always something going on.

TRACY SHARP I used to sit in that huge room upstairs at Walnut Tree Farm and study, and he would mark what I was doing. On one occasion, I saw one of his many cats dragging a pheasant across the lawn. Suddenly from downstairs came, 'Tracy, Tracy? Do you eat pheasant?' And that's what we had about two hours later for our late lunch.

EMMA BERNARD My dad, Oliver Bernard, came to Norfolk in the very early sixties and spent a lot of time being an outsider and a real weirdo. Various poets hidden away in East Anglia began to find each other. When Roger turned up, my dad was like, 'There's this new guy from London and he's all bouncy,' and so they had this funny relationship where my dad slightly took the piss out of him because Roger was incredibly enthusiastic about everything. They had a good friendship. At school we called him Mr Deakin but out of school we called him Roger. Me and my friends would go and stay at his house in the holidays and have bonfires and build things in the field. One winter we made a snowman with legs. Because Roger would get so absorbed in a task like that he wasn't like most grown-ups who go, 'Oh, now we need to make dinner.'

There was a group of sixth-form girls who he was really matey with, including Tracy and Jo. They would hang out with Roger as adults whereas we would hang out with Roger as young friends who were up for doing whatever Roger wanted to do, and quite a lot of babysitting Rufus. Today, having some fourteen-year-old girls to stay would be suspicious but it didn't feel weird at all. He was like a slightly older kid and he always had some girlfriend on the go; they were always beautiful and we always really liked them. I used to think, I wonder why he didn't stay with that one, he's got another one now.

ALISON MITCHELL, *who had a relationship with Roger in 1979* My memory is of being in his bed and listening to the house creaking. I don't remember him ever being in it. He's that absent. There was the pond and the geese around the pond. The geese were slightly terrifying, they made a hell of a mess. It was rather a magical place but it was very, very raw. There were no frills, no creature comforts. Roger was an only child. That was a bond for us. We understood each other on that level. We came from the same place. But it still doesn't make it possible to connect and neither of us knew how to make that connection work. We were both like on islands and we didn't have a boat to get across.

TRACY SHARP During one Wednesday lesson, Roger discovered that none of us had seen the north Norfolk coast. 'How come you've never been to Holkham beach? Well, we need to go. We'll go for the dawn.' So some of us stayed, and then five of us set off in the dark in his big Citroën, taking a kite to play with on the beach. On the way home, he said, 'I'm feeling a bit tired, I'm going to pull over and have a little cat nap,' and he pulled over and closed his eyes. We were packed in his car and it was hilarious but we couldn't really start laughing; we had to wait, with no idea whether this was going to be two minutes or twenty minutes. He was so absorbed in what he was thinking or doing that he was unaware of how he would be perceived, and that was hilarious for a young person.

MARY TODD Tracy was sitting next to me giggling, going, 'What if he doesn't wake up? What do we do?' He fell asleep for a few minutes, woke up and drove us home.

TRACY SHARP I felt it was a very positive message: sometimes you just need to do what you need to do, and you don't have to endlessly consider everybody else's feelings.

*

ROGER, *CV, 1978–1982* Campaign consultant for Friends of the Earth; planner for the whale campaign, events organiser and editorial consultant. Edited with Michael Flood *The Big Risk* (1981) on nuclear power, and *Solar Prospects* (1983). Planned 1979 whale rally in Trafalgar Square with Peter Scott, David

Bellamy, Spike Milligan, Bob Geldof, David Steel. Produced and directed *The Save the Whale Show* for FoE at The Venue, London.

GARY ROWLAND I've never met anybody who was so universal – universally creative and confident to do whatever needed to be done; identifying the little universal bit in everything that you can join together to make all these things happen. Roger never finished Walnut Tree Farm 'properly'. Some of Roger's friends still say: shall we do it properly or shall we do a Roger? Doing a Roger is not necessarily what looks good but is actually using the appropriate technology – appropriate means, appropriate materials, appropriate to the budget, the time, the place, the space, the end result. He wasn't a guru, he was a collaborative protagonist, and if he didn't know how to do it, he'd do it.

JULIA BLACKBURN He was a sort of start-up. He came from nowhere, he'd done the fairs, he was stepping out of being a hippy into something else, but he was still not quite sure what.

GARY ROWLAND Roger and I did Save the Whale!, the anti-whaling campaign, which brought good results. Greenpeace were getting in front of the whaling ships in the *Rainbow Warrior* at the time and we created a poster, a shot of a fin disappearing into a big sea, and it said, 'The Last Whale?' That was poignant, and a beautiful picture. And somebody donated billboard spaces so it was up on billboards at the time it was debated in Parliament. We were young and excited and excitable and we got on with it.

CAMPAIGN MAGAZINE, *1979* Friends of the Earth, the conservation society, will next month mount its biggest Save the Whale! campaign with ads in four national newspapers and twenty other magazines and journals. The campaign, created by Roger Deakin, ex-creative director of Interlink, appeals for donations to aid the Friends of the Earth anti-whaling work. As well as the press ads, the campaign involves a 110-foot inflatable balloon resembling a whale.

'Who cares about the whales?', Diss Express, *8 July 1979* There are no whales in south Norfolk. But this does not absolve local people from responsibility for their fate. This is the belief of those who will leave Diss on Sunday morning to take part in the Whale Rally in Trafalgar Square . . . There are still a few tickets left for Sunday's trip. They cost £2 each and can be obtained by ringing Mellis 400 [Roger's number].

The Whale Declaration, written by Roger Deakin, and delivered by actor
Christopher Timothy at the Save the Whale! Rally, 8 July 1979

It would be strange indeed if a society which seems to believe that big is beautiful were to consign the largest inhabitants of the globe to extinction.

By extinguishing these generous giants, man himself would be diminished. In 1868 Buffalo Bill massacred 4,280 buffalo in one year – and people called him a hero. The Indians thought it made him the smallest man who ever lived. Now there are no buffalo left to roam the plains of America – only Cadillacs.

Whales are like mountains, and clouds, and great oaks. They are part of the majestic backdrop against which we play out our lives.

What we have to decide is whether life is a little, cautious grasping affair, or whether it is wonderful. If it is full of wonder, then let it include the whales, which of all creatures show us that to be truly mighty and powerful is to be gentle and generous.

The slaughter of the few remaining great whales would be a great meanness. It would be going too far. It would be excess. It would also be foolish; for what do we know of these enormous, mysterious mammal brothers and sisters of ours?

If we are prepared to stand by and watch the disappearance of the most majestic creature in creation – the great Leviathan himself – then we are prepared to accept an impoverished world for ourselves and for our children.

'*Save the whales! Britain acts*', Daily Mail, *9 July 1979, front page* Britain is to join the international Save the Whale movement. This week, the Government will officially ban the importation of sperm whale oil and join the ranks of those nations fighting to save Earth's largest mammal from extinction . . . Ten thousand people demonstrated in Trafalgar Square calling for a ban on whaling.

'*Friends of the whale gather in protest*', Guardian, *9 July 1979* Supporters travelled from all over the country for what was a classic Trafalgar Square event, thick with colourful T-shirts and banners and with platform performers. Colin Welland and Joanna Lumley read some poems, David Bellamy, Sir Peter Scott and Spike Milligan formed a trio of speakers, while Christopher Timothy, television's James Herriot, read a eulogy on whales, accompanied by a tape recording of a whale's own remarkable song.

GARY ROWLAND When Roger first left advertising, he was on a retainer with the National Coal Board. Working for the Coal Board and Friends of the Earth was never a conflict for him. Global warming wasn't known about and carbon emissions wasn't a concept that you thought about either. He believed that if you used coal responsibly it would be all right – if it needed filtering, you filtered it. One of the first things I did with Roger in the seventies was an eight-foot-high Coke can for a recycling campaign. He had this idea to deliver it to the American Embassy, on the back of a horse and cart. It was bonkers. And I made the Coke can, and we delivered it with the message, 'If Coke can, you can.'

*

The evening a policeman came to the door and told my seventeen-year-old self that my father had died that afternoon might have been the moment that made me into a conservationist. When I was a teenager writing poems such as 'Gentian' and later fighting for Cowpasture Lane, I was wanting back what I had lost. I wanted my father back. I didn't want to lose anything more. I had lost such a big part of my life, I needed to compensate by holding on tightly to everything else. I wanted not to lose Cowpasture Lane. It was traumatic to lose part of it. I reacted strongly. This may be the source of my passion for conservation. Does this matter? Is it too personal a base? Too emotional a base? Not philosophical enough? Is it even the wrong reason?

Cowpasture Lane is a medieval green lane running along the western flank of Walnut Tree Farm, connecting the villages of Mellis and Thornham Magna in Suffolk. It is broad, up to ninety feet wide in places, and flanked on both sides by ancient boundary ditches, hedgerows and trees. In spring, there is a snowy mountain of blackthorn and wild plum blossom and chiffchaffs singing in the hedges. In summer, the lane is a cool green tunnel. In autumn, owls hoot their cool oboe-notes in the lane, before committing volicide or shrewicide on a moonlit night. Wood blewits, inkcaps and giant puffballs materialise in the margins.

And in the winter of 1980, a 400-yard stretch of Cowpasture Lane was threatened with obliteration when a local farmer bought the land to one side of it, claimed ownership of the lane itself and announced his intention of filling in the boundary ditch, uprooting the hedges and trees, and ploughing up the lane to join a much larger cereal field. By doing so, he would gain one and a half acres of arable land worth thousands of pounds.

The history of the countryside is far more of a history of skulduggery than has been generally recognised. Written records are of only moderate usefulness in delving into the past: most of the real action was never recorded because it took place on the wrong side of the law.

Cowpasture Lane is probably thousands of years old, and in its thirteenth-century heyday it was a busy droving road, linking the markets of Burgate, Botesdale and Redgrave with Mellis and the Roman road between Ipswich and Norwich to the east. Later, it was a back door for the poachers of Mellis into Lord Henniker's estate at Thornham.

The shaping of the ancient oak, ash and hornbeam pollards on the lane was probably very gradual, and surreptitious: branches covertly removed by villagers for fodder or firewood, possibly by night or very early morning. But people helping themselves to hunks of common property grew audacious and industrial in scale in the twentieth century. When I arrived in Mellis in 1970, local farmers had recently conspired to redraw the parish to their own convenience, downgrading byways to footpaths at the stroke of a pen. One farmer helped himself quite brazenly to two and a half acres of Cowpasture Lane beyond the railway, uprooting the hedge and dynamiting the more spectacular oaks. This 'improvement' to create a prairie field that endures today was assisted with a grant from the Ministry of Agriculture, part of a nation-wide act of breathtaking skulduggery during the late sixties, seventies and eighties as thousands of miles of old hedgerows were grubbed up. In what other area of work except agriculture could people get away with such obvious vandalism?

William Battell, the farmer proposing to remove the section of Cowpasture Lane between the common and the railway line in 1980, was a neighbour, so I discussed it with him, pointing out the great antiquity of the lane, its status as a footpath of great natural beauty, its value as a wildlife habitat in an area of spreading wheat prairies, and its importance as a link for both humans and other creatures between Thornham Woods and Mellis Common, which is the largest in Suffolk. He replied frankly that he disliked trees and hedgerows, which he regarded as obstacles for his machinery and harbourers of wildlife, which he saw as a threat to his livelihood. He also pointed out how uneconomical it was for him to leave one and a half acres uncultivated.

In January 1981, when the farmer began cutting down some of the hedge-row trees in the lane to three-foot stumps — often an ominous sign that they are to be levered out and uprooted by a digger — I applied to the district council for a Tree Preservation Order (TPO) to save Cowpasture Lane. I pointed out natural evidence of its antiquity such as its fifteen different tree species, its importance as wildlife habitat and the fact that its whole width is a public footpath and to grow crops on any of it would constitute an obstruction to the public highway, an offence in law.

The council's Landscape Officer inspected the lane, and recommended a TPO, which was to be discussed at the council's planning meeting. The committee had twenty-six members and I phoned each one. To them, it was simply 'Item 16' on a crowded agenda. I made the case as briefly as possible, answered their questions and asked if they would support the TPO at the meeting.

At the meeting on Friday 6 February, the council decided to put a TPO on Cowpasture Lane, and this was briefly reported in the *Eastern Daily Press* on Saturday. On Sunday, the village awoke to a dawn chorus of chainsaws as the farmer and two allies cut down as many trees as time would allow in the one day they knew they had before the TPO – a legal document hurriedly drawn up by the council's solicitors on the Monday morning – was served on them. By the end of Sunday, they had felled every tree and the whole of the hedge along one side of the lane, and most of an oak–maple–blackthorn–hazel copse at one end.

When the Landscape Officer arrived at midday on the Monday to serve the order on the farmer, the lane was a tangle not only of felled trees but of reporters, photographers and TV cameras falling over themselves and the trees to tell the world. Powerless to prevent the cutting of the trees, short of chaining myself to them, until the TPO had been served, I had spent much of Sunday and Monday telephoning press, television and radio contacts both locally and nationally, as well as informing Friends of the Earth, who also spread the word.

ROGER DEAKIN, *quoted in the* Diss Express, *10 February 1981* The fact that the landowner has cut down many of the trees is, of course, regrettable but it is only a temporary setback in the long life of Cowpasture Lane whose boundary hedges and trees have probably been coppiced at regular intervals since medieval times.

WILLIAM BATTELL, *quoted in* The Times, *11 February 1981* It is my land and I am entitled to do what I want with it. You were too late.

WILLIAM BATTELL, *quoted in* Norfolk & Suffolk Journal, *13 February 1981* I would never dream of saying a thing like that.

By the end of the week, the story had not only appeared on the front page of *The Times* and elsewhere but, most importantly, it was headline news in the local newspaper alongside an editorial deploring the farmer's action. WOODLAND ORDER IS TOO LATE was *The Times* headline, but this was not altogether true. The hedgerow and trees down one side of the lane still remained. Far more significant, though, was the fact that even though many of the trees felled were thirty feet tall, they were coppice trees, and would have been coppiced like this countless times.

Since 1978, when Sladden Wood near Dover became known as Horizontal Wood after its new owner tried to beat a TPO like Battell did, the order applied to the rootstock and stumps of trees even when they had been felled, provided they were capable of regeneration. So the roots on Cowpasture Lane were still protected, and could grow back.

But the battle only intensified. Battell enlisted the support of the Mellis Parish Council, most of whom apparently felt that private property is the owner's to do what he likes with, even if the public have a right of way over it, and chose to ignore its value as wildlife habitat. He employed an influential firm of land agents to represent him, and appealed to the district council to overturn the TPO.

In the weeks leading up to the next council committee meeting on 4 June, I failed in my attempt to persuade the Mellis Parish Council to withdraw its objection to the TPO. So I visited every house in the village with a petition to preserve the lane. Most villagers were amazed to hear that their parish council was objecting to the Tree Preservation Order; ninety-two of them signed the petition. Within a couple of weeks, 302 local people had signed my petition. I enlisted the support of local historians, the Open Spaces Society, the Ramblers' Association and the government's wildlife agency, the Nature Conservancy Council, whose local field officer wrote a report on the lane's wildlife value. I phoned each member of the Mid Suffolk Council committee again.

BOB MARSHALL-ANDREWS Roger was permanently at war with the local farmers who were busy turning that part of Suffolk into prairies. I was a barrister and he called me up and asked for my help. He said, 'The council aren't protecting this lane.' I was down there, had a look at it and said, 'Let's try the threat of a relator action.' I had discovered this old-fashioned legal tool called a relator action which doesn't exist any more. If you wanted an authority to do something but only had an interest in it – you were related to it – you could try to make them do what you wanted. Roger owned the land next to Cowpasture Lane so he had an interest in it. Now, I've no idea whether it would've stood up in court but we got a London solicitor to write fierce letters to the Mid Suffolk planning officer, and it seemed to work. Roger was a serious hero in that respect, surrounded by these very powerful farmers.

When the council committee met on 4 June, Cowpasture Lane was eloquently debated, and the vote was seventeen to four in favour of confirming the Tree Preservation Order on the lane. The local paper's editorial was entitled 'A Wise Decision'.

Even as the lane began to recover, its 'coppiced' trees growing to six feet after two summers, William Battell did not give up. He took an appeal against some of the conditions imposed in the TPO to the Department of Environment. It was 1985 before the Secretary of State finally decided that the burgeoning tree 'stumps' were living coppice stools and refused Battell's final bid to uproot them. Two decades later, in 2005, I joined the abstruse legal process of a two-day public inquiry to determine whether Cowpasture Lane could be restored as a BOAT: a Byway Open to All Traffic.

RICHARD MABEY We had an amazing day out together with the local planning officer when we did a kind of Shakespearean double act in trying to persuade her how marvellous Cowpasture Lane was. Roger was no fool as a naturalist. He absolutely knew his stuff. There wouldn't be much botanical knowledge I had that he didn't have. But he had a lovely phrase where he talked about Cowpasture Lane being 'old land'. A very simple thing that seemed to catch simultaneously the scientific idea of ancient countryside that the woodland ecologist Oliver Rackham talked about but also a cultural idea of a place, rooted in old local traditions. I rather treasure that phrase and use it sometimes as a register for things that won't fit into 'scientific' assessments of the natural value of a place. Old land.

We won, and Cowpasture Lane became a Byway Open to All Traffic again. It meant that none of it could be ploughed up and the section south of the railway line that the farmer amalgamated into a prairie field of wheat in 1970 could also potentially be reinstated. In future, I imagine a continuous green tunnel once again running from Thornham Woods to Mellis Common.

*

ANGELA KING, *friend* I was wildlife campaigner at Friends of the Earth and Roger appeared, calling himself creative director. He put on amazing events to raise money for Friends of the Earth: the Save the Whale! event; the Save the Krill sketch.

SUE CLIFFORD, *friend* That sketch was Michael Palin and Terry Jones, it was absolutely hilarious. Angela was the first person to bring Save the Whale! this side of the Atlantic in 1971, before Friends of the Earth or Greenpeace even existed. So the groundwork was done by her. In the early 1980s we talked about how everybody was spending time on the special, the rare, the endangered and the spectacular and yet none of that would survive unless the ordinary survived. Angela drew Roger into the conversation and he said, 'Well, we should start an organisation.' He was the impetus for actually getting into being. So in 1982 we set up Common Ground and in 1983 we became a charity.

ANGELA KING Roger was very keen on calling it the Hedgerow Society because of Cowpasture Lane. He was engrossed in Cowpasture Lane. But we thought that was a little restricting. We rang up Richard Mabey and said, 'We're going to form this organisation and we think we're going to call it Common Ground, do you mind?' Because he had a book called *The Common Ground*, and was nothing to do with it. We later lured Richard into editing a book and he joined the charity's board, like Roger.

RICHARD MABEY I met Roger through Common Ground and I thought he was wonderful. He was an exceptional lateral thinker. Because Common Ground were always looking for ways of reframing old customs, Roger in a board meeting was a fountain of ideas, and of course contacts via his legendary and invaluable network of acquaintances. But I also realised something fantastically important about Roger: he was a comic person. He refused to have an overburdened tragic or serious view of life. Even his most serious writing is tinged with comic undertones. It's comic in the Shakespearean sense, not always laugh-out-loud funny, although it was often that. It was comic in the sense that he appreciated and loved the muddle of things, and always believed that they could be partially resolved. He was a profound optimist. While everybody around us were purveyors of deep environmental gloom, Roger would have none of that. He always believed that things could be done.

SUE CLIFFORD We argued like mad with Roger about Common Ground's first statement. We wanted to argue for the ordinary, which meant we couldn't use scientific or economic arguments. So the idea was to work with poets and painters and writers and musicians and draw people in through cultural routes. We were a catalyst, not a pressure group, and Roger introduced us to all sorts of interesting folk from the advertising world he'd virtually left behind, particularly the art director David Holmes who became a treasure for us.

ROGER, *letter to Angela and Sue, 11 May 1982* Now, about this new draft of the manifesto. First sentence is the real problem; I think it's too much of an echo of the old FoE membership leaflet: 'Every day this that and the other dreadful and doom-laden disaster is overtaking us, wives are being battered, battleships sunk, smaller boys tripped over by bigger ones in playgrounds everywhere . . .' the catalogue-of-disaster formula . . . The hardest subject we have to tackle [is] expressing the artists-for-nature part. Wordsworth and Coleridge tackled it in the Preface to the *Lyrical Ballads* and even those two had a spot of bother pinning things down.

SAMUEL TAYLOR COLERIDGE, Biographia Literaria, *1817* Mr Wordsworth . . . was to . . . give the charm of novelty to things of every day, and to excite a feeling analogous to the supernatural, by awakening the mind's attention to the lethargy of custom, and directing it to the loveliness and the wonders of the world before us; an inexhaustible treasure, but for which, in consequence of the film of familiarity and selfish solicitude, we have eyes, yet see not, ears that hear not, and hearts that neither feel nor understand.

Common Ground prospectus, 1982 Common Ground aims to:

— foster a new attitude to the countryside and its guardianship
— promote the importance of common animals and plants, familiar places and our links with the past
— promote practical links between nature conservation and the arts
— give inspiration and courage to people to conserve their local surroundings
— disseminate practical advice on conservation at the local level
— reach a wider audience by exploring new outlets and distribution networks.

ROGER, ANGELA *and* SUE, *draft preface for the Common Ground prospectus* Our countryside is losing its local character, identity and distinctiveness. We are losing our familiar places, our wild life and the records of the past. We do not wish to fossilise our countryside, but we believe that changes that have taken place in the last forty years have been too insensitive and often quite unnecessary. The aim of Common Ground is to motivate and help people to conserve their immediate environment – their locality or parish – and to encourage people in the arts to overtly celebrate and defend one of their main sources of inspiration – the countryside and its wild life . . . Wild animals and plants and landscapes may be able to exist in isolation from us, but if they are not a part of our experience we are less likely to be motivated to save them.

Common Ground prospectus, 1982 In an attempt to conserve what remains of the best of our countryside and wild life, scientists have concentrated on saving the special and rare, on establishing national nature reserves and national parks – and the countryside outside these special areas has been devalued as a result.

SUE CLIFFORD You've no idea what prejudice we met with. The established environmental charities weren't campaigning for 'ordinary' local nature. We were lucky to find some scientists who were keen. Roger taught us to aim high – go for the best, whatever the noise is. Roger always dared to do. He was Mr Derring Do, he would have a go if he thought it was the right thing or he was interested.

ANGELA KING He wouldn't hold back if he wanted to contact somebody.

SUE CLIFFORD In part I think it was a naivety. He was always quite wide-eyed. People are many-faceted and he was also quite contriving. So that the two seemed to work well with him.

In the very early days, we put on a series of lectures at the ICA, which was the place to be at the time. We had folk like Melvyn Bragg speaking. Roger was terribly excited by this. During the launch of our *Second Nature* book, which was edited by Richard Mabey, I sat by Roger and he kept whispering, 'You've got to say this, that and the other,' and I was being typically reticent. 'You do it, Roger.' Eventually he got up and said, 'Common Ground is really proud to have brought these people together and to have people queuing round the corner unable to get in. I'd just like to say thank you, and you ain't seen nothing yet.' I thought, oh no, don't say that, but it stuck with me: it was aim high, do it well, get it out there.

ANGELA KING There was a freshness of approach about him. He was a joy to be with: very direct and brave. That's the main thing.

SUE CLIFFORD We were on the same train, arguing that people had to take control of their own localities. But he wasn't a campaigner, not like Angela had been and how we continued to be. Over the years, through the work of Common Ground, we introduced Roger to artists such as Andy Goldsworthy and David Nash, which he was very influenced by, and we introduced him to Oak Apple Day and Barry Juniper, who traced the descent of the 'English' apple from the wild apple woods of Kazakhstan, which was ultimately why Roger travelled to central Asia for chapters in *Wildwood*.

ANGELA KING It worked both ways.

SUE CLIFFORD The first writing of his we came across was when he wrote a chapter on Cowpasture Lane for Common Ground's book about local activism, *Holding Your Ground*, which was published in 1985. This was our first attempt to say the ordinary is worth taking care of, although we got braver – and more ordinary – as time went by.

ROGER DEAKIN, *'Raising a Barn', in* PULP! *(1989), an anthology of trees in newspaper form, edited by Roger for Common Ground* I have just finished building a timber-framed barn. It took a long time: hundreds of hours, I imagine, although I never actually noted them, because making it was such pleasure. Building in wood is particularly satisfying. When you first raise a timber frame, it has an abstract quality that a brick structure lacks. The wooden beams outline the space like lines drawn on paper. As you look up at them, silhouetted against the sky, they sketch the way the finished building will enclose the air, yet, like a conjurer, you can pass through the walls as though they weren't there.

SUE CLIFFORD We spent the best part of two decades trying to persuade him to write. He was more than capable, certainly a lot better at it than we were. We kept saying, 'Roger, why don't you write?' And there he was, busy making films, trying all these other things out, stretching his wings in various ways but not writing, really.

As a toddler, Roger remembered being parked in his pram outdoors: his mother wanted him to grow vigorously, like a plant in the sun. But perhaps this wartime encounter with pigeons was at the instigation of his father, who observed how pigeons gave children 'the early habit of fondness for animals'.

Young Roger was fascinated by all creatures. 'As an only child, relationships with other animals were hugely important to me,' he wrote.

SURNAME _DEAKIN_ BORN _11.2.43_ PREVIOUS SCHOOLS I. _Wellington St., 1947–_ AGE (on entry) _10.7_ DATE _Sept. 1953_

FIRST NAME(S) _Roger Stuart_ R.I. _C_ HOUSE _S_ 2. AGE (on leaving) DATE

YEAR and TERM	Abs.	Late	FORM	Posn.	SPECIAL MERITS or FAULTS, HEALTH	E	H	G	Fr	L	M	B	C	P	A	M.T.	MUS.	P.T.	Games	ACTIVITIES, ETC.

Roger's report card from Haberdashers', aged ten to fourteen, when he was a 'rather excitable' schoolboy. Praise for his 'most efficient' charity fundraising but increasing frustration with his 'casual attitude to work'. When he was fifteen, the report concluded: 'Relies too much on charm.'

Roger's parents, Gwen and Alvan Deakin. They married late by the standards of the day and Roger was their only child. Gwen was domineering; Alvan rather shrank from view.

Roger and Tony Axon (*right*), his lifelong friend. 'Tony is one of life's great adventurers, a Don Quixote with a gift for self-mockery,' wrote Roger after celebrating Tony's sixtieth birthday.

Clockwise from top left: Dudley Young, Roger, his then-girlfriend Sarah Dickinson and friend Jules Cashford, photographed in the mid-sixties at the cottage Dudley rented in Whittlesford near Cambridge. Charismatic Dudley 'hypnotised a lot of people', according to friends. Roger was impressed by Dudley but later reflected on his habit of seeking 'strong guru friends' whom he 'looked up to in an infantile way'.

'I've been mostly in Norfolk, driving about 800 miles in ten days mostly in first gear, instead looking for the house,' Roger wrote to a friend in 1969. Here he photographed his house-hunting companion, girlfriend Jenny, who became his wife.

Roger's leaving do at Interlink, where he stepped down as creative director in 1974. His lover at the time, Jo Southon, is on the far left. 'I worked for fifteen creative directors. He was easily the most charming,' said art director John Bayley (*second left*).

'My name is Roger. Roger Deakin,' was Roger's introduction to his class when he became an English teacher at Diss Grammar School in 1975. Roger was an emissary of the sixties in a school fossilised in the fifties.

Mr. Roger Deakin, of Walnut Tree Farm, Great Green, Mellis, with his son Rufus, and the goat presented to him as a farewell gift.

Some pupils cried in 1978 when Roger resigned to become a freelance consultant for Friends of the Earth. His class presented him with Dylan the goat. Two years later, Roger helped Nerissa – as he preferred to call her – give birth.

Roger fell in love with Serena Inskip in 1980 and they were together for a decade. Here Roger photographed Serena on a north Norfolk beach after a couple counselling session – therapy he later disavowed.

Roger was a self-taught carpenter, and always had restoration projects or creative woodworking tasks on the go, as here in the 1980s at Walnut Tree Farm.

For many years, the 'moat' at Walnut Tree Farm was too muddy and overgrown for a dip but Roger had it dredged in 1990 and it then became his swimming pool – when it wasn't frozen solid.

Margot Waddell, the 'golden thread' in Roger's life, according to one friend. Roger proposed marriage to her in the sixties but was turned down. They became lifelong friends and finally partners after his split from Serena. When the relationship ended in 1995, Roger found solace in a new project – 'The Swimming Book', which became *Waterlog*.

Roger by the back door (there was no front door) at Walnut Tree Farm with Millie, his favourite and tamest cat.

Roger enjoyed using an outside bath at Walnut Tree Farm. 'It's so much my promised land, so much a product of my imagination, that I feel complete there as nowhere else,' he wrote of his home in a letter to Margot.

CHAPTER 10

The Impresario

A secret valley in France – falling in love with Serena – working together on the land at Walnut Tree Farm – Carole King and the Aldeburgh Festival – bringing folk to the festival – problems with Planxty – the sack – tensions and therapy – a big row in Rhodes – struggling on and the split from Serena – 'I couldn't take my eyes off her shoes'

I know a river and a steep valley of chestnut woods in the south of France within the golden circle Cyril Connolly described as his paradise on Earth, roughly encompassing the wooded hills and valleys of the Dordogne, the Lot and the Aveyron rivers.

All of us, I believe, carry in our heads landscapes we shall never forget because we have experienced such intensity of life there: places where, like the child that 'feels its life in every limb' in Wordsworth's poem 'We are Seven', our eyes have opened wider and our senses have somehow heightened. Returning the compliment, we accord these arenas that have given us such joy a special place in our imaginations. They live on in us, wherever we may be.

My particular river and valley, owned purely by right of familiarity and deep affection, are downstream of the little hill town of Souseyrac, high above Saint-Céré, in an almost alpine land of woods, walnut orchards, hillside beehives and farmyard guinea fowl.

I know a place, down a lane beyond a kink by a half-derelict watermill, where there's level ground at the top of the chestnut wood just wide enough to nudge in the car and make a camp. Rising up through the trees day and night is a sound that might be a freshening breeze in the leaves but is the rushing water of what locals call a 'torrent'. 'Torrent' neatly sidesteps the difficulty of distinguishing in English between a gentle enough summer stream that turns into a river the moment there's a thunderstorm in the higher hills, or into a raging cataract in the spring when the snows are melting.

I found this place in the summer of 1980, when I half-lived in the old Citroën DS Safari for July and August. The beauty of a Citroën is that you can stretch right out and sleep in it, curl up and read in it, spread out your dinner in it, carry a library in it. You can drive all night in it with a friend, taking it in turns to sleep in the back. Some people have prim little curtains across the rear windows but I carry an air-force silk parachute and spread it over the car when I'm in residence. It works like net curtains in the suburbs; I can see out but people, or just as likely cows, can't see in. It also diffuses the light beautifully, prolonging sleep by softening the intensity of sunrises. One morning I heard some early walkers. *'Mais alors, ils sont venues en parachute.'*

My stay near Souseyrac began when I nosed the DS's frog-mouth bonnet into the little chestnut clearing and set up camp under the shade of the parachute, which undulated like a swimming stingray at the slightest summer breeze.

Each morning, after a leisurely campfire breakfast, I would descend the steep valley wall through the trees, holding on to saplings and low branches like Robert Frost's swinger of birches until the stream came into view and I could drop down on to a tiny flood-meadow, pooled in warmth as the sun rose up over the treetops.

The moment the meadow lit up, it also filled with insects: delicate blue-and-green damselflies with barred wings, big emperor dragonflies, flying iridescent shield beetles and wasp-mimicking flies of all kinds, busy in the big white or yellow flowers of the umbellifers: the fennel and aniseed that filled the place with their Bassett's Allsorts liquorice scent.

This meadow, perhaps forty yards by twenty, was really a sandy, pebbly island formed by the force of the stream at times of flood carrying down stones from higher up the valley. The stream swung round it in a wide arc, with rock pools and miniature bays and beaches that immediately aroused all my latent boyhood desires to emulate the water in its playfulness.

For us as children, water, and its close relations mud and sand, always invited play. It turned us into natural engineers and sculptors. Here beside the stream, the rising August heat of the morning was an added stimulus to water engineering, and I would set about the construction of a bathing pool, tugging the stones that lie about the island into a natural neck between two rocks, damming it to raise the water level in the pool so it was deep enough to swim against the stream, making no headway in the powerful current but not falling back either, as trout often do, with so little effort they hardly seem to flex a fin.

Thus wallowing in my aquatic version of an exercise bike, I could swim for miles, or rather I could chill my blood and clear my hot and bothered head, then clamber out again on to a rock and back into my book. Reading beside the dancing water of a stream, and cooling yourself in it from time to time, must be the summertime equivalent of reading beside a fire in winter, warming yourself by its flames, adding a log to stimulate the flow of warmth.

Nobody else ever came to this place: the only disturbance was a pair of buzzards mewing overhead, or the occasional raucousness of a woodpecker. In autumn there would be the gatherers of chestnuts and mushrooms edging along the contours of the narrow woodland paths. And in winter, the hunters whose red *CHASSE PRIVÉE* notices adorned the tree trunks here and there. But in high summer I was utterly alone beside this pool, glinting with golden flecks of mica, flickering with damselflies. Then, as the sun shifted over the treetops on the western side of the valley, I could climb up to the camp, relight the fire, drink tea, and think about supper.

SERENA INSKIP, *Roger's partner 1980–90* It is very strange reading Roger's account of our expedition, for of course we were together. And this became his practice. Yes, we would drive through the middle of France in the Citroën DS, laden with all the accoutrements for survival in the wild. There were long poles for the parachute tied to the roof of the car and inside was baler twine and old fertiliser sacks to put things in: clothes, rugs, duvets, pillows, sleeping mats. The car was like a very old person with fragile joints. Its hinges, windows and handles were a bit rickety and Roger would reprimand me for throwing the door open when I should do it more carefully. We'd drive into a wood, drape the parachute over the car, and sleep inside. On the first night in France I got really scared but Roger said it was OK, he would drive further into the wood, and it was all right. Another time, we slept in the car in a lay-by and a man woke us and brought us strawberries.

Near Souseyrac, we drove down narrower and narrower lanes, crossed a little bridge where a ruined house stood, looked down through the trees and saw a flat, grassy spot. So we parked the car beside the road. We slipped and slid down, wondering what we were doing, but we were full of an impetuous urge to discover what was there: a meadow in the loop of the river.

We dashed into town, bought food and returned, hauling our things down in fertiliser bags. We rigged up the parachute as shade. There were large tussocks of grass and it hadn't been grazed so it was very uncomfortable to sleep on. You had to squeeze your body between the tussocks. We made a dam in the river to wallow in and discovered a deserted miller's house. There were bags of flour, a coat on a hook and plates on the kitchen table. It looked like people had just walked out, but the cobwebs were so thick, and covered in flour, it must've been many years since anybody lived there. It was a very powerful experience. We stayed in the meadow for two weeks and nobody ever came by. It was dreamland, because we were fantasists and nostalgics.

ROGER, *poems for Serena to mark their first anniversary, 1981*

> Twenty-one beehives on a hillside,
> shaded under the trees.
> One has a tin-can ventilation shaft,
> others have plastic fertiliser sacks,
> weighed down by stones, to keep them dry.

They face across the valley
like soldiers on a ridge.
Down in the pasture, cowbells,
loud as a prison riot,
and the bees come and go,
subdued as the day.

*

A rusty plate proclaims the maker's name,
a firm now long extinct in Saint-Céré.
He must have trundled it, brand new,
the ten miles and the thousand feet
along a road that tracked the river,
up through a green canyon of hornbeam
where he would venture on a Sunday
to hunt boar, or ceps, or meet a
charcoal burner, whittling on a pole,
up over the little meadow
with the dragonflies
and the green shield beetles
and the golden mica-flecked pools,
home to the proud mill
where the shining chestnut stallion
drank deep at the pond before the door
as the proud miller stepped from his cart
and the late bees struggled into the
attic skeps.

JULIA BLACKBURN I found him complicated. I'll give you an example. He and Serena went to France and had a wonderful time, and he came back with boxes of living cicadas and crickets which he put on the window ledge, where they died. And I thought, is this nature study? He loved the beauty of them. But he didn't want to acknowledge that this possession was also destructive. That stayed with me as an oddness of character. He was very ambivalent in lots of ways – we'll eat you up, we love you so.

Serena came like an apparition of absolute beauty. She was as lithe as a weasel. She was extraordinarily beautiful and energetic. She was very confident at that time because she was so exquisite that nobody could resist her. If you went with her to the sea, she'd perform cartwheels on the beach. But she had all these complexities about who she was, as much as Roger.

BUNDLE WESTON I remember Roger telling us about Serena. She was this goddess! She was wonderful! She was amazing! Oh, how could he be worthy of her? His heart was inflamed. It's these wretched drops in the eyes that Shakespeare doles out in *A Midsummer Night's Dream* that make us see quite differently. We've all been like that. It was very sweet. I don't know quite what we were expecting but when we met her we both went, 'Oh, hello Serena.' It is in the eye of the beholder, really.

SERENA INSKIP The first time I noticed him was when he spoke about nuclear power from the pulpit in the Friends Meeting House in Diss. I was very impressed. I was driving back to my home in Suffolk from London on New Year's Day 1980 and I called in on Walnut Tree Farm, and knocked on the door. I understood he was single at the time, he had a son, and he was working with Friends of the Earth.

He said, 'Hmmm, oh hello. Come in.'

That was the beginning of it.

He'd been to a party in Suffolk and had a hangover; I'd been to a party in London and had a hangover; we both laughed because we both had hangovers. He must've shown me around and I loved the land and I still do love the land. He had goats, which I love, and chickens and geese and sheep. I'd always wanted to have animals. We were together within the month. I thought I'd got together with a farmer who had a nice bit of land to cultivate.

I had moved to Suffolk three years earlier with my two children after I split from their father, who I had been with for fifteen years, since I was seventeen. I was young and innocent and slightly deprived of an education.

I was born in 1943 while my father was away in the Royal Navy, and the eldest of three children. After the war, my father became a 'captain of industry', having inherited his Viscount title in 1947 from his father, Thomas Inskip, an MP, barrister and then a judge, rising to Lord Chief Justice. My father and brother both went to Eton but I was sent to a boarding school for upper-class girls that didn't even offer A levels. I was a tomboy, I liked riding a pony and wearing jeans, and suddenly I was among sophisticated girls from stately homes who were shaving their armpits, hair in rollers. They all went on to be debs, my mother had been a deb, and so that's what I did.

My husband was a wine merchant in the City, and in the seventies with friends we founded Dingwalls dance hall in Camden Lock. Together we got to know a whole range of musical, radical, political and creative people but I had no self-esteem and didn't speak very much. I came along, looked pretty, wore the right clothes, and hung out with the right musicians. At home, I hand-washed my husband's fine cotton shirts because that's what my mother had done, and I ironed them a second time if they were not smart enough.

When my marriage ended in 1976, I wanted my children to have a country childhood like my own but I hoped to live communally with other families too. Most of my friends thought I was mad but there was a bunch of us looking for a big house. Eventually, I drove up to Southwold and it felt like going home, and I ended up buying Valley Farm, a beautiful old farmhouse near the village of Bramfield, with friends from London who used it for weekends and holidays. It was my dream: a farm with barns and twenty acres. I was probably longing for a relationship that would remake my family. I was feeling very alone.

As soon as I moved to Suffolk I got to know hundreds of new people through the fairs. There was a community and a culture with the Barsham and then Albion fairs, and then I joined the organising team. We held the Wild Dream Fayre on our land. It was really exciting to get to know all these funky people. I did yoga and joined environmental campaigns, including against the second nuclear power station at Sizewell. We grew vegetables and kept ponies and guinea pigs. Then I met Roger. I was a very curious person and I had not met anyone like him before.

Roger had a moustache when we first met. I didn't like it; I might have persuaded him to take it off. We both dressed in clothes from the Quartermasters' Stores army-surplus shop in Diss: thick cotton collarless shirts, traditional farmers' workwear, which I wore with dungarees. Roger was a totally whacky person. He had these Speedos, and Rufus and I were totally embarrassed by them. So I took Roger to Lillywhites on Piccadilly and bought him a pair of Indian cotton swimming shorts. I think he went back to the Speedos when he did *Waterlog*.

*

In May 1980, nearly two years after my class 3Z gave me Dylan, or Nerissa as I came to call her, she gave birth to her first kid, a beautiful black-and-white billy, with a little help from me. Being there in the goathouse with her, doing all the James Herriot stuff, was such an exciting hour. In a quiet and modest way, this was quite as satisfying as climbing a difficult mountain. The remarkable thing about that morning was the degree of communication, first between the goat and I, and then between the goat and her kid.

Almost as soon as I went to see her, she began her labour – as though she had been waiting for someone to give her a hand. She lay on her side in the straw, and two white front hooves appeared followed by a black snout with the tongue sticking out to one side like a concentrating schoolboy. Having heaved her kid thus far, the goat took a rest, then began heaving away again, whinnying each time with the effort and, I suppose, the pain. But she couldn't seem to push the kid any further, so I gently took hold of the kid's front legs behind the hooves and pulled evenly each time she heaved. At first this didn't help at all, but each time I said something encouraging, and the goat muttered back and sometimes licked my hands, she seemed to relax a little more, until suddenly the kid's face and head emerged. Its body seemed to flow from the mother, twisting slightly as it came, and then shivering, and then shaking its head like someone waking up. Once the kid's head was in the world, the rest was swift and almost effortless. Nerissa made an enormous amount of noise as the kid was actually born, but there was a note of triumph in her voice.

Then, with the kid lying beside her, she began licking furiously from its head down its body, talking to it in little muttered phrases all the time, and being extremely thorough. Supporting it slightly in my hands, I felt its heart jolt into action, revving away. The lungs simultaneously sprang out and in, and I heard breath snuffling in the nostrils. Within twenty minutes, the kid was on its feet and suckling, and I was retiring, grateful and exhausted, to the kitchen for a cup of tea.

Delivering the kid was quite extraordinarily hard work, both emotionally and physically, and as I had encouraged the goat she encouraged me back in the same way as she encouraged her kid into heartbeats and breathing – by licking me. She licked the sweat off my face and she licked her own wetness off my arms and hands, and she licked her own side where it bulged and strained. It was licking language – and it worked.

Flopped out on the kitchen chair afterwards, I felt, as they say, as though I'd given birth myself. It was, of course, a most intelligent day on which to have a kid; dry, warm and sunny. Equally it was not the kind of day to be sweating round a field carrying a good-sized billy kid in your belly.

SERENA INSKIP We loved Billy the Kid. He used to climb on the back of Roger's sheep. Self-sufficiency was the thing, and I learned to milk the goats. Roger was virtually vegetarian when I met him, living on beans and rice. I got bored of that and encouraged him to branch out into game. We bought everything from coots and moorhens to ducks from Gislingham game parlour and had these big roasts on the Aga. Partridges, pheasants, hares, rabbits. We ate some of the goats as well. I learned to kill the chickens and the geese – I hope I did it well. As a child at my father's side, we skinned and eviscerated rabbits and plucked pheasants. I was well prepared for a simple life.

SERENA INSKIP, *letter to Roger, May 1980* I keep feeling big surges of love, and hope, and warmth and all-over completeness. No fear, no anxiety, no despair – it's deliciously exciting. But not mad and wild and unreal, very real, very secure, and dear. I never felt like this before. I hope other people get it sometimes.

ROGER, *letter to Serena, July 1980* I'm back here at Rendham churchyard again, on the stone step under the doorway, only the gutter has stopped dripping, and the grass is up to my shoulders, and there are skylarks and swallows, and even a swift, and it is warmer than it was that evening when I sat in my overcoat and you appeared sudden and beautiful before me, and I noticed the evening sun lighting up the henna in your fine hair as you spoke.

All these months later I only want to tell you how much all the feelings I had then for you have grown and confirmed themselves in me, so that being here feels like being in a blessed place. It's like one of those bits of wall you measure yourself on as you grow up, putting marks and dates. Returning here I find I've grown so much in love and happiness with you.

SERENA INSKIP We enjoyed cooking. Roger wasn't one of those men who said, 'Leave the kitchen to me'; we did it together, and we had friends over for meals. I loved the trains and Roger liked them too – other lives, another world, rushing past. I absolutely loved looking after the land. We dug out ditches and planted hedges. Later, we turned the small triangular patch of land by the railway into a wood, planting the ash, oak and hornbeam saplings by hand. We planned to coppice the wood after twenty years; eventually the hornbeams would become stout and sinewy and wild flowers would grow under the coppice.

We went to the local auction houses, reclaimed timber yards and old farm sales. I bought a tractor, a little grey Massey Ferguson for £450 from an auction in Eye, so we could cut the hay. We bought an old shepherd's hut together, did it up and slept in it. Sometimes we slept in the middle field in an iron bed. One night there was a thunderstorm and we had to run indoors.

The auctions traditionally held when a farm was to change hands at Michaelmas made for memorable public theatre. One such occasion stuck in my memory. I was sitting in drizzling rain in a Suffolk field in the Waveney Valley. Beside me on an old wooden tool-bench sat my friend Margaret, holding back the tears as the contents of her parents' farm were auctioned. Set in neat rows up and down the home meadow the whole history of the farm lay displayed, labelled and numbered as lots: ditching spades, scythes, pitchforks, harrows, ploughs, hay-tedders, an old iron-wheeled swathe-turner, a clutch of rusting milk-churns, cattle troughs, a two-man saw, a faded-blue Fordson Major tractor. The crowd of bidders shuffled round with the auctioneer, whose bantering incantation drifted across the field as he worked his way along the row to the next lot, a wooden stack ladder and a length of rope. 'Fifty pounds. Fifty pounds anywhere? Start me in at thirty, surely you will?' But I was listening to my sad friend, who kept up her own quiet commentary as each item sparked fresh memories of her childhood here. She poured out a vivid spontaneous history of the farm's life and times, evoked in the details of each lot-numbered item in the sale. 'The men used to thatch the stacks off those ladders with reed from the Fen,' she said.

*

SERENA INSKIP I had a lurcher, Bat ('Out of Hell'), who was biscuit-coloured, unruly and untrained. When I lived at Bramfield, I would go poaching and hunting hares with Bat and a few friends. At Mellis, I walked Bat on the common and he would sometimes chase an old lady who cycled past on a very old bike. That was very naughty of me. Roger had never had a dog before, and this became a bit of a bone of contention. But Roger was more than happy for Bat to lie on his lap and creep into our bed.

Roger loved cats. They were 'barn cats', he said, not house cats, and he wouldn't really feed them on principle and just threw occasional scraps at them. At the same time, they were allowed to come into the kitchen and would walk across the table seeking food. Then he would get annoyed because there were so many on the table: he'd pick them up by the scruff of the neck, open the front door and throw them out on to the lawn. It's true that cats land on their feet but it shocked the children and friends when they witnessed it, and me too, but I knew to keep quiet.

The kitchen was never finished, and beneath the sink was a grotty space where the rubbish and recycling was kept. By morning, mice would be in the rubbish bin and couldn't get out again. I would take the bin on to the front lawn, call the cats and tip the mice out, and the cats would have breakfast. I told my friends about this to shock them but I can see now that I was allowing myself to be drawn into Roger's way of being with nature.

I felled my biggest tree at Valley Farm, Bramfield. It was an elm which had succumbed to the disease and overhung the road and a barn. Because it was right next to one corner of the barn, it was imperative it be felled accurately along the line of the hedge, or just to one side of it inside the field. I succeeded but still remember the heart-in-mouth feeling as I cut deeper with the *coup de grâce* of the higher chainsaw incision from beside the barn. Had the tree fallen on the barn it would certainly have crushed it.

SERENA INSKIP My family was always quite held-in and Roger was the antithesis, so that was exciting and a huge relief. But that was a gut reaction. It wasn't an understanding of him. After a year or so together, I arranged to sell my share of Valley Farm, and arrived at Walnut Tree Farm with a van carrying my things, which I thought we had agreed. 'All that stuff!' said Roger. I'd never seen a man's face fall so low. 'There isn't room for that in my house.' He insisted we put it in the barns, where my furniture got damp and some of my books and papers were devoured by rats. Mutual friends expressed concern but I chose to just live with it. There couldn't be any discussion.

He was attached to Walnut Tree Farm through his belly button. It was so important to him that it was very hard to see it as my home. I was excited when we began to research starting a herb farm at Mellis. We met horticulturalists to discuss the project, but when it came to actually doing it, Roger wandered around in his dressing gown, saying, 'I can't be dealing with this.' He didn't want to be a farmer. He wanted to have the freedom of being a creative mind and to do things when they came to him. There were all these conflicts within him – of money and work, and being free, and not being held down by any circumstances or by anyone. He didn't want to have a smallholding or anything so banal as that. There was a lot of 'I'm a poet'.

VICKY MINET That nothingness of living in the country and just digging potatoes – that wasn't for him. He was an ideas man. And he wanted to be getting kicks from the next new idea, new adventure, new person, new angle.

*

GARY ROWLAND Was Roger a music producer, a promoter, a documentary maker or impresario? He wouldn't want to be any of those things but he was all of those things; he wanted to do it all.

STEVE ASHLEY, *friend of Roger and folk musician* Rog booked me to sing at a benefit concert for Friends of the Earth at the Roundhouse with John Williams. When Rog and I got talking at the end of the concert, it was really sweet. He gave me a little mug that had been turned by his friend Tony Weston. We hit it off and I did various gigs over there in Suffolk. Rog would often promote things in obscure pubs in the middle of nowhere. He put us up for the night and blewits, big mushrooms from his fields, hung from the kitchen ceiling. He cooked them up, they were fantastic, and he'd brew up cider. It was an amazing place. He had an ability to set fire to other people's imaginations. And he was non-stop.

The touring circuit for folk singers and bands in the seventies took in Colchester Arts Centre or a venue in Ipswich, followed by the arts centre in Norwich. I began to phone band managers and agents, or sometimes the band themselves, persuading them to play a gig in the Waveney Valley on their way through. We'd put on nights in Eye or at the Scole Inn, or arrange ceilidhs at a village hall, selling copies of the *Waveney Clarion* or raising money for the fairs. Then, with Friends of the Earth, I began organising much larger charitable gigs and the Save the Whale! concerts.

Barley from the fields of Suffolk was once shipped to continental Europe from Snape Maltings, a complex of Victorian warehouses on the banks of the River Alde. The buildings were converted into a concert hall for classical music by the composer Benjamin Britten and his partner, singer Peter Pears, and opened by the Queen in 1967. It was an important venue for classical music but in the autumn of 1981 I pitched to bring folk, rock and pop to the Aldeburgh Festival.

I told the festival I would approach American artists of the calibre of Joni Mitchell, James Taylor, Kate and Anna McGarrigle and Paul Simon. To persuade any of these musicians to visit Britain, or more particularly Suffolk, would take more than money but I thought it possible that the position, history and quality of the Maltings as a venue might prove attractive. I hoped the soon-to-launch Channel 4 might fund a concert that could be broadcast live on TV; I suggested seeking sponsorship from a local brewery. Jack Phipps, the general manager of the Aldeburgh Festival foundation, liked this vision, and took me on.

JACK PHIPPS, *letter of engagement to Roger Deakin, 1982* Aldeburgh Foundation's Special Projects Advisor, £1,750 per annum; commission 10 per cent of gross box office revenue; expenses guide at £250 per quarter.

ROGER, *quoted in the* Ipswich Evening Star, *1982* I think that the reason why they asked me to do the job was that while they were keen to promote popular music, jazz and folk they wanted to be sure that the acts that came here would be . . . well, tasteful. I have been able to realise some of my private fantasies. I used to promote concerts locally but on a much smaller scale, and I often used to lean up against a bar somewhere and dream of putting on people like this. I never really thought it would happen.

Carole King was a global star, first as the co-writer of songs such as Aretha Franklin's '(You Make Me Feel Like) A Natural Woman' and then as a solo artist. Her 1971 album, *Tapestry*, sold more than 10 million copies, one of the half-dozen biggest-selling records in history at the time. When I heard of her plans to perform in Europe for the first time in more than seven years, I phoned her agent in the States and explained why Snape should be her first destination in Britain between shows in Dublin and London.

The 800-seater hall at Snape quickly sold out so I phoned her agent again and persuaded Carole to put on an extra performance. Snape sold out again. Carole's rider for her eight-piece band was undaunting: tea and coffee, herb teas, fresh orange juice, fresh fruit and the 'best in regional beers (cold)'. I put Adnams Pale in the fridge. Shortly before she arrived, she asked one thing I couldn't deliver: the attendance of the Prince of Wales and Diana, who was pregnant with her first child.

ROGER, *letter to Buckingham Palace, spring 1982* I realise that this invitation comes at very short notice indeed, and have pointed out to Carole King that we should not hold out much hope of an acceptance. I should be grateful, however, if you would kindly pass on the invitation to the Prince and Princess of Wales, with Carole King's warmest hopes.

GARY ROWLAND Serena was Carole King to Roger's Loudon Wainwright III.

SERENA INSKIP How did he get Carole King? I think it was sheer chutzpah. He had friends in high places in the rock business and he was also always putting on events for young people – gigs, folk music, supporting his former students' bands. He was hired to bring a new audience to Snape. This was Roger's dream job, and when an old friend of ours suggested he might 'smarten up' a bit, Roger allowed us to escort him to Grey Flannel, a menswear shop in London, to kit him out with three suits. I'm not sure how often he wore them! I was still quite starry-eyed and everything he did seemed amazing. He enjoyed the glamour of putting on the McGarrigle sisters and Loudon Wainwright, and he knew how to entertain musicians. He had a long row of knocked-up sheds at Walnut Tree Farm, got these big barrels and made this powerful cider. God, it was wonderful.

IPSWICH EVENING STAR, 1982 Roger Deakin, who organises the concerts, had just the right pedigree to appeal to the foundation. Having operated on the fringes of the pop record business, he knew the ropes and it was his excellent contacts which enabled him to scoop Carole King from under the noses of a number of envious promoters.

That autumn, I brought the Roches over from the United States, the Chieftains from Ireland, and the McGarrigle sisters, Kate and Anna, who reached Snape despite being told by their American agent they would be playing 'Snake Maltings, Aldburger, in Germany'. Their contractual demands were exacting: eighteen microphone stands and adequate power 'to deliver 120db of continuous sound with an absolute minimum of total harmonic distortion' as well as whisky, Courvoisier, beer, wine, pots of 'hot' coffee and tea and 'at least 3 dozen 8oz. Cups'. The McGarrigles enjoyed the Suffolk countryside, especially when they were sent by a fellow hotel resident to Dunwich. 'We didn't know it was under the sea,' Kate told the local paper.

Mick Brown's reviews in the *Guardian* – 'The Roches are a peculiarly New York preppy-turned-bohemian sensibility with a mixture of cuteness and cynicism and a belief in their own cleverness which may sometimes make them irritating but ensures they are never dull' – reminded me of the self-consciousness of Leigh Hunt on Keats 200 years earlier. Critics used words such as 'charming', 'cosy', 'homely' (or 'homespun') to describe the McGarrigle sisters and mentioned them wearing odd socks or being 'idiosyncratic'. These observations applied to anyone lacking the self-conscious surface of what they aptly called a 'polished' performer. The McGarrigles were uninterested in either surface or polish. They wrote mostly of personal experiences in a straightforward emotional way that I wish we English weren't so embarrassed about.

IPSWICH EVENING STAR, *November 1982* Mounting debts of £200,000 may threaten the future of the Aldeburgh Festival.

In spring 1983, I booked a talented group of Irish folk musicians called Planxty to play at Snape. At ten thirty on the morning of the gig, their manager rang me to say they wanted to cancel the concert. They had played in Glasgow the night before and hadn't realised that Snape was 424 miles away. Their manager magnanimously allowed me to sort it out, on an Easter Bank Holiday Monday. A bus or train would take too long, so I chartered a plane to fly from Norwich airport to Glasgow, pick up the band, their manager, sound engineer and support, and fly back to Norwich. Meanwhile, miraculously, I found a PA system for hire in Cambridge and arranged for it to be driven to Snape. The band were due into Norwich at 4 p.m. but didn't arrive until 5.30. The local football derby, Norwich City versus Ipswich Town, had finished and traffic wedged through the city and down the A140 south towards Ipswich. They reached Snape shortly after 7 p.m.

Unfortunately Planxty's keyboardist had funked flying in the Cessna. He was scared of small planes. Even more unfortunately, he was the creative lynchpin of the band: half their repertoire was unplayable without him. Eight hundred people were made to wait outside the hall while the band undertook their soundcheck, breaking a solemn promise to appear on stage at 9 p.m. The group finally took the stage at 9.30 p.m. by which time several people had cashed in their tickets, and many others were losing patience.

Letter of complaint to Snape Maltings, 1983 I am writing to express my disgust at the very inept performance my wife and myself along with a few hundred other people experienced at the Planxty concert on Easter Monday.

ROGER, *letter to Planxty's booking agent, 1983* Their concert at Snape Maltings was, to put it mildly, an embarrassment to everyone concerned – not least themselves.

Letter to Roger from Kenneth Baird, general manager of the Aldeburgh Foundation, cancelling his contract with Snape, January 1984 The concerts have contributed in the past little if anything to our general overhead costs.

According to Roger's calculations, his 1982–83 concerts commanded an average attendance of 89 per cent, took £25,999 at the box office, with artists' fees of £18,336, earning him £4,346 with a surplus of £2,435 for Snape.

SERENA INSKIP Roger might not have brought Snape a lot of money but he brought them a lot of people, and they've carried on having a mixed programme ever since.

*

ANDREW SANDERS, *friend of Roger* Serena was very practical and appreciated the soil in the way that Roger did.

GARY ROWLAND Serena is an amazing woman. She has a real spirit and Roger loved that spirit. She is a wild child, which I mean in a complimentary way.

JOAO SMITH, *friend of Roger and Serena* Our dinners would last until 1 a.m. We had fabulous, exciting, dynamic conversations, from politics to the environment. I came alive with Serena and Roger. They had a fantastic relationship. They were incredibly compatible. It was one of those relationships where you feel a healthy tension. There was never any negative feeling, it was a great but edgy warmth between the two of them. Serena was edgy and Roger was edgy too.

TONY AXON She and Roger were always having these terrible rows. Serena was great fun and we liked her but we didn't always enjoy the relationship.

BUNDLE WESTON It was just so obvious that girlfriends had to do what Roger wanted. We were there one freezing-cold weekend and Roger came in and said, 'Oh, we've got to unblock the ditch. Come on, Serena – now.' And I thought, it would be interesting if Tony said that to me. I would've said, 'I don't think so.' But Serena went meekly out like a lamb and did it, and I thought, blimey, I'm glad I haven't got a relationship like that. Tony would've unblocked it but he would've never dreamed of asking me to do it.

SERENA INSKIP Money was always a concern for Roger after he gave up teaching and became a freelancer. We didn't have a proper arrangement about money. We weren't any good at that. Because I had the guilt and he had the rage. I had stocks and shares. He couldn't bear the fact that I had money I didn't earn. He used to rage at me about inherited wealth.

There was money and there was sexuality. I had a relationship with another girl at boarding school and it was discovered. I was told I was evil but I wasn't expelled because my mother had been at the school as a child and she was a lady. None of my friends ever mentioned it again; nor did my parents. It was kept in a box, and I began to live a compartmentalised life: relationships with girls at school and boys in the holidays.

Before I moved in, I wrote to Roger about this whole other part of my life. During our early years together, Roger was setting up Common Ground, and I enjoyed the presence of Angela and Sue, who as a couple created a good balance for me, in my silent ambiguity. Roger seemed quite easy with them, rather than threatened as I feared he might be. But it soon turned out that Roger felt threatened by my sexuality; even though I'd done my best to forewarn him, I was a complete mystery to him. He had outbursts and no control over them. He used to terrify me. I didn't know what to do with these explosions. I didn't have any experience of how you 'hold' someone when they are having a tantrum. I didn't know what to do with Roger. My childhood was filled with the tantrums of my younger brother, who our parents were totally unable to deal with, which was terrifying for us all.

Afterwards, Roger would pretend they hadn't happened or tell me not to make such a fuss. When I brought up what he did, he would tell me, 'You're lying. You must be mad.' He hit me around the side of the head with a mug and there must've been a chip in it because it cut my ear. The next day I said something like, 'That was a bit much,' and was told, 'You're just being dramatic.' Another time, I wrote down what he had said to me – it was something untrue and irrelevant but brutal and bullying – and the next day I read it back to him and there was this huge silence. He walked away and we never discussed it. People who are in pain are very good at creating another reality to protect themselves from the pain.

Frequently during arguments he told me I was 'a fucking lesbian'. I loved digging the ditches and he'd go, 'Why are you out here and not cooking the fucking lunch?' Another time he'd say, 'Why aren't you outside helping me?' During one row, he threw my camera on the floor and smashed it. More than once, he would throw me out and drag me back by the arm, scaring me into silence. He didn't like me walking Bat on the common. 'We've got twelve acres here – you don't need to go out on the common.' He was constantly wary of me talking to the neighbours – worried about his reputation. He didn't trust me to portray the image he wanted. When I had a rip in my jeans from the hedge, he'd say, 'You're not going into town like that.'

'Like what?'

'What will people think of me?'

I remember one particular outburst. He had agreed to have a television, which he hadn't before, but once threatened to throw a brick at it, yelling at the kids, 'Why aren't you outside playing?' He pulled out the plug and banned any more watching. To this day, I remember the children's faces. The rage was out of proportion; I saw it as unacceptable behaviour but I didn't know how to negotiate.

ROGER, *diary, March 1981* At Mellis collecting signatures for Cowpasture Lane, then back to Bramfield late at night to an awful row. S. out with Julia all night. Oh dear.

SERENA INSKIP The farmer was going to remove the ancient droving road of Cowpasture Lane and Roger did brilliantly to get the media there and stop it but I got the back hand of it because it seemed that I wasn't adequately enthusiastic. I didn't know enough about the environmental movement and the importance of hedges or non-violent direct action – that you could do something construct-ive to change things. When he raged, I was in a complete blind panic and I called Julia and Hein from a phone box and went and stayed with them.

JULIA BLACKBURN The sense of him as a person was of claustrophobia. Even the swimming, it was all to do with claustrophobia – must get away from this or that. He was a very curiously explosive person. Sometimes when you met him, you could hear a kind of ticking: click-click-click.

I saw him a couple of times exploding with rage and I thought, a-one, two, three, four, five, six – is it over yet? I only saw it with Serena. On one occa-sion, my husband Hein and I and Roger and Serena were all stuffed in one car travelling from Bramfield to Mellis. Serena's kids wouldn't come, they'd gone off, and Roger exploded by driving so fast around blind bends that I thought, gosh, this is the end. Another time we were living in Dunwich and Serena and Roger came over and he'd hit her on the head with a frying pan but he was contrite. They came to say what was to be done? I sometimes might have felt tempted to hit Serena on the head with a frying pan. It's that thing, isn't it? It takes the two to tango. She was moving towards realising that she loved women more than men, and he saw that as a threat, and they built up this ter-rible bubble of rage with each other.

VICKY MINET I think Serena tormented him by being half gay. That drove him absolutely bananas in terms of being very frustrated about whether she cared for him or not.

JOHN FARLEY, *friend and neighbour* We went over there once and Serena was in pieces, anticipating him getting really angry because she'd lost a hedgehog that he'd had in a box on the Aga and she knew that this was really gonna be fireworks time.

JENNY FARLEY, *wife of John* Serena would get upset with Roger. She would turn up here in tears and have a cup of tea or she would have breakfast with us. It took her a little while to calm down. I got the impression that a lot of it was to do with Roger's way of life and collections. There was a sideboard in the kitchen with innumerable animal skulls that were covered in dust. They hadn't been touched but must've been very precious to him.

SERENA INSKIP Once, when Roger was really frightening me, I went to his friends Peter and Kate Campbell, who lived in Eye. Kate, who was a very controlling woman and worked as a production manager for Merchant Ivory, managed everybody. She said, 'I'll deal with this,' and took me on one side and gave me a brandy. 'Tell him next time he does it that you will leave.' So, the next time it happened, I told Roger and he looked so relieved, and I realised that we had to draw lines. It helped, for a while.

I knew that it was very important that I got therapy. I knew I wasn't coping but at least I could help myself grow. Margot Waddell, Roger's old friend who was now a psychoanalyst, encouraged me, and recommended Joan Hall, a therapist who lived in north Norfolk. When I first went, Roger seemed to see it as an aberration and a threat. 'What a waste of money, what a waste of time.' I was deeply grateful when he agreed to have therapy as well. I knew it wouldn't be easy and it wasn't easy because he knew I'd already talked to Joan a lot, and that triggered a deep fear for him about women together – remembering his mother and her sisters, saying things behind his back, which he had told me about in quieter times. Roger was also fearful that therapy would emasculate his poetic voice, stop him being free to express himself. A lot of men of that era felt that anger was justified by being a creative person.

ROGER, *notebooks, 1996* A drive to Stiffkey reminds me of my endless pilgrimages when I was taking psychotherapy from a delightful woman on the north Norfolk coast not far from Blakeney. A kind, good woman, but all the time I kept thinking, I don't need to pay for good conversation.

MARGOT WADDELL, Inside Lives *(1998)* The aim of psychoanalysis could be described as seeking to make available to the patient more aspects of the self.

JULIA BLACKBURN We hadn't seen them for two years and they came to the farm and Serena had put on weight and looked as though she had been kept hidden away in a box. She looked so miserable and Roger looked so cross, and it was an absolute change. Something had happened. I think she was doing therapy; maybe he was doing therapy too. That doesn't say much good for therapy.

JAYNE IVIMEY He spoke about taking Serena to therapy for five years up in north Norfolk and so he understood about unpicking the past. He was like a child who was always finding out new stuff about how you behave, coming up against little problems and going 'waaaaaaah'. I'd meet him and he'd say, mystified, 'I don't know how that happened but I got really angry with him or her.' I know a lot of people had awful experiences with him. He could be really nasty. But I'm sure it was just the child in him. He didn't know what to do.

*

SERENA INSKIP In the mid-eighties, some friends of mine, a family with two kids, were returning to live in New Zealand and we arranged one final summer holiday with my sister and all our children in Greece, where we had holidayed many times together before. I told Roger and he was immediately upset. He said he was already planning in his head a trip to the Greek islands with Rufus. I said, that's a lovely idea, why don't you have a week with Rufus and then come and join us. He furiously replied that was impossible because Rufus would want to be with us all the time. I didn't want Roger to feel not wanted but I didn't want him to come if he was feeling an outsider, which he might because of my shared history with these friends. So I let him decide, and the holiday began with this tinge of anxiety and fear.

RUFUS DEAKIN We went on holiday to Lindos in Rhodes in 1986, staying with Jos and Roger Morton and their children, who had a beautiful house arranged around a courtyard like a Moroccan riad. There was a lot of friction between Dad and Serena in particular. Some rows were really fucking full-on and that wasn't just down to my dad. Serena liked a row. One evening, Dad and Serena had this mega-row. They were on the rooftop terrace throwing shit at each other. I didn't see it but I remember the noise of stuff being thrown around, and then screaming.

SERENA INSKIP It was the worst Roger ever was and it was all to do with him not being in control because it was a holiday with my friends and my family.

He was making physical demands on me that were unreasonable and I was yelling for help, and my sister eventually came up and rescued me. The rest of the holiday was fraught with tensions and silences.

ROGER, *notebooks, 1 a.m., 31 July 1986* Serena, I write in the hope of recording for you my feelings just now – feelings of the deepest hurt and despair.

I have walked out of the restaurant under the mulberry tree in abject despair of you and of us – yet at the same time because somewhere I hold, still, tremendous and limitless hopes for us, and don't wish to do any more damage, verbally or physically, than I have already, unwittingly and utterly against my better judgement, done on this tortured holiday.

We have both been racked on our histories, and especially on all your rich experience of the incredibly beautiful and above all <u>sensual</u> life in this place. The acute and present knowledge of it all in every unknown detail has put me to tortures of the most exquisite loneliness and apartness from you. A feeling that I am but a recent and latter-day adjunct to your life's former glories and mysteries as enjoyed and expressed in this place – from whose beauties you have unconsciously excluded me. You'll say this is paranoid rubbish yet it is true that you have made not the slightest effort to introduce me to the beauties of the church, of the Acropolis, the colosseum! That's over the top and exaggerated, I know, but it leaves me feeling still an <u>outsider</u> to all this. A failure at making things work socially.

And desperately lonely. Tonight I appealed to you. I asked you to help me in a moment of total isolation. The children didn't want to know me. The others didn't want to know me. I was desperate with loneliness. Yet you refused to give me even one crumb of love, or of solidarity. All day you froze me out, with a poker face and grim determination to sacrifice yourself by driving me miles in almost total silence over the most beautiful country.

Tonight, over dinner, hurt beyond endurance, I appealed to you for some affection, some help, some understanding, some solidarity. I got nothing – worse than nothing. I got abuse and a systematic, torturing coldness that is like a bullfighter's cold knife in my breast at every turn.

I sit here, still hoping for the sound of your cough or your foot on the stone stair, in spite of it all, yet I feel a fool for it. It is all so undignified. My heart beats as though it would pop out of my chest. I'm so wound up, I could spring all the way from here to the Socrates Bar, where I assume you are carousing with your mates as though nothing had happened.

What am I to do? You asked me here. You strenuously wanted it to be good, as I did too. Yet you made no effort to make it good. Indifference, tension and excuses about your various states of health was all I got. You were apparently in a perpetual state of exhaustion. You <u>accused</u> me of desiring you. You <u>berated</u> me for showing affection.

SERENA INSKIP When I first spoke with Patrick, in 2020, we met at Walnut Tree Farm, invited by my nephew Titus and his wife, Jasmin, who now own it. I was in a very raw state, having never told 'the whole story' to anyone. I had spent my life since then holding it all in, for fear of upsetting friends of Roger's and of mine, many of whom had indicated or said, 'Do not tell this . . .' I was afraid of being accused of 'bad behaviour' and being told that 'skeletons should remain in cupboards'. It has been very hard to stomach some of the adulation without qualification that has been expressed about Roger. So then, to be sitting in that garden, beside the famous moat, a lot came out in a big splurge. I was still angry, and full of unprocessed pain.

I didn't know about the contents of Roger's 'Lindos' notebook from 1986. I had become aware of its existence soon after his death, but couldn't read it at once, couldn't face more pain – it had been bad enough him dying and us never resolving anything. It wasn't until the last moment before this book went to the printers that I found the strength. The notebook is addressed to me. It was shocking, but not devastating. It confirmed much of what I knew already, and what others had told me. I even felt grateful that he'd written like this, so copiously, and not destroyed it. I had not been aware of the full extent of his anguish and his complex processes of self-justification, self-deception and denial. What most shocked me was the extent of his efforts to swing all blame on to me for his own 'unwitting' tyrannical abuse, which of course in all cases is unacceptable. For the record, the notebook begins with one page of 'The Good Things about Lindos' then four blank pages. Perhaps he'd hoped to add more? But they remained blank.

After we had this terrible row in Lindos, Roger went off to see his friend Jules Cashford, who happened to be on holiday there too with her daughter.

JULES CASHFORD I took my daughter to Rhodes with her friend and I was walking up the street and I saw Roger and Serena. We arranged to meet the next day and went swimming together. The next evening, I was walking up the hill to the place where we were staying and I met Roger and Rufus. And Roger said, 'Oh, we've got nowhere to stay. Can we can we can we come and sleep on your roof?' So I said, 'Well, yes, of course it would be lovely to have you.'

I did Jungian analysis at the time and Roger asked if he could talk this through. I was very wary about doing it with a friend so I tried not to. But he said, 'Oh come on, I'm in a real muddle.' So we had a conversation, and he seemed to feel a lot better. In a strange way, he longed and suffered and tried to figure out what was best for everybody, himself included. And it wasn't always easy for him, or others. Intimacy of the real kind was, perhaps, something he insisted a little too much on, which is strange, because he wasn't an insisting person. But I did feel that his longings got the better of him sometimes. So that he couldn't bear that they weren't fulfilled. You might think he was a romantic, and that called him to wonderful places and allowed him to see nature alive. But it was difficult when there was a person who was also there with things that they did or didn't want. I don't think he ever could have been knowingly cruel. But I think he sometimes found it a bit difficult to understand the other person's point of view.

ROGER, *notebooks, Lindos, August 1986 [addressed to Serena]* I don't think it would be good for me, or for you, or for us, for me to accept your version of what happened the night we argued so frenziedly, or of what happened over this holiday.

The version of events, and of my behaviour, that you gave as we climbed up the Acropolis was untrue, and unfair to me. I believe that you have treated me most unjustly – that you have gone along with a general move within the group – something that swept through it – to make me the scapegoat for whatever didn't work within it. By siding with the rest against me, you betrayed me as your partner, and betrayed all the trust and love we had so patiently and lovingly built up over this last year to the point of considerable solidarity.

I am not the evil person you told me I am, and I do not accept your description of me and my actions. I am neither bad nor mad, and if I were to accept that I was, and apologise to you, and agree to be defeated in that way, I would be accepting the role of my own defeated father – and thus be of no further interest to anyone. To myself, or the world, or to you.

*

ROGER, *notebooks, 22 August 1986* Serena came to dinner at Mellis. The first time I'd seen her since Lindos. She arrived and carefully turned her car round, parking facing towards the road, and close to the entrance – something she would never normally do – like preparation for a getaway. That felt hurtful; that she could feel that intimidated, be so careful and wary.

SERENA INSKIP It was 'hurtful' that I was 'intimidated'? Imagine: I was going to dinner, alone, with Roger at Walnut Tree Farm. I'd called him up and suggested a meeting and he'd invited me over but of course I was terrified – still existing in a frozen state, yet determined to give us both a chance to talk through the truths of what had happened: how much he had abused me in Lindos and how much I'd been traumatised by it. I hoped he could take his chance. And for my own wellbeing I needed to face him. I trusted him enough to offer him that opportunity but little knowing how completely he had with such skill written his own scenario which, by then, apparent from the notebook, must have been cemented in his mind, and in his whole psyche and reason for being, to such an extent that to park my car facing the way out was an *insult* to him. The outcome of that meeting wasn't fruitful. I still lacked the presence of mind or the courage to confront him with the truth.

ROGER, *notebooks, 22 August 1986* She began by saying that she hadn't changed her mind at all about any of what she said at Lindos on the last day – that she had felt crystal clear then about what she wanted. She cannot any longer live with the restriction and controlled feeling that I give her – that she had to break out from being with me and have the solitude and freedom to find and be herself; that she cannot live with the threat of intimidation or anger or violence she feels from me. That what happened in Lindos is so traumatic it will take a long time to heal and it will totally change the nature of our relationship, if to continue forever after; that, yes, she feels hope for us and for our relationship, and does love me, as I love her.

SERENA INSKIP We split up for several months after Lindos and then we met up again and couldn't remain apart. It was a fatal attraction. It was wonderful and awful. In the autumn of 1986 after I left, Roger built a curved brick wall at the west end of Walnut Tree Farm to create a walled garden for me. When I returned, I planted flowers there.

Because of the tensions at Mellis and Roger's difficulty in accepting me as co-habitee, after discussing it with him I had bought a house in St Thomas's Gardens, Chalk Farm, in 1985 so we each had a house and I could provide a base for my children. It meant that we could have separate lives as well as together lives, and we'd often had to stay in my parents' flat when we were both working in London.

ROGER, *notebooks, 1997* The best of the men of my generation bore the brunt of the feminist revolution and suffered and learned from often painful changes in their lives. They grew with the women, and benefited too, in the long run, even though in the short run it was hell.

SERENA INSKIP Nearing the end of our relationship, I was trying to find my way in life, make new friends and try new things. In London, I attended drama improv classes which certainly fired me up, much to Roger's irritation! I would get up early once a week to play tennis with a woman friend and Roger would become absolutely furious because I wasn't staying in bed with him.

TIM RAYNER, *friend* I went to dinner at Chalk Farm one time. When I got there, Roger had lost his wallet when he arrived home. He was making the most godawful fuss and Serena was placating him. It was a total disaster because he'd lost his wallet.

CHRISTINE SMITH, *friend* Serena and Roger came for a meal in the mid-eighties and Serena got quite agitated. 'I keep saying to Roger he should do more because he could be really great!' Meaning that he was talented and could work harder.

ROB PARFITT, *husband of Christine* Instead of wasting time fiddling around with tractors.

CHRISTINE SMITH He could really make a name for himself. Of course, she's been proved right. But at the time it sounded like she was saying he was dreaming instead of getting on with the job. There was a lot bubbling about in his brain that he could do.

VICKY MINET Serena felt very insecure about herself and her own identity, quite apart from her sexuality. Now, if you're going to be hard about it, that wasn't his problem, but she blamed him for her own feelings of insecurity. Whether he could have been more encouraging and said, 'Yes, do an English degree, go and try this,' is a different matter. It's quite likely that he could have been. But living at Mellis was always going to be on his terms and not hers. There would have been no compromise.

SERENA INSKIP My mother said, 'You and Roger are only really happy when you're away together, aren't you?' Travelling was best and we seldom argued.

In Dordogne one year, we found an abandoned riverman's flat-bottomed boat, baled it out, made paddles out of driftwood, tied up our things in a fertiliser bag, and set off with the flow downriver. Pure delight together. Such collusions made life together worth living. We flew to Agadir before Christmas 1986, travelling inland to remote pink-coloured villages in a beat-up Renault 4. We made two trips to Portugal, hitch-hiking south – I hopped on to the sheepskin-covered back-shelf of a lorry cabin while Roger talked to the driver. We had to stop in the road for a troop of Gypsies and their horse-drawn carts and wagons and flocks of sheep and goats with bells on, and people waving.

Another time we took Gwen, Roger's mum, to Portugal. She nearly died of the cold in the huge marble hotel room in early spring, but we knew she enjoyed the adventure too. She had been living in Bournemouth and Roger worried about her a lot because she'd had a stroke. I'd suggested that she moved nearby. She wanted a bungalow in Diss but he was horrified. 'I can't let her have one of those.' He wanted her to live in a timber-framed cottage. Eventually they found one in Eye, three miles from Mellis, and it worked well. It had a lovely garden and she loved gardening so she was very happy.

Gwen put a lot of fear into Roger when he was small. The boy who took all his clothes off and ran down the garden really needed to be wilder than he was allowed to be. He was terrified of being tamed. I was an eternal reminder of that.

GWEN DEAKIN, *card after her eighty-first birthday, 27 September 1989* My very, very dear Roger & Serena, It is true what they say about love, not only does it make the world go round but it gives new life. Today I feel alive, refreshed and still warm from the love I felt around the four of us yesterday. It is a day I shall cherish always.

*

ROGER, *letter to Tony Barrell, December 1990* Imagine my surprise when, two weeks into the craziness of researching, writing and preparing six half-hour TV programmes in the space of five weeks, Serena takes me out to dinner at Andy's [restaurant] and tells me she's decided it's all over between us, forever, from here to eternity, starting now . . . There has been a good deal of pretty excruciating pain in parting with Serena – and that is a story I'll tell you when I see you. (There was, and is, of course a story behind her apparently sudden announcement at Andy's . . .)

SERENA INSKIP Sadly, I wasn't strong enough to leave until I was involved with someone else – this time a woman. In order to break the news to him, but without danger of more physical battles, I suggested we go out for dinner at Andy's. As soon as I told him, Roger got up, and said, 'Well, that's it,' and threw a pint of cider over me and stormed out. Afterwards, I can't tell you how many people said, 'Oh you know Roger's broken-hearted' and I had broken his heart. 'Oh really,' I said. He had already broken my heart, again and again. You put your life into trying to make a life with someone and in the end it doesn't work.

So many questions still pursue me. It was hard to know how to be loved by him. And it was hard to know how to love him. 'I love you' wasn't said often in my childhood. It was seen as a bit soppy. It was a tragedy in the relationship – neither able to accept and be comforted by what the other was offering. Maybe we were both idealising each other. We were really two kids flailing around in the dark. It was years before I understood these things.

SERENA INSKIP, *letter to Roger, 25 May 1990* Dear Roger, After seeing you last week for dinner, I felt that we'd actually had a reasonable conversation – I had felt very clear about my own decision, able to explain to you how I felt, and why (a little bit) I had finally come to the conclusion that I could no longer live with you. I was impressed by and grateful for the way in which you listened – it felt quite unfamiliar! . . . As I've already explained, I am unhappy about our relationship but it is also that I find your relationship with the world generally most uncomfortable to live with – your anger at the human race, your impatient disregard for countless individuals, your fear of what people may inflict upon you, or not appreciate in you: it all adds up to a bitter taste and an atmosphere of panic.

ROGER, *notebooks, account of attending a memorial service alongside Serena for a neighbour in London, June 1990*

I couldn't take my eyes off her shoes, beautiful turquoise-blue shoes with pointed toes and feet in new black stockings. I remarked on them.

'You've got some lovely new shoes.'

'They're my daughter's,' she said. 'I borrowed them from her. She doesn't wear them, doesn't like them.'

. . . At dinner at the Spanish tapas bar I found my eyes returning again and again to a new Latin American-looking bracelet, all bright colours, that she was wearing.

'You've got a new bracelet,' I said.

'Yes,' she said, 'I was given it.'

And it was quite clear who it was who gave her the present. That it was a love-present, and that she was quite unconcerned at wearing it before me, even flaunting it.

We walked together to my car separate and silent at first. Then, in silence, she put her arm into mine and held my hand. The joy of it, surging through me. I held her hand, tight and warm, and we walked on in silence, neither wanting to break the good, warm feeling with any words.

At the car we embraced, holding close, cheek-kisses, stroking heads and hair, then home.

. . . [The next day] As usual, I feel fear but also weariness begins to come on. All these sleepless hours (woke at five thirty this morning, got up, and drove over to tiptoe into St Thomas's Gardens and deliver a bunch of white ox-eye daisies on the doorstep). This is probably crazy, and just the kind of romantic gesture S doesn't need. But anyway, so what – it's what I need to give, so I shall do it!

After Roger and Serena split, he took the basement of her house in St Thomas's Gardens in lieu of £30,000 he had lent Serena for the renovation of the house. As part of their agreement, over the next few years, he turned it into a garden flat that later became his base in London. Serena returned to East Anglia, living with her new partner, Cee, and started a degree at the University of East Anglia in 1991. She sold her part of the Chalk Farm house in 1995. In the copious notebooks Roger wrote from 1997 to the end of his life, often looking back, he never mentioned Serena.

MATT MARCHBANK, *friend* They were in love for a long time. When they broke up, he slept on my sofa for a week or so and ate nothing but grapes. Serena was lovely but she was rather dismissive of Roger's feelings at the time, I thought.

DUDLEY YOUNG He was seriously depressed by the bust-up with Serena. It's my quiet opinion that there's nothing worse for a man's sexual self-esteem than to have his girlfriend go off into the arms of a woman. It doesn't do you any good at all.

ANGELA KING He was very upset about Serena. Their relationship seemed like a grand passion and he was beside himself.

SUE CLIFFORD Was that because he wasn't seeing what was coming?

VICKY MINET Who left who was irrelevant. She had to leave because somebody had to move out of the farm, and it wasn't gonna be him. But really, he wasn't abandoned, because by then, their relationship had broken down.

CHAPTER 11

The Film-maker

*'We discovered we were in love' – bliss in Jura with Margot – filming the Bolshoi –
A Beetle Called Derek – making documentaries, 'social adventures into fascinating
backwaters' – persuading the train to stop at the Roger station – weekends with Margot
at Mellis – tiptoeing around Margot's professional life – split between Suffolk and
London – 'Come along too'*

ROGER, *letter to Tony Barrell, December 1990* I made my way to Margot's that night, arriving on her doorstep at midnight. Come in, she said. Here was sanctuary from the storm. That was in mid-May, and I've been here ever since.

All through June and July we lived together as we always have – in cheerful platonic harmony. Then, in August, we went away to Scotland, Margot, her children Nicholas and Anna, and me. We stayed where they've stayed every summer for the past six years, at Ardpatrick, a beautiful house and farm on the far western tip of the mainland by the sea, looking out across to Islay and Jura. On mature reflection, we discovered we were in love (and probably have been for the twenty-three years we've been such friends), and decided that any course other than continuing to live together simply wasn't an option. So here I am, and here we are, in December, at Cardozo Road. I have come round to the idea of long engagements. The history of our friendship means our children have known each other, and us, all their lives, which only adds to the general feeling of the naturalness of it all. So, here I am at last, unable to believe that life can really be like this, and wondering what I've been doing all these years. Growing up, I suppose.

Margot works as a psychotherapist, running the adolescent department at the Tavistock, as well as seeing private patients, and writing and lecturing a good deal. Even without two children and her stepchildren, her life would be unbelievably hectic. Add me, and of course it's mad, paradoxically. I spend the week, or most of it, here in London, and we all go to Mellis at the weekend. Being in London has the added advantage of enabling Ru and I to see a good deal more of each other . . .

I'm sorry to be so unremittingly cheerful in this letter, and I know what incredibly boring reading relative satisfaction with life makes.

MARGOT WADDELL I knew Roger inside out because I was also on the inside of him and Serena, as a helpmate. When they finally broke up and I went to stay at Mellis there was a different atmosphere. I woke up one day and he'd made a beautiful arrangement of white stones across the entrance which said, 'Margot, with my love,' and something changed. I never thought of it like that because Serena was such a presence but suddenly I was a presence.

JENNIFER SILVERSTONE, *friend of Margot*

You with jet-black hair piled high
Huge flashing silver rings

Silver rope necklace around a long neck

Pale skin

Tall, a demanding presence that filled the air, gifting it with a sense of thinking and listening, always listening, always thinking.

JOAO SMITH Margot was a kind and beautiful woman, beautiful inside and out.

MARGOT WADDELL, *foreword to* The Tavistock Century *(2020)* From an early age, I wanted to be a clever and effective person, like my wonderful father (a working-class scholarship boy from Edinburgh whose own father had fought in the trenches and whose grandfather had regularly driven the Flying Scotsman in four hours from London to Edinburgh). Mother had been brought up under the Indian Raj. It was she who taught me how to speak and engage with the literary qualities of life . . . I ended up at Cambridge, loving the experience and going on to do a PhD on George Eliot and her intellectual history background. Halfway through my research, however, I suffered a crisis of conscience: what was I doing in academe when some of my close and talented friends were in the local psychiatric hospital and two of them had committed suicide? I wanted to leave and become a psychiatrist, but my parents couldn't afford that. A good friend suggested that I ask her godfather for advice: 'His name is John Bowlby and he works in London at a clinic called the Tavistock.' That was the beginning of the rest of my life.

NICHOLAS WADDELL, *Margot's son* In the early 1980s, when my parents didn't get on, my mum would throw us in the car and we'd head off to Muddy Boots Roger's, and that was part of her escape from London and my dad.

ANNA WADDELL, *Margot's daughter* Our dad, Bob Young, split from Mum when I was about one but he lived around the corner and our garden backed on to his. He was obsessed with whether Mum was getting together with someone. We would go for weekends at Mellis as friends in the 1980s. It was known as Muddy Boots Roger's, and there was Bat the dog and Serena, her two children, and Rufus. Mum would go away without Dad quite a lot. He didn't go to Mellis. Given how clear it was that Roger always loved Mum, I'm not surprised. When Roger moved in, he became Roger the Lodger because he had a little room downstairs. When he and Mum got back together, my sisters found it hilarious because it was old Muddy Boots Roger who was this eccentric guy we used to visit at weekends.

217

*

ANNA WADDELL Mum and Roger were both in utter bliss when it was just the two of them.

ROGER, *'A Journal from Jura', given to Margot, 1991* It is hard for me to think, up here, of anything except how much I love you. Crossing and recrossing burns, new tarns coming into sight each moment. And the brilliance of the blue, the brown, the greens, the greys. And all the time this clear, clean icy wind. And even when I do begin to think of other things, they all soon come round to you, and how much I love you. I'm walking down the riverside to the north coast of the island now, to Loch Tarbert, and I drank for you, and from the very head of the stream where it breaks ground, full of bright green mosses, in the saddle between Beinn an Oir and Beinn Shiantaidh, the highest watershed on the island, a place we gazed at together from the Point Hut in the summer.

ANNA WADDELL We stayed in cottages at Ardpatrick on the west coast of Scotland. They were part of a big old estate owned by a family of brothers who were our friends. The Point Hut was a wooden hut on the furthest reach of the land looking over the bay to Jura. Mum and Roger stayed in the hut while us kids were somewhere else. We would spend all day out rampaging around, Mum would write for most of the day and the children would troop up to the house for a meal. Sometimes a big yacht would pull up and everyone would pile on, and the adults would drink a lot of whisky.

MARGOT WADDELL We drove up in convoy, Roger in his brown Citroën, and me in my white one. We would stop en route and roll out a futon mattress in the back of each car and sleep.

ROGER, *'A Journal from Jura', 1991* Crossing over on the ferry there are white horses, yet it felt calm on the boat, with a fierce wind and a dazzling sun burning a furrow across the water. I lunched on grilled herring and mashed neaps. The Paps of Jura look rather dauntingly high and steep from here. The sun is on them whenever the clouds pass over, but clouds do seem to flock in to them from the Atlantic, and roost. The Paps are curiously steep and striped, with streaks of white down their rounded summits, as though gigantic prehistoric chickens roosted and shat on them for millions of years. From here, leaning on the windy rail, the heather looks soft enough to lie down in and sleep for hours. We'll see. It reminds me of summer bike rides on the mainland. Sitting out on deck on the lee side of the boat and missing you, I begin to feel what Andrew Marvell meant when he wrote:

My vegetable love should grow
Vaster than empires, and more slow . . .

I can feel it growing in me all the time, and it bears on everything, like a blessing.

As Virginia Storey observed last weekend at dinner, you and I are a pair of Aquarians, and having our birthdays so close makes us brother and sister. No wonder there was such a taboo. And no wonder we both love the West of Scotland, with its waters, lochs, tarns, streams, rivers, bogs, rains and sea. No wonder I found Jura so utterly enthralling, with water springing everywhere, above me, below me, beyond me, wherever I looked, and whenever I felt thirst.

*

ANGELA KING He wanted to be a film-maker so he spent a lot of time on that.

Most of us in the sixties wanted to be film-makers. Plenty of people from the advertising world around me in London moved into feature films: David Puttnam to Alan Parker and Ridley and Tony Scott. By the eighties, they had reached Hollywood, while I began by making environmental documentaries: about the wildlife of the Thames and the return of salmon to the river, for Friends of the Earth and Thames Water. Other commercial films followed. In 1985, I brought in my friend Mike Southon to make a thirty-minute film about Laura Ashley for the company, and in 1991 I called Mike again to film a cinema advert I was producing for Tactel with the Bolshoi Ballet.

MIKE SOUTHON First we had to fly to Palermo to meet with Yury Grigor- ovich, the Russian choreographer who was then head of the Bolshoi's touring division. We arrived at the Palermo opera house and were greeted by a sea of very old men in black suits. All down the side of the chamber stood men with guns. Rog had some cheese biscuits in a bag. I said, 'Whatever you do, don't pop it.' Because it would be the end of a Tarantino film. We had to pitch this idea that we would visit Moscow and pick a boy and a girl dancer to come to London to be in this commercial. Grigorovich said yes and we flew to Moscow with Nicole Farhi who was doing the costumes. We had a week to choose our dancers. These days, we would be given twenty minutes but Rog always knew how to do things properly. And it gives you a chance to think. Some producers you work with say, 'Oh, what? You want some food?' But travelling with Rog, it was always, 'Now we'll go and have lunch.' He wanted to look after everyone. There are two kinds of producers: the nuts-and-bolts producers who literally put the stuff together and pay the bills, and the creative producers who put their signature over a whole slew of things, by hiring the right people and saying the right things and inspiring people. They are a joy to work with. And that's the sort of producer he was.

Opening for A Beetle Called Derek, *ITV series, 1990–91*

Imagine yourself in a tropical rainforest, netting insects.
In a few hours, you would probably capture a species unknown to
    science.
It would have no name.
So you could name it yourself.
It might be a beetle
You could call it Derek.

TIM RAYNER Andrea Arnold was a really forward-looking, fast-thinking, ambitious young presenter. She sold the idea of an environmental series to Television South, and I agreed to direct it. I got hold of Roger as a consultant and assistant director because I knew him and knew he was an environmentalist. He was very useful to me in my understanding of the script, although he didn't have a natural flair for film-making. We had a decent budget, and Benjamin Zephaniah, who is a joy, did some poems for us, and we had a lot of fun. Roger was splitting up from Serena and was coming down to Maidstone and sleeping in his car, turning up unshaven and unwashed at the TV studios. That was difficult to handle.

ANDREA ARNOLD We were all very much a team and everybody did everything. Roger did some filming and lots of research; he was one of the gang. I loved Roger. Everybody loved Roger. We became friends, I kept in touch and used to stay with him at Mellis. Roger was like a new land for me. I'd come from a working-class background and worked in TV, and that had been my experience of life. I didn't know anyone like Roger when I first met him. He really meant everything he said so interactions felt a very genuine exchange. He was passionate and funny, really knowledgeable, and he used to wear jackets. He was quite posh; in my book he was quite posh, anyway. I don't know if he'd done much TV but he worked in a completely different way – he was a lot slower but he cared and that was his style, because he cared.

I was about twenty-nine at the time and Roger's friends were all older, and they were all fascinating. I went to his fiftieth birthday party at Margot's house. There were loads of people in her living room, a varied gang, and that was Roger. That's why I liked going to his things; they were always full of interesting people.

JOHN CLEESE, *actor and comedian, card to Roger after dinner at Margot's, April 1992* Roger, you are an ACE!!! Wordsworth noted. If anything from Tennyson occurs, call Melanie on etc. will you? Or I can just wade . . . With thanks, John.

*

A FRIEND OF MARGOT The Cardozo Road house was a bustling vibrant home with pots of bean stew on the Aga and endless vigorous conversations. Margot parented with absolute honesty and empathy and gave young people complete permission to speak their thoughts and feelings and respected them for it.

MARGOT WADDELL Roger had a study downstairs at Cardozo Road. He'd come down to London for bits of the week. He didn't really like being there because in those days there was quite a lot of Bob in the house. 'Why do I have to live with Bob Young's books?' he'd say. On the whole, he really wanted us to go to Mellis for weekends.

Much of my first book, *Inside Lives*, was written when Roger and I were together. He discussed it with me, and was always incredibly generous. I don't remember him making me feel small or pathetic in the way Bob did the whole time. Roger could be supportive but he didn't really want me to be in any sense famous or known, not that I felt any of those things.

ANNA WADDELL Like quite a lot of men Mum has been with, Roger didn't like her being interested in her work but Mum definitely had a role in inspiring Roger and feeding his interests. She gave him a lathe for his birthday, so that he could turn bowls and explore wood. It paid dividends in terms of the number of wooden objects she received as presents.

ROGER, *writing to Margot in memory of her father, undated* This lathe he gave me jointly with you is about as fine a memorial as any I can think of, working as it does through circles and roundness, yet solid and four-square. I like to think his spirit is in that lathe, hand in hand with yours, of course, and when

I'm in my happy work-trance with the engine purring and the wood-shavings flying off the chisel into the darkness beyond the Anglepoise in the perfect arc of a cockerel's tail, or like the plumed wake of a planing speedboat, this is the song I can sing to him:

> Thy firmnes drawes my circle just,
> And makes me end where I begunne.

MARGOT WADDELL The lathe, which was my idea, was such a major change in his life. We picked it up, and he started woodworking. We talked about the films he was making, about allotments and music. He was remarkably busy. He spent a lot of time thinking about allotment-holders, and how people made their music and where.

*

Making documentaries mostly for TV enabled me to go on adventures – social adventures mostly, into the backwaters in our land that have always beckoned and fascinated me. Allotments, Southend and Canvey Island, the last true end-of-the-pier show at Cromer.

ROGER DEAKIN'S *documentaries for Anglia/ITV*

Ballad of the Ten Rod Plot (1992) – on allotment life
Southend Rock (1992) – on the underground rock scene
Crystal Palaces (1993) – on conservatories large and small
Cowboys Stay On Longer: The Country Legend of Hank Wangford (1993)
North Sea Follies (1994) – on the Cromer end-of-the-pier show
A Telegram from Hollywood (1996) – on singers at the Aldeburgh Festival

ROGER'S VOICEOVER, *Ballad of the Ten Rod Plot, 1992* To most of us, the allotment world is a hidden one, glimpsed from railway carriage windows, minding its own business. An unmistakable patchwork landscape whose improvisations and ingenuities amount to a kind of folk art. If popular culture is about free self-expression for the artist in everyone, that's exactly what these modest places are. You can't help feeling when you visit an allotment that you're stepping into another country, a haven from hurry, a realm of robins and rhubarb, a principality of pea-sticks and potterers.

STEVE ASHLEY Rog asked me to collaborate on a film he was doing for Anglia TV on allotments and I did a few songs for that. We went around the allotments while all these conversations were being filmed with these old gents sitting by their forks. It's a cracker, a classic Roger construction, really. He makes these lovely connections. Ronald Blythe was interviewed and there were little chapter headings throughout the film – David Holmes painted a little watercolour vignette to title each section. Roger did a lot of films. He was incredibly accomplished in all kinds of things.

TERENCE BLACKER, *friend* Roger was a good film-maker, an interesting film-maker, but for me it did not seem his natural medium. With *Ballad of the Ten Rod Plot*, there was something slightly effortful about it – it looked as if he was trying whereas his writing just seemed to flow.

SUE ROE, *friend* I wrote a poem about a girl who came from the Moulin Rouge to dance at the end of the pier at Cromer. It was based on a true story, I told Roger about it and he absolutely loved it. My poem had crabs and whelks dancing underneath the pier and that idea really appealed to him – people and animals dancing together – and also because Cromer was so run-down in winter he liked the idea of it coming alive for *North Sea Follies*. He just loved England's crumbling old seaside towns; that they had been left as they were and hadn't been interfered with. *Southend Rock* is about the music emerging from the plastic bottles of vinegar and neatly folded napkins in the café – all these wonderful details he homes in on. He's interested in how people express themselves – the kinky boots, the tattoos – and there's one song lyric, 'Do anything you wanna do', that is Roger's mantra. *Cowboys Stay On Longer* is kind of the same thing. Roger's films seem to begin nowhere in particular and end nowhere in particular. They are just a slice of life in these wonderful, unspoilt places with people speaking from the heart.

HANK WANGFORD We spent between two and three weeks shooting *Cowboys Stay On Longer* in Suffolk. Roger was extremely easy to work with. Everything was pretty much first take, so there was a spontaneity about it. It's really the nicest thing I've ever done. There's other things I've done that make me squirm but I'm not in the least embarrassed by that. Roger hired an American truck which I drove for the film and we filmed me in an old wagon, where I'd lived for a year, and he organised a sequence at Snape Maltings and got the string section of the Suffolk Youth Orchestra to play my song 'Anyway', one of the prettier things I've written. There was a lovely reveal, where the camera swings around and there's no audience – nobody there.

*

ROGER, *Filofax, Margot's work commitments, 3–6 June 1991*

Monday M – staff meeting 8.30 p.m. to 10 p.m.
Tuesday M in Leeds – back at 9 p.m.
Wednesday M teaching evening till 10 p.m.
Thursday M back at 10 p.m.

MARGOT WADDELL On a Friday night, I would drive Anna, Nicholas and sometimes Rufus up from London for weekends at Mellis. It was a hell of a drive, quite frankly, and I'd done a full week's work. It wasn't what I wanted to do. There wasn't a huge amount of time that wasn't taken up with being there at the weekend with the children. They loved Roger's tractor and picking blackberries, making crumble, creating Andy Goldsworthy-style sculptures with leaves and stones, and swimming in the moat. Roger promised Anna when she was about nine that he would take her scrumping for apples in the nearby orchards and that's a lasting memory for her – that Roger actually did go scrumping with her.

He was very good at getting on with lots of people, including the drivers of the train from London to Diss. I don't know how he managed to do this but on one occasion he talked them into dropping us off at the level crossing by Walnut Tree Farm. They slowed the train right down and we jumped off. I can't imagine anyone else doing that. He assumed that doors would open for him. And they did.

Mellis was absolutely his. He didn't share it, really. But he also recognised that I was completely committed to my work and so wasn't going to move out of London. Whenever we went for a walk it was distinctively his land and his timing. It was his world. That was OK for a long time but it wasn't OK forever because I didn't have any say in it. He tended to take over the cooking and he had to light the fire himself. He didn't want to entrust it to anyone else. I could light a fire perfectly well; I had been a Girl Guide.

NICHOLAS WADDELL These weekends at Mellis were incredible fun but not without tension. Roger would throw open the doors to assortments of teenagers and my large family but he was a mix of a hugely generous and ambivalent

224

host because he liked things just so and he was threatened by the chaos and energy and wilful independence that everyone brought. He partly loved it but the reality of hosting was sometimes challenging – when someone lowered the arm of the record player too roughly and scratched his Toots and the Maytals record.

One of the signature things we did was to go on to the railway, put pennies on the rails, stand back, and wait for the trains to squash them. It's such a mad thing to let children do. Roger would sometimes be there, supervising it, but we would be allowed to be up on the tracks without him. It wasn't a molly-coddled approach to childhood and it was brilliant taking friends there. Very magical, very fun. But I was always aware my mum was trying to manage Roger, manage us, make it work, make it add up, fulfil his hopes of what he wanted to be for his friends.

ANNA WADDELL Roger was excited by the world – like a puppy some-times with his bouncing hair and bulging eyes – and he always had interesting friends. He liked to tell us how interesting all these people were, so of course as tweens and teens that made us marginally less impressed, although when the principal dancers of the Bolshoi Ballet came to Mellis I was very impressed.

MARGOT WADDELL He had a magnetic appeal to a lot of people. All kinds of really fascinating people used to come and stay with him. He had a great gift for friendship. We saw quite a lot of his rather creative and wonderful friends, such as Richard Mabey, and Roger was incredibly good to him because Rich-ard was very depressed for quite a long time.

BRIAN PERMAN We visited Roger when he had got together with Margot Waddell. I remember saying, 'This is marvellous. This might be it.'

BUNDLE WESTON Margot was the love of his life. There's no doubt about it. She was the one who went through his life like a golden thread, from when he was in his early twenties to when he was past fifty. She was just there, unattainable.

ANNA WADDELL Roger was hugely ahead of his time and charismatic and wonderful in all sorts of ways but he was a tricky dude. The fantasy was so intense with him. It was wonderful when it was all in line with where he was and you could all do things together. But then you weren't allowed ketchup on the table because it wasn't right.

In every family there are these tensions but Roger was so in his own track, he wouldn't meet the other person where they were. You were either in this world – this life – or not. He wanted everyone to be part of his life but not to bring who they were or what they needed. And this meant that Roger could be oblivious to someone else's needs.

I was quite fussy and wouldn't eat Roger's weird dishes and Roger wouldn't compromise so we would drive up for the weekend and have to fix our own food. He would be very upset. And then the next day, on Saturday morning, Toots and the Maytals would be on, and the sun was streaming through the window and we'd lark about, picking potatoes, swimming in the moat, driving cars around the field. There were treehouses and magical things. It seemed all ramshackle and easygoing at Walnut Tree Farm but it was not. It really worked when we were playing on the ice on the moat or going scrumping for apples in the dead of night. Doing the things that were his thing. But most of the time we children were a bit of a pain to him.

MARGOT WADDELL I think that was what separated us in the end.

ANNA WADDELL Oh God, sorry.

*

MARGOT WADDELL, Inner Lives *(1998)* The achievement of a committed partnership only represents a port of re-embarkation. It simultaneously marks the distance already travelled and the distance yet to go. And so it may be that it is the very imperfection of these unions that could be said to represent not so much arrival as potential for further development . . . [The unease in novels such as *Middlemarch* poses] questions of whether, and how, individuals can go on growing up within a partnership; how they can achieve or attain independence of mind; how they can come to experience and to tolerate the chosen other as they really are, as opposed to how they may have been wished to be.

ANNA WADDELL Roger started to take on a sort of stepdad position and I'm sure this was hard for him. From my perspective we already were a team – Mum, me and Nicholas. There wasn't a separation between the adult world and the children's world – we would sit up with grown-ups around the kitchen table. Mum was working very hard keeping the show on the road, up terribly early and terribly late. Roger was the newcomer. From his perspective, we were the newcomers.

TONY AXON Roger said that if he was spending the night at Margot's house he had to leave at 5.45 a.m. because her patients couldn't see him. It seemed like another tense relationship.

BUNDLE WESTON Margot was calling the shots like mad. Roger was literally having to tiptoe around. There were rules about when Roger could enter the house and when he could not, because of the sanctity of the therapy room. You couldn't have footsteps in the corridor, you couldn't have anybody upstairs, Roger was banned.

ANNA WADDELL That's what we all had to do. It's interesting that he took that so personally. My brother and I became floorboard ninjas, we knew where every creak was, because patients tried to find out about Mum's life and would call at all hours of the day and night. There was something fair about Roger's resentment because Mum was very focused on her work and her life was big and complicated and there wasn't space for everyone. He was central for the time he was central but he couldn't have absolutely all of her.

MARGOT WADDELL And he couldn't bear that.

ROGER, *letter to Margot, undated* Now and again, there is a heady moment when I need not be hidden, and we can even go out together like other people do, and be what I would dare to proudly call a couple, and dance, and mingle together amongst your friends to most of whom I am a shadow, a private shadow to your public self, a bit dazzled by the sudden glare but mostly glad of the opportunity to acquire some substance in their eyes.
   Imagine my dismay when, in the midst of this precious moment, just as we are getting into our dancing stride for the first time for months, you approach another man, engage him in earnest conversation, bid me leave you alone with him, and fall deeper into lengthy, intimate, private professional discussion in a corner of the dance floor while I wander off . . .

*

MARGOT WADDELL, Inner Lives *(1998)* The difference between maturity and immaturity hinges not on the fact of chronological years but on a person's capacity to bear intense emotional states; on the extent to which it is possible to think about, and reflect on, psychic pain as a consequence of having found, and sustained, a relationship with external and internal figures who are able so to do.

The contrasting response is to adopt all sorts of means to avoid engaging with painful matters. Those means often seem more exciting and compelling than their alternatives. And in many ways it is easier to define maturity in terms of what it is not, than to find a way of expressing the contrapuntal intricacies of anguish and joy, action and thought, fire and calm which underlie the capacity fully to engage with experience. Wisdom would seem to be more to do with living and feeling than with acquiring knowledge. It is not a case of believing oneself to have grown out of infantile impulses and longings, but rather one of knowing and understanding those undeveloped aspects of the self and, as a consequence, being alert to their potential effects, particularly their self-destructiveness.

ROGER, *notebooks*, *1997* I divide my time between Suffolk and London – it means you only live a fraction of your life – half of it. And you end up with a fraction. You know those bits of litter you see blown about on the sides of motorways? That's my brain, scattered between Mellis and London and my too-frequent peregrinations.

DUDLEY YOUNG For a lot of the time with Margot, Roger was commuting from his flat in North London to Mellis every weekend in his car. I'd say, 'Rog, for fuck's sake, why don't you just move in? You're burning up a lot of petrol and you're basically becoming distracted. And you know, if you want Roger, he's on the A12, somewhere between London and Mellis. That's nowhere. If you're on the road between the two of them, you're nowhere, mate.'

BUNDLE WESTON He wanted Margot to give up everything and come and live with him and be his love. But she was never going to. The phone used to go and it was Roger and I would think, 'This is going to take a long time.' You'd have to give yourself to him. I would hear it all and then I'd say, 'Roger, you're not going to change, are you?' 'No.' 'Is Margot going to change?' 'I suppose not.' 'So what are you bothering about? You've got to make the best of it – either throw in the towel or get on with it.'

DUDLEY YOUNG Something that Bundle and I share is having put in a long innings on the curing-Roger-of-the-Margot stuff. I'm a shit like everybody else but I did him a good turn on that one. You haven't done a good turn unless it has actually impoverished your time. Roger was being smothered by Margot or smothering himself through her and, listening to Roger, I said, 'You're dying. You're dying under this relationship. You've got to get out of it.'

VICKY MINET Roger said that Margot didn't give him anything at all. She had her life. She had her patients. She had her way. She had her children. She had a relationship with her children's father who lived over the wall. And Roger could fit in with that. They did have some good, fun times at Mellis but it was impossible for someone like that to be a good life partner for him.

ROGER, *notebooks, undated* What's been happening over the past months could be summed up as 'I don't want you, but then on second thoughts perhaps I do.' Since your letter in October, I seem to have experienced a gradual process of demotion – your birthday no longer celebrated at Mellis, our birthdays no longer celebrated at Mellis – as though you know how central you are for me – and I now begin at last to realise how far off-centre I am for you.

ROGER, *notes from Dictaphone, 1995* I've loved you not wisely but too well. In the end it is exasperation at all the thousands of miles I have driven – when did you ever get up at six thirty in the morning for me [but you] get up every day at six thirty for a patient?

ROGER, *notebooks, 1997* What was it I felt in Marrakesh with Margot when we went to the souk? All the things she wanted to buy were for her, for Nicholas and Anna, herself; they weren't mutual things. She wanted to buy separate bowls, separate everything for herself. She didn't want to share anything.

MARGOT WADDELL I remember my impatience with him not being able to just be with the children. Mellis was a lovely experience for Nicholas and Anna, racing around and jumping in the moat, but they both had quite an uneasy sense of Roger wishing they weren't there. I thought he should be interested in my children. I was there for Bob's three children and I was there for Rufus.

He couldn't cope with the fact that he wasn't the only one in my life. He needed a particular kind of attention that I couldn't give. I remember the last row. We'd gone up on Friday night. The children were there for supper. They wanted ketchup on their dinner. He really didn't like that. I said, 'If you can't cope with ketchup on the table because these children are in their early teens, I don't know what to do.' And that was the beginning of the end.

ROGER, *quoting Margot, in a short poem to her, 1995*

> 'We're going to Scotland
> We're going to Australia
> We're going to Capri
> Come along too.'

BUNDLE WESTON 'Come along too' was Roger's line. It was very good for Roger to hear that from Margot.

*

MARGOT WADDELL, *card to Roger from Melbourne, August 1995* I find myself very tearful a lot of the time and the solitude between events is very welcome. I have, as I said, been thinking and dreaming a great deal about us. I don't know whether to talk to you about it because I don't know whether you want to 'hear' such things. I want to be as honest as possible with you but also to respect your limits and not cross into the country where you no longer want me to be. My love and my love, M.

CHAPTER 12

The Swimmer

Drowning in ideas – 'The Swimming Book' floats to the top – swimming starts in Cornwall – the Gogmagogs musical theatre and a winter visit from Lucy Bailey and Errollyn Wallen – a trip to the Isles of Scilly begins a summer of swimming – in love again – the descent into Hell Gill – the death of Gwen Deakin – writing up – a bold restructure, and Waterlog *takes shape – the battle for glidders and uvvers*

It began when I heard about a retired major who lived next door to my friend Tony Axon in Freckenham, near Newmarket. His obsession was swimming in open water across East Anglia. He was found floating face down in a pond one Christmas Day. For many months, 'The Swimming Book' was one idea among many. What if I swam my way through Britain? Not around its coast-line but really in it – along rivers, in lakes, across estuaries; beauty spots, secret spots, forbidden places. Our landscape is made by frozen water travel-ling to the sea, ice sculpting valleys and river beds. Water doesn't follow the contours of the landscape; it makes them. Even the rising of the sap in the trees is part of the flow of our country that begins with rain and ends in waves. That is why I began my book in a rainstorm and ended it in the North Sea.

The notion of a swimming journey was also inspired by John Cheever's classic short story 'The Swimmer', made into a film starring Burt Lancaster, in which the middle-aged hero, Ned Merrill, decides to swim eight miles home from a poolside party on Long Island via his neighbours' swimming pools. I have always found swimming a great liberator of the mind, a kind of medita-tion, so to travel amphibiously, joining the pale blue lines on a map, offered an opportunity to learn about our land from a new perspective. The swimmer and the writer in me shared a single aim: to leave our baggage behind on bank or beach and float free.

D. H. Lawrence, 'The Third Thing'

Water is H2O, hydrogen two parts, oxygen one,
but there is also a third thing, that makes it water
and nobody knows what that is.

Our bodies are mostly water: salt water. It is one of the secrets of our buoy-ancy. To swim is to experience what it was like before we were born: the first nine months of our lives were afloat in the amniotic ocean of the womb. At birth, we swim into the world; babies are born swimmers. During his travels in the South Seas, where it is still unheard-of not to swim, Herman Melville describes his delight at witnessing an infant barely a few days old, 'which at first I took to be an uncommonly large species of frog', swimming in a stream with her mother. 'I am convinced that it is as natural for a human being to swim as it is for a duck,' he wrote.

When we swim, what we're really doing is flying. It is what people dream about, and there is little difference between flying in the water and flying in the air. Swimming and dreaming go together. In our nakedness or nearly so, we become much more like the mammal we are, and the child we were. We lose some of our self-consciousness; we gain playfulness. 'I'm just getting changed,' we say, and indeed we are. We are about to defy one of life's great tyrannies: the law of gravity. Lightening up, we return to an aboriginal state.

There is certainly something deeply atavistic about what Paul Valéry called '*fornication avec l'onde*' in the wild. Our sense of the present is overwhelming, as it is for every animal. It must be the origin of the trance-like state in which I often find myself on a long swim, my mind floating free as though I had swum into subconsciousness. It is why swimming is such a source of renewal and inspiration. I invariably return from a dip with some new idea in my head.

Floating free, and taking part. The line on Keats's grave – 'Here lies One Whose Name was writ in Water' – reflects his idea that a poet should be within the world, not set apart from it; his individual being formless even while his words take form. The swimmer, dissolving himself in water, immerses himself in the natural world and takes part in its existence.

Swimming is always a rite of passage, a crossing of boundaries: the line of the shore, the edge of the pool, the surface itself. Breaking the surface, entering this new element, you experience a kind of metamorphosis.

*

JANE TURNBULL, *literary agent* Out of the blue, in the nineties, Roger got in touch with Brian, my husband, whom he knew from school, saying, 'I want to write a book about allotments.' This was before allotments were cool. I spoke to a few publishers about allotments and absolutely nobody was interested. I talked to Jonathan Burnham at Chatto about Roger and Jonathan said, 'He looks like an interesting man, has he got other ideas?' I must have said to Roger, 'Chatto are really keen but what else can you do?' He talked about swimming in his moat and it started from there.

JAYNE IVIMEY It was Margot's idea. She said to him, 'Why don't you stop talking about it all? Why don't you just swim round England?'

MARGOT WADDELL I don't remember if it was my idea but I certainly wanted him to do it.

JULIA BLACKBURN In the eighties, we had gone to live in Amsterdam and Roger came over with the express purpose of talking to me about writing a book. I remember him saying, 'How are you doing it and how does it go?' but I don't remember him saying what his book was about, except that clearly it would be about the natural world. He was looking for a voice. And with *Waterlog* it was the chicken before the egg or the egg before the chicken; I imagine that in his frustration about finding a voice he went swimming a lot and either he or someone else said, 'Why not? This is your journal.' He always kept diaries before that and *Waterlog* is a diary, isn't it?

TERENCE BLACKER One of the first times I saw him was at Ling Farm, the house I then shared with my first wife, Caroline Soper. I thought, who is this prat who's talking all the fucking time? He's so bloody full of himself. If Roger was keen on something, he would talk more than is polite about it. He wouldn't pick up others' restiveness in the way that most people would; when they were thinking, Roger, that's enough. There was a slight social awkwardness. It was only when I got to know him that I tuned in to him; I realised that he was bloody interesting. He was kind, loyal and very, very good at friendship.

There wasn't some great change where he said, 'What I really want to do is write.' There was never a moment of crisis in Roger's life where he said, 'What am I going to do? How am I going to get my career back on track?' He seemed to have an inner confidence. I remember sitting in his garden when he first said, 'I'm going to write a book,' and it was a complete surprise. I thought, yeah, how many people say that? He talked about the John Cheever short story and said, 'I've got this idea. I want to swim across Britain through ponds and lakes and swimming pools.' I was enthusiastic, and said, 'That is the most brilliant, marketable idea.' And he said, 'I know . . .' He knew that he was on to something.

JOHN CHEEVER, *'The Swimmer' (1964)* He was not a practical joker nor was he a fool but he was determinedly original and had a vague and modest idea of himself as a legendary figure.

*

Roger Deakin, proposal, May 1996, 'The Waters of the Wondrous Isle – Swimming Round Britain'.

I have been thinking how best to approach a book about native swimming. I think it should be an aquatic version of Cobbett's *Rural Rides*, with a similarly discursive style. I would keep the itinerary as simple as possible, swimming or dipping as cheerfully as an otter in fresh or salt water . . .

I spent some hours in the Map Room at the University Library in Cambridge the other day, hoping for the same experience as John Cheever's Neddy Merrill in 'The Swimmer': 'He seemed to see, with a cartographer's eye, that string of swimming pools, that quasi-subterranean stream that curved across the country.'

I concluded that although I could certainly swim across Sunningdale or the stockbroker pools of Leatherhead like that, or combine hiking and swimming across parts of Wales, the Lakes and Scotland, where you could more or less draw leylines through the blue marks on the map, most of Britain's interesting swimming places are more haphazard in their distribution.

I think I should go by car, and my course should meander, like the Severn, with many a detour to visit this or that fen, village bathing hole, beach, waterfall, moat, burn, pool, creek, sandbar, cove, tarn, even the odd interesting swimming pool . . .

This would be, above all, a personal journey; a kind of quest for a remaining sense of a land and a people with a deep instinctive affinity for water . . .

I am not proposing an attempt on *The Guinness Book of Records*. Returning to Cheever's swimmer, my impulse is essentially the same as his: 'The day was beautiful, and it seemed to him that a long swim might enlarge and celebrate its beauty.'

As to a title, I'm sure it would come to light in the course of the work.

JONATHAN BURNHAM Jane, who is an excellent agent, pushed him to come up with other ideas. Now we call it wild swimming. That was his passion. It was also my obsession. I would jump in a river or lake whenever I passed one, and Roger's absolute commitment was exciting to me. I was immediately impressed by his proposal – the vitality of the prose, the observation was unique. It gave me the confidence to go with the book.

JANE TURNBULL, *fax to Jonathan Burnham, publisher Chatto & Windus, 26 June 1996* SWIMMING BOOK Roger Deakin. This is to confirm that we have agreed the following terms on the above book, which will consist of approx 120,000 words and will be delivered on 1.1.98 unless otherwise mutually agreed. Advance £20,000 . . . He is absolutely delighted to have you as his publisher and the Chatto imprint on his book and asked me to say that he really would love to give you lunch and a swim in the moat when you are next in Suffolk.

MAVIS CHEEK, *friend, letter to Roger, July 1996* Terence Blacker tells me you are going to swim around GB & write a book about it. What a fabulous thing to do.

*

Hayle Bay – Newlyn – Polruan, August 1996

I began my aquatic adventure by driving the sometimes reliable Citroën to Cornwall to stay with my old schoolfriend Brian Perman and his wife, now my literary agent, Jane Turnbull. In Polruan, I decided to swim the mouth of the Fowey River. I knew it was not going to be easy. The root of the problem is that ever since the days when Daphne du Maurier and her dashing chums lived here, it has been a place for showing off. The moment you go on the water, you're on stage. Polruan is stacked up the hill like a grandstand, and it bristles with binoculars and telescopes. Everyone has a scenic window, the kind that would cost a fortune if you broke it, and everyone is watching everyone else. There are coastguards on patrol, pilots leading enormous cargo ships up and down the river with china clay from St Austell, tugs, ferrymen, water taxis and the Fowey Yacht Club, all keeping a weather eye on the cut of your jib.

After much debate with Brian and Jane, I decided the best place for a crossing would be the harbour mouth, from the rocks below the ruined castle to Readymoney Cove on the Fowey side, a distance of about half a mile. If things went well, I said flamboyantly, I might swim both ways. That afternoon, on my first attempt, I swam out into the harbour mouth on high tide simply to get a feel of the water and currents. I hadn't intended it to be more than a short trial run, but was just settling nicely into the rhythm of the swim when I was intercepted by the coastguard. A big grey powerboat a-quiver with antennae came sprinting across the water out of nowhere and snow-ploughed to a halt like a skier a few yards off.

'Are you all right?' they called.

'Absolutely fine, thanks,' I said, trying to strike the same note as you would for 'Just putting the milk bottles out'. 'Just taking a swim.'

They explained sternly that I shouldn't swim in the harbour without permission from the harbourmaster, and told me to turn round.

'But I'm halfway across already. I might as well keep going to the other side,' I suggested, feeling like a fish arguing with an angler.

They disagreed, and it was getting too chilly to engage in debate, and so I headed back to Polruan, my spirits a little dashed, to the amusement of my friends on shore.

Over dinner that night at their cottage, I discussed the plan of action with Brian and Jane. The regatta week was about to begin, and there would soon be far too many sailing boats to make a safe crossing. My only option was to swim concealed from the coastguard by Brian's boat, hoping, if caught, that they would forgive me.

Next day, we took the boat to the appointed spot and I went in off the rocks. Brian and his children, Holly and Joe, chatted as I eased into a steady breaststroke, keeping to the seaward side of the boat, out of sight of the harbourmaster's office. The necessary subterfuge added to the fun. If this were a Channel-swim report, I would add that I was swimming at twenty-nine strokes per minute and had set off at 4.25 p.m. I swam a workmanlike breaststroke, always the most sociable way if you want to hold a conversation with your friends. It is also the best way to see what's going on around you. The children in the boat kept watch for jellyfish, but none appeared.

I swam into Readymoney Cove and waded through the clear sandy shallows on to the little beach. It had been a straightforward crossing, so far unnoticed by the coastguards. Not wishing to cool off in the cool breeze, I plunged back in and struck out for Polruan still shielded by the boat.

We were a couple of hundred yards from the other shore, and congratulating each other on giving the slip to the coastguards, when they suddenly appeared from nowhere, bearing down on our little unofficial combo with a determined air. For a moment things looked tense and we saw a loudhailer being tuned up for maximum embarrassment, if not worse. Their opening salvo came as something of a relief.

'Oh my God, not you again!'

'It's all right, we're on our way back now,' we said quickly, and apologised for any inconvenience we might inadvertently have caused. They were remarkably good-natured, giving us a slightly tongue-in-cheek telling-off, the nautical equivalent of being let off with a caution.

JANE TURNBULL The harbourmaster that day was the nephew of one of my clients. It was his first day in the job, and so a very young man in his uniform and boat with the blue light normally with very little to do came across Roger. The poor young harbourmaster had to tell him off. Roger didn't swim in a wetsuit and he was absolutely freezing.

*

My friend Lucy had recently moved from a sixteenth-century house in Walberswick to an elegant flat high up on the fourth floor of one of the great buildings of the 1930s: Berthold Lubetkin's celebrated Highpoint in Highgate. Lucy is a serious swimmer and I had wondered how she was going to cope with the sudden loss of the sea. I found my answer when I peered gingerly from the vertiginous balcony. Looking down into the gardens, I caught sight of the ripple and glint of a swimming pool.

> LUCY MOY-THOMAS, *friend* He came to my flat at Highpoint and I took him swimming in the pool there. He was collecting. He collected people who could add to his name and big him up – he sort of added them to him – and he collected fashionable places. Highpoint was a very fashionable place at that time and so he managed to get that in his book. On another occasion, we went for a beautiful swim at dawn at Walberswick. The sky was pink and reflected in the calm sea as we swam. I said to Roger, the sea was amniotic. About ten days later, he had a little piece in the *Guardian* and there was one good word in it – 'amniotic'. And he didn't once say, 'Lucy, that's a wonderful thing to say.' He just used it, and I felt used.

Jaywick – Dungeness – Camber – Romney – Mellis, October 1996

In October, I travelled to Jaywick Sands in Essex, the first place I ever went on holiday. It was only a year or two after the war and I was probably about three and a half. It must have made a big impression, because I remember aspects of it quite clearly. Most of my uncles, aunts and cousins were there, and we rented one of the wooden houses on stilts by the bay. I was lifted up to touch the ceiling by an uncle, and I paddled about in sandy pools beneath the forest of soused wooden stilts that held up the houses. The smell of sea and seaweed permeated everything, and my cousins and I spent a lot of time running up and down the wooden steps that led to other houses, jumping off into the soft wet sand. It was like living in our own sandcastle. I was enchanted with this shack city, and have been in love with shed-life ever since.

My most vivid memory of the Jaywick holiday was of catching my first fish. My Uncle Laddie, the prankster in the family, fixed me a simple fishing rod with a bent-pin hook and took me down to the beach, where I landed an enormous plaice almost instantly, borne back to our shack villa in triumph, and enjoyed by one and all for lunch. It was some years before I learned the truth; how Laddie had bought the biggest plaice at the fishmonger's and attached it to my hook by sleight of hand. The benevolent conspiracy provided me with the highlight of my holiday.

Fifty years later, I walked fast along the beach to warm up after my swim, trying to imagine the exact spot where I'd caught that fish. The sand shelves gently, so the inanimate plaice would have slid ashore easily enough. For all I know, it was already gutted and filleted too. It made a passable metaphor for a middle-class boy's progress. You think each success is your own, but they're all illusions, set up for you by the system.

A FRIEND When I read it, I thought, fuck me, that's my story. That really did happen to me – the first fish I caught had been bought at a fishmonger's and put on my line. It may be true for Roger too but I wonder if I told Roger that and he pinched it. All these stories feed into building up the aura of Roger and making him into this great man. He was a brilliant, brilliant storyteller.

*

My desk looked like a nervous breakdown over the winter of 96–97. I resisted invitations to parties and followed the literary recommendations of my friends, picking up trails in the University Library in Cambridge and wandering them, often taking unpredictable turns. From Annie Dillard's *Pilgrim at Tinker Creek* and *Teaching a Stone to Talk* to J. B. Priestley's *English Journey*; Tom Graves's *The Diviner's Handbook* to Keats's *The Fall of Hyperion*.

ROGER, *notebooks, January 1997* Did a big spring clean of kitchen and living room after returning from Cambridge at 9 p.m. Finished at 2 a.m. Errollyn and Lucy Bailey came up at twelve thirty with baby Billy – highly imaginative and resourceful toddler. What a joy to have a boy-bird in the house, appreciating everything – every detail, every drawer handle, every floor brick and the open fire!

ROGER, *Filofax, 1997*

Saturday 22 March Lucy Bailey & Errollyn & Billy to Mellis.
Sunday 23 March Lucy & Errollyn staying.

LUCY BAILEY, *theatre director* I had been looking at a way of working with musicians that released their physicality when I received a letter from an undergraduate at Cambridge called Nell Catchpole who said, 'We're a string ensemble. We'd like to work with you.' I wanted these musicians to be as physically in tune with each other as they were with their instruments, and create music that was written around movement not stillness, and make it sexy music. Why not have classical music for youngsters? Why not get them on their feet, laughing and interacting? Our first show, *Introducing the Gogmagogs*, was at the ICA in 1994. We went on to the Purcell Room, then the Royal Court, then Sydney Opera House, Italy, Germany, Brazil, New York.

I asked Roger to be a trustee of the Gogmagogs in 1995 because of his film contacts and I felt he was this interesting polymath. He filmed one of our shows and edited it. He came to London for meetings and the shows. *The Gogmagogs-a-go-go* was a collaboration with the composer Errollyn Wallen and I think Roger was in awe of us lot – me the director, Errollyn the musician – because we were the artists doing it all. He lapped it up vicariously as something he yearned to be.

Errollyn and I and my young son, Billy, went to stay with Roger at Walnut Tree Farm. We went to a little film festival in Southwold and Roger carried Billy with him almost all the time, loving having this child in his arms. I had a furry coat on, Errollyn wore a leopard-print coat and we looked like Londoners. Errollyn was the only black person there. Billy, a little boy with curly hair, looked like he could be the child of Roger and Errollyn. Roger was in his element with this little boy and us girls on each arm.

We'd left a fire burning in the field at the farm; Roger was often lighting fires out there to keep us warm, and when we got back there were three fire engines parked around the house, blue lights flashing, and a mass of smoke.

That night was something out of D. H. Lawrence. The firefighters left but said we had to stay up and make sure this fire didn't flare up again. We took turns to go to sleep, leaving someone on watch. It had a romanticism to it; it was exposing and beautiful. A triangle of people around the fire and the little boy sleeping inside who we would check upon. Two young women, and this person we felt immensely tender for. Roger was this very kind and charismatic presence. I think Errollyn and Roger were beginning their relationship and I could really feel the pull between the two of them.

MAVIS CHEEK He absolutely loved the Gogmagogs and they loved him.

In the beginning was Gog and he begat Magog, son of Gog, also known as Gogmagog or Gog Mac Gog. They were giants, at least 4,000 years old, and kings of one of the nomadic tribes who wandered the lands around the Black Sea. Being giants, it was but a short walk to Britain. They conquered it, and soon became known as the original Sons of Albion. They gave their names to the Gog and Magog Hills in Cambridgeshire, where Daniel Defoe stood in 1724 to view the Fens from a safe distance in case he caught malaria.

The Gogmagogs began life through a common desire to explore and release the physical expressiveness of the classical musician. Music is essentially dramatic, and it *moves* us, because it affects us physically as well as emotionally. I can't emphasise too strongly that this was no gimmick: it was not merely about making music 'more accessible'; it was about the invention of something entirely original on stage.

*

Scillies – Marazion – Talybont-on-Usk – Covehithe, April and May 1997

In April, my swimming adventures resumed. I was off in search of water as others travel in search of sex. There was no difference, except that my sublime aim was to consort with the naiads, goddesses, no less. Mother Nature. And to do that one must be pure in heart and chaste, like other great naturalists: Kilvert, White, Mabey, Lawrence, Durrell, Waterson.

When Keats described 'my teeming brain' what was the metaphor? What was that teeming? I open a dustbin and the bottom is teeming with maggots. I turn the compost and it is teeming with worms. Is it that kind of image? Or is it an African lake teeming with flamingoes?

I covered great distances, alone, as quickly as I could. I bought Pro Plus tablets from Boots. When I rose early one morning to drive from Suffolk to Cornwall to catch the ferry to the Scillies, I totted up 377 miles in five hours, an average speed of 75 miles per hour.

MAVIS CHEEK He had this wonderful Citroën which he could sleep in, and in which he also kept a dress suit wrapped in plastic and a bottle of champagne. Just in case. The car was a big old thing. And it held everything.

JULES WILKINSON, *radio producer and friend* I loved his slightly worn towel and swimming trunks always in the boot of his car, always ready like an emergency kit, like a defibrillator.

ROBERT MACFARLANE, The Wild Places *(2007)* The boot held, as it always did, a bivouac bag, a trenching tool of some sort, and a towel and trunks, in case he passed somewhere interesting to sleep, dig or swim.

JAYNE IVIMEY *Waterlog* wasn't one journey because his mother was dying so Roger was coming back all the time. He said it was awful because he had to plan these swims between her bouts of illness. Everyone romantically reads into it that he swam from one place to another but he had to come back, do jobs, earn money, go and see his mother, try and sort out her affairs. It was hectic, that book.

ANDREW SANDERS I was on a film shoot in Cornwall and Roger was down there for *Waterlog*. I was at Rick Stein's with one or two people I was working with on the film and then this guy turns up who looks like he's just come out of the river, and he had. I was so pleased to see Roger but the people I was with were somewhat startled by this guy who turned up actually soaking wet. At that time he was incredibly anxious about his book; he was having tremendous difficulty writing it. He sat down at this table, a soaking-wet figure, in a state of turmoil.

ROGER, *Filofax, 1997*

10 May Mum very weak in bed.
11 May RD in bed all day with flu bug.
29 May Errollyn 10.30 p.m. to Mellis.

RUFUS DEAKIN I liked Errollyn a lot.

TONY AXON I thought she was delightful.

BEN BARKER-BENFIELD She was wonderful and such a nice person. I was very impressed with her. She was as open and smart and talented as he was.

ANDREW SANDERS Errollyn had buckets of charisma but their relationship was quite incongruous. There was Roger in his worn-out clothes and hobnail boots and there was this girl with the most amazing gold make-up and completely outrageous attire which was totally unsuited to being in the country. And no attempt at wearing wellington boots or anything like that.

ROGER, *notebooks, 1997* Margot: 'Thales, the pre-Socratic philosopher who thought principal element in the world is water'. Errollyn: 'Endolphins'.

ROGER, *Filofax, 30 May* To Covehithe – swim sea and mere – cold windy east wind. Walk then Benacre marsh reeds etc. – return to Mellis exhausted!

ROGER, *letter to Errollyn, undated* I still love you like I did when we walked to Covehithe beach and you peeled me out of my wetsuit and told me swimming in cold water would give me a rush of endolphins, and we sat on the steps of the wooden bird-hide together in the sun, and walked through the marshes and saw a pair of huge marsh harriers skimming the reed-tops and stood still and held our breath as a flock of greylag geese flew low just over us, and you called them jet lag geese. I love your wit, the funny words you make up, and above all else I love your honesty and straightforwardness.

*

Waveney – Winchester – Windrush – Rhinnogs – Mold – Cambridge,
June 1997

Trespass is a key ingredient for a good swim. In June, I reached Winchester. Approaching the Itchen along College Walk, I came eventually to the water meadows and two or three piebald horses grazing by the river. I vaulted a low fence, steadying myself on a PRIVATE FISHING notice, and crossed the meadow to a convenient willow, where I changed into bathing trunks and a pair of wetsuit boots for the return journey, and sank my rucksack and clothes into a patch of nettles. At the chalky, gravel bank I confirmed William Cobbett's observation, made on 9 November 1822, that: 'The water in the Itchen is, they say, *famed* for its *clearness.*' I plunged into the river, which was three to four feet deep, with here and there a shallow, sandy bank cushioned by water-crowfoot. The current was fast enough to make it slow-going if I turned and struck out upstream. But I rode downstream with the river in a leisurely breaststroke, keeping my eyes open for whatever might be round the next bend. I was rewarded with the sight of a water vole crossing over and disappearing into the reed bed on the far bank. The river swung round in a long arc through the water meadows, and very sweet it was too. Here and there I saw the dark forms of trout, and minnows hung in the sandy riffles. This was very fine swimming.

I had climbed out of the river and was strolling back through the lovely water meadows when a shout rudely intruded. 'Do you realise this is private property?' The horses looked up for a moment and resumed their grazing. I decided to ignore the two irate figures on the fenced footpath and pressed on with all dignity in my bathing trunks towards the hidden clothes in the nettle patch. It crossed my mind to make my escape across the water, but then I thought of Cobbett and what he would have done, and that settled it. I was going to stand up for my rights as a free swimmer.

I got changed as languidly as possible, then casually leapfrogged the fence and sauntered off along the path, whistling softly to myself, as an Englishman is entitled to do.

'Excuse me,' came a voice, 'does that fence mean anything to you?'

This was unmistakable school talk, and I turned round to confront two figures straight out of Dickens; a short and portly college porter with a beard and an Alsatian, and a gangling figure on a bike with binoculars, strawberry-pink with ire: the College River Keeper. I introduced myself and enquired the cause of their disquiet. They said the river was the property of Winchester College, and full of trout for the pleasure of the Old Wykehamists who sometimes fish there. It was definitely not for swimming in by hoi polloi.

'But surely the countryside and all the beautiful rivers in it belongs to all of us?' I said. The River Keeper practically fell off his bike laughing at that one.

At this point things turned nasty. They accused me of scaring away the trout and the porter muttered about calling the police when I said I contemplated swimming naked. If I frightened away the fish, I said stoutly, and perhaps unwisely, then I was doing them a good turn, since if they stayed they would only be murdered by the Old Wykehamists. I told them I swam in the Waveney all the time in Suffolk in a place where bathers and anglers have co-existed happily for at least a century. And anyway, I said, why not designate one stretch of the river for bathing and another for the Old Wykehamist fly-fishermen?

'We couldn't possibly do that because the water quality is too dodgy,' said the porter. 'Upstream of here they spray pesticides on the watercress beds and there's a sewage works discharging what should be clean water, but isn't always, into the river.' He urged me to leave immediately and have a shower with plenty of hot water and soap to wash off all the pollutants. People had been getting skin rashes, he said. Wishful thinking on his part, I fancied.

'But if the water is so evil and polluted, why aren't the trout all dead?' I asked. 'And why have you fenced in this footpath in a straight line miles away from the river instead of letting people enjoy winding along the lovely banks? Isn't that a bit mean?'

'I'm not wasting any more time with this,' he said, and flounced off, the Alsatian casting hungry looks over its shoulder.

*

The experience that became the introduction to *Waterlog*, a swim in my moat during a summer storm, came on Wednesday 11 June 1997, a year after its billing in the book. The conditions were ideal: I was in love but alone; at home and yet deeply focused upon my adventure. When I wrote down my sensations soon afterwards – eyes at water level like a frog's; rain sinking the floating pollen, rain pummelling the surface of the water like grapeshot – it encapsulated everything that made me begin my swimming adventure. Swimming in the sun-warmed moat beneath the rain, I had the curious sensation of being safe, dry, and invited in by the pond goddess. Come in, she said. Here was sanctuary from the storm.

Later that month, the pond goddess in the form of my old friend Tony Barrell delivered my title, when he proposed a characteristic Barrell pun: waterlogging. A year later, after much discussion, 'The Swimming Book' took form as *Waterlog*.

*

Buscott – Hathersage – Arncliffe – Ingleton, July 1997

Over breakfast at Bernie's Caving Cafe in Ingleton, I shared a big table with a group of potholers tucking into chip butties and sausages. The Full English was very much in evidence. Considering that in potholing your life can depend on the ability to squeeze through a letterbox crack or a hosepipe cave, I was mildly shocked. Yet I've learned that the very people you expect to look after their bodies often don't appear to care at all. I once had to meet Yury Grigorovich, artistic director of the Bolshoi, in Palermo where he and the cast of *Swan Lake* were on tour, and partying after the show. He drank us under the table, while outside in the hotel corridor the dancers boozed and chain-smoked until five in the morning.

To walk up Hell Gill Beck on a sunny afternoon out of the Vale of Eden was my idea of heaven. Gavid Edwards, an Aysgarth potholer I met in Bernie's Caving Cafe, had recommended the descent into Hell Gill as well worth the trek to this wild forsaken moor; something between potholing, swimming and rock-climbing.

I eased myself into the first of a series of smooth rock cups four or five feet in diameter and of variable depth. The Hell Gill gorge was like a

245

pothole whose roof had cracked open. It plunged almost vertically down the hillside for about 400 yards in a series of waterfalls dropping into overflowing cups. The rock was smooth and wet and a beautiful aquamarine. It was slightly pockmarked, giving the effect of a moonscape, and I slithered and squirmed down the tunnel from one cold bath to the next in one long primal scream.

Everyone I had talked to about this descent said that once you're in, you must keep on going down, because you can't climb up. I was glad of the rubber boots and the grip of their soles as I slid down this stone uterus, deafened by the rush of the water, with sheer rock rising to sixty feet above me and a crack of sky. The water was cupped and jugged, saucered, spooned, decanted, and boiled in its descent. So steep and labyrinthine, it was impossible to know what was to come next. It was like a dream of being born.

I was conscious that I shouldn't really be doing this alone. I had impetuously broken the first rule of potholing or climbing – that you let somebody know where you're heading before you set out. The feeling became acute as dusk fell and I reached a waterfall perhaps 150 yards down. It sounded as if it dropped some way. The river slipped over the rocky lip of a saucer and disappeared into nothing, like something out of Edgar Allan Poe. A rope ran along the roof of rock above, bolted in here and there, leading down over the void to a lip in the ceiling beyond. It was impossible to see where it led, or where the next foothold might be. I had no equipment at all, not even a rope, because the rocks were all too smooth to secure it.

I pondered my dilemma carefully. Once over the edge and dangling from the rope, there was no going back. I would have to go hand over hand down it. But how far? I was no potholer and stupidly short of information. And I didn't fancy being stuck in a freezing beck all night. On the other hand I had been told it was impossible to climb back up. I decided to try anyway, and flopped and clambered my way up like an exhausted salmon, resolving to return some day with a companion – and a little more local knowledge. The experience was so utterly primeval that I still dream of Hell Gill Beck.

You look back on where you have gone and realise that unconscious connecting forces have been at work. Or were they acting somehow from outside? Are you following some natural pattern you instructively recognise, but at a pre-conscious level? Did I know, when I went to Hell Gill, that it would represent such atavistic forces? Life and death, being born and descending back into the earth.

Hoxne – Ely, eels and the Fens – Fladbury Mill – the Avon – the River Dart –
Holbeton – the Erne Estuary – Isleham – Dartmoor –
Padstow – Penzance – Plymouth – Burley-in-Wharfedale – Bolton Abbey – the
River Wharfe – the Leeds and Liverpool Canal – Beesley Falls – Ingleton –
Kirkby Lonsdale – Holkham, July and August 1997

In August, I took to Ilkley Lido before tea with Errollyn Wallen and various members of her unofficial fan club, assembled for a first performance of her magnificent *Chrome* by the National Youth Brass Band at the Harrogate Festival. At Betty's of Harrogate we took on what we swimmers call ballast, and departed clutching chocolate teddy bears that promptly melted in the heatwave. The kids in the audience loved *Chrome* and after the concert kept coming up to Errollyn to congratulate her and ask for her autograph. The next day, I swam in the Leeds and Liverpool Canal before heading south again.

A few days later, Dudley Young came over to Mellis for dinner. We sat by the moat and watched newts floating in their firmament, and I was surprised that one of my most brilliant and learned friends thought that newts turned into frogs, since he had never seen one on dry land. We had our usual long conversation about life and love, men and women, women, solitude and the bachelor existence and Dudley stayed the night. We talked of my mum, getting weaker and sicker, eighty-nine now, and dying. There's a sense with Gwen of 'He taketh away the sins of the world through his suffering on the cross'.

Next morning we rose in the glowing dawn and drove to north Norfolk. For a while, on the way out of Norwich, we found ourselves following a lorry belonging to Harwich Reclaim, Textile Collections – 'Working today to save tomorrow from yesterday'. This is how copywriters can cause road accidents.

Dudley was an old swimming companion, and the prospect of enhancing the day still further with a swim together from one of the best beaches I know was stimulating. We followed the path through Overy Marsh towards Burnham. A butterfly went past over the sea lavender. I said it was a swallowtail. Dudley thought it was a cabbage white. 'That's the difference between us,' he said. I kept my eyes firmly on the sandy path ahead, hoping to find a lizard out sunbathing. Dudley would probably think it was a stick, but I would know it was a lizard.

We stripped off to wade and swim alternately in the general direction of Wells, accompanied by a posse of oystercatchers and several sandpipers, who scampered after invisible delicacies with desperate urgency as the tide went out, uttering little cries of discovery. We came to a place where people were vigorously body-surfing into the shallows. I thought of Byron, who 'wantoned' in the breakers in Italy at Lerici. We threw ourselves into the naked buoyant tumbling, and gloried in the abandonment in wave after wave, happy as the bathing pigs of Kythnos we had once discovered sailing across the Aegean in a small wooden sloop. We rode out a stormy night in the shelter of a providential cove and awoke to a rosy-fingered dawn and a perfect sandy bay. There was not a soul in sight. But the beach was not empty. In the shade of a tin shelter on driftwood stilts, occasionally strolling into the sea for a dip and a roll in the shallows, lolled a dozen ample sows. I hope those pigs still have the beach to themselves.

DUDLEY YOUNG Roger wasn't a sailor but he would've liked to have been, and he was willing. We had a nice couple of summers sailing in the Greek Islands. He loved the swimming pigs. And then one day, the boat caught loose, and started to float out to sea. And we were on the beach. It was a dangerous moment. The boat was fucking off. So I jumped in the water and started swimming after it and Roger ran along the shore to the point. And I got the boat. That suggests to me that Roger was not then a classy swimmer. But he picked it up. I never went swimming with him, except we did have a big day together at Holkham. It wasn't a swim, it was a day walking and bouncing around but not much swimming. When we met the naked people, that was great fun.

*

The Little Ouse – the Wissey and the Wash – Bamburgh – Jura – Ardpatrick – Easedale Island – Loch Awe – Belnahua, August 1997

Before I set out on my long-planned trip to gather some Scottish swims on the west coast, I visited Mum at her cottage in Eye. Then I drove north, swimming in the Wissey before finishing the day with a dip in a flat sea off Bamburgh sands. It took a long time for the water to deepen but then I cut through the oily calm in a soundless dream of swimming. Behind me, the castle stood like a cloud in a continually changing sky.

As I crossed the wide, puddled sands, the sunlight fell from the castle and it was revealed as grey and forbidding. Gulls floating on the sea looked airborne, lifted on a mist that painted out the horizon in pale grey. Rain came, just as I was getting dressed, and I felt suddenly lonely and ridiculous on this glorious expanse of beach. I threw my rucksack over one shoulder and ran hard, barefoot through the dunes, marram grass stinging my wet calves as I ran, slowed by the cloying soft sand. The halving of each stride by the sand made the running dreamlike, as the swim had been.

The Farne Islands hovered like planets suspended in the mist. I felt far wetter than in the sea. The car was misted up. I felt miserable. But when I dived through the deluge into a phone box in deserted Bamburgh a rainbow appeared over the heavenly castle. It was all absurdly magnificent and sad. I drove on in my own mist to Lindisfarne, spinning across the causeway, not caring whether I were cut off by the tide or not.

ROGER, *diary, Sunday 17 August 1997* 9.10 p.m. Mum died. I am on Lindisfarne in the Abbey graveyard.

Before Mum died, I had telephoned Kate Campbell, who lived near her in Eye and had been looking after her, from that phone box near Bamburgh Castle. I worried that sudden thunder could alarm Mum. When I phoned from a call box in Tarbet the following evening, I could tell something was wrong. 'Take a deep breath,' Kate said, 'Mum died last night.' She had died very suddenly and peacefully – she said, 'I'm just going to let it wash over me' – and let go. I think she wanted to release me as well as herself.

I wondered whether to go straight home but Kate said I should carry on because that is what Mum would have wanted. I phoned Sue Clifford, who was very kind, and then spoke to Margot. A few days later, confined in the pup tent by midges on Jura, I discovered what it was like to be a prison writer and had a nightmarish dream. A man had been murdered and I somehow colluded by moving the body and covering it up. People in the neighbourhood were suspicious. The Citroën CX was involved. A detective arrived and the dream was unresolved when I woke to discover mist down to the sea and my mattress pushed out from under the tent. There was an immense silence, with only the sound of the sea breaking gently on the pebble beach.

After a spartan breakfast of burn water, biscuits and an orange, I veered inland on switchback deer tracks, climbing steadily until I was level with the first of a string of swims that winked in the sun, stretching in an imaginary leyline across the island. Feeling no modesty before the deer, I entered the ineffable softness of Lochan Mhic-a-phi. If some Fenland rivers are gin clear, this was like swimming through single malt whisky. The loch turned my body to the dull gold of a carp, and bore me up as if in water-wings, as I crossed 200 yards of the finest water in the world, tasting it at intervals. To feel its balmy softness in every limb, at every stroke, was a kind of heaven.

Mum gave me all this – this love of outdoors – by allowing my menagerie at Randon Close, and my *Observer* books, and *I-Spy* books, and rabbits and Cosy Cabin. Her great gift was a kind of detached tolerance – or rather involved, in the sense that she was proud of what I did and perhaps relived her own childhood vicariously through what I did, retelling the stories of my exploits to her neighbours, sisters and friends. I took two striated purple-and-grey stones home with me, both heavier than a camera, walking all over Jura with them in the rucksack.

Driving back on the M74, I thought of ringing Mum. 'I'm ringing up to say how much I love you. I'm asking if you had a lovely day.' A serenade to my mother, a Mother's Song, that's what it is. I love you, Mother. Then the mist comes down and she's not there.

TONY AXON When his mother died, he didn't return for about ten days. I hadn't realised how much she'd meant to him because it was never apparent, really. But for Rog, something snapped. He went into a depression and he didn't want to come back. He had to be dragged back almost.

BOBBIE, *cousin, condolence card, 1997* Gwen was a fantastic, brave, intelligent lady who coped with so much in her life and was so independent. She was a lesson to us all, she was a great sister and friend to my mum and much loved. We have had our mums for such a long time, and been very lucky in that fact for they were not exactly young when they had us.

ANGELA KING and SUE CLIFFORD, *condolence card, 1997* She must have been very proud of you. It is a great shame that she didn't live long enough to read the book you are working on.

Roger did not mention his mum's illness or death in Waterlog.

Farleigh Hungerford – Henleaze – St Just – Treyarnon – Frenchman's Creek – Bryanston – the Stour – on the Riviera: Bournemouth – Fordingbridge – the Avon, September 1997

Driving through the New Forest to Bournemouth reminded me of trips out with my mother, when she lived here. We would take out sacks and collect horse manure and take it back to put in her garden.

Memorial service for Gwen Deakin, 27 September 1997

TONY AXON There was a memorial service at Walnut Tree Farm where everybody said something about Gwen.

ANDREW CROOK, *cousin* Most of us deal with bereavement through some formality. This was unusual because we sat in a circle on the grass, and people made random comments off the cuff. It took a few people by surprise but it was quite touching.

VICKY MINET We all sat around in a circle at the back of Walnut Tree Farm. I thought, oh my God, this is going to be so embarrassing. But it was lovely, and Jenny was there, and Rufus, and Jenny's daughters as well, who were in tears, and the whole thing was a big success.

ROGER, *letter to Ben Barker-Benfield, October 1997* Now autumn has set in with a certain chill and pallor, so I'm at the desk, fully clothed, with the trunks hung up, still dripping, beside me. Today is really grey and nippy, but the weekend was Indian summer and I managed to get up to a spot north of Norwich on the River Bure near Blickling Hall called John's Water. Despite the dubious name, it was a marvellous place – a brisk mill pool and ball-threateningly cold – but with hills of watercress and forget-me-not all round, and the clearest water imaginable. I might have frolicked there all day had I a thick enough blubber. It's going to take some getting-used-to, this living without my mum – and of course the whole experience brings back a lot of memories of my dad too.

John's Water: the Norfolk Bure – Islington – Droitwich Spa Brine Baths – Somerset Levels – Medway – the RAC Club, Pall Mall – Walberswick, October, November, December 1997

I was at my desk all the spring and summer of 1998 writing up my log and swimming in the moat, which helped clear my mind, rendering the recollections of my wanderings more lucid. All the most sacred places are secret and I swam in countless places without revealing where they were. This is the advantage of writing a novel. When I wrote *Waterlog*, I approached it like a novel.

*

Tuesday 11 August 137,130 words written.
Wednesday 12 August 16½ hrs' work 9 a.m. till 1.20 a.m. Revised 1st draft.
Thursday 13 August Printing out the book; Oliver [Bernard] did the page numbers. I hole-punched it etc. Working on opening chapter – MOAT.

ROGER'S *first draft of* Waterlog, *chronological structure, beginning with:*

Knee-high on the Red River, 13.8.96 Hayle Bay
Crossing the Fowey River, 16.8.96 Polruan
Swimming with Trout, 4.9.96 Stockbridge
etc.

JAYNE IVIMEY He got into the most terrible muddle and state about writing it all up. It was so confusing. All notes were out of kilter. He was in a right state. There was so much information.

DUDLEY YOUNG As he was writing it, he sent me a bit and we talked. I'd say, 'Rog, it's all about you and your crypto-religious relationship to the water, which I'm quite interested in. But we want more people.' And I said, 'Beware the devils of narcissism. They're closing in on everybody.' And he would look a little vaguely out the window and say, 'Yes, dear.'

ROGER, *notebooks, 1968* D's assertive magniloquence. The need to hold forth, to have an audience, to have a mirror, preferably gilt and fairly decorative, for violent attacks on narcissism.

MAVIS CHEEK We talked about writing quite a lot. We talked about the I, the me, in *Waterlog* – that it needed to go in.

TERENCE BLACKER, *note to Roger after reading his first draft of* Waterlog, *September 1998* It's a terrific piece of work – always interesting and original and with some strikingly good pieces of writing. I love the way you've combined all sorts of different passions and views about the countryside, history, literature, music and so on without losing coherence. I'm sure that it could be both well received and commercially successful. But the more I read it, the more convinced I became that what you have here is raw material and that for the book to be as good as it could and should be, you need to think in terms of a radical rewrite. What you've got at the moment is a series of scenes and impressions, some of them spectacularly good, which don't have any kind of structure or story or shape. They're a series of dips, rather than one long, satisfying story.

REBECCA CARTER, *editor* I was in my late twenties and *Waterlog* was my first big editing job. When I read his manuscript in late summer 1998, I had this feeling of, oh goodness, this is going to be really tricky, because I had been so looking forward to it and yet after a few chapters I got bored. It was a diary, and it was repetitive. The swims were in the slightly haphazard order that he'd done them in, over eighteen months. My initial concern was, how are you going to stop the reader putting this down? I was very worried about breaking it to him – that radical restructuring was needed.

I put a bit of preparation into a first meeting with him. I spread maps all over my floor to find out where his swims were and what could be put together – curating a slightly fictional journey for him that could take place over one year and through the seasons. I looked for interesting juxtapositions between different swims. It was a massive jigsaw puzzle. I planned what I was going to say to Roger and took the train to Diss. I brought my swimming costume but disappointingly I was not invited to swim in the moat. We sat at a table outside and went through the book in what was perhaps the most intense day I've ever had with an author. I felt each chapter should have a thematic point. He said, 'I don't think in themes.' But I gave him notes on how he might reorganise it: to make the most of the geography, the seasons and the moods.

Rebecca's restructuring, fax, 21.10.98

1. Introduction – the moat and a swim; Mellis in spring; maps and kit
2. Scillies, Marazion, St Michael's Mount
3. Stockbridge, Winchester – trout – fishing – river access
4. Cambridge: the Cam, the Map Room research, in search of a cold bath (Madingley), Map Room (con't)
5. Ely and the Fens – the lark

6. Mellis – early summer (+intro to summer?)
7. Holkham and the Norfolk coast – Stiffkey (night)
etc.

This was the structure that Roger adopted for Waterlog.

REBECCA CARTER There was also the question of trying to slim down sections that were overwritten, or conversations with rich and important friends that meant a lot to him but probably wouldn't endear him to readers. He always wanted to point out who he knew of influence. I was probably over-insistent in the way that young editors are who haven't yet learned the tact needed to work with authors.

I missed my train in the evening so he drove me back to London and we continued to talk about the edit during the two-hour drive. I got home late and exhausted but it was such a fruitful conversation because he took up my suggestions for the restructuring.

I remember seeing this incredible book emerge. It was such an exciting editing experience – learning that we could transform something like the Hell Gill section by putting it in the right place. I thought of *Waterlog* as a piece of music – leitmotifs and recurring themes and climaxes. Maybe then I got a false sense of security. I became a bit too confident when sending him the line edit that he would see where I was coming from.

Rebecca's line edit, 12 November 1998; some examples

Waterlog *draft, original title for Chapter 7* Beachcombing.
Rebecca Carter's suggestion Title about tides + currents?
Final version Tiderips and Moonbeams.

Waterlog *draft* I immerse myself like the fox when he rids himself of his fleas by leaving just the tip of his nose above the surface, then ducking away underwater. I leave my devils behind on the waves.
Rebecca Carter Cut 'by leaving . . . etc.'?
Final version I immerse myself like the fox ridding himself of his fleas. I leave my devils behind on the waves.

Waterlog *draft* I listened to the sea percolating into the marsh, sliding up every little meandering mud canyon, between the glidders and

254

uvvers – the mudbanks – trickling about the mycelium of creeks, gently rocking the glistening samphire.

Rebecca Carter [underlines glidders and uvvers] Names for mudbanks? Mycelium – this image won't be vivid for people who don't know the word 'mycelium' – like me!

Final version All retained.

ROGER, *letter to Rebecca Carter, 15 November 1998* I am afraid that if you are to home in on every ounce of wit or poetry like this, the very heart of the book is in danger of being taken out. If this kind of thing is a problem, and I am not providing the kind of book you want, I think the sooner you make it clear what it is you want instead, the better. But it may not be a book I am qualified to write.

This is not about my ego as a writer; it is about the fundamental authenticity of the book, as described in my proposal, and on the book jacket.

If a less different, less poetical, less allusive, more literal-minded book is what is now required, and this is indeed the view of Chatto & Windus, then I think we are heading for a considerable problem. I find it hard to see, in the circumstances, how I can rewrite any more of the book until we have reached a clearer mutual understanding.

REBECCA CARTER When the fax came in, I had no idea he had been so angry about my suggestions. I thought I was doing him a wonderful turn, giving him all that time and attention. It was upsetting because I'd emotionally and creatively engaged with the book. I was trying to help him take out the digressions that distracted from its essence. Whenever he disagreed with me, all his friends would be commandeered to give advice.

ROGER, *fax to Jane Turnbull, 15 November 1998* I took the advice of Richard Mabey and Terence Blacker, who both agreed that Rebecca is savaging my work – possibly through sheer insensitivity, who knows? – and both suggested I must take action straight away because we are just clearly on a collision course . . . She doesn't seem to have the faintest idea how to enthuse, encourage or inspire an author to yet greater heights. I had rather withdraw it than see it bowdlerised by such prosaic ignorance and – Richard's word for what she is doing – impertinence.

JANE TURNBULL Roger was a nightmare during the edit. Poor Rebecca. I think it's seared on her soul. I said to him, 'It's always your book. An editor is there to help you.' It was a first book. Normally people are a little bit more humble and open-minded about it.

ROGER, *another fax to Jane Turnbull, 15 November 1998* I have just had a very long telephone conversation with Rebecca Carter about my letter. She was very apologetic about what she felt on reflection were rather hasty notes. She felt she should first have prepared me for the fact that all her marks on the page were meant to be <u>suggestions</u> and not prescriptions. I believe she is genuinely enthusiastic about what I'm writing, even though her margin notes didn't convey that to me.

REBECCA CARTER Roger was a baptism of fire for a young editor learning how to work with authors. We had a very tight deadline, and he was so all-consuming. I would cycle round to his flat in Chalk Farm, delivering edited drafts and picking up original artwork for the chapter headings. Jonathan Burnham, who had acquired the book, had moved on, and Roger's book had been a little forgotten about at Chatto. Roger didn't see that I was doing so much work behind the scenes to convince my colleagues that this book could be big – the general attitude was, 'What, a little book about swimming? That isn't going to be a bestseller.'

ALISON SAMUEL, *then publishing director at Chatto, fax to Jane Turnbull, January 1999* I'm currently reading the revised manuscript, which is wonderful. I think Roger's done marvels – it has just exactly the blend of magic and water and eccentricity and powerful evocation of place that we all envisaged.

ROGER, *notebooks, 2004* Short-changed – that's exactly how I felt I was treated by Rebecca, and even more so by Alison Samuel. I never felt properly appreciated by either. So acute was the feeling that in the end I felt forced to write a letter to Rebecca pointing out how blind she was to what I was trying to do in *Waterlog*; blind to (this is hard to put down with any semblance of modesty) – the poetry. She wanted to cut out the moorhens walking like little girls at a party trying out their mothers' high-heeled shoes. To me, such images were the very essence of *Waterlog*. To her, they were excrescences; superfluous, getting in the way of the narrative. She seemed to want a 'travel book'. I wanted something more like a meandering river of a poem.

CHAPTER 13

The Author

Naughty swimming at the Oasis – friendly views of Waterlog *– 'Beware fama':
Dudley makes an enemy – courting Ronnie Blythe – Richard Mabey's* Nature
Cure *– conquering Radio 4 –* The House, The Garden *and* Cigarette
on the Waveney *– a new agent*

Waterlog was sent into the world in the spring of the century's final year with a party at Oasis, the outdoor council pool behind Covent Garden. London was breathing, clicking and buzzing under an orange sky. There was music, speeches and swimming. Floating on my back in the pool and looking up, I saw the balconies of council flats and bright offices lit up with people at computers in the windows and, up above, a black starry sky with now and again a jet. As a swimmer, I felt connected to everyday life in a way I never do in an indoor pool. Here I was in the centre of London, gazing at the stars in the utmost luxury of a heated outdoor pool. The place had a Roman feeling about it, and rightly so, because this was the height of civilisation.

JULES WILKINSON They played Loudon Wainwright III's 'The Swimming Song', and we swam and lots of his lovely friends were there. It felt like this was the beginning of Roger moving to a different phase, and it was.

LUCY BAILEY Errollyn was there looking extraordinary, I had white peroxide punky hair and I remember his pleasure in us being there. He loved being around the Gogs, full of optimism and mad fun and mischief. It was a buzzy, great event, Jacqui Dankworth was performing, and we did really naughty swimming.

REBECCA CARTER All the Chatto people who went to the party were buzzing afterwards about how wild it was. All these guests were hanging out in their kaftans. But I couldn't face it. I was hurt and I made some sort of excuse to Roger about why I couldn't go.

BRIAN PERMAN It was a rather cool evening in late May and it was a low-key affair. We were all standing around rather awkwardly. It wasn't a really riotous evening but this was a first book by someone who no one really knew. There was no reason for Fleet Street to turn out en masse and they sure as hell hadn't.

DUDLEY YOUNG The party was quite fun. Terence Blacker was the man, the one who was pushing Roger and pushing the book. He was a London figure, he had a column in the *Independent*, and he made a nice little speech too, saying, 'This is my mate, Roger. And here we go.' And Blacker was right. The book did catch on.

*

ROGER DEAKIN, Open Book, *Radio 4, 23 May 1999* I think the swimmer is in some ways expressing the child in themselves.

MICHAEL HOLLINGTON, *English professor and friend* My reading of *Waterlog* is that he wants to be a boy again.

OLIVER BERNARD, *letter to Roger, 1999* The combination of erudition and a child's sense of wonder had me smiling over and over again.

RICHARD MABEY He was not an ideologue in any sense, he was an anarchist in the best sense of the word. I don't think he agonised about his writing style, it flowed like an improvised jazz solo. Not being a swimming person, some of the eulogies to the effects of water caused me to raise an eyebrow. They seemed to venture into what I would call 'woo' territory. But then he'd diffuse a bit of portentousness with a terrific pun – when he talked about the endorphin rush from swimming in cold water, which he called endolphins. That is a classic Roger move. It was warm and it was, literally, light-hearted. I may have done some innovative things but I've never, ever achieved the lightness of touch and intimacy of his prose, which I think at its best is a wonder.

TERENCE BLACKER What made *Waterlog* so good was that the tug of sadness at the start is always there. But what really amazed me was what a brilliant writer he was. There was a flow in his writing, it had a complete swing to it, immediately. You sense in *Waterlog* a writer who is beginning to feel: this is what I was put on Earth to do. As he goes along, he realises, I have hit my stride. Most of us have a slightly buffed-up version of ourselves in a book but Roger was completely genuine. He wasn't a phoney at all.

MARGOT WADDELL I think he needed to realise his own fantasy of who he was. He was absolutely writing his own story. A friend said, 'It's very beautifully written but he never swims below the surface.' Did he choose not to? I don't think he quite realised that there was a choice.

SERENA INSKIP We all read it and said, 'Where's Roger?' There was a huge gaping hole. There was a lot more to him than that, but he couldn't get it out. It was too frightening. I'm still learning about being frightened out of being yourself in your early years; I can understand that side of him.

JULIA BLACKBURN It's all to do with that escaping from one element to another, whether that's the element of childhood or the element of into the water from out of the day.

*

In some ways, I suspect *Waterlog* may have been a kind of requiem for the long time with Margot. Naturally, there was much sadness – and a long swim turned out to be as good a cure, or coming-to-terms, as any. But I didn't want the book to turn into one of those fashionable tomes where you climb aboard the couch, pour out your heart and various inadequacies to the world, and probably go on about football at the same time.

In the months after *Waterlog*, I lived relatively modestly in a Thoreauish sort of way on something of a shoestring – sawing up logs for exercise, eating muesli and scrumping apples from friends' orchards, driving about in a grubby old Audi, and writing for the *Independent* 'Country and Garden' pages and other journals with 'country' in the title.

Out for a constitutional round the lanes on my bike, I was very nearly mown down by the mobile library. It came too fast round a corner behind me and had to slam the brakes on hard and swerve. I thought of the headline in the *Diss Mercury*: LIBRARY SLAYS LOCAL AUTHOR. Then I imagined the scene inside the van: Tibor Fischer sent flying, Nigella Lawson tumbled into a heap with Bill Clinton, Bill Bryson jammed beneath the clutch pedal.

*

ROGER, *notebooks, 1969* Scott Fitzgerald thinks that men who succeed at twenty ascribe their success to their star shining. Men who succeed at thirty, however, tend to take a more balanced view of fate and the will working together. And men who succeed at fifty ascribe everything to the will.

> '*Writer makes a huge splash*', Diss Mercury, *May 1999* A writer and teacher has made a huge splash with his book about swimming the length and breadth of the UK ... The Mellis man has shot to fame appearing in newspapers, magazines and on television and radio programmes.

Fan mail delivered to Walnut Tree Farm

> 'Roger Deakin, the Moat House, Dis'
> 'Writer, the house with the moat, near Diss, Norfolk or Suffolk'

ROGER, *notebooks, summary of* Waterlog *in the media, 1999* Over fifty reviews and features in the press and more than twenty-five radio interviews. Three-page feature in the *Daily Mail*; *Independent* magazine feature; *BBC Wildlife* magazine six-page colour feature; *The Big Breakfast* on Channel 4, *Sky Book*

Show, *Bookworm* feature with Griff Rhys Jones; Hay-on-Wye, Ways With Words, Edinburgh Festival.

ROGER, *Filofax*, *20 July 1999* W'log sold 3,300 to date (50 a day last week) (7 weeks 472 per wk = 78 per day).

ANGELA KING   He sent me all his press cuttings from book reviews, he was so pleased and proud.

SUE CLIFFORD   He loved it. We all said, 'Oh Roger, we told you you could do it,' and then he'd done it, and he kept on doing it.

JULES CASHFORD   He had a special expression on his face when he said, 'Oh, so and so said such and such.' He'd found his voice and he was amazed and grateful that it rang a bell with everybody. And he'd worked hard enough for it, in obscurity, and so that would answer the longing of the little boy with his mum, finally, to be recognised. But he had worked through that by then and what really mattered was the joy of writing the books. He really loved the writing and he really cared about a sentence.

LUCY BAILEY   I saw him give a talk at the Edinburgh Festival and I felt, oh my God, Roger, this is just where you want to be: to feel like a celebrity. It was really sweet for him to suddenly be a writer and an artist, and to combine it with his love of nature was perfect.

ERICA BURT   I met Roger again in 2000 after he had given a talk at Dartington Hall, and he was ever so concerned that they hadn't written to him to say thank you. What had he done wrong? It surprised me because I thought, oh, come on, you've made it. But he was very worried. Having been a teacher and knowing what we know now, I would say he was definitely on some sort of spectrum. He was easy with people but he could easily fall out. He could be very, very sensitive, and quite insecure.

VICKY MINET   He was always ill at ease, Rog, on some level because he was an outsider. So he really basked in the kudos of the various glitzy social things he did. But actually, it wasn't him at all.

DUDLEY YOUNG   I would enthuse, and say, 'How's the paperback selling?' and blah-de-blah, and then I would do my puritanical number, and say, 'Beware *fama*. Fame is the last infirmity of the noble mind.' That's a famous line from Milton. I never became famous – a lot of it has to do with luck – and I'm very glad I didn't. And I warned Roger about it. I kept saying, 'It's all a load of crap.' It's quite a good book but I didn't become a cheerleader. And so that meant I was envious. Oh come on, man! An inversion took place. He became the big fella and I became the little fella. And I wasn't having that. The last few times I went to Mellis, the computer had taken over; it was big, and it was expensive, and Roger had become a Writer.

CAROLINE CLIFTON-MOGG And what did Dudley want to be?

JULIA BLACKBURN Roger came to all my book launches, and he was much nicer to me than I was to him. He was perplexed by his own apparent success, as nervous as ever but with a slightly different air. Talking to people who organised literary festivals, they'd say, 'Oh my goodness, he was so enthusiastic, he was absolutely the leader of the pack.' He would come with gifts, he would go for supper, he was full-tilt charming. And he had this showman style. He was fascinated by status. He sought the ballast of other people having reputations – of having fame, success, all these funny words – which he wanted to lean on a bit. But that's not malicious; that's a need.

TERENCE BLACKER There's a school of opinion, which I'm not part of, that Roger was a bit of a star-fucker. He liked famous people. He liked the attention that came with *Waterlog* but he didn't become a pain in the arse. If you've been knocked around and suddenly had this success, you don't go bonkers. He probably was a difficult author. But then anyone who's any good is a difficult author.

ANNETTE KOBAK, *writer and partner from 2000 to 2002* Admiration from his peers, whom he hugely valued and respected, was, along with admiration generally, top of his list. And being modest at the same time. These things are quite compatible.

RICHARD MABEY I've always found it slightly distasteful when writers have cults around them, and certainly a cult formed around Roger. He was a bit of a sex god.

JANE TURNBULL People behave so differently when handed sudden unexpected success. Obviously this delight in celebrity was latent in him and he went for it. He loved it. It distracted him from where his real talents lay.

*

ROGER DEAKIN, The Garden, *radio programme* I've got a weakness for scythes because they are such beautiful things and so finely made. The thing about scything is it isn't a sweeping action so much as a drawing action, and you're drawing the blade parallel with the ground; a slicing action. There's also a rhythm to it which is your own rhythm and you lose all of that as soon as you begin to use a machine like a strimmer, and you notice this in terms of the fatigue you feel from using a scythe. The weariness is a very sweet weariness because you've stayed within the rhythms of your own body and mind all the time.

JULIA BLACKBURN Ronnie Blythe is one of the figureheads of Roger's encounters. I was at that time very close to Ronnie and he told me that he thought Roger was the most beautiful man in all the world – Oh! Vision!

One day, Roger bought one of the very best scythes you could get as a present for Ronnie, and he didn't knock on his door. Ronnie came out and there was Roger – whippt, whippt – with the scythe. There you get the theatricality of the man and also his wooing. He wooed everybody, because he wanted steps. He wanted steps to get to wherever it was; I don't think he knew where he wanted to go.

VICKY MINET When he realised that I knew Ronnie, he really wanted to meet him. So I got them together and we had a meal with Colin Ward [the anarchist writer], who is in Roger's allotment film with Ronnie. Roger really admired Ronnie and took him a scythe when he met him for the first time at Ronnie's home. Roger had an absolute reverence for Ronnie, and rightly so. Ronnie is very much the genuine article, raised in the countryside, and he knows what he's talking about more than anybody else. Whereas Ronnie viewed Roger more sort of coolly, I suppose; he wasn't so interested in what Roger was doing.

ROGER, *Filofax*

29 March 1998 Dinner, Ronnie Blythe.
5 June 1999 Introduce Ronnie Blythe at Southwold Literary Festival.
15 August 2000 Vicky and Ronnie for lunch.
29 September 2000 To Ilkley Literary Festival with Ronnie.

In the summer of 2001, I made my way south towards Wormingford from the dentist's, where I'd had the elusive, long-suffering crown fitted properly at last. Few people think of Suffolk as rolling country, but here I was, floating along a ridge high up above the Stour Valley, turning off the road and diving along the familiar bumpy track down a green tunnel of hazel in the deep holloway that follows the contours of a hill to a farmhouse, first down, then up and round past a sprinting rabbit or two, then down again and around one final twist to arrive beneath a row of oaks by an old boarded garage-cum-garden-shed that hasn't actually housed a motor car for decades.

When I arrived at Bottengoms, Ronnie Blythe's old yeoman's house that is much like mine, he was at the gateway, talking to a departing publisher bearing a John Nash painting for the cover of a new edition of one of Ronnie's books. Ronnie gets so many visitors, so many demands on his time. Because he lives alone, people are always inviting him to drinks or dinner after a church service. In the previous two days, he had written a 2,000-word story for a BBC Radio 4 series. An idea had come to him in the vegetable garden and he sat down and wrote the story straight off. He had also rather grudgingly written an introduction to a book of stories by a farmer.

RONALD BLYTHE, '*Word from Wormingford*', The Church Times *(2008)*
[Roger] would arrive unexpectedly, looming into my low rooms, happy and expectant like a dog. Where shall we go? What shall we do?

Ronnie's washing was on the line stretched between a pair of old apple trees, a biscuit tin full of wooden pegs beneath on the lawn. In much of what he does, Ronnie is keeping alive the traditions of ordinary life in Suffolk: hanging out washing with wooden pegs, picking barrows full of plums, not mowing his lawn so much as scything it, walking everywhere or taking buses or trains, and the occasional taxi, not having central heating until a year or two ago, and still warming his house with open wood fires. He is like a one-man folk museum, except that there is nothing in the slightest self-conscious about all this. It is what he is used to doing, and what he likes.

We had tea and Ronnie's home-made cake in the drawing room, with a huge grand piano in one half of it, and an alcove lined with books. When we climbed the clover hill opposite the house we could look across the rolling Suffolk countryside along the border with Essex at a landscape which is substantially unchanged since Constable's time.

RONALD BLYTHE He was a lovely man. We'd go for walks around the countryside around here. I'd tell him about Gainsborough or Constable, local things as it were. We had much in common: the same kind of house, an interest in crafts and the countryside, and also a knowledge of furniture.

Vicky Minet has talked a lot of sense about how Ronnie deliberately limits his life: he doesn't drive a car and hardly ever goes shopping – people do it for him. This is how he is able to write about a sense of place so well. He isn't constantly on the move, as most of us are. He stays put, people come to him, he contemplates the world; has no partner, is solitary but by no means a recluse. He is highly sociable, his emotional life is involved in his friends and he cares very much about them. He combines a breadth of learning and wisdom with a deep innocence and limitless compassion. This is not to say that he can't be acerbic and satirical too.

I promised to coppice a couple of hazels that are blocking the view of the little valley and the hill and planned to visit again in the winter with a triangular bowsaw. Ronnie needed a new scythe blade too, to cut down some of the many nettles, and the ubiquitous horsetails.

ROGER, *notebooks, 2005* James Hamilton-Paterson [the writer and a friend of Ronnie's] coppiced a pair of big hazels, and chainsawed all the dead elder and fallen crack-willow boughs around the ponds below the house when he came over from Italy in his Land Rover in the spring, bringing his chainsaw.

On another visit, I was struck by how Ronnie and Richard Mabey are both priest-like in character: Ronnie preaching sermons; Richard preaching flowers and birds; both wanting to communicate the sacredness of the Earth.

RICHARD MABEY I met Roger through Common Ground but I also met him after working with Terence Blacker in the early 1980s on a short series of proto-nature-writing books for Hutchinson. Terence invited me up to the Waveney Valley one weekend to stay with him and introduced me to Roger again, and Roger took me on my first visit to Redgrave Fen. I thought he was wonderful.

ROGER, *letter to Richard about his new book,* Whistling in the Dark, *1993* I like your descriptions of the nightingales' song very much – as oratory, as having silences, not unlike Kipling. Your description of the 'natural amphitheatres' they seem to seek out, 'serving song' from the baseline of an old tennis court, and the word 'epicentre' stunningly evokes the explosive urgency of the song, and the widening ripple of its immobilising effect . . . It is wildly romantic, beautifully descriptive, and deserves to be as great a success as Beatrice Harrison's 'tinned nightingales'. *Whistling in the Dark,* however, will pose a serious problem to the booksellers. Should they display it under Natural History, Biography, or Popular Song?

RICHARD MABEY, *card, 28 October 1997* Dear Roger, Glad you found the Desert Island on your dial, and that you felt the programme worked. So did I, despite spending a fortnight in a cold sweat writing for it. Alas, am in an inexplicable biochemical low again, so haven't had the energy for much walking. So DO come over when you feel up to it, and we can totter out over a short course together! Love and thanks, Richard.

ROGER, *Filofax, 11 July 2000* Ways With Words, Dartington, 3.30 p.m., event with Richard & Ronnie.

RICHARD MABEY Roger *adored* attention, and played up to it a bit. We did quite a few events together, with Ronnie as well. Roger and I would take trips to Ronnie and go for walks. That was hysterical and also got a bit competitive because Ronnie, when he was on form, was an incredible spontaneous narrator, so wherever you walked he knew every little detail of the landscape – what writer had lived in that house on the hill, what their furniture was like, where the Bury St Edmunds martyrs were killed, what really happened in the Red Barn Murder at Polstead. Roger was quite a talker as well so it became a narrative contest. On one walk, Ronnie fell in the Stour. We got him out. He was quite fit then.

ROGER, *Filofax, 2001*

5 September Richard Mabey, St Andrew's Hospital,
Northamptonshire.
5 November Richard coming to Mellis.

RICHARD MABEY The next significant thing between me and Roger was when I had my bad bout of depression, and felt that it was necessary to leave my home in the Chilterns. My instinct was to come up to East Anglia but I had no kind of preconceptions about where it might be.

ANGELA KING Roger was in awe of Richard and his writing, and when Richard was ill he was terribly concerned. Really upset, and wanted to help him a lot. 'He's one of our best writers and we must do what we can to help him.'

In June 2002, I drove up the M1 to see Richard in St Andrew's Hospital, Northampton, a lovely pale sandstone Palladian house where John Clare lived for years to the end of his life. Richard and I sat in the sun on the terrace and looked out across acres of mown grass and park trees. Big, mature acacias, cedars, sycamores, copper beeches. As we sat there, for two and a half hours, different shifts of birds came and went, feeding on the lawn; first a half-dozen blackbirds, then wood pigeons, then a pair of crows, a wagtail, then magpies. A hen sparrowhawk had been hunting up above too. Later came the rabbits, dozens of them all over the lawns outside the hospital. Richard had watched one roll in the grass on its back like a cat the day before.

FRIEND, *email to Roger, July 2002* I'm sure Rich will love being with you for a few days.

RICHARD MABEY I spent a few weeks living at Roger's, with his wonderful cooking. He made food in the way he made the house – it was improvisation of the highest order – a bit of fish, chickpeas, half a bottle of some obscure Greek wine. So that was huge fun. And we ranged about the country a bit together around here.

I was driving around the area with Roger and we found a sign for a corner of Hartismere Hospital in Eye that does acupuncture, the Complementary Health Centre. On the road sign it had been misspelt as 'Complimentary Medicine'. So we had a hysterical time working on the conversations that you would have with a Complimentary Doctor. 'Oh goodness me, your liver disease is quite admirable.' Silly stuff like that. And of course Roger had more Diss jokes than anybody else. The railway station had been named the Dissjunction. There was Diss Tress, the hairdresser. Roger was eccentrically creative and had this comic warmth.

ROGER, *'Local Disstinctiveness', poem for Richard and Polly, undated*

> Dissappointment: a fixture where neither party turns up.
> Disslocation: selling up in Islington, buying in *au paysan*.
> Dissguise: Range Rover, green wellies and a dog or two.
> Dissorientated: on the train from Liverpool Street.
> Dissengagement: a one-night stand.
> Dissoluble: shoppers in the queue ahead of you.
> Disscombobulation: sexual intercourse.
> Dissinterested: having no interest one way or the other.
> Disspute: a punch-up at the Sun.
> Dissolve: anagrammatic code in local vole-catcher's lingo
> Denoting the aggressive indigenous strain,

Based on the quaint folk-belief that
Voles listen in to human speech.

ROGER, *notebooks, August 2002* I lie here in the shepherd's hut, reading, drifting in and out of consciousness after a fortnight of intense demands, more, three weeks of nursing and cajoling, observing his sudden pains and tensions, offering the solace of apple juice or cups of tea whenever unnamed cravings appeared.

RICHARD MABEY I was much better when I stayed with Roger at Walnut Tree Farm and I was learning to live again properly. He wasn't overtly maternal but he did a lot for me before I got my car back: he drove me around and he cooked for me quite often. Occasionally I cooked for him. At that stage I wasn't really needing to talk about my depression, and he wasn't terribly inclined to talk about his emotions. I never ever witnessed him being depressed about anything. He got angry, quite often, but he never really got down, in my experience.

After staying with Roger, friends found me a little cottage at the edge of Wiveton in north Norfolk. And then Roger came up with a suggestion: he was great friends not just with Terence but with Terence's ex-wife, Caroline Soper, and Roger told me that Caroline needed someone to look after her place and her cats while she was working in London. Living in a sixteenth-century farm-house with three cats was my idea of heaven, so I stayed there for nine months until June 2003, when my partner Polly and I bought a house together close to Roydon Common.

ROGER, *notebooks, 13 February 2003* A sunny, cold but almost springish day. I can't resist pottering outside, re-erecting the rose on props of ash and hazel, burrowing away the ash-cuttings in piles from under the ash arch. Then I cut some firewood with a bowsaw at the bench, then go for a bike ride. I'm climbing the hill on a bend towards Burgate out of Gislingham when Richard Mabey comes up behind me in his jeep and pips the horn. I wave him on, not realising who it is, then stop and talk to him. We're both exploring lanes and pollard trees round Burgate Little Green. Richard sets off down Furzeway and Stonebridge Lane, with his jeep parked by a stunning old ash pollard on the green.

RICHARD MABEY He lost his temper with me once but it was entirely accidental. It showed how short his fuse was. He was out on his bike and I was out in my car driving, I think I was on my way to see him and he wasn't home and I went down the road towards Gislingham and saw Roger on his bike. I slowed down and tooted very softly at him and stayed behind him and he got off and started raging at me before he saw who it was. That's entirely understandable; if I had somebody doing that while I was on a bike I'd probably do the same.

Even though he appeared to live like a hermit, he was contagiously garrulous. We had both been to the Words by the Water literary festival in Cumbria and we visited the Pencil Museum at the site of the Derwent factory in Keswick. Roger would go straight up to anyone who was around, particularly the women, and say, 'Hello, what are you doing? How do you enjoy your job?' He was like a sort of agreeable census-taker wherever he went – demanding, in the friendliest of ways, wanting to engage with total strangers. I think that was significant.

ROGER, *notebooks, March 2003* I wake up from a wonderful wet dream of the lovely girl on the Schumacher course. I almost feel I should write and thank her. I wake at eight having blissfully slept past 5.45 a.m., the moment I was awoken these past two days by the sudden boom of RM's TV set through the hotel bedroom wall. He doesn't sleep for long, and must be far too fidgety to lie in bed awake for a single moment.

*

JOHN BAYLEY, *advertising colleague from 1974* I can still remember his voice.

SUE CARR-HILL, *friend from schooldays* The thing that I remember most is his voice. He had a very interesting voice. He was one of those people with a laugh in their voice when they are talking. You never forget it.

VIVA ROWLAND, *friend* His voice gave you a sense of stability and peace and quietness; an awareness; which is how he captivated people.

ANNETTE KOBAK He had a most beautiful radio voice.

SUE CLIFFORD He had a lovely voice. Apart from his little cough. There'd always be an urggh-urrgh and he'd get into this little routine of clearing his throat that didn't need clearing.

ROON HUTTON He had the most awful nervous cough. 'Huh-huh-ahum, ahumm, harrumph.'

JULIA BLACKBURN He had this extraordinary tension about him which came out when he was talking. Except on his radio programmes you don't hear it at all. He's so relaxed.

JULES WILKINSON I read a small article about Roger swimming around Britain before *Waterlog* was published. He sounded so interesting that I tracked him down to Mellis. Straight away I thought it would be great to get him on the radio. We started plotting radio series including one of him swimming with people and talking as he swam, and the commissioning editors rejected it. At that time, wild swimming was seen as the preserve of crazy eccentrics and Ironmen. So I tried to do it by stealth.

He loved the radio and was very keen. His voice was soft and very mellifluous and his descriptions were so vivid. His accent was not RP but sort of *Boy's Own*, up for an adventure; very open, a real curiosity. He had a lovely laugh, he was fantastic on location – brilliant at standing in a chalk stream and talking – and his years in advertising gave him a sense of what was wanted, and he didn't mind being chopped up or edited. Listening to him on the radio feels like it is just you and him, and that's how he conducted his friendships as well.

I got him on to the radio talking about the night sky and on to a programme called *The Charm of Birds*, talking about the natural world. Then I left the BBC but he was now on the radar of the BBC's Natural History Unit in Bristol.

In April 2003, Sarah Blunt came over from the BBC Natural History Unit in Bristol to record sounds in my house – the squeal of the bathroom cold-water tap, the complaint of the bedroom door hinges. But the warbler which sang by the moat in the mornings had fallen silent. Sarah came again in June, at 4 a.m., to catch the dawn chorus. It was amazing to hear it through the ultra-super-sensitive, boffin-class recorder and headphones. Sarah took the recorder into the meadows amongst the grasshoppers and bees, even recording the wing-flaps of a passing butterfly. And instead of strimmers or lawnmowers as noises off, snatches of a recorder being played by one of the neighbouring children were occasionally audible on the breeze. Millie, my cat, killed a red-legged partridge and I was most distressed. It was deeply embarrassing. After tea, I slept for half an hour of complete bliss in the railway wagon, an ash tree sweeping its branches back and forth across the roof like the sound of waves. A sea of long grass, ox-eye daisies and a cooing of wood pigeons.

SARAH BLUNT I met Roger at a meeting with Jules Wilkinson and first went to his home with the sound recordist Chris Watson to interview him for a programme called *Tranquillity*. He swam in his moat and talked about the healing quality of being in water, relating it to being back in the womb. He was deeply in touch with the natural world around him. I gave Roger a recorder to do self-recorded pieces, which is commonplace now but was unusual then, and I visited him twice to record sounds for *The House*. I was struck by how it creaked, and I went around all the rooms and shook the windows, flushed toilets, put plugs in and out of baths, and went up the stairs. He talked about it being like a ship and it was. If you have a ship in a storm and you're inside that ship, you're in this safe bubble. And it was this safe place.

ROGER DEAKIN, The House, *BBC radio programme, 2004* The whole house seems to sigh. You feel that you're living inside a great beast, it's like living inside the skeleton of a whale, or something like that.

SARAH BLUNT When I recorded him for *The House* it was interesting how he spoke. He would say things and then, because he was a writer and so aware of words, he'd correct himself, honing and refining his sentences. You heard this writer thinking very carefully about the words he wanted to use. I found that fascinating, hearing someone thinking and finding their words. I kept a little of that quite subtly in the programme. He wasn't very happy with that. He wanted the last take; he didn't want that thinking. After that, with the second programme, *The Garden*, I was careful not to put those earlier takes in.

ROGER DEAKIN, The House You can hear the owls right across the county. They're calling from wood to wood across the fields. The Thornham owls calling to the Gislingham owls and they're calling to the Rickinghall owls and the Botesdale owls and the Redgrave owls, and across the fen and out into Breckland and up the Peddars Way all the way to the north Norfolk coast, I expect. It must be a terrifying night to be a mouse or a vole or a shrew, and I'm lucky to be a human [chuckle] and lying in bed snug and safe.

*

ROGER DEAKIN, Cigarette on the Waveney, *BBC radio programme, 2005* Across the meadow, there's a favourite place for puffballs, giant puffballs, to grow. Sometimes there are so many of them they look like the rows of the bare bottoms of swimmers getting changed [a music-hall comedic pause]. Great. Big. Puffballs.

LUCY MOY-THOMAS When I sold my house in Walberswick, I had nowhere to put my stuff and I asked Roger if I could put some things in his great big barn. One of them was a canoe, which really belonged to my friends, the Ropers. So that beautiful bit of recording on the Waveney – that was that canoe, and I never got it back afterwards, and absolutely no credit, no thanks, no nothing.

SARAH BLUNT For *Cigarette on the Waveney*, Roger went downriver in his canoe, called *Cigarette*. It was in his shed. Unfortunately, we went to retrieve it and discovered it had a rather large hole. Various things had nested in it. So we had to hire an enormous canoe instead that was large enough for the both of us. I sat in front, and Roger sat behind. He had a mic on him, so I could record him without looking at him, and we both paddled. He had this very distinctive voice, very warm, and very rich. He could be very serious but it was wonderful when he found something to laugh about.

A colleague drove us in a van to one spot and we would paddle downstream. We had to lie down in the canoe to go under low bridges and paddle really fast so we wouldn't get stuck in the shallows. There was wire fencing across the river at one point, hissy swans, weirs and a lively field of very young heifers. I'm not very good with cattle and I was very nervous.

ROGER DEAKIN, Cigarette on the Waveney I'm now being followed by a small herd of cows, inquisitive cows, or rather probably incredibly bored cows. Nothing much happens in the life of a cow, grazing beside the river. I suppose this is a bit of a major event. And are they excited. Goodness me, they can hardly contain themselves. They are actually skipping with excitement [laughing]. It's all right, girls, it's not that exciting. Cows in the sunset going completely bananas, skipping and prancing with the sheer joy of our encounter. Hello, girls [laughs again]. Sorry, it's just me and *Cigarette* taking a spin down the river.

SARAH BLUNT We did it over three days. On two nights we took Roger home but on one night he wanted to camp out so we left him in his tent in a field by the river. There was humour but iron and steel as well about what he wanted. I loved what he wrote, so I would give him as much rope as I could. The programmes had an amazing reception, from both commissioning editors and audiences, and there would have been more. It's one voice talking to you and opening up. He's got a very special way of giving you that insight because it's all done through his passion for the natural world. He doesn't tell you about himself but you get an insight into the man through what he tells you he's doing.

ROGER DEAKIN, Cigarette on the Waveney It's quite a strange feeling approaching the end of a canoe voyage because you've been in this entirely different world for quite a while, and you've been in a different dimension of time. You've gone native. Stevenson said, it's a form of meditation. Your self does go somewhere else.

*

JANE TURNBULL *Waterlog* got very wide coverage and did very well. Everyone was saying what are you going to do next? He did get *folie de grandeur* when he was on telly a bit. He saw himself as the new David Attenborough but younger and more attractive. He left me after *Waterlog* because he wanted TV and he went off to Georgina Capel who had been my assistant when I was a publisher.

ROGER, *Filofax, 21 February 2001* Meeting with Georgina Capel.

GEORGINA CAPEL, *literary agent* Moving from Jane to me was obviously very painful for everybody. When Roger first came and sat on my sofa and said would I take him on, I said, 'I don't know whether I can,' because I had worked with Jane. We had a back-and-forth of me feeling pathetically guilty and then thinking, of course, I've got to take it on.

JANE TURNBULL In March 2001, I took him out to lunch to talk about the future. I remember saying, it's time for a biography of a place and I think you should write the story of Walnut Tree Farm and your long love affair with it. Gilbert White meant most to him and I always felt that Roger's talent was very similar. He had that empathy for very small things.

ROGER, *letter to Jane Turnbull, 13 March 2001* It was good to see you for lunch. I have since been thinking hard about our conversation and what I should do next. You will appreciate that I find myself at a turning point in my career where I feel I could either go up or down. Having put so much into *Waterlog* for relatively little financial return, I simply have to take a hard commercial look at where I am going and what will be best for me in both short and long term. I have a livelihood to make and it is vital that I realise the potential everybody keeps telling me about, but which is far from evident in my bank balance . . . After much thought and anguish I have decided that were I to enter discussions with any other agent without having first left you, my position, and yours too, would be invidious and uncomfortable, so I think it best to leave you first in order to be free to move on.

JANE TURNBULL I thought it was a weaselly letter. It wasn't very brave and I didn't like that.

BRIAN PERMAN He suddenly decided that he was such an important talent that he needed a bigger and better agent. That really pissed me off. There weren't better agents than Jane at the time. It was not to do with business – it was to do with loyalty. I wrote to him and told him he was making a big mistake. I'm sad that I was never reconciled with Roger after we had this falling-out. I shouldn't have sent that letter. Roger was hurt by it. I think he genuinely believed we would say, 'Absolutely, Roger, you're in the big time now and you need a big-time agent.'

CHAPTER 14

The Heartbroken

Walnut Tree Farm in the early 2000s – Errollyn Wallen – Peter Pan in the family –
falling for Annette Kobak – the Psychoanalytic Train to Ukraine and
Poland – adventures with Robert Macfarlane – 'a classic strong, healthy and lovely
quite broad size 8 with a very high instep' – Green Shoes and Alison Hastie

ROGER, *notebooks, 2002* Tony Weston showed me a new poem and gave me a mug. The poem, 'Brides and Grooms', is about being married for forty years. What an amazing thought.

ROGER, *quotes collected in his notebooks, 2003*

A. W. Schlegel and Otto Rank After all, poets are always Narcissi.
Oscar Wilde 'I wish I could love,' cried Dorian Gray. 'But I seem to have lost the passion, and forgotten the desire. I am too much concentrated in myself. My own personality has become a burden to me. I want to escape, to go away, to forget.'
Vladimir Nabokov Everything in the world is beautiful, but Man only recognises beauty if he sees it either seldom or from afar.

JAYNE IVIMEY, *letter to Roger, June 1997* You by your nature (which I love and in NO way criticise) give so much gold to so many people that you would find it hard to have enough left for one person, because you thrive on the browsing. You have such a range of relationship possibilities, more than anyone I know!

JAYNE IVIMEY Roger couldn't let go of people and needed support of many kinds. He was like a collector with a kaleidoscope, every turn of the scope revealing someone that interested him.

While the rest of the world has been playing musical chairs all around me, I have stayed put in the same house for more than half my life. It's not that I don't like to wander, but somehow I feel easier in my freewheeling knowing that this place is here, a fixed point. I am located by it, as Donne's lovers are the twin points of compasses in his poem 'A Valediction, Forbidding Mourning':

> Thy firmness draws my circle just,
> And makes me end where I begun.

You reach Walnut Tree Farm across the common, a great inland sea of rippling grasses that rises like a tide towards haymaking in July. When I first saw it, I thought it must be a fantasy, a form of East Anglian mirage, and I still do. Its grip on reality, its relation to the rest of the world, remains tenuous at best.

Crossing the moat on my return here, and making my way past the ash and the walnut that throw shade, algae and mosses on to the roof, and dam the rainwater gutters with composting leaves, I approach the house past a little concrete frog and a squirrel, which I had when I was a boy. One of the frog's glass eyes has dropped out. They are called Frog and Squirrel.

Everybody comes in through the kitchen door which faces south, towards the rear moat. You step on to the herringbone brick floors that run throughout the house. I may be the last man in Suffolk without central heating and so inside everything revolves around the Aga. It is always warm in the kitchen. I still burn oil in my Aga, which heats my water, cooks my breakfast and dinner, and it exudes an agreeably maternal air of comfort and goodwill. On the rare occasions when it goes out I feel bereft and, somehow, unloved. Clearly it is standing in for all sorts of other needs besides the purely practical.

I have lived with other creatures ever since my Cosy Cabin filled with slow-worms was my refuge in childhood. My home is probably another version of that cabin. Toads, frogs, snails, bumblebees, wasps; they all enter my house, and are observed and then helped outside once again. I don't get rid of spiders, or their webs, out of respect. These are my friends. They patiently weave these impressive structures and it seems wantonly destructive to remove them. They are very beautiful when they catch the light and much more interesting than having bits of flypaper dangling around.

JULIA BLACKBURN Everything in the house had a talismanic quality. He had his own psychological and physical history in objects and his safety was there in the objects too. They were anchoring. The house as an extension of who he was. 'I am the house. The house is me.'

JULES CASHFORD He attended to every small thing. That's what I liked so much about him. He'd see things that you might not notice, and he'd care for them and his heart widened. And everyone had a place in this farmhouse. Everyone being – animals, insects, bees, wasps and woodworm; everything.

RICHARD COOK There were these disconnected things in his life but the inside and outside were not disconnected in Mellis. The normal division between inside and outside was not there. It was certainly living with nature and that clearly was the thing that mattered to Roger.

VIVA ROWLAND His house was beautiful but it was also completely filthy. There were things growing out of the fridge. He was quite often ill with stomach upsets – it was the food that was off. We stayed there a lot, and being the German housewife I am, I thought, I'll wash the curtains and clean a bit and tidy.

GARY ROWLAND She killed all his friends, the spiders.

VIVA ROWLAND And he went mad. But he could also have arguments with me because ultimately he respected me. He had an incredible warmth as a person.

RAMONA KOVAL, *friend* It was bonkers. There was no animal that wasn't allowed in if it wanted to be inside. It was a complete mess but apparently everything had to be where it was; you couldn't move anything. There was stuff everywhere, things he collected, things hanging, and cobwebs. It was fantastic, it was eccentric, it was funny. And we'd have afternoon teas and people would come. It was lovely. He was lovely.

My twelve acres are a little bit of old Suffolk, the hedgerows and trees conforming to ancient maps. Each of my four meadows is like a room, enclosed by the tallness of my near-mile of hedgerows. This is one very good reason for not assiduously laying every inch of them: I would be like the man painting the Forth Bridge.

The fields, the wood, the house and the cabin are all one in my mind. So are the workshop, the barn and shepherd's hut. In the lee of a south-facing hedge and a big ash is my hut, perched on iron wheels. It was made in about 1920 and inside is a simple chair and table where I often write. There are oil lamps and candles, sun-faded curtains, and a wooden bed with a space underneath where sheepdogs and orphan lambs would once have curled. Here, I sleep coffined in grainy pine, knots like boulders standing up in the riverflow of the sap. Lines of grain ripple and eddy from the eye of each knot.

Above my head, the hut has a barrelled roof of corrugated tin and, inside, a wooden boarded roof like a pine tent. When it rains, the whole vessel responds with a tattoo. Sleep through that, and you could still be woken early by magpies clattering along the corrugated rooftop like Cajun washboard-players.

The open door frames a wall of green: the hawthorn hedge, ash, nettles, graceful flowers of grass all sway in the hot breeze. Dust-mites flicker and drift in the window-light. Cows low in the distance across the common.

RICHARD MABEY, Nature Cure *(2005)* Roger is a true commoner, not just by dint of living on a common, but just, I think, by living. If it wasn't so pretentious I suspect he would put it down as his occupation. His life is suffused by the belief that, with ingenuity and a bit of respectful give-and-take towards fellow dwellers, anyone can do anything, in almost any company. Thirty years ago he rebuilt a derelict sixteenth-century farmhouse from scratch, learning everything from timber-hewing to plumbing as he went along. Now the farm is like a surreal Arcadia: fields being teased back into meadowland, patches of new woodland (but many of the trees in rings not rows), barns full of corrugated iron and turned wood, found stones, the cockpit of a Canberra bomber, home-grown David Nash-style ash sculptures, graveyards of old Citroëns, vegetable patches and tree nurseries round the remains of an abandoned wood-mill ('the weeds help keep the roots moist'), converted shepherds' huts for sleeping in when the weather is too hot, and just in case the morning moat-crawl seems too forbidding, an outside bath. Roger is a believer in the layered life. Confront him with a group of leylandii conifers, say, and his first instinct would not be to incinerate them, but to cover them with roses. He tacks round problems, almost always choosing the long, and therefore most eventful, way round.

ROGER, *notebooks, August 2003* Richard Mabey appears unannounced in the morning with Rowena Dugdale from *BBC Wildlife* magazine. I give them tea, then show Rowena around the fields. We visit a giant puffball at the far end of the Long Meadow. On the way back I show Rowena the inside of the shepherd's hut. 'Lucky you're chaperoned,' says Richard.

LUCY MOY-THOMAS I can remember an evening sitting in his house and we were about to eat and he had a guitar leaning against the wall and there was a lovely thing that the strings vibrated with his voice in that space. That was wonderful, and the house was wonderful. There were a series of semi-abandoned love-nests – to put it politely – dotted around his small estate.

AN ADMIRER, *card to Roger, 2005* Your domain is completely magical: the roses; wild flowers; ramshackle overgrown cars; beautiful trees; meadows; woods; moat; damselflies; fierce cat, sweet cat, stone collection, antique bath-room taps, and BEST OF ALL the little house on wheels in the field! How I'd love to sleep in that!! You are very lucky and very special. PS. I'm also deeply impressed with your culinary skills . . . delicious apple pie, perfectly al dente asparagus and no slugs in my lettuce. Heaven! Xx

LUCY BAILEY You couldn't help but be . . . enchanted is too soppy a word. I fell in love with Walnut Tree Farm. I fell in love with that space that was Roger.

ANDREW CRACKNELL I always thought that Walnut Tree Farm was unbeliev-ably seductive.

*

I also have a railway wagon, which I hauled on to one of my fields years ago. Working or sleeping in my railway wagon is like embarking on a journey. When I light the candles in the three Moroccan lanterns, I think of something the artist Roger Ackling said to me, quoting Thoreau: 'Electricity kills darkness, candlelight illuminates it.'

JAYNE IVIMEY Roger went to visit an artist friend of mine called Roger Ackling on a research trip. When I met my friend again he said, 'Yeah, Roger's a funny bloke, he made me feel as though I was his best friend and we had SO much in common and I never saw him again.' Roger was a magpie. He also had no boundaries, which is a characteristic that usually only children have. If he saw something interesting, he wanted it, and he was going to have it.

Slowly being swallowed by the billowing hedges of bramble and blackthorn are an old green truck in which I once took the sixth-formers of Diss Grammar on impromptu school trips and my two Citroën Safaris. These old machines are like the cast-off skin of a dragonfly. Each time I cast one off I emerged into a new existence, armoured in a gleaming new car. People are fond of saying my car looks like a compost heap – well, these cars are compost heaps.

A FRIEND He always had these Citroën cars. Walnut Tree Farm was littered with them. He couldn't be arsed to get rid of them but he'd turn it into a romantic story that they were where chickens could live. He could turn something into fantasy and an amazing story that people would be utterly charmed with.

BOB MARSHALL-ANDREWS Tony Barrell used to call it the Safari Park. The truth is that it turned into a bit of a rural slum.

*

ROGER, *Filofax, 25 May 1998* 1 yr since E and I got together!

TONY AXON That relationship fell over, sadly. She would've done Roger a lot of good.

BEN BARKER-BENFIELD I was the same age as Roger was and you run into someone like Errollyn – Jesus Christ, you're a lucky person.

JAYNE IVIMEY Errollyn was amazing. They were all such lovely women, but having an intense relationship with Roger would have been a nightmare.

VICKY MINET He admired Errollyn as a composer immensely. And so she was 'incredible'. She was very much a London person and not a country person at all. I couldn't see where the connection was other than the fact that Roger really really admired her and thought she was amazing.

ROGER, *letter to Errollyn, undated* I love the sound of your piano coming through my door when we are both working. I love the mysterious scrawl of your music, and the proud way you show it to me, and how you enjoy the visual delight of the notes on the page . . . And of course I love your songs, and the music that pours forth from you, the notes that tumble on to the page, the beautiful, tentative, unfolding of things. The faith you have that it is in the air, in your generous heart.

ROGER, *Filofax, June 1998*

Saturday 20 Wedding, 3 p.m. Miserable! Stroppy message from E.
Sunday 21 Miserable!
Monday 22 Miserable! Wrote to E.
Tuesday 23 Miserable! Telephoned E. – v. unfriendly. Work – useless.
Wednesday 24 Miserable!
Thursday 25 Wrote again to E. Miserable! Work dragging desperately.

ROGER, *letter to Errollyn, undated* I am miserable without you. I am eating myself up, having myself for breakfast, lunch and tea. I have been observing a tiny fruit fly, how it wanders in the air so gracefully like a person in an art gallery, and how it finds its way by tiny olfactory antennae to the very place I knew it would: the rim of my empty red-wine glass. How I identify with that little fruit fly because you are the red wine in the glass. That rim, that minuscule drop of wine, is where the fly must be; what it is put on the good Earth for. Nothing else interests it in the slightest, yet it doesn't make a beeline for the wine. It is far too subtle and sensitive for that . . . And yet. It has a purpose. And one of its purposes is to show that purpose doesn't have to go in a straight line. True purpose moves in mysterious ways and doesn't necessarily declare itself straight off, like a rocket does. Its trajectory is much more like an arrow, like the shafts soaring off skywards at Agincourt, then raining down to find their mark in unexpected ways. I'm trying to say that I'm always the fruit fly or the Agincourt arrow where you're concerned.

ROGER, *Filofax, Sunday 28* Lunch – Errollyn at Le Pont de la Tour.

> LUCY BAILEY It was like Don Quixote and Sancho Panza. They were both wonderful people but very different. Roger had an artistic temperament, slightly neurotic, and he could be a very worried person. There was a spoilt child in him sometimes. He could have tantrums. My feeling is that happened with Errollyn a few times.

*

ROGER, *notes for a memorial tribute to his cousin, Adrian Turton, 1999* One theory about Adrian – that he was a complete Peter Pan. He was never out of shorts, refused to get out of them, refused to grow up. He was about to reach fifty. To him, growing up meant death. Why? The idea of being forever young is very prevalent in our family. Vi wanted to be forever young. Laddie did (note name). My mother did. Margaret did. So did I. The need to be young equals immortal, equals a fear of death.

> JANE TURNBULL Roger was one of those Peter Pan men. He was extraordinarily attractive if you felt your life was a bit humdrum and a bit staid. At that moment, Roger would say, 'I'm going to go off in a campervan and see the sun rise.' Boyish charm was his absolute go-to mode and he was very charming. He looked like a marvellous proposition. The fact he went from relationship to relationship was quite odd from the outside but you can see you would have been suffocated.

> A LOVER At the beginning we had a very hot sexual relationship but then we became like brother and sister. And I'd lie with him in bed in a purely platonic way and we'd talk for hours on end and then we'd go out for a walk. The bedroom smelled of apples in the autumn, it was so romantic. It was what I needed. I needed comfort, I didn't want the tangled stuff that he was having to go through. And he also needed comforting too.

*

ROGER, *Filofax, 7 June 2000* 6–8 p.m. Society of Authors party.

> ANNETTE KOBAK I met Roger in the sixties when he came for dinner with my friend Philippa Fox-Robinson at the flat we shared. I had ordered a brass bed

from a barn in the Cambridgeshire countryside and very typically for Roger he said, 'I've got a van, I can pick up the bed.' He brought it to London. He had that mass of curly hair, a big smile and was always very eager to help. I think probably Roger thought this true – he got more attractive in looks and character as he got older, and we didn't connect in a romantic way at that stage because I was engaged to Reg Gadney. When Roger and I did connect, we really did, and it was quite a romance for both of us.

It was 2000 and I came to London after our children had left home and I had split from Reg. I could see that the Thames was opening up and I bought a tiny flat in Borough. In June, I met Roger at the Society of Authors party. He'd come back from Australia and he looked haunted, haggard and grey. And then we got to know each other very fast. Looking back, we were madly in love. I'd never said 'madly' about anybody, but there was something in that. It was lovely for both of us because it always is, that falling-in-love thing, particularly at that age.

ROGER, *notebooks, June 2000* Last Friday at a fish restaurant with Annette Kobak in Bermondsey, an interesting conversation about being an 'only one'; only child. It makes you into someone who chairs everything, in order to control things, because you never learned from siblings about relaxing into give and take, rolling with the punches. A. has dreamy eyes and lovely straight fair hair, and slender, elegant ways, and a deep, almost husky Czechoslovakian voice.

ANDREW SANDERS When Annette appeared on the scene, Roger was very excited because she had been this unattainable person when he was a student at Cambridge.

ROGER, *poem, 2000*

Are Such Things Possible?

This is how it is
A pair of tousled napkins on a blue tablecloth
Your white nightie, my white shirt
warm themselves before the Aga.

This is how it is
Lying side by side with you
I write love-letters in my head:

Dear Annette, I have never been so serious
or so light-hearted
scarcely needing to breathe
reading a lullaby of Eric Rolls
spouting dour old R. S. Thomas at dead of night:
'One night of tempest I arose and went
Along the Menai shore on dreaming bent.'

'A plaintive wren,' you say,
its querulous tiny overture
threading like thin silk through the dark.
A moorhen, then blackbird, first notes,
'We are singing the birds awake.'

Too wide-eyed with longing
cells won't lie down.
I gaze into the bedroom black
watching you at work in a world of green,
netting weed.

This is how it is
Red deer surprise us on our bikes
hurdling nonchalantly off
like two champagne corks
over rows of corn.
Deer dreaming in long-ploughed Suffolk.

This is how it is
Swimming through rain
living on air
just-touching eyes, lips, noses, fingertips, we're acrobats
trapezing to the zenith of two upward swings
across a circus tent, everyone breathless,
no safety net.

Perhaps, since you bumped your head on a beam,
all this is a dream.
Did we run with the stunned hare

headlong into each other's headlights?
Something or other must have
knocked us both for six.

This morning rain falls on the sunlit garden
from a clear pool of sky.
It slaps the mulberry leaves,
Tattoos the moat
As we dot-paint each other
lightly with our lips,
Sketching outlines to which we will return
and flood the ochre in.

Are such things possible?

*

ANNETTE KOBAK I'm astonished that we actually kept a relationship going. He was very tolerant because at the time I didn't have proper income, I was freelance and reviewing books for the *TLS* and the *New York Times*. There was an awful lot on for both of us.

I'd written a biography of Isabelle Eberhardt and when we met we were both agonising over new book projects. He was thinking, should he do something on wood or something on parks? I was stuck on *Joe's War*, a memoir about my father, who was born on the border of Czechoslovakia and Poland, and fled from the Nazis and then the Soviets at the start of the Second World War. It was a mark of Roger's generosity that he said, 'Why don't you go on this journey through the Carpathians in the footsteps of your father?' and it was interesting to him as well. In March 2001, we both went to the Ukraine and Poland. That journey was jolly difficult, it was really quite grim, but it was a big gift that each of us gave to the other.

ROGER, *Filofax*, *14 March 2001* Go to Prague; on to Lviv, Ukraine.

Prague railway station, like the rest of the night city, appeared to be lit by a single forty-watt bulb. It may have helped create atmosphere, but not when you're struggling to read a railway ticket with your reservation details in Czech. Prolonged scrutiny with the tiny Maglite I learned to carry in Eastern

Europe revealed our sleeping car was number 315 and we clambered up the steep iron steps and tumbled into our home for the next twenty-four hours clutching a bottle of Mikulovsky Muller Bohemian white wine bought on the platform.

We had a compartment to ourselves, and explored it much as you would try out a new Swiss army knife. Everything folded or slid away and, yes, you could get two people into one bunk, but it was a squeeze. We drew the net curtains, turned on the bedside reading lamps, poured out the wine and trundled through the blackness towards the Carpathian Mountains.

Later, lying on our backs in our separate bunks like knights in effigy on tombs in Westminster Abbey, we drifted into sleep as we swayed wildly round sharp bends, climbing steadily into the Tatra Mountains. Sleeping in a train at night is extraordinarily like swimming. The train teases you by first lulling you to sleep then, as you're dozing off, jolting you awake in a sudden lurch and a crashing and jarring of the bogeys beneath.

Woken again, and talking into the night, Annette and I hit on the idea of the Psychoanalytic Train. It would begin in Vienna, of course, and head east through Slovakia and the Ukraine all the way to Odessa and the Caspian Sea. It would be full of patients and analysts lying parallel in their bunks, one above the other, their subconscious fantasies freed by the heartbeat of the wheels, the rhythmic passing of telegraph poles, and occasional plunges into uterine tunnels.

After staying in Lviv in western Ukraine, we took an afternoon train to the Polish border and then a bus to the remote hamlet of Ustianowa. This was where Annette's father had left the train from Lviv during his flight to rejoin his parents in his home village of Baligród across the border in Poland at the outbreak of war. He had been studying in Lviv and found himself cut off from his family with no passport. The eighteen-year-old student risked his life by walking home across country, travelling by night to escape detection by patrolling guards. Annette's idea was that we should walk the same fifteen miles in her father's footsteps.

ANNETTE KOBAK, Joe's War *(2004)* On our walking map for this part of the Bieszczady Mountains, we've highlighted the tracks we need to follow across the hills, and our path takes us down into the valley and up the road we've seen from the station. Roger's only concern is possible encounters with wild dogs, having seen the whites of their eyes in the Romanian mountains a while ago, so he looks out for fallen hazel branches and whittles them into dog-fencing staves with a penknife bought in Lviv. My concern is about finding a bed for the night.

We crossed a rivulet and, hearing farmyard dogs, paused in the hedgerow to cut a pair of stout hazel walking sticks to defend ourselves against their inevitable attentions. Dogs are the one universal annoyance to walkers all over Central and Eastern Europe. The best defence against them is to cut a stick just over four feet long and point it like a magic wand at any animal that threatens you. In a firm, unquavering voice, you should also issue instructions along the lines of 'Down, Rover, and jolly well keep your distance.'

ANNETTE KOBAK, *early draft of* Joe's War The track is long and uphill and it's getting dark. We've been walking for seven hours, with backpacks. There are still no lights or signs of life anywhere to be seen in the hills all around. Once we reach the top of this hill, we shall know if Baligród lies the other side or not. If it doesn't, we shall have to go back to the hateful church, and I may abscond. In spite of the endorphins stimulated by the sheer walking, it's been hard-going today and Roger manfully (used with full feminist awareness, and still used) insists on carrying my backpack as well as his own for this part of the journey. I'm not sure I could have done this last leg without that. As we breast the top of the hill in darkness, we look down and see a brilliant sight: the twinkling lights of Baligród some two miles away down below. It's a great moment.

*

ANNETTE KOBAK There was a clear end to the total involvement with each other. I had a lot of claims on my attention at that time. Roger didn't have family around and I did in spades – I was going to Australia practically every year to see my parents; I had my children, and then grandchildren, and *Joe's War* to write. There were certain parts of Roger which overlapped hugely – I loved the countryside too – but although I was very much involved in the sixties, I'd never bought the whole hippy thing. That wasn't quite me.

He was very attached to friendship, and his friends, and he had very, very good ones. But they were necessary pals, like a soldier. He relied on them a lot. Roger had this writer friend, Ramona Koval, come over from Australia and stay with him for three weeks while we were technically in the middle of our big love affair and he didn't really tell me. He held a party for his friends at Walnut Tree Farm and I drove Richard Mabey up there, not knowing what I was going into. She wasn't a girlfriend – Roger said, 'No no, not at all' – but it was kind of juvenile, stupid and humiliating, and it was a question of trust. In my mind, I left the relationship at a hundred miles an hour.

I'm not a confining type of person. I walked myself to school from the age of four so it's not in my nature to be confining. Roger had a real, absolute compulsion to get out of boundaries. Compulsion is a silly word because it's a lovely thing, it's glorious, and that was 95 per cent of his charm – his terrific urge to meld with countryside. And having an open house was part of this psychological impulse, part of what was very good in him. An open house was absolutely a prerequisite for him, and that was true to a degree which I haven't seen in anybody else of our generation.

RAMONA KOVAL Annette didn't like me being his friend and she was suspicious. On one of my trips to Britain, Roger picked me up from Heathrow and took me to Walnut Tree Farm. You know how long it takes to get from Melbourne to London, and in economy? You're completely fucked when you get there. And Roger said, 'We've got people coming to dinner tonight and I would like you to cook borscht.' I once wrote a Jewish cookbook and gave it to him, so he had everything I needed and I made this fantastic pot of borscht. There were loads of people there, it was a great big table, I was beyond hysterical because I was so tired and I sat next to Ronald Blythe. Was he about ninety? He was gorgeous, he was flirtatious, he was charming, and we had the best time. I didn't even say very much to Roger. I must've slept till about 11 a.m., and Annette had already left and they'd had an argument. Roger said that she was really upset that I had made borscht. He set me up and he didn't realise it – I don't think he had a very sophisticated understanding of the human condition.

ROGER, *notebooks, August 2002* Racked by anxiety all night, waking at 4 a.m, with a pain in my right wrist, as in the Hank Wangford song, and thinking about cancer. Yesterday I posted off Annette's glasses in a Jiffy bag, feeling very sad: 'Here are your glasses, mine are full of tears.' Better to have said, 'Here's a dry pair; mine are very wet today.' It is 4 p.m. and the sunshine slants into the wooden hull of the hut, and I lie alone on this bed where I might have made love to Annette in kindlier times. Now there are too many pillows. An emperor dragonfly soars and dives about amongst the nettletops outside. At night, the crickets have begun their song in the field.

I dreamed as I slept in the shepherd's hut of a pair of beautiful great northern divers, and I had a gun and impulsively fired, and immediately wished I hadn't. I watched the pair of birds wheel on across the sky, desperately hoping I hadn't damaged them, but I knew I had hit one, and sure enough it faltered and fell out of the sky and its mate landed too, and the wounded bird hobbled along, dragging a wing pathetically, and I felt deep dread, and guilt, and sorrow, like the Ancient Mariner. I woke with a deep feeling of anguish, and felt convinced that the lovely bird represented Annette, and that I had wounded her dreadfully – as I do feel, but don't know what to do, because she keeps on wounding me too, so we both end up feeling winged and hobbling through life like the bird in the dream.

*

ROBERT MACFARLANE He blew into my life like a storm. He was a huge shaping force for my books, as a way of seeing the world and being in the world. I read *Waterlog* in 2000; he was part of my enchantment of the British landscape before I met him. I asked for Roger to be sent proofs of *Mountains of the Mind* [Robert's first book, published in 2003] and met him when I was in the audience for a talk he gave at Waterstones in Cambridge. He'd been in the Cam and he squelched as he came on stage.

ROBERT MACFARLANE, *email to Roger, April 2004* Thank you so much for your unstintingly generous, miraculously unterritorial, and unfailingly sensitive help with the 'British Wild' book [which became *The Wild Places*]. Several moments and angles in that proposal would, as you will have seen, never have existed without your help and intelligence.

ROBERT MACFARLANE He was such a huge part of my imagination and horizons at that time. How did we become such good friends so quickly in such a short period? We probably only saw each other maybe twenty times. I was in my late twenties and he was the great senior partner. I remember being amazed and touched that he would trust me to talk about things with him. I didn't want to fuss him too much and felt quite a bit like 'Why did he want to be my friend?' He was everybody's friend.

JULIA BLACKBURN It was like a Greek ideal of the older man and the younger man, striding hand and hand into the Walt Whitman sunset.

BUNDLE WESTON I don't think it was a father–son, it was a meeting of equals, but in view of the age difference, Rob would've been the perfect boy for Roger.

In the summer of 2004, I set off from Cambridge for Dorset with Rob Mac-farlane. The previous autumn we had agreed to go together in search of the sunken lane where our hero in Geoffrey Household's *Rogue Male* went to ground. I spent the entire morning rushing about at Mellis packing things in the car that might come in useful: tins of sardines and mackerel, nuts and rai-sins, junk chocolate and biscuits, Bourbon creams especially, and a solitary tin of baked beans. Also tools: a slasher, a fearsomely sharp billhook, a triangular bowsaw, an iron griddle for our fire, a corkscrew, secateurs and the trusty beech-handled Opinel knife from the Dordogne, where all the farmers and lorry drivers carry them and eat with them in restaurants. I also took my pup tent, sleeping bag and matches. On the way down, we stopped at Stockbridge and leaned over a railing to admire the brown trout, suspended in the River Test. We bought muffins and gourmet sardines at the delicatessen, none of your 45p-tins-from-Tesco nonsense.

ROBERT MACFARLANE, The Wild Places We got lost several times on the way. When he was unsure of the correct exit to take on a roundabout, which was nearly always, Roger tended to slow almost to a halt, and squint up at the exit signs, while I assumed the crash position in the passenger seat.

After staying the night with friends in Dorset, discussing *Rogue Male* and burrowing into the soil, we continued towards Chideock. Suddenly, we breasted the ridge of the horseshoe of hills Household describes, and all was clear. A deep half-circle of hills with the horns resting on high cliffs by the sea, with Chideock and North Chideock nestling in the centre.

ROBERT MACFARLANE ET AL., Holloway *(2012)* *Rogue Male* was our guide to the holloway's location. Household's novel is about a man who – fleeing the mysterious pursuers intent on killing him – decides to go to ground in Dorset, somewhere in the half-moon of hills that encircle Chideock. He searches out a deep holloway that he had discovered earlier in his life, its bottom 'a cart's width across' and its sides, 'with the banks, the hedges above them, and young oaks leaping up front the hedge . . . were 50 feet of blackness'.

We left the car in the leafy, shaded car park of the Catholic chapel of Chide-ock Manor. It was a well-wooded, secluded place, reached along a tall box hedge and past the spreading arms of laurels, limes, planes and oaks. The chapel was dedicated to the five Chideock martyrs who were hanged at Dorchester in 1594. All its traditions – of hiding the Chideock martyrs, the

Catholic priests, from the authorities – are about concealment; outlaw, covert activities. The Chideock martyrs hid in the woods for several weeks.

GEOFFREY HOUSEHOLD, Rogue Male *(1939)* The deep sandstone cutting, its hedges grown together across the top, is still there; anyone who wishes can dive under the sentinel thorns at the entrance, and push his way through . . . But who would wish? Where there is night, the nettles grow as high as a man's shoulder; where there is not, the lane is choked by dead wood. The interior of the double hedge is of no conceivable use to the two farmers whose boundary fence it is, and nobody but an adventurous child would want to explore it.

We set off up the hill towards Venn Lane, which we entered about midday. Past Venn Farm, going north uphill, it soon became deeply sunken and damp, with evidence that the rains flooded it. Sticks were jammed into little beaver-dams, and the plants of stream banks, brooklime and water mint, grew in profusion, as well as various sedges. Further up the lane we found ourselves walking between 'steep, high banks reaching to fifteen or twenty feet with the hedgerow trees growing along the bank' as described by Household.

Towards the high point of the lane, the going was getting harder than ever as the brambles, bracken and 'shoulder-high nettles' closed in to form a deep, dark tunnel. Roofed by hedge, and diving through tunnels of brambles and thorn, I kept getting hooked like a fish by the scalp. Vertical bramble lianas dangling like fishing lines in our path. We wove through the lane like a pair of hapless fish, like two gourmet sardines on our way to be hooked and tinned. Brambles and thorns were impossible to complain about, however, because they were such a vital part of our defences.

We persevered, and came to a place beside a huge, slightly ragged ash tree with a trunk some twelve feet in girth. The bank wall of the lane to the east here was fully eighteen to twenty feet, and to the west, the hedge was so dense that it would be possible to sit within its cover all day observing the comings and goings in the valley below without ever being seen.

Here, we decided, was the most plausible spot for our hero's hideout, burrowed into the sunken lane. However, in terms of strict textual accuracy, we were unable to find solid sandstone here, only ochre sandy earth. Could a burrow be safely constructed in such earth? We lit a fire in the lane having dug a little fire-pit with our garden trowel and made a hearth and fire-back out of some old logs of oak. We were anxious about the smoke giving us away to the farmhouses on the far side of the valley overlooking the lane, so followed the Vlach practice of making a tiny wigwam of sticks, all of small calibre, in order to produce the maximum heat as quickly as possible.

ROBERT MACFARLANE, The Wild Places We cleared nettles and briars, moved loose trunks to make seats, and then Roger built a fire to cook supper on – a pyramid of small sticks, with a hot centre of tinder, that produced an intense and almost smokeless fire.

Once it was going well, we kept an eye on the valley downhill to the west which was unfortunately where the breeze seemed to want to waft our smoke. But the denseness of the hedge formed such a filter of greenery that the smoke was indistinguishable from evening mist by the time it emerged and rolled downhill. Only the cows noticed it, and came up to investigate.

ROBERT MACFARLANE He was very proud of the smokeless fire that he made. It was all part of the *Rogue Male* cosplay that we engaged in – 'We have to camp out and build a smokeless fire in the style of our hero.' Later, I got a rude letter from a sharp-elbowed man about the 'Vlach method' of fire-making. He said, 'This was typical Roger, he would always make more of the lore than he should.' Roger was just having fun, and it was loads of fun.

We cooked spaghetti, and were puzzled by the dark brown hue of the water until Rob realised he had left a teabag in the cooking pan. We added chilli con carne to disguise the taste, most successfully.

ROBERT MACFARLANE, The Wild Places We ate a spicy tagine that Roger had made in advance and carried up with him. Firelight flickered off the walls of the holloway and on the hedge canopy above us, and set complicated shadows moving in the leaves.

We lay in the bottom of the lane, reclining on bracken and grass, sipping Glenfiddich and spooning up spaghetti, Tuareg-style, out of the same cooking pan. Then we made tea, stoking the fire for warmth and light as dusk and then night came on. Pudding was to have been the banana we roasted on the embers, but Rob stepped on it, perhaps because I had earlier made use of it as a demonstration model in a short impromptu lecture on male circumcision in Aboriginal initiation ceremonies.

ROBERT MACFARLANE, The Wild Places Campfires prompt storytelling, and Roger, never slow to start a story, told me how he had once been shot at by a hunter in the Polish woods, because the hunter thought he was a bear. The conclusion of the story, it turned out, was not Roger's outrage at having been fired on, but his delight at having been mistaken for an animal.

At last we left the dying embers and clambered up the steep bank past the ash tree into the higher field to the west above the lane. Here we camped, well concealed in the lee of the thick cross-hedge that divided it from the rough pasture that ran uphill to the summit. We pitched the pup tents side by side on an almost-level sward and slept soundly in the silence under a mackerel sky perforated by stars.

ROGER, *email to Robert, July 2004* It was a magnificent adventure, somehow falling into place just so without any conscious planning. You were a superb, generous companion, as ever, and the gods obviously thought whatever we were doing was a good idea.

ROBERT MACFARLANE, *email to Roger, July 2004* Those martyrs were wonderful; such an unexpected and apposite start to it all . . . Talking of martyrdom, I am still pulling thorns from my scalp.

*

ALISON HASTIE, *partner* In 1981, when we were in our early twenties, my university friend Sarah and I took one cutting board and some tools to the women's centre in Totnes and, with £600, set up Green Shoes and started making shoes for children. We had no money but we sold shoes at Glastonbury and other festivals, gradually building up the business, and eventually setting up a shop in Totnes. In January 2000, we had a sale as we always did. It was quite late in the day, I was making shoes at the machine and this guy appeared down the passageway, opening up shoeboxes and looking for shoes. I thought, what the hell's going on? In Totnes we get interesting customers, pushing boundaries, and here was another. He was good-looking but you get a bit steely in Totnes because there are all sorts of chancers, although Roger did not have a ponytail and yellow jogging pants; he wore a lovely tweed coat and had very beautiful grey curly hair. He began trying on practically every pair of shoes in the shop, but the great thing was he bought some. He said he was staying in the area, writing, and he had written a book, *Waterlog*. I hadn't heard of it. Later that week he came back, round two, for more shoes, so we were all saying, 'Crikey, who is this person?'

ROGER, *notebooks, January 2000* Green Shoes – ask names of the girls there. ALISON, LIZ, BOBBIE & STEPH. Olof Daughters boots conversation – boxes of shoes piled up at the back. Girl at sewing machine.

ALISON HASTIE Roger's feet were a classic strong, healthy and lovely quite broad size 8 with a very high instep and slightly turned-up big toes. According to old shoemakers, a high instep is a sign of being an artist while turned-up toes is a sign of intelligence. It was all a bit of fun when measuring his feet, and it was also fun baiting him about his choice of footwear – he chose a Christopher Robin-style bar sandal, not realising or being bothered by its status as a women's style. Clearly a man comfortable in his own skin.

Then he came to Dartington for the Ways With Words literary festival, and I had been divorced for three years and so the women I worked with were saying, 'He's coming to Dartington, Alison, you should go and listen to him,' because they could tell I was a bit smitten. So I went with my best friend Julia.

Ways With Words, festival brochure, Dartington, July 2000. Event 46, 'Know Your Place', Ronald Blythe, Richard Mabey and Roger Deakin, Great Hall, £7. These three eminent writers write vividly and movingly about the countryside immediately around their homes. They believe that daily life is enriched by observing, appreciating and recording what is on your doorstep and prove that familiarity breeds respect.

ROGER, *notebooks, July 2000* At Dartington: met Jane Beeson, Miranda Sawyer, Alison from Green Shoes, Alice Oswald – ring her. Satish Kumar. Lucinda Lambton.

ALISON HASTIE The three Rs – Roger, Richard and Ronnie – did their thing and Julia and I had a tea party with them in a tent. Roger had been into the shop and I wasn't there. Steph said, 'That chap Roger's been in, he thinks he needs his shoes resoling, he doesn't need his shoes resoling, what's going on?' He was going out with someone else and I lived in Devon and he was a man who needed time to write. He was very wary of being in a relationship which would take him away from his writing.

We wrote to each other and it turned out that my mum lived eight miles up the road from him. When I visited my mum, I called in on Roger and that's when I felt that I'd been there before. In the mid-seventies, I'd grown up in Suffolk and used to go to the Barsham Fairs as a teenager, which were fabulous. One night, after a gig at the Scole Inn, I'd ended up at a party at Walnut

Tree Farm. It was a load of people in a house, mattresses on the floor, one big room upstairs. I didn't know whose place it was, and I don't remember Roger; I was probably very shy. Then Roger realised that he remembered my friend. There were all these connections.

ROGER, *letter to Alison, 23 August 2000* Dear Alison, Thank you so much for your letter. I had meant to write and thank you for bringing my wonderful boots all the way from Devon, and to apologise for having been so wound up with writing my radio talk. It was really good to see you here and discover this wasn't your first visit!

ALISON HASTIE We gradually crept towards knowing each other. At that point, he was seeing Annette, so I was just being a bit curious and probably putting on some nice clothes when I went to Walnut Tree Farm, and smiling. It was always very interesting to visit, and he would write lovely letters.

Then he came down to Devon to do the piece in the *Independent*. That was the courtship piece.

ROGER DEAKIN, *feature for the* Independent, *March 2001* It is not so very long since every town and village in this country had at least one shoemaker – 'shummackers', as they were called here in Suffolk . . .

In recent years, the tradition of the local shoemaker has been re-invented in Devon by Green Shoes of Totnes. The firm was founded in 1981 by Alison Hastie to hand-make shoes to a high standard . . . all the shoemakers have always been women for the perfectly simple reason that the half-dozen of them have always worked well together in an atmosphere you recognise the minute you enter the shop as at once convivial and creative.

In the workshops behind the shop and upstairs Alison, Flora, Liz, Steph, Mirren and Gillian work amongst stacked rolls of coloured leather: green, blue, grey, plum, brown, red. Another member of the group, Hilary, makes leather bags from home. A radio plays. Jam jars overflow with buckles, rivets, eyelets or ski-hooks. Skeins of shoelaces hang around the walls, pale blue lasts are pigeonholed in rows, and on another set of shelves is an array of children's lasts. Liz is seated at a sewing machine stitching the uppers of children's T-bar sandals in green, apricot and red. Customers' orders, with drawings of their feet attached, lie beside a cutting board. Even the Apple Mac computer sitting in one corner does nothing to detract from the robust air of low tech about the place . . . I discovered the shop in the High Street a couple of years ago, tipped off by a couple who have ordered twenty pairs of boots, shoes and sandals between them in recent years. I live in a pair of donkey-brown sandals from Green Shoes day and night all summer, and the firm's handsome ten-hole Dartmoor boots in winter. I have yet another pair, chocolate brown, warm and figure-hugging, which I wear about the house.

ROGER, *letter to Alison, 2 March 2001* I was delighted that you took me to Branscombe beach, and the elusive, invisible potato-hut, and the elusive fossils, and the blinkered hut with the criss-cross balcony – and the flotsam trainer.

My latest theory about taking the long way back is that a) I was unconsciously hoping to loop back and find myself in Devon again, or b) that it was such an inspiring two days that any journey back to day-to-day realities would have been very long and arduous.

ALISON HASTIE I was intrigued by this man but he was taking phone calls from previous girlfriends and nothing was happening between us. The thing about doing anything with Roger was it was always super-fun because of his curiosity and enthusiasm. He was making connections all the time, with people and things, to make life more interesting. It's like embroidery – making it richer, and appreciating it as much as you can.

One of the things we shared was a similar aesthetic. He really appreciated Green Shoes. He completely got it. And that was great because we're not super-trendy. He helped copywrite the website and the brochure for Green Shoes and he really increased my own sense of confidence. That was a great gift. For me, personally, he absolutely arrived at the right time. It sounds stupid but a letter each week can really fuel a thing. His letters were hardly ever posted with a normal stamp, it was always a picture stamp.

ROGER, *letter to Alison, undated* Here are some thoughts on product names. You have a great name in Green Shoes, and you have staked your claim to the high ground of ecological shoemaking. If we care about the Earth, what could be more important than the shoes that connect us to it? SHOES WITH ATTITUDE might be at least a concept and even a summing-up of all that you stand for. (You go on to state all the reasons for not buying shoes made by cowering ten-year-olds in sweatshops in Indonesia.) . . . Just a few developing thoughts, and please don't worry at all about completely ignoring them. Love, Roger xxxxxx

ALISON HASTIE The marketing man was never far away and he often tried to give me advice about marketing. It is sometimes a bit challenging when people tell you how to do things but it was fine from Roger because he was far enough away and he wore the shoes.

ROGER, *notebooks*, *23 August 2002* Alison and I walked up and over Hameldown and down to the Miner's Pool; we found an old mine-working pit, with a great mossy sallow and some rowans growing out of it. A tangle of twisted branches groping out of the dimness for light – disused mine was at West Combe. The combe was full of oaks, rowans, sallows, all mossy and bent.

ROGER, *notebooks*, *24 August 2002* A great walk with Alison from Batworthy Farm across towards the stone rows (two parallel rows of stones running north–south, which must have been processional routes for rituals or celebrations close to Scorhill stone circle). We then turned due west and walked across open moor to the bend in the Teign and swimming hole known variously as 'Teign Turn' and 'Turn Teign' and 'The Elephant's Tail'. Lovely six-foot-deep pool some thirty feet long, with level picnicking grassy banks either side.

ALISON HASTIE It was a slow-burn. As time went on, he valued our connection a bit more. We would see each other about every six weeks but we'd speak every night on the phone. When I visited him, there was fish and chips in Dunwich, the occasional day out to Aldeburgh and suppers with Terence Blacker and Angela Sykes or Andrew Sanders. We had the odd argument and one of us went and slept in the shepherd's hut. Roger was fighting against the idea of wanting to be intimate and close, fearful of what that might mean. He was pretty terrified of a big commitment at that stage because he wanted to write and, bloody hell, sometimes making the next date with him was impossible because he would have this list of things that he needed to do. As you become more 'famous' you must have to be so fierce with your time if you're going to get anything done. Roger was always being invited places so holding the line and keeping the diary empty was essential. At the same time, he loved quiet, not-too-demanding company.

He would drive down to Devon and it usually involved something happening such as a festival at Dartington, or teaching at Schumacher College, or a research trip. We would go for walks, visit people, go on escapades. For me it was great: my daughter was sixteen and didn't need constant supervision, and he didn't have commitments, so we could take off. We visited the sacred groves of Devon, and looked for carvings of Green Men in village churches. And the thing about Roger, as evidenced by his entrance into my life, was that he could knock on a door and just talk to people, and they would open up to him.

CHAPTER 15

The Traveller

Australia, 2000 – the first shoots of 'Touching Wood' – leaving Chatto, finding Hamish Hamilton – globetrotting in search of trees – 'a somewhat disorganised (very much in a hurry) romantic Englishman' – Kazakhstan and Kyrgyzstan – a second tour of Australia, 2002 – struggles to finish 'Touching Wood' – 'Obscurity is what a writer needs to get on with work' – the god of small things – sickness and loss – 'Mellis has gone to the dogs'

ROGER, *notebooks, 2004* I am well on the way to becoming a tree myself. I put down roots. I sigh when the wind blows. My sap rises in the spring and I turn towards the sun. My skin even begins to look more like bark every day. Which tree would I be? Definitely a walnut; an English walnut, *Juglans regia*, the tree with the greatest canopy. A kind of tree-doctor to the ailing human race, with nuts full of goodness and healing.

Arriving for my first Australian adventure in the English spring of 2000, I was struck by how the birds did not sing so much as chortle, whistle, guffaw, scream, shout from the treetops of the macadamias, bottlebrushes and jaca-randas in Sydney. There were birds that sounded like a car-engine starter motor on a frosty morning and others like rusty pumps; all somehow mechanical. Some couldn't quite be distinguished from cricket song, which sounded like the hot water burbling in the plumbing, heated by my Aga.

It was the screeching of a pair of red-tailed cockatoos that woke me from a fitful sleep beneath eucalyptus alive with nesting budgerigars and ring-necked parrots in the red centre of Australia. It was like camping under an English pet shop.

I lay on my back and watched the big cockatoos gliding and swooping, red feathers in the thick, black tail of the cock bird flashing as it banked and landed in the river red gums that grew along a creek where the land dipped into shadow. I was rolled up inside a canvas swag and I lay listening to the mad, abandoned cries of flocks of pink and grey galahs that rolled and tumbled, revelling in their early-morning aerobatics.

I was travelling the desert parts of Central Australia west of Alice Springs with my friend Ramona Koval and we camped with ethno-botanist Peter Latz in the bush outside Alice Springs. Ramona's keen sense of the ridiculous and her unfailing humour in the face of the hardships and uncertainties of desert travel meant that we muddled along in a state of continuous hilarity at the curious out-back world around us. Her sense of the ridiculous began with me. On our first day 'out bush', she had spontaneously pointed at a flock of budgerigars in a tree and I had patronisingly explained that instead of pointing, which could disturb the birds, she should give a more discreet verbal indication of their whereabouts, preferably out of the corner of the mouth. Thereafter, 'budgerigars at three o'clock' became a private watchword throughout our trip.

RAMONA KOVAL We met in a yurt at the Edinburgh Book Festival while I was waiting for a cab to take me to the airport to fly back to Australia. Roger gave me a copy of *Waterlog* and I read it on the plane home and thought, this is fantastic. I'm going to interview him. We emailed each other and he said, 'I'm going to come to Australia,' and I said, 'Look, I know some fantastic people you might be interested in meeting' – Peter Latz in Central Australia and John Wolseley in Leather Arse Gully, Victoria. Roger said, 'Would you like to come to Central Australia and introduce me to these people?' and I thought, why not?

So this guy I didn't know arrived in Australia and we flew to Alice Springs and hired a car. Roger had all those English affectations we Australians see on television. He was very proper, he was very polite, and I think he found my directness very amusing. Anyway, he tolerated it.

It was like a road movie with these two protagonists who were completely mismatched but generous with each other. We were brother and sister. There was absolutely no romance involved. I wasn't his type and he was too eccentric and not grown-up enough for me, even though he was much older. He had all these rules, nature rules. Because I'm not a nature person, I'd say, 'Oh look at that!' And he'd say, 'We don't point!' and he'd get really annoyed with me. I thought it was hysterical.

ROGER, *notebooks, 2004* Are Australians notably different from the Americans? *Wit* is what distinguishes them. A tendency towards solemnity and reverence in the American often spoils their otherwise impeccable prose. Barry Lopez, for example, rarely breaks into a smile.

RAMONA KOVAL He had all these rules when we were camping. We had to turn our shoes upside down and put them on sticks so he took my shoes and he put them on these two sticks, because of scorpions, he said. He knew how to make a Boy Scout fire. I'm not a big camper but I had been camping with Aboriginal people before in the arid zone. They would make a little fire but they would get a long tree trunk that they'd drag over and they'd work out where the wind was coming from so that the wind blows against this log, keeping the flames moving along the log all night so the fire gets fed as you sleep. I said, 'This is how we're going to do it.' He said, 'Oh no, oh no. We can't possibly. That's not how to do a fire, THIS is how you do a fire.' So he makes this funny little English Boy Scout fire and of course it's hopeless and doesn't work.

We both had a swag and he would set mine over there and his at a proper distance. He would make my bed as well. He was very gentlemanly. And he would wear these stripy Wee Willie Winkie nightshirts that came down to his knees. I never saw what was underneath them. Because it was cold at night we wore caps so he wore a cap with his nightshirt; he just needed a candle to see him to bed.

I liked the deep, red centre, sleeping under the stars and, on waking, metamorphosing out of the swag in my Sybil Bird nightshirt and wandering off barefoot across the dew-damp sand. I would decipher the delicate calligraphy of tracks: skink, goanna, snake, kangaroo mouse, beetle, millipede.

I swam everywhere in the red, hot centre of Australia, in Redbank Gorge, Ormiston Gorge, in Palm Valley, in the superb, dramatic 160-foot pool in Alice Springs, which would soon close because locals considered a sunny autumn day of 26°C too cold to swim. In the delicious clear deep waterhole on the Finke River close to our camp, I floated on my back gazing up at a pair of wedge-tailed eagles who were nesting in the top of a river red gum on the opposite bank, seizing the advantage of the mass of birds and animals flocking to the river. We went fishing and caught spangled grunters, Australian perch, which had suddenly filled the Finke waterholes since the rains, hatching from dormant eggs and growing at astonishing speed, breeding and burying more eggs in the sand to carry their species beyond the next drought. We dined on the excellent spangled grunters, grilled over the fire, and ate spangled grunters for breakfast too.

RAMONA KOVAL It was starting to get warm again and the little pools were getting smaller and smaller so the concentration of these tiny little spangled grunters was getting higher and higher. When he said we caught spangled grunters you basically walked into a pool with your frying pan and they jumped on to it. That was fishing for spangled grunters.

*

ROGER, *notebooks, June 2000* Over drinks at St John in Smithfield with Richard Mabey I discussed book ideas with him. He feels British woods are too much the same. Not enough people in woods, either. Could work if I visit more bizarre habitats, like the stunted hazel woods of the Burren in Ireland, or chestnut woods in France, or walnut groves in Morocco.

ROGER, *notebooks, October 2003* When I was thinking of writing this book I mentioned the idea to a friend as we strolled in his wood. 'You know, I'm not sure it's such a good idea: I mean, when it comes down to it, one wood is much like another,' he said. Fortunately, I ignored the advice and went ahead to discover that the truth, as I suspected, is the very opposite.

ROGER, *notebooks, November 2003* I pick up my rucksack and as I walked out one midsummer morning is how Adam [Nicolson] sees my journey. He sees the interludes at home as being OK too. In a way, you end up writing about home when you travel away.

GEORGINA CAPEL When we first spoke, *Wildwood* was fairly unformed at that stage but I thought, that's a completely and utterly brilliant idea.

TONY BARRELL, *email to Roger, November 2000* The genre we're in is 'narrative non-fiction'. It has to have an artificial forward momentum imposed, either some grand theory (which can be tedious), or great journey (which has to be interesting) or it becomes some endless digression which I do really well, guv.

ROGER DEAKIN, *proposal for 'Touching Wood', which became* Wildwood, *September 2001* 'Touching Wood' is the natural sequel to *Waterlog* in that woods, like rivers, and the sea, are the last truly wild places in the landscape. The book will be a continuation of my pursuit of the wildness I believe is still to be discovered everywhere if only we will stop in our tracks and look. It will be a voyage of discovery from wood to wood, from tree to tree, beginning in my own broadleaved wood in Suffolk and journeying through Britain, Europe and across the world following the Dionysian spirit of the Green Man.

My accounts of the places, people, wildlife and trees I meet along the way will be a mixture of travel narrative, natural history, history, and personal memoir. I have no pretensions to write an authoritative or comprehensive work. My approach, as with *Waterlog*, will be strongly personal and elemental. It is through trees that we see and hear the wind: woodland people can tell the species of a tree from the sound it makes in the wind. If *Waterlog* was about the element of water, 'Touching Wood' will be about the element of wood, as it exists in nature, in our souls, in our culture and our lives.

I believe this is the moment for a passionate, personal account of our closeness to woods and trees; for a book that asserts the vital affinity with trees and wood that is humankind's greatest hope of ecological salvation, preparing the way for a return to symbiosis with nature instead of exploitation. We touch wood when we speak of the future. Trees *are* our future.

GEORGINA CAPEL He did want to be a successful writer; he wanted to be recognised and wanted to sell. Without being one of those 'oh God, they are selling and I am not' authors, he was aware of other writers and he wanted to be in the canon. One felt you needed to make it right for him and get the good deals. He wanted the money and he wanted a publisher who really believed in him and would really go for it.

It would have been very easy for me to ring up Chatto and say, 'How much do you want to offer? Oh, £20,000, thank you very much.' When I rang Rebecca at Chatto and said, 'I am sending it out on a multiple submission' [to several publishers], she was very upset. I felt she was intimating that she'd practically written *Waterlog*. All the work she'd put into it. All the effort she'd gone to. Editors quite often think this.

REBECCA CARTER When the reviews of *Waterlog* came out and they were so fantastic, I naively thought he would recognise that it might not have happened without me. Then I was on maternity leave, I wasn't aware that Roger had changed agents, and I was incredibly shocked when Georgina Capel sent me the proposal for the woods book and said, 'I've sent this out to other publishers.' I felt a kind of cold anger at that kind of behaviour from an agent. I said, 'If you don't give us twenty-four hours to consider this exclusively I'm not going to read it.' I was a young editor and really idealistic, and felt that as Chatto had put so much effort into making *Waterlog* a success we should be allowed a first option on the next book. I was quite surprised at myself for being so assertive but everybody backed me up in Chatto because, I think, by that point he was notorious in the company for being quite difficult.

GEORGINA CAPEL When you get that kind of aggressive hard-ball from a publisher who assumes some sort of special right to publish a book, one always feels a bit aggressive back towards them. If publishers love authors you don't sit and wait for years until they are ready to do their next book, you get on top of it. I felt Chatto had lost their moral imperative to publish his next book. I don't think they quite got him. I think they were irritated by him, in the way that publishers get if an author doesn't deliver a perfect manuscript on time.

TONY BARRELL, *email to Roger, September 2001* Publishers have to learn the hard way. Chatto should have been beating a path to your door asking what was next, making suggestions even. They sound like followers rather than leaders.

REBECCA CARTER I said to Roger, 'Your agent hasn't sent this to me exclusively.' He said, 'But you never asked me what I was doing next.' That was a real lesson in publishing's hard knocks. He was right. I had been so exhausted by the process of publishing *Waterlog* alongside all the other books I was working on and having my first child that I hadn't been in touch with him to talk about new projects, and I should have been. Roger taught me so many things, about our emotional relationship to nature, and the nature-writing tradition he was in dialogue with, and about the magic that can sometimes happen in an editorial process. It's a shame he didn't see that.

ROGER DEAKIN, *book deal for 'Touching Wood'* £50,000 advance (£25,000 advance payment on signature with £12,500 on manuscript, and £12,500 on hardback publication).

GEORGINA CAPEL It was definitely not one of those 'Oh dear, that's all we got' advances. He was pleased, and he was thrilled with Simon Prosser from the beginning. Simon was wonderful from beginning to end and truly loved Roger. So I felt I'd got him a decent deal.

SIMON PROSSER, *editor* Wildwood I found him utterly charming. How could you not? His original proposal had a lot of things about his family names and his feelings about wood, and there were some lovely exploratory, digressive thoughts, many of which end up in the book. Roger wanted to travel, he loved travelling, and he wanted to break out and be abroad. Because I knew *Waterlog* and knew him from Suffolk, my hope was that the core of the book would be rooted here.

ANDREW CRACKNELL I told Roger he should call it 'Log Log'.

*

My delivery date for 'Touching Wood' was spring 2003, which allowed me time for the travel involved but not too much time. As with *Waterlog*, I wanted to leave scope for the full play of serendipity in the journey, to be in a constant state of what Keats called 'mystery, doubt and uncertainty' as I travelled. I already knew quite a lot about woods and wood but I wanted to be surprised at every turn, one wood leading to another. Ruskin said 'the imagination is naturally active in the obscure and indefinite daylight of wood scenery'; I hoped it to be true.

After signing the deal, I travelled to the Pyrenees with Andrew Sanders, and to Dorset to see the low-impact eco-community of Tinker's Bubble. In

2002, I coppiced hazel at Vicky Minet's farm to build a bender for friends on an island in the Thames, visited the chestnut woods of Olargues, the olive groves of Lesbos, encountered the withies of the Somerset Levels, hilltop sycamores, the carved Green Men of Devon and the ancient trees of Petworth Park, West Sussex. In September 2002, I made my preparations to visit Kazakhstan. I was unusually nervous about this trip but exhilarated too.

GEORGINA CAPEL   Suddenly, he got the visas and travelled to the apple woods of Kazakhstan and the walnut groves of Kyrgyzstan, and then he was in Australia. The question was where do you stop? I was having conversations with him about Californian redwoods as well. Of course there are amazing trees all over the planet.

BARRIE JUNIPER, *plant scientist, email to Alison Hastie, 1 October 2002*   I have been trying to help a somewhat disorganised (very much in a hurry) romantic Englishman by the name of Roger Deakin, to travel to some very funny places, and to meet some very surprised, but generally friendly people.

BARRIE JUNIPER, *email to Alison Hastie, 2 October 2002*   We were appalled that Roger D. was trying to organise in a week what took us the whole winter to set up not a few years back. However, thanks to some very well-disposed friends in Central Asia, who are now getting used to insane Englishmen dropping in on them, at very short notice, and asking them impossible questions, it looks as though things are turning out all right.

On the streets of Almaty, I spied an advertising hoarding for Sovereign cigarettes showing a red London double-decker bus, a number 12, passing through a Cotswold village with a destination board that said it was on its way to Westminster via Oxford Circus and Camberwell. Since the English are prepared to believe that Kazakhs all roam about the steppe on horseback and live in yurts, which only a minority of them do these days, the myth that the English hop on double-deckers in the Cotswolds and head into the West End seemed a reasonable exchange.

Everybody took a great interest in me, since I looked neither Kazakh nor Russian and was probably the only man in Almaty wearing brown corduroys. Everyone else wore blue denim. I was even the subject of a bet. 'I tell you, he's not Russian,' said the woman, and when I confirmed she was right, she turned and slapped the hand of her lover triumphantly, demanding her money.

After visiting the wild apple woods of Kazakhstan, I travelled on in the deepening autumn, towards the walnut forests east of Jalal-Abad in south

Kyrgyzstan. Inside the labyrinth of the Jalal-Abad bazaar, my translator and guide Zamira and I encountered a vast, shadowy hall in which mountains of huge green-and-yellow melons twice the size of rugby balls were being vigorously weighed up. In workshops around the margins of the bazaar, various artisans plied their trades. One was a dressmaker's, full of seamstresses busy at ancient sewing machines, lovely women in bright, long dresses and headscarves over gushing black hair. They invited us in for tea. Dozens of women gathered round in friendly curiosity, most of them young and intensely attractive, all black eyes, flashing gold teeth and earrings. Having established I was English, they asked if I was married with such sudden directness that I fell into a trap by answering that I was not. One of the older seamstresses immediately invited me to help myself to a bride, calling forth a series of frankly stunning young women and commending their beauty to me. They needed no recommendation in their elegant, Gypsyish dresses of azure, purple, green and crimson. 'Take Asil. Look how beautiful. Take her with you to London.' I had stumbled into one of the fashion temples of Jalal-Abad, and for a moment actually dreamed of staying there forever like Paul Bowles in Tangier, settling down with one of the proffered brides in heavenly exile.

Later, in the walnut forests, I felt moved and elated by the universally cordial atmosphere: we shook hands with everyone we met, so that the black stain of the walnut juice became a badge of friendship and hospitality in this place. Everyone gave us walnuts, choosing their biggest, most prized nuts. Our pockets swelled. At bedtime I fished out walnuts from every pocket like a squirrel and stashed them at the bedside. Everywhere we went, we kept some of the best nuts as seed: from the forests of Kurslangur, Arslanbob, Jayterek, Gava and Ortok. In my rucksack were several film cans filled with the carefully labelled pips of wild apples, and walnuts, destined to be sown in my Suffolk garden, as a living reminder of the wild fruit forests I had encountered on my travels.

*

At the end of the year, I visited Australia for a second time to visit the ancient forests of Tasmania, via Ramona in Melbourne, and the artist John Wolseley. I spent an afternoon visiting St Kilda cemetery, searching for the grave of my distant relative, Alfred Deakin, the second prime minister of Australia and one of the principal authors of the constitution of the new nation that was founded in 1901. The son of William Deakin from Northamptonshire and Sarah Bill, a Welsh farmer's daughter, Alfred grew up in Melbourne in 1856.

At school, he was a leader but also a dreamer, 'thin-skinned, wayward, emotional', and he loved acting and adventure stories from *Robinson Crusoe* to *Gulliver's Travels*. As an adult, Deakin was elected to the Victorian state parliament aged twenty-three. One of his early roles was to become Commissioner for Public Works and Water Supply. He travelled to the western United States to learn their irrigation techniques and later introduced laws nationalising water rights and providing state aid for irrigation. Deakin served three short terms as prime minister, but retired in 1913, suffering from a loss of memory that may have been vascular dementia or early onset Alzheimer's. He wrote in anguish about his failing mind and in 1919 he died, aged just sixty-three.

RAMONA KOVAL Roger wanted to see Alfred Deakin's grave and so we went to find his memorial, which is not a cross but an open book. He was keen on Alfred Deakin. He noticed that there was a tree there, it was blooming and it had weird red flowers. In the last few months of his life he kept saying to me, 'Can you please go back? Can you please go down to St Kilda and get me some of that tree and send it in an envelope?' But I never found the time to do it because it was the wrong end of the city and I had the kids at home, and he didn't tell me that he was sick.

I was laid low in Tasmania with what I later understood to be vestibulitis, a drying-up of the sinus and nose-vestibule and consequent infection, caused by extreme dryness – often at altitude or in dry, hot conditions. It reminded me of the forest fires of the Pilliga. A desertification of the nose. When I returned to Suffolk in early 2003, I was wiped out too. I missed my friends in Australia, and I missed the sunshine. One fine January day, I stripped to the waist and sat outside on the kitchen doorstep before a mirror propped on a cane chair and cut my hair. It felt good, even rejuvenating, to strip off the professor-like abundance of locks and to feel the sun on my skin.

JAYNE IVIMEY Something happened in Australia. That's when he started to get ill. When he came back, everything was very, very stressful for him because he had to write that book. He would ring me in the middle of the night, waking me up, and say, 'I don't know what's happening, I've got such a terrible headache.' Twice I drove out from Norwich to Diss at one in the morning to be with him because he seemed so distraught.

SIMON PROSSER The extent of the Australia trip did surprise me at the time and I worried that it would overwhelm the project or prevent it being ever finished. It became a question of, when can he finish this book and how is he going to finish this book? *Wildwood* was a potentially unending book and Australia just increased that possibility. He clearly loved being in motion and there is a palpable skill in the way he writes about entering a different place, and he captured a lot of the excitement of going to a place, going on an adventure, exploring, connecting with people.

GEORGINA CAPEL The coaxing of Roger was how I'd be with any writer – enthusiastic or gushing, 'It's all going to be all right,' and we'd have another lunch. Some of these books do take a long time. When we talked about the book it didn't strike me as anything unusual. It's just the struggle that some writers have with some subjects. *Wildwood* is a more unwieldy book, not like *Waterlog* which has a much simpler narrative journey. He also wanted to get it right, needing it to be a book that was going to sell, and that added to the rabbit in the headlights.

When you're young your mind is running really fast, like a camera overcranked to produce slow-motion film, so the days and weeks and summers seem incredibly long. When you grow old, the mind slows down, doesn't clock so much sensory stimuli, so the days and years flash by. The same kind of thing happens in a day. Morning time seems longer because your mind is whirring. Evening time goes by faster, because you've slowed down.

Obscurity is what a writer needs to get on with work. To be under the glare of lights is the last place you want so, moth-like, you burrow away into some basement where you can talk to yourself, pace about and think. In the days of letter-writing and penny post or earlier, it was easier. Forster, in *Howards End*, speaks of a world of 'telegrams and anger' inhabited by the Wilcoxes, and it is the quieter, less accessible world, closer to dreams and sleep, the writer needs.

Above all else, though, writers need not to think too much about what they're doing. 'If poetry come not as naturally as the leaves to a tree, it had better not come at all,' says Keats. Running two at a time downstairs you are fine until you start to think too much about what you're doing, and stumble. I blame the Romantics for all this self-consciousness about landscape and inspiration. Wandering lonely as a cloud may be the last thing you need sometimes. Going round the corner for breakfast in a steamy café may be much more like it.

In 2003 my first deadline for 'Touching Wood' came and went. I continued to research and write. When I turned to T. H. White and read him for an hour in the early morning, my mind grooved on to him and I found myself writing away downhill as if guided and balanced by his invisible hand at my elbow. I didn't have to even think about a thing. Just push off and freewheel.

I described to Jules Cashford getting up and sitting in a bit of a daze for half an hour writing in longhand what's in my head, or I didn't know was in my head. 'That's your unconscious, Rog,' said Jules. 'It's much better than you are.'

*

ROGER, *notebooks, 2003* You could spend a lifetime studying a hedgerow, or a pond.

> JANE TURNBULL When he was talking about the things that interested him, it was always the very small things, and he was spellbinding. He was a miniaturist and he was a proper naturalist.

ROGER, *notebooks, Midsummer's Day 2003* The perfect morning for it. Wood pigeons cooing in the young elms and ashes surrounding the garden in deep shadow. Spider's gossamer threads glinting in the sunshine. Robins on the lawn. There's a goat's-beard head stuck in a jam jar swivelling in the breeze at the open window of my study. An earwig explores the window frame, and an ichneumon fly elegantly strolls up and down the windowpane. A distant cockerel across the field and even the neighbour's distant barking dogs, or Michael's crop-scarer across the common, sound benign this morning.

ROGER, *email, April 2004* The book's going well but taking longer than I planned, simply because there's so much material and I'm trying to wrestle it down into the right length and shape.

*

My writing was interrupted. One day, I was thrown into deep confusion by my inability to find my two Rotring ArtPens. I remembered taking them out of the pocket of my rucksack because it had a hole in it, but I didn't know where I put them. I cleared my desks in the study, I looked in the car, but not a sign. I get very anxious when I can't find things, especially pens, the tools of my trade. I continued writing with a perfectly good pen but why do I always need to have more than one of things? It must be my deep fear of loss. My assumption that I am going to lose things or people leads to a deep need to protect myself, insure myself, against the loss of one pen by owning two or three. It's the same with shoes, or my computer. I'm scared of the pain of loss. It is unbearable to me, so I hedge my bets against it, and double up.

It was also interrupted by life. In June 2005, I spent four days on the Waveney in a canoe for BBC Radio, then drove to Worcester to give a talk at a Woodland Trust conference, and then on to Dartington for a week's teaching on a Schumacher course, when all I really wanted to do was stay at Walnut Tree Farm and write. There were still crucial chapters of my book to complete.

Later that summer, I found the usual sawing and raking and hedging at Mellis utterly knackering. One day, I lay half-feverish with a swollen knee after bashing it on something sharp as I carted hay. I kept losing tools. Where's my fucking shears? I wondered, as I pruned various plums and roses and bushes and lit a good bonfire.

Another morning, I woke feeling terrible and decided to go straight to the pool in Diss. I drank half a cup of tea and headed for the sauna. It felt very hot, but, strangely, I didn't sweat at all. I felt cold inside. After a steam, I swam ten lengths, not too fast, sat in the sauna again for a minute or two, but soon felt very sick and ran out in the gents to throw up. On the way home, I had to stop three times, and stood violently retching by the hedge, trying to look as if I was botanising when cars went by. I went to bed, and my ribs still ached two days later.

ROBERT MACFARLANE, *email to Roger, July 2005* Dear Rog – I can't bear it any longer! Are you all right? I've been holding off and holding off emailing, knowing how much you've had on your plate these past couple of months (Waveney, Schumacher, and through all that, the book), but am missing hearing your voice, even electronically mediated, ever so much – and also just have the faintest worry that you might not be OK.

ROBERT MACFARLANE, *email to Roger, August 2005* It was just so good to hear from you again. Though the news is not so good from your end. I had worried about the cost of those two big commitments – Waveney and Schumacher – on you, at such a stage with the book, but hadn't thought it would be so high . . . I hope so much you've found some writing rhythm again, and some privacy.

Mellis Common has gone to the dogs. Cat people sit patiently for hours, watching. Dog people are always striding about, huffing and puffing, straining at the leash. I rarely see people walking along on the common now unaccompanied by at least one dog. Women in pressed jeans with little dogs on elasticated leads, like yo-yos. People have more and more dogs.

July 2003 The affluent have dogs and go 'dog-walking'. 'I'm just going to walk the dog down to the post,' they say, unhooking the Barbour from its peg by the door. Later they will drop off the kids at school in the 4WD.

August 2003 Three people on the common with dogs on leads. Seen from a distance they could be wielding metal detectors, pausing, adjusting, looking up a reference, continuing, the dog-detectors combing the common. They are all 'dog-walkers' in Mellis now. A dog is a status symbol.

April 2004 At the eastern end of the common, you have increasing numbers of people and their pet dogs and cats, all disturbing the common in one way or another.

July 2004 A blackcap sings sweetly somewhere offstage. And the infuriating, unhappy, neurotic dogs across the field, cooped up in a cage all day, bark incessantly, miserably.

May 2005 The repeated firing of the gun is symptomatic of the new selfishness, narcissism even, of the 'country person' who affects green wellingtons and 4WD, and festoons their home with security lights that will flash on at the least movement of an owl, a badger or a hedgehog. And they have dogs, usually several of them, for no reason except to bolster their master's illusion that he is a true son of the country, master of his piddling demesne?

July 2005 Should I build a big haystack as a sound barrier against the barking of the next-door dogs? Perhaps it might absorb some of the sound. My neighbours and I have tried everything, short of dog-murder, to shut these dogs up. They never seem to stop, and now we are so used to them that we all suffer a kind of dog-tinnitus, imagining we hear the barking even when it isn't there, like a ringing in the head. I suppose this is what is meant by 'barking mad'.

*

ALISON HASTIE The material for *Wildwood* was endless, it was such a vast thing, and everybody was always chipping in, 'Have you heard of this?' He felt under pressure – it's your second book, were you a one-book wonder? He would read bits to me – that was lovely, that was really special. But I think the last year of his life was seriously uphill.

ROBERT MACFARLANE, *email to Roger, February 2006* I wonder how your meeting with Georgina went, how the revisions to the Great Work are now going.

ROBERT MACFARLANE We had two or three 'How's the book going?' conversations that ended with Roger saying, 'Well I just can't quite . . .' There were several versions of that conversation and Roger never seemed to have moved it on much next time around. 'Why don't I come over and we'll talk it over and try to get it right?' I suggested but he became evasive about this. If there had been no illness one would've thought, that's just writing, it's hard, he'll get there in the end, which he did so brilliantly with *Waterlog*. But he seemed to recognise that something was beyond his capacity.

VICKY MINET He'd become more chaotic than usual and also slightly solitary. He didn't ring up so much. And the whole book thing became very difficult to talk about. He was very much struggling with his book. In the end, it was 'Don't mention the book'. He couldn't get it together.

ALISON HASTIE He was always saying, 'God, I feel so tired,' and we put it down to the book deadline. He was needing to get the work done. That was masking the beginnings. You realise that being on your own and writing is quite dangerous.

TERENCE BLACKER If you look at Roger's notebooks, his focus gets more and more local, and small. In the end, he was simply writing about the pencil on his desk. So the nightmare project for someone who's doing that is a book as broad as *Wildwood*. The tragedy of it is that if you go into a strange mood and you lock yourself away, that's seen as part of a writer's life. That's what we thought was happening with Roger – he's going through the pre-deadline shit. And so everyone left him alone. He was probably in torment because he was trying to make sense of something that his brain wasn't allowing him to make sense of. Because he wasn't seeing people, he was pretty far gone before anyone realised.

I swear there's a singing newt in my study. It generally bursts into song around ten o'clock at night, and seems to live somewhere near the woodstove, possibly behind the mantelpiece. Its song is a high-pitched squeak like a piece of delicate machinery in need of a spot of oil. I have heard it before, rising out of the bottoms of drains, or the rainwater traps at the feet of drainpipes. In one instance, I tracked down a plaintive newt-song I kept hearing in the garden to the depths of a water-drain stopcock sunk in the lawn and, by lying down and plunging in my arm as far as I could, actually succeeded in capturing the tiny songster, and liberated it in the vegetable patch. A few nights later, however, it was back again on its perch in the hydrant practising scales. The song of the newt must count as the most subtle, and least known, of all nature's musicians.

CHAPTER 16

The Dying Man

Where am I? – Japanese translators invade Walnut Tree Farm – diagnosis – the short fight to beat the glioblastoma – Alison takes care – the mission to see Jayne's exhibition – a last walk to Burgate Wood – where there's a will, there's a Wildwood *– 'We need to get our stories in a little sooner, don't we?' – last rites – the mind looks back*

ROGER, *notebooks,* 2004 'And this our life, exempt from public haunt, finds tongues in trees, books in the running brooks, sermons in stones, and good in everything. I would not change it.' Shakespeare, *As You Like It.*

ROGER DEAKIN, Wildwood *(2007)* There's more truth about a camp than a house . . . because that is the position we are in. The house represents what we ourselves would like to be on Earth: permanent, rooted, here for eternity. But a camp represents the true reality of things: we're just passing through.

Sometimes when I wake, I see a window or a wall and wonder where I am. Whose house is this? Which country am I in? Is this a hotel or the bedroom of a friend or lover? Then, slowly, I remember I am in my own house, and it is just another bedroom. I sleep around, you see, moving from one bedroom to another, alternating vacant bedrooms in my house, or visiting the satellite dens in the fields.

Here, now, in Suffolk, in January 2006, there is barely any light in the mornings until ten, and it is dusk from half past two. Last month, I attended the funeral for my neighbour and friend Christine Popescu in Mellis church, wearing a huge, black overcoat weighing half a stone. The dead have such secrets. Now he is dead I think of so many questions I should like to ask my father. But then, he has been dead ever since I was seventeen.

It seems hardly worth getting out of bed. Grey after grey, day after day, and fucking cold too, but no snow or ice thick enough to skate on, the most miserable weather on record. I hardly remember what the sun looks like. In the cold grey half-light, everything is so still that I can hear the stillness, like the sound of my rabbits in their cage in the mornings before school, chewing on the hogweed I collected along the lane. I'm still finishing 'Touching Wood' but my mind keeps remembering. The custard-dish weather-station scaffold pole and anemometer in the back garden. The minnows and carp in the pond. The Hornby wind-up train set round the garden. Bees in the snapdragon. The first red bicycle. Jokari, my yellow RAF box kite.

Wallpapering was planned and agonised over for months in advance. Tomes arrived at the house, full of samples. They were leafed through in the evenings and discussed, patterns compared, colours considered.

The dog that could strike matches. It became an arsonist and set fire to the paint factory at Wealdstone.

Hatch End: the Gang.

'Hello Hatch End 183. Roger Deakin speaking.'
The twins: Virginia and . . .
Douglas Catterell – smoked a pipe.

*Roger's notebooks fall silent in 2006. Through January, February and
March, pages are unfilled. We don't know what is on his mind. His last
piece of writing is in mid-March, a customary summary of a drive to
Bristol and Cheltenham, where he visited relatives and attended Steve
Ashley's sixtieth birthday party with Alison Hastie.*

9.45 a.m. Bristol from Mellis. Tank ¾ full.
Sunday 12 March. M25 at 11.05 (hr 20 mins).
12 noon at J10 on M4 144m from Mellis. 10-minute break at Reading
at 152m.
ARRIVED at Bristol stn at 1.30 p.m.
Saw badger at Aldington at 330 miles on verge on way to Burford at
8.06 p.m.
9.06 p.m. on to M25 (389m).
We've lost 66% of our ponds in the last 100 years.
Mellis arrived at 11.05 p.m. The journey to/from Bristol–
Cheltenham–Painswick–Gloucester–Stroud–Oxford–Mellis, 502
miles. Tank ¼ full after adding another 22 litres. £20.04. Summary:
500 miles travelled on approx 50 litres total.

ROGER, *notebooks, 16 March 2006, final entry*

'Be elusive, but don't walk far.' D. BOWIE.

*

ROBERT MACFARLANE My friend from Cambridge Leo Murray and I visited
in early spring and it was sunny and we went in the moat but Roger sat on the
bank and watched us. It was bloody cold but that was no problem for Roger
normally. We wondered why he didn't go in.

TERENCE BLACKER It was the most ghastly time. Because he didn't recognise
that he was in the shit. He didn't recognise he was dying until really late on,
which was merciful. We had been leaving him alone because he was up against
a deadline, and he just wanted to finish *Wildwood*. And so I hadn't seen him for

a long time, and I was writing my biography of Willie Donaldson. I was driving down to London and I talked to Roger on the phone and he said something rather weird to me. He said, 'The house is full of translators. Japanese translators of *Waterlog*. And they've gone to the WI stall in Eye but they're going to be back pretty soon.'

ANGELA SYKES, *partner of Terence* Roger said, 'They're driving me mad, these bloody translators.'

TERENCE BLACKER I thought, Japanese translators of *Waterlog*? That does seem quite unlikely, and quite unlikely that they would go to the WI stall in Eye. Then he said, 'I was over at Cheltenham seeing Steve Ashley, and I saw on the side of a bus a poster of Willie Donaldson. Willie with Jonathan Miller.' And the one thing I knew about Willie was he never had his photograph taken. And why would he be on the side of a bus in Cheltenham? So when I came back up from London, I went over to see him. I took over a bottle of wine and I said, 'Have you got a corkscrew?' And he picked up another utensil and gave it to me. I gradually realised that he wasn't with it. There was something seriously wrong.

SUE CLIFFORD I spoke at a conference in Snape Maltings on Thursday 6 April and stayed with Roger that night. I arrived and there was no one in. I hung around and finally I tried the door and it was open, so I went inside. It felt like someone was there. I helped myself to a cup of water, and then I heard something upstairs and fairly soon afterwards Roger appeared. He had been fast asleep, had forgotten about something he'd put in the oven for us to eat, and it was all burnt. He didn't seem at all right. I hadn't seen him for a long time. He sat in a chair and his cat, Millie, sat on his chest; she was comforting him. As we talked, I became more and more upset by our conversation. He seemed not to have talked to anybody for ages. I got Alison's phone number from him because I was so disturbed and talked with her. That's when she came back up there, and she was extraordinary, and she got him to go to hospital.

TERENCE BLACKER One of his Common Ground friends had been staying with him the previous night and I called Andrew Sanders and Alison to see if they had been in touch.

ANGELA SYKES You asked Roger if he had been to the doctor, and he couldn't find the doctor's number in the book.

TERENCE BLACKER And the milk was all sour. He obviously hadn't been eating very much. The whole thing seemed really odd.

ANGELA SYKES You rang him on the Saturday morning to check he'd called the doctor and there was no answer so we decided to go round, and we rolled up with real dread because we felt something might have happened such as a stroke. We knocked on the door and called out and there was no answer and then he peered out of the window and said, 'Oh hello?'

TERENCE BLACKER He was still in bed. Which was really unlike Roger. I rang the local doctor. Saturday morning, locum doctor. Useless bastard. He was very reluctant to see him. I managed to get an appointment and drove him to Diss. Roger couldn't remember the way. I said to the doctor, 'Look, this guy thinks he's fine. Believe me, he's writing a book, he's an author and intelligent, and he's not making any sense at all.' But Roger was in complete denial about it. He thought he was fine. The doctor said, 'He's tired. He just needs a good meal and a rest.' So we took him back and Alison came up over the weekend and she took him to his doctor on Monday.

ALISON HASTIE I was in Devon and he phoned me one evening and said, 'Where are you? Are you coming to supper?' 'Roger, you've just rung Devon,' I said. 'I'm coming up.' Later that night, Terence rang. I don't know how he got my number but thank God he found it. And Roger was really relieved to see me when I arrived the next day. I could see that he was frightened. It was frightening for all of us.

We saw the doctor. 'Sixty-three-year-old man, a bit confused' – they are not very interested. They did blood tests but it was going to take a week to come back. Then we came home and Jayne Ivimey came for supper. Roger was on the other side of the kitchen table and he was so confused. His immediate memory, the order of things, was not right.

JAYNE IVIMEY I spent hours on the phone to the Macmillan nurses and doctors trying to describe his symptoms because he was quite gaga then, he was semi-conscious really, while we were trying to have this supper and we both got terrified.

ALISON HASTIE We rang 111 and the person said, 'Take him to A&E,' and I went with him to the hospital in Norwich. They asked questions – 'Who is the prime minister?' – to see whether he was with it or not, and then they called the neurologist. People on A&E said it was like calling down God. Roger had a brain tumour.

At first, the doctors said they thought the tumour was operable, but the following day they found that it wasn't, which was really horrible. It was a glioblastoma, a grade-4 tumour: the fastest-growing kind. Some brain tumours are very localised and can be removed; others are called diffuse and don't have a clear boundary between the tumour and the normal brain tissue. Roger's tumour was like honey fungus in wood: there was a mesh of tendrils wrapped around every bit of the brain.

Roger was kept in hospital and then it was Easter and clever old Angela said he doesn't need to stay in hospital, so we got him home and that was much better.

ANGELA SYKES They gave him steroids because it was the pressure on his brain from the tumour that was causing him to hallucinate, and that had probably only been happening fairly recently.

TERENCE BLACKER We took him out of the hospital with Alison and I said, 'What about all that stuff about the translators, for God's sake?' I told him the story about the Japanese translators and he said, 'I really did believe that. I was absolutely convinced by that.' In a typical Roger way. So he had the awareness. The steroids kept the thing at bay and then suddenly, in the way of cancer, you saw his face change, and the cancer was no longer messing around.

*

RICHARD MABEY Ronnie Blythe got the right words, as always. He said Roger was stunned by what was happening to him. His life had not been prepared for that sort of thing – his optimism, pretty much his enduring good health. It was inconceivable.

ROBERT MACFARLANE I still remember the horror moment when Terence told me, 'It's terminal,' and I sat there absolutely shattered.

TONY BARRELL, *memoirs* My last email from Roger came on Easter Sunday 2006, from Mellis, where he was still waiting for spring, and finishing his book. He had suddenly discovered he had a brain tumour, but even in the midst of that horrific shock, his parting shot was not about his illness ('Don't worry – the best people are on the case') but 'Weather here certainly hasn't improved, MUCH. A tiny sprit warmer, but considering it's SPRING, there isn't a single bit of green anywhere except on the fields. Woods still as bare as brushes.'

JULES CASHFORD After the first time ever I had written to him and he'd not written back, I rang him, and he said, 'I've got a tumour in my head.' An interesting way of putting it. And I stayed with him and he didn't look as if he was about to die. He didn't look anything like that. He was not stricken at all at that time, just a bit odd, like we all are sometimes.

RICHARD MABEY I was driving down a remote mountain road in the middle of Corsica, miles from anywhere, and the mobile phone rang and it was Terence saying Roger had been diagnosed with an inoperable brain tumour. In the early stages of his illness, Roger expressed to me a belief that the cancer was 'his fault', and that in some way it was a kind of punishment for 'living wrongly'. I tried to persuade him this was an absurd idea and he never elaborated on where he felt he had strayed.

*

ALISON HASTIE That spring and summer I was mostly at Walnut Tree Farm but I didn't stop work completely, and occasionally I'd come down to Devon and then I had to make sure Rufus or somebody else was with him. At the beginning of his illness, I answered the phone and said, 'Mellis 400,' and this woman went, 'Who are YOU?' I said, 'Er, I'm Alison,' and she said, 'Hummmpf,' and hung up. There were quite a lot of women for whom Roger was theirs.

MEG AMSDEN Alison was very protective of him. She said, 'You can stay for five minutes.' She sat there with him and with me, and she was called away and we started having a proper conversation. Poor woman, she was in a very difficult position because he had a lot of relationships with women. She didn't know if I was one of *those* women; I wasn't, we were just friends, but she didn't know. Then she came back and said, 'You'll have to go now.' Someone was coming to do this, that or the other, and Roger took my hand and he said, 'Don't go, don't go.'

BUNDLE WESTON Alison was his absolute saviour. She really, really was. I don't think he realised what a jewel he had. She didn't know anybody because Roger hadn't introduced her to anyone, and these people were all turning up and there she was, holding the fort, looking after this dying man, doing all the cooking and cleaning and generally being wonderful, worn to a thread.

VIVA ROWLAND A lot of Roger's girlfriends were too complicated for my liking. And the person who was really fantastic was Alison. She was amazing and she really, really loved him, unconditionally, which is why she cared for him so beautifully until he died.

TONY AXON What was so sad was that he met Alison late in life. She is delightful, an absolute rock, lovely and constant, and she knew how to handle Rog perfectly. Rog said to me, just before he got ill, 'I wish I'd met Alison twenty years ago.'

*

TONY WESTON, *poem*

The Short Straw
For Alison Hastie and Roger Deakin

I don't know whether Rog has mentioned me?
The voice is diffident yet somehow quite assured.
Thing is, she says, *I wonder could I stay the night.*

Of course we know her name. Rog sings
her praises all the time. She makes great shoes
and few demands, this Devon girl of his.

She has no pattern
and no last for this and yet for months she puts it all
on hold – her life, her work, her hope of love – to send
him properly shod into the shining firmament.

ALISON HASTIE, *diary, 2006*

April 20 Bed finally ready at 8ish, arrived Addenbrooke's Hospital 10.
April 21 Roger had biopsy at Addenbrooke's 4.30, visited briefly.
April 22 Visited a.m. – bed rest as heart murmuring. Met Rob Macfarlane, visited 4.30–8 p.m.
Sun 23 Visited 12–8. Andrew Sanders visited, Tony and Tere Axon, Rob p.m.
Mon 24 Long day waiting for prescription, return from Addenbrooke's.

BUNDLE WESTON We really knew nothing about Alison. She phoned Tony and I to say, 'Roger said I could phone you and you might look after me,' and we said, 'Yes! Come round.' She stayed with us for a few days while Roger was in Addenbrooke's. We really got to know her and we all sat and bit our nails and held hands while we waited for news.

TONY WESTON, *poem*

Villanelle for Roger

Trees showing green, things growing as we speak,
we sit and read the papers in the sun,
you out of hospital barely a week

and seeming much yourself – our good old Dekes.
Someone addresses pigeons with a gun.
Trees showing green, things growing as we speak,

you stand. You walk away to take a leak,
so boyish, tall – life a serious bit of fun –
you out of hospital barely a week.

They took you down to have a poke and a peek
inside the magic-lantern of your brain –
trees showing green, things growing as we speak.

It's anybody's guess – we're all unique –
a year, two years, don't let's say one.
You out of hospital barely a week,
trees showing green, things growing as we speak.

ALISON HASTIE, *diary, 2006*

April 26 Eye for me and WI market. Vicky for lunch. Quite a lively day.
April 27 Tony W came. Roger pretty tired.
April 28 Roger resting a lot. Tony Axon came. Went for a walk to look for pulmonaria [lungwort, a spring flower] in Burgate Wood, slow stroll.

April 29 Roger new pills less steroids, went to Eye, Jenny and Joe
Kember came 12.30. Late lunch and sleep. Andrew came to supper.
April 30 Roger up at 12 for Jo Rolfe lunch and then back to bed.
Caroline, Mandy and Dave for tea. Out to supper at Andrew's, good
fun, R on great form.

ALISON HASTIE There were so many visitors, it was pretty full-on. It was
new to us all. If this happened now I would say, 'Go away.' But there was hope-
fulness. It was completely bonkers but they said he might have a couple of
years. 'Ah, I think we should drive to Italy,' he said. Roger bought a suit
because my son Luke was getting married in June, and he was going to come
to the wedding. In the end, of course he wasn't well enough to go.

VICKY MINET Before radiotherapy, he couldn't get words out but the radiotherapy worked well, it shrank the tumour, and he got his speech back. He was
articulate again. Language, of course, was him, and so he was being very positive that it worked. 'Look, I'm back to my old self now, and I'm well.' And I
went with that.

ALISON HASTIE Roger was much loved, and revered by his friends, and all of
them wanted to save his life. And there is this school of thought around cancer
that 'we can beat it'. I don't think Gary Rowland would mind me saying this,
Gary was adamant that Roger wouldn't be dying. It was totally not happening.
Almost on a daily basis people were bringing me things – has he done this? has
he done that? We tried some ghastly green things – a mixed special concoction –
and contacted clinics, and it's really crap because he wanted to live but there
are some fights that aren't even fights. There was a bit of railing and tears but
he was astonishingly pragmatic. He was really sad but he was also really quite
settled.

GARY ROWLAND I took him to hospital for treatment one day and I said,
'Doesn't it annoy you, Roger, that your own brain is killing you? You've lived
by your brain.' He accepted it better than I would've. I wasn't trying to wind
him up but I'd say, 'Come on, let's . . .' He did fight it but it was an unwinnable
fight. He was so gracious a man that he could accept his own death graciously.

TRACY SHARP I was part of the group of friends who took him to hospital for
treatment. On the way, he talked about how very interesting this brain tumour
was, and when he'd seen the scan how the tumour looked extraordinarily like

the roots of a tree in his brain, and that's why they couldn't operate. Even that he saw as something to be fascinated by.

*

ALISON HASTIE There were aspects which were super-fun like the day he came back from hospital and we realised we'd locked ourselves out so we had to get a ladder and I had to climb in an upstairs window. We laughed about that. We tried swimming in the Waveney once and it terrified the living day-lights out of me. Fortunately I took a rope and stayed on the bank so I could haul him out.

JAYNE IVIMEY Over the previous year, we had talked a lot about an exhibition I was holding at Salthouse church on the north Norfolk coast. He insisted that he wanted to see this exhibition but he was really ill. So Alison arranged that they would drive over and stay at a nearby hotel. And it was so awful. She drove him and they stopped in Aylsham because he wanted to go to the loo, and he was so long that after about half an hour she went in there and he couldn't get his trousers up and was in a really bad way. They got to the hotel, she put him to bed and rang me and said, 'Come over and help me decide what to do.'

ALISON HASTIE That was awful. We'd booked a really grand hotel and I knew as soon as we got there that I was out of my depth. I couldn't cope. In the end you don't want to be rescuing people from loos, trust me you do not. Poor Jayne, we wanted to go to her exhibition and we did get there in the end, on another day, but it was a bit frightening.

JAYNE IVIMEY Somehow, he made it to the show. He'd completely lost it, but he looked at the show.

ALISON HASTIE Roger wanted to be at Walnut Tree Farm. That was his fam-ily; that was his safe place. Eventually he could settle down and die in the house that he loved, in the place that he loved, and hopefully that's what would be one of the best things you could do for any of us.

*

ANDREW SANDERS One time when Alison was away, I stayed at Walnut Tree Farm for five days. He was mostly bedridden but could still walk and quite late one evening he said, 'I'd like to go for a walk.' There was no point asking him where he wanted to go because he knew, and I had to follow him. We set off and went all the way west down Mellis Common. There was a wonky old bridge crossing a deep ditch and then a cornfield. 'Come on,' he said. The clay soil was dry and very cracked and he was very interested in the cracks, as if they were going to open up. We walked around this field and then through another field and I said, 'Come on, Roger, we must get back.' It was beginning to get dark. 'No, no, we've got to go on.'

The place he wanted to go to was Burgate Wood, a very important place for him. Roger loved it. I walked there with him a number of times. It was a medieval wood of coppiced hornbeam, and it was spooky even in the daytime, and in the middle was the remains of a medieval manor.

We didn't reach Burgate Wood. It was almost dark and it was very difficult to turn him round but I had to lead him back. He was very reluctant to go home because he was at the end of his ability to walk. He had these longings; ordinary things that he was immensely fond of.

*

ROBERT MACFARLANE Terence and Alison had obviously had a discussion and Roger rang me to ask whether I would become his literary executor. I said, yes, of course, and that was the closest we came to talking about him dying. When it came to finishing *Wildwood*, nothing was written for him; what was needed was shaping the book into what became three sections. A bit of topping and tailing and ordering to get things in the right sequence. Roger had done most of that and then Terence, Simon and I became involved.

BUNDLE WESTON There were a couple of occasions where there was a brainstorming about *Wildwood* with a group of friends and they got that first chapter sorted out, which was wonderful because that was so necessary for Rog's wellbeing as much as anything else.

TERENCE BLACKER Roger was really concerned about *Wildwood*. We arranged a meeting with Roger and Rob and Simon Prosser in August. We wanted Simon to tell Roger that his book was all right; that it was going to get published. This was when Roger did realise he was on the way out. So it was an incredibly difficult meeting. The book needed a lot of work but Simon was really impressive. He was a grown-up. He said, 'You don't have to worry about it, it's all in and we're really happy. It's fantastic.' And he did a really good job because he reassured Roger.

ALISON HASTIE   We delivered the book, that was the thing for Roger. And we were so lucky because that August was beautiful and he was able to sit in the garden, under a tree, and just be there. He did say that he thought that if this was going to be it then that was OK. He was very accepting of it.

GEORGINA CAPEL   A few weeks before he died he told me he was struggling with horrible constipation from all the drugs. We had a call, he was outside in the garden, and I was in London, and I knew it was the last call, which is not something I've ever had before or since. I told him rather pathetically that I loved him and I promised to do everything I could for his books, and then we said goodbye.

ROBERT MACFARLANE, Underland (2019)   The first time I heard anyone speak of the 'wood wide web', more than a decade ago now, I was trying not to cry. A beloved friend was dying too young and too quickly. I had gone to see him for what I took to be the last time. He was tired by pain and drugs. We sat together, talked . . . That day I read aloud a poem that was important to us both, 'Birches' by Robert Frost, in which climbing the snow-white trunks of birches becomes both a readying for death and a declaration of life. Then he told me about new research he had recently read concerning the interrelations of trees: how, when one of their number was sickening or under stress, they could share nutrients by means of an underground system that conjoined their roots beneath the soil, thereby sometimes nursing the sick tree back to health. It was a measure of my friend's generosity of spirit that – so close to death himself – he could speak unjealously of this phenomenon of healing.

TONY BARRELL, memoirs   As dawn was breaking on a clear day in August, the phone rang from Suffolk: Roger's son Rufus with the news that his father's condition was getting worse very quickly and that he would like to speak to me. I was shocked and surprised. When my mother died of a brain tumour she too declined quickly, but had not been able to communicate at all in her last weeks. But although he sounded slow and spoke with little energy, Roger was lucid and engaged, and we had a 'normal' conversation, as we often did, about how the weather, or the climate, was going at opposite ends of the planet. Roger asked after Jane and Klio, my health and work, and then said simply, 'Don't worry. I'm not scared.' He felt a little tired, so we said goodbye. We both paused, wondering who should put down the phone first.

*

August 7 Bed arrived.

August 8 Rufus arrived.

August 11 Meeting with Simon Prosser. Reasonable night.

August 12 Visited Terence and Angela. Roger sleeping a lot.

August 13 Ru and Em left at lunchtime. Roger v. weak. Didn't get up today. Vicky and Ronnie p.m.

VICKY MINET I went to see him and took Ronnie with me. I thought it would give Roger pleasure and he seemed pleased but also slightly ill at ease, as if he didn't want Ronnie to see him in a weakened state where he couldn't have a decent conversation. But Ronnie knew exactly what to do, of course.

RONALD BLYTHE, River Diary *(2008)* The little window opens on to the mite of grass and the cool moat in which Roger swam all the year round, writing the Preface, as it were, for his strenuous masterpiece *Waterlog*. Now he whispers, his familiar voice a kind of human susurration in tune with aspen leaves, and we listen hard to catch his words. He looks if anything rather astonished, as do we in our different ways. When he drove from his ancient farmhouse to mine he would bring a present, a fine cup, a fine grapefruit sapling he had grown from a pip, and once a wonderful new scythe from Stowmarket . . . I have brought John Clare's poems with me. I read 'The Nightingale's Nest' and it describes Clare being torn between his need to come close to the sitting bird and his longing not to scare it. How can he communicate his not being like other men, or rather boys? It is a long poem and Roger's ears, I realise, are not at all dying at this moment. He is listening to Clare as keenly as we listened together to the nightingales at Tiger Hill.

VICKY MINET Ronnie is so philosophical about death. He is completely accepting of it. With Roger, I felt there was a hole in our conversation that we couldn't address. Why did he not say he was dying when we all knew it was happening? He didn't acknowledge that there was a problem at all, perhaps because he would rarely acknowledge any problem. We didn't have that conversation ever, about death. He wouldn't face it. And if he didn't bring it up, I couldn't.

RUFUS DEAKIN After he was diagnosed, Alison came round and she was incredibly helpful in looking after Dad after he was sick. He suddenly rallied for four or five days and he and I swam in the moat and we walked to Burgate

Wood. But the last few weeks were really shitty. The cancer had got into his stomach and he was in pain. At least he was at home, where he wanted to be, and it was mercifully quick. There's a strange sort of relief at the end with someone with terminal cancer. Particularly with him because he was losing his mind and he was someone who relied on his mind so much.

Alison Hastie, *diary, 2006*

August 15 Roger in chair. Tony Axon.
August 16 Tony Weston visited.
August 17 Roger stayed in bed.
August 18 Roger very frail. Tony Axon, Terence Blacker, Andrew Sanders.

TONY AXON I used to go up two or three times a week. There was not much you could do; it was just chatting, really. In the latter stages, he'd doze off a lot. One afternoon, an NHS van rolled up, the driver got out and said, 'We've come to deliver a bed for Mr Deakin. Where do you want it putting?' It was electric, with an adjustable back, and it was so he wouldn't have to go upstairs because he was quite weak. It didn't hit me until I was driving back – that was his deathbed.

ALISON HASTIE Did Roger pay me romantic compliments? He would say I looked nice. When we were at a dinner party he would look across the table and he would smile at me. It sounds ridiculously small but trust me, lots of men don't do that. At the very end, he was lying in the hospital bed in the sitting room at the bottom of the stairs and Jenny Farley, a local friend, was helping for the first time. I came down the stairs and Jenny said to Roger, 'Isn't she beautiful?' and Roger said yes. We need to get our stories in a little sooner, don't we? But he got it in. Time runs out and we don't realise.

TERENCE BLACKER I saw Roger on his last day and Roger said, 'It's OK.' But he was very, very weak.

ANDREW SANDERS That afternoon, Alison rang to say she was very tired and could I sit with Roger? So I went over. The sun was streaming in, and Roger was in a hospital bed in the sitting room. There were a lot of flies, so he had this plastic red fly swatter. When I arrived, he was trying to swat the flies but he had no strength. You could press a button on the bed and it could go up and down and he constantly needed it put up or down because he was very restless. He needed to be given sips of water every ten minutes, and they were tiny; that was all he could take. His mouth had completely cracked up.

He asked for a piece of paper and a pencil. You could hardly hear what he had to say. It was a whisper. There was a little notebook lying about. And he very, very laboriously did this drawing. And the drawing looked a bit like the head of a bird and then underneath what might have been the beak he did a whole lot of stabbing dots. And then he said, 'Do you know what this is?' I said, 'No, Roger, I don't know what this is.' He said, 'It's a game. It's a game.' I said, 'Well, what's the game, Roger?' 'Can't you see?' he said. 'It's the bird, and it's pecking. And do you know what those are?' 'No.' 'They are the microbes.' After he said that, he drew a scratchy thing. 'It's a black cloud,' he said. He was observing what was happening in himself and he was concerned that I didn't quite understand what was going on. So he thought he'd have a go at explaining it even though he was unable to read, let alone speak. He spent all his life constantly observing and constantly communicating and he was still trying to do it with his last breath.

Paul Bayley, Ricky Wright, Pussy Pratt, Simon Holmes, Diana Chapman, Susan Little, Julia Holborn, Elizabeth Moxon, Ian Keynes.

Lofty the Vicar. Rev. Moxon.

Ricky Wright's chain-smoking parents, and his kind big sisters. One worked for Radio Caroline.

High-explosive sodium chlorite pipe-bombs. Bikes outside Giles's. Dansette record players. Buddy Holly. Elvis. Fats Dominio. Dizzy Gilspy – 'Do you mean Gillespie?' Lonnie Donegan's 'Cumberland Gap', the 'Rock Island Line'.

The squirrel-tail saddle cover. The tandem. The tandem trailer and double bass. CAUTION. LONG VEHICLE.

Boys who were injured became instant heroes. Steve Dormer, concussed when knocked from his bicycle. Willie Watson with a torn ligament in his leg.

Mr Stimpson the bailiff.

'The Rec' – the model steam railway on brick plinths at one end of the Rec near the bowling green. It had a viaduct over a stream.

The memories are engrained in me.

The ecology of language and literature; the forest of early books. *The Land of Counterpane*, *Parlicoot's House*. The Scouting books.

Hatch End. Track bikes in the woods – a dirt-riding circuit. Soapbox trolleys in the Highgate woods. Treehouses in the spinney, and dens. Fire in our den. 'The main den'. Clay balls flung on whippy sticks of ash. Wooden fences. Listening in to Mrs Crawley, or Cracknell, ranting at Hitler behind the fence, when it was really us.

The quarry in the ditch, and the bridge.

The weather station.

The aquabike.

The Trafalgar Square pigeons.

The Windmill Theatre.

Tree frogs.

Praying mantises.

ALISON HASTIE, *diary, 2006*

August 19 2.40 a.m. Roger died. Terence arrived 3.30 a.m. and stayed night. Gary and Andrew arrived a.m.
August 20 Westons – Gary – Terence – Angela. Rufus and Emily arrived. Tony Axon.

JO SOUTHON, *letter to Roger, 18 August 2006* Dear Rog, I break my thirty-year silence because Mia has told me that you are very ill. I am so sorry. I unearthed your letters and poems and read a few for the first time in decades. They have the same brilliance and power to tug at the emotions as when they were stashed. Rog, I was head over heels and loved you with a passion. Love has come in softer, smoother ways that have been easier to live with. You changed my life – I became an English teacher and a strong swimmer. Whenever I glide through green depths of lake or sea I shall think of how you made me feel alive.

ALISON HASTIE After Roger died, Tony and Tere came with one of their grandchildren, a little boy of about eight, and we walked up the Long Meadow. It was a quietish day; the three of us and the little boy skittering about. Then, suddenly, this white-faced barn owl came swooping down in front of us. I had never seen a barn owl there before. It was just, it was Roger. It was.

CHAPTER 17

Ripples in the Moat

The funeral – the memorial celebration – Roger's archive – what would Roger say today? – Roger's ripples – the spirit of Roger and his special place: Walnut Tree Farm

ROGER, *notebooks, 2001, after a visit to Cromer* If I play my cards right I may get a memorial built to myself like Clement Scott – a horse drinking trough in granite, full of pansies on the Overstrand Road.

STEVE ASHLEY The funeral was very moving. It was a lovely humanist event with foliage all over his coffin.

BUNDLE WESTON Tony Weston took the ceremony, Tony Axon did the eulogy and then it was open house for other people to speak.

ROBERT MACFARLANE, Landmarks *(2016)* The coffin he lay in had a wreath of oak leaves on its lid. Just before it glided through the velvet curtains and into the cremating flames, Loudon Wainwright's 'The Swimming Song' was played, full of hope and loss.

Roger's ashes were spread by the largest oak on the footpath to Burgate Wood after leaving Mellis Common, and in the middle of the wood. Some were also scattered beside his moat.

*

ROGER'S *last Will, 8 August 2006* I give the sum of £70,000 to the Authors' Foundation and express the wish (without imposing any legal obligation) that they will use these funds to sponsor an annual award in my name . . . My Trustees shall hold the whole of the Trust Fund for RUFUS DANIEL DEAKIN.

After this gift to charity, and a smaller gift to Alison (amounting to less than 5 per cent of his estate), the rest of Roger Deakin's savings, his flat in London and Walnut Tree Farm, went to his son, Rufus.

GARY ROWLAND, *joint executor* It was surprising that when he died he had a lot of investments – stocks and shares and pensions – which I hadn't expected him to have. He was not a dark horse but it was a really sensible thing to do.

*

ALISON HASTIE A year after Roger's death, Rufus put on this incredible party with a big-top tent at Walnut Tree Farm.

TONY AXON The memorial service was a wonderful day.

GARY ROWLAND It was a flaming June day and Walnut Tree Farm was looking at its best. The turnout was tremendous, and speeches by Alison and Rob Macfarlane were particularly moving. We showed a loop of Roger's film work too, which was very entertaining and everyone jumped in the moat at the end.

RUFUS DEAKIN Loads of mostly lovely people, lots of cooking. Gary put together a cool video of some of Dad's work which played in the open-fronted barn. Tony Axon and Rob Macfarlane gave the best speeches. Mum, Margot and Serena got up together and spoke together which made me cry.

MARGOT WADDELL, *memorial address, 2007* I was told that the night Roger died he spoke of being able 'to see a very deep hole'. Whatever he meant by that he certainly has left a very deep hole – but out of it, as today attests, came some wonderful things, all bound by the richness of his very distinctive personality.

SARAH DICKINSON His memorial service was really moving. It was an old circus tent. We all sat on straw bales and there was copious amounts to drink. Various people spoke and the very last item was an extract from a radio programme he made. He was saying, 'I'm lying in a tent and what you can hear now is . . .' There wasn't a dry eye in the tent. Quite a few people stripped off and plunged into the moat and came out covered in weed hanging from their appendages. It was very funny. He created a lot of joy and a lot of angst for us all.

KATE WESTBROOK The memorial was in an open marquee. We performed a William Blake song, one of Mike's [Westbrook] settings, and Harvey and the Wallbangers did a number. People die in the wrong order. Roger should've had more time.

TERENCE BLACKER I played 'The Swimming Song' rather badly on the banjo. I remember a willow warbler singing in the hedge by the tent and thinking how appropriate that was. There was a great atmosphere of love for Roger, but not great keening.

JULES CASHFORD Roger's memorial service was permeated with a deep sadness, great respect, and shock – shock that all his enthusiasm and excitement, always brimming with life – projects, plans, visions for a happier Earth – could not somehow have kept him, of all people, alive. For he, of all people, was needed.

*

335

ANGELA SYKES After he died and for a long time, there were so many times when we'd be walking around here and we saw something and we'd say, 'Oh, I wonder what that is.' And we'd say, 'If only Roger were here.'

TERENCE BLACKER He is one of those people who stays with you, whose presence and whose sensibility and approach to life stays with you and shapes your own.

ROBERT MACFARLANE There was a long time when I was always thinking, what would Roger do or think about a certain thing? That was always a good question to ask and it remains a good question to ask.

*

In 2007, Rufus sold Walnut Tree Farm to his childhood friends, Titus and Jasmin Rowlandson. Four years after Roger's death, his literary executor, Robert Macfarlane, sorted through his papers and notebooks before they were given to the University of East Anglia, where they are kept in a literary archive.

ROBERT MACFARLANE, Landmarks With Titus and Jasmin's generous help, I began the process of working out what Roger had left behind. Digging through boxes; brushing away mouse droppings and spiders' webs; scanning letters from friends and collaborators; putting letters from lovers and family to one side unread. Each box I opened held treasure or puzzles: early poems; first drafts of *Waterlog*; a copy of the screenplay for *My Beautiful Laundrette* sent to Roger by Hanif Kureishi; word-lists of place-language (*tufa, bole, burr, ghyll*); a folder entitled 'Drowning (Coroners)', which turned out not to be a record of coroners that Roger had drowned, but an account of his research into East Anglian deaths-by-water. It was hard not to get distracted, especially by his notebooks. Each was a small landscape through which it was possible to wander and within which it was possible to get lost. One had a paragraph in which Roger imagined a possible structure for *Wildwood*: he compared it to a cabinet of wonders, a chest in which each drawer was made of a different timber and contained different remarkable objects and stories. The notebooks, taken together, represented an accidental epic poem of Roger's life, or perhaps a dendrological cross section of his mind. In their range and randomness, they reminded me that he was, as Les Murray once wrote, 'only interested in everything'.

*

TERENCE BLACKER After his death, Roger became a kind of green saint. And he wasn't a green saint, he was much more interesting.

SUE CLIFFORD I feel so sad because he would've loved all the attention. Loved it! He would've revelled in it, nicely. And it hadn't really hit the levels it seems to have hit now.

REBECCA CARTER I meet people all the time who say, 'Oh my God, *Waterlog* is my favourite book!' when they find out I worked on it.

CAROLINE CLIFTON-MOGG He'd be amazed and pleased that people are doing all this wild swimming. He might say, 'Oh, it's all become a bit Sunday supplement,' but he'd think that it was healthy, for body and mind. And he'd probably giggle at the number of people who now know who he was but he'd jolly well like it.

JULIA BLACKBURN I'm curious to know how ambivalent Roger would've been about his own success. Either he would've been turned into a kind of grand guru, a Laurens van der Post, 'How true, how very true', or he'd have stepped back and said none of this really matters.

SARAH BLUNT Everything in Roger's life would inspire a radio programme. If he had lived longer we would have loved to make a programme about green lanes. We talked about recreating his boyhood nature camps in the New Forest with his old teacher and a programme on tree-climbing or living in trees. It would have gone on and on.

ANDREW SANDERS If he had lived I think he would've become much more political. He could've been a very, very powerful voice. He was very angry – about farming, about roads, about the countryside – but he was very articulate about why he was angry.

BOB MARSHALL-ANDREWS I'm absolutely certain that he would've been in Extinction Rebellion and could have been a significant figure in that movement.

SUE CLIFFORD He would have been powering up the Thames, demanding things.

*

GILBERT REID Roger was an extraordinary person, prophetic in some of his interests, complex, with an almost saint-like facade – and also deep inside – and with a wry sense of humour.

337

LUCY BAILEY He was this Renaissance man, truly impressive in his different abilities and interests. He had this voracious interest in the world and he translated that into oneself so he had enormous charm – and women fell for him and loved that – but he also loved us for what we did, and he was incredibly generous.

JULES CASHFORD I see Roger's legacy as calling us beyond the customary boundaries of what is possible – in ways of thinking and ways of being – caring deeply for all creatures great and small – whether studying a fly, a spider, or a fungus, or travelling through continents to meet an oak tree of singular magnificence, or diving into a swirling river in winter searching for otters, or walking so fast he was almost impossible to keep up with, striding up hills as though they needed someone to stand on their very top and celebrate the whole landscape as far as you could ever see, stretching endlessly, leading to everywhere.

RUFUS DEAKIN His public legacy is wild swimming, not that he invented it, but *Waterlog* will stand the test of time and still inspires people to get out into the wilds and strip off. He was genuinely ahead of his time in lots of ways, from Common Ground to documentaries seeking to inspire children about nature.

JENNY KEMBER Roger's legacy – the first and much celebrated modern book about wild swimming. A beautiful natural history writer and an early and passionate environmentalist. Personally, my wonderful son, but tainted at the time by sadness and disappointment.

SERENA INSKIP My perceptions have evolved over this time of reflection. This is how I feel today.
　'The Good Things' I am grateful for:

The beautiful chest of drawers that Roger made for me, from old oak boards, full of poems handwritten after the first Dordogne trip. And a coffee-pot handle crafted by Roger.
I knew I had a lot to learn, and here was where I learned, a lot.
Wherever possible, I've always had the best support from all my family and friends.
Bat is buried in the far corner of the middle field at Walnut Tree Farm, with daffodils.
My tractor is still running at the farm too.

I am alive and I told my bit of the story.

No one is to blame. *Je ne regrette rien.*

JULIA BLACKBURN The energy that made him into a writer is the energy that whipped him up into furies, or got him confused. But out of that, he found that way through the confusion or through the pent-up-ness. He was certainly utterly genuine in his striving to find peace within himself and also to find words to put not his love of nature but what he got out of it for himself, in the way of finding quiet, and that's very valuable.

ANNETTE KOBAK There's a lovely review of a Richard Jefferies book by Roger. This is Roger writing about him: 'Never simply viewing the land through a study window, but always placing himself and his reader, foursquare in the open air, writing with an intense intimacy, proving his observations on the pulse, as Keats puts it, Jefferies "takes part in the existence of things" very much as Keats did. Jefferies is hopelessly in love with what he calls the divine chaos of nature. For in its absence of design, he sees limitless hope and possibilities.'

That could have been a manifesto, for Roger.

ROBERT MACFARLANE Roger's legacy, in short: a rippling, branching ability to inspire love and wonder at the living world; a Green Man who still speaks to us in leaves.

RICHARD MABEY His legacy could be summed up in his phrase, 'seeking the extraordinary in the ordinary'. And his writing style was an inimical template for loose-limbed, free-associative, fiercely attentive wordplay.

ROON HUTTON Despite the calumny and the ridicule that he sometimes endured in the sixties, the main point was how cool Roger Deakin was. The swimming around England, the forests, his deep love of nature – there's nothing more cool than that. Roger was cool and he'll always be cool, and I bet he didn't realise that, bless him.

ANDREW CRACKNELL And he was fucking good company!

*

PATRICK BARKHAM The long grass still ripples like water on Mellis Common in midsummer. The swimmer takes a sudden left by the sallows and bumps on to the track that leads to a copse and a glimpse of an old brick chimney. Sheltered by the guardian ash, and the spreading canopy of the walnut, is Walnut

Tree Farm, long, low and slender, with its roof of red pantiles fossicked from surrounding ruins.

Here is wood, pasture, shelter, fire, water.

The rear end of Roger's ancient grey Ferguson tractor protrudes from the barn. Between the elegant curve of the brick wall Roger built for Serena and an enormous pair of blacksmith's bellows gently decaying against the west end of the house, the path skips around to the warm southern side, where Roger's favourite rose, the 'Rambling Rector', throws its creamy fragrance with abandon. The door is open; the bees are busy.

It takes a moment for eyes to adjust to the inside of the house, its green-lit windows like a bower deep in the woods. A hefty ginger cat, disturbed, dashes from the Aga and under the big kitchen table. There is a wall of pictures, postcards and mementoes, like Roger once had. He is still here too, curls and grin, in one of the photographs. Beyond, the low-ceilinged sitting room where the cavernous open fireplace smells of last winter's woodsmoke. A floor brick bears a prophetic inscription made by the potter and poet Tony Weston when the house was first restored by Roger in the early seventies.

> This house was built by my true friend
> His work stands up, his labours end.
> By this place he will be known
> To those who never know his face.

A bumblebee diverts from rose to sitting room, and then out again through the window, into the dazzle and over the herringbone brick patio and rough green lawn adorned with purple ground ivy and yellow cowslips in spring and ox-eye daisies in summer.

Garden warblers and peacock butterflies and people are held safe in this glade of oak, ash and thorn. Its fortifications, the billowing hedges of black-thorn and field maple and holly, grow ever more generous. Nothing of the village beyond is visible although the wider world occasionally takes shape in sound: cows lowing at Hall Farm, a tractor, the tinny buzz of a 50cc motorbike heading to Eye. When silence returns it seems deeper than ever.

Every twenty minutes or so, time is marked by a faint 'woo-uh, woo-uh, woo-uh' rising from the level-crossing gates half a mile distant heralding the London train, a ten-second rush of noise arriving and departing through the trees. On a winter's night, the lit windows of carriages flicker through the bare branches like the fleeting projection of an ancient movie.

Across the lawn, between coppiced hazels, lies the moat, its moods as varied as the sea's. In winter, its banks are open and its water is clear, traced with silver and gold in the pale sunlight. In summer, it is wrapped in green leaves and coiled with tresses of ranunculus. Great-crested newts hang suspended in the water like a mobile dangling from the ceiling of a child's bedroom.

At this time of year, the swimmer can be heard but not seen through the rosebay willowherb that springs up along the bank. They glide along, surveying the top of the house that runs parallel as swallows dart above and moorhens parp below.

The water is always cool but also unexpectedly soft and sweet, an upwelling from the aquifer. Last year's hazelnuts, blackened by their dunking, bob on the surface like water snails. The duckweed tickles and each stroke propels it downwards into the dusk. The swimmer scatters it in all directions but by the time they turn for another length it has reunited into a bowling green once again, as if maintained by a very devout groundsman.

A young frog kicks down and away. Diving deeper, the bottom of the moat at the east end is soft clay, smooth and firm to touch. In the depths of the west end an aquatic trampoline of leaves and twigs has accumulated.

Pulling themselves out via the rotting half-ladder fixed to the bank, the swimmer feels cool water and hot blood; calmer than before and perhaps more alive than ever, for a few seconds at least. Scattering meadow browns, they walk south through the four fields that Roger bought from Arthur Cousins, each its own thickly hedged room, and, from the air, virtually the only pattern in this part of Suffolk that still conforms to the old maps. The western edge of the farm is most tree-fringed of all, for this is Cowpasture Lane, and its endurance, as a medieval motorway, a long green, an accidentally coppiced woodland, may be Roger's greatest physical legacy.

In early 2020, the current owners of Walnut Tree Farm, Titus and Jasmin Rowlandson, worked with the landowner, Nigel Battell, the son of William, the farmer Roger once fought to preserve Cowpasture Lane, to reinstate the section of the lane south of the railway line that had been ripped out and ploughed up fifty years before. Dozens of local people and some of Roger's old friends replanted a native hedge and trees at the grand width of the original lane. Roger may have preferred natural regeneration but the trees needed a little assistance. Today, they are stretching up towards the sky.

At the southern edge of the middle field is the old shepherd's hut that was Roger's best farm-auction bargain of the early eighties as the old agricultural life came to an end in this part of the world. Inside the hut, the panels of warm pine are fixed into a peak like a miniature chapel. It is maintained as Roger kept it, with a bed, desk and woodburner to revive the chilled swimmer.

Out here, luxuriantly starred nights are dark and quiet, interspersed with the passing drama of the trains. Mornings are bright. Craneflies bash limbs against the hut's half-sash window; wasps mine flakes of exterior wood; birdsong spills in. Is that drill of notes a nightingale? Is that somnolent purr a turtle dove? Both vanishing species still occasionally pitch up in this sanctuary mile of hedgerows, in whose vale echo the inept harmonies of competing wood pigeons and a melodic wall of blackcap and blackbird sound. At first light, the fields belong to the rabbit who chews grass, the muntjac who saunters beside the blackthorn and the male pheasant with his ridiculous red eye-mask who parades proprietorially past.

Walnut Tree Farm is still suffused with the spirit of the man who held the piece of paper that gave him freehold here between 1970 and 2006. The green BMC truck in which he proffered lifts to pupils from Diss Grammar is just visible, decaying in the hedge. Tear into the bramble and ivy and the skeletons of two pale Citroën DS Safaris emerge. Wood salvaged from skips in seventies London, bottles of home-brewed cider from the eighties, old car batteries from the nineties and miscellaneous other detritus may yet be stumbled across.

This place owes much of its present-day magic to the ad man from London who wanted to be a teacher, whose dreaming brought him to Suffolk; who liked soft outlines over hard, preferred ruins to homes, chose pencil strokes, not pen; snatched conversations; fantasy; mystery. He put down roots but remained restless too. He shaped this hidden world and inhabited it with utmost sincerity but it was this place before he arrived and it is this place after he departed. He was, as he wrote, just passing through.

This modest patch of north Suffolk is not a museum. It is not preserved in aspic but reverberates with the art and design and dreams of others from the past and the present, most particularly its current owners. The swimmer's imagination may also detect the singing spirit of John Clare and Ronnie Blythe and Rooster Byron and Steve Ashley and Serena Inskip and Rufus Deakin and Robert Macfarlane and many others who have shaped how we see rural England or simply laughed in Walnut Tree Farm's kitchen and gasped in the moat and lay in the long grass and left a piece of heart or mind with the bees or the barn owl that still ghosts across the meadows at twilight.

To the slower beat of a longer time, trees grow up and trees die back. The oaks that Roger planted across the middle of the Long Meadow are mature trees. His Railway Wood, a small triangle against the line that was newly planted in the eighties, is all grown up. The great elms that rose above the hedgerows succumbed to disease in the seventies; some of their replacements, self-sown ashes of grace and height, are dying back because of new disease. The seasons turn. Plants and animals and people; we come and go, brightening the place with a momentary firework of drama, a quick dance of life.

ROGER DEAKIN, *notebooks*, 2002 Eddie comes on his tractor to cut the hay. I point out that I've planted a row of five young walnuts across the field and he grunts.

'Why did you have to plant them right across the field?' he asks.

'Because they will look beautiful when they're grown up,' I say.

And if you ever visit Walnut Tree Farm, you will see that they do.

INDEX OF PEOPLE

MEG AMSDEN and TIM HUNKIN Meg and Tim are friends of Roger from Suffolk in the 1970s and 1980s and, like Roger, settlers from London. Meg, an artist, founded a puppet show company. Tim, an inventor, engineer, cartoonist and creative collaborator, worked with Roger on various advertising films in the 1980s.

CHARLES ANSON A friend of Roger at Cambridge University and for several years afterwards, Anson joined the Foreign Office and eventually became press secretary to the Queen.

ANDREA ARNOLD Now an acclaimed film-maker, Andrea met Roger when she was a children's TV presenter. They became friends after working together on the ITV environmental series *A Beetle Called Derek* (1990). Arnold's short film, *Wasp*, won an Academy Award in 2005; her feature films include *Red Road* (2006) and *Fish Tank* (2009).

STEVE ASHLEY A much-loved English folk singer-songwriter whom Roger got to know through arranging a charity concert. Roger hired him to provide the soundtrack to two of his documentaries in the 1990s and the pair remained good friends.

LAURENCE ASTON The former manager of Mike and Kate Westbrook, Aston became friends with Roger and they worked on several musical and artistic projects together.

TONY AXON Roger's oldest friend, who met Roger when they joined the same class at Haberdashers' aged ten in September 1953. Worked for *The Economist* and later ran his own publishing company. Married Teresa, whom he met in Cambridge on a night out with Roger. Roger was best man at their wedding and they continued to see each other regularly – despite Tony mostly living in Spain – for the whole of Roger's life.

LUCY BAILEY Theatre director and co-founder of the theatrical music group the Gogmagogs (1995–2006), during which time she met and became good friends with Roger, who served on the board of the Gogs.

IAN BAKER A friend from Haberdashers', Ian studied the sciences at A level and joined Roger on his New Forest camps. He later became a vet.

GRAHAM 'BEN' BARKER-BENFIELD Ben was a friend of Roger and Tony Axon at Haberdashers'. He became a historian based at universities in the United States for most of his working life.

KEN BARRELL A teacher at Diss Grammar School during Roger's time (1975–78), and a rare friend of Roger in the staffroom. Roger joined Ken on one of his regular student trips to the Lake District. His wife, Di Barrell, also knew Roger.

TONY BARRELL Roger's friend and flatmate at Queen's Gardens from 1965 to the early 1970s. Barrell was a freelance copywriter and songwriter with Roon Hutton. He later moved to Australia with his wife, Jane Norris, and became a broadcaster with the ABC. Roger visited Tony on both his Australia trips, and Tony and Jane visited Walnut Tree Farm when they were in Europe.

DEBBIE BARTLETT A pupil of Roger at Diss Grammar School from 1975 to 1978, Debbie was a member of his sixth-form group who were later given extra tuition by Roger at Walnut Tree Farm. After Diss, Debbie got a place at Cambridge.

JOHN BAYLEY An art director at Interlink from 1973 to 1974 who was part of the creative team working under Roger as creative director.

PETER BERGLUND A pupil of Roger at Diss Grammar School.

EMMA BERNARD The daughter of Oliver Bernard, a poet who moved to East Anglia a decade before Roger, and became an important friend and influence on Roger from the seventies onwards. Emma was also taught by Roger at Diss Grammar and became friends with Roger too.

JULIA BLACKBURN Julia is the award-winning author of fiction and non-fiction including *Time Song: Searching for Doggerland* (2019) and *The Three of Us* (2008), a memoir about the domestic violence in her bohemian upbringing. She met Roger through her friend Serena Inskip, and for many years lived nearby in Suffolk. Roger sought out her advice about writing in the early 1990s, particularly impressed by her 1991 biography of the naturalist Charles Waterton.

TERENCE BLACKER Author of fiction for children and adults and a biography (of the writer and satirist Willie Donaldson) as well as being a national newspaper columnist for sixteen years and a musician. Terence got to know Roger through his first wife, Caroline Soper, who was friends with Serena Inskip. The Blackers had a second home in the Waveney Valley and Terence later moved permanently to Norfolk. Became close friends with Roger from the mid-1990s. With Alison Hastie, Terence edited *Notes from Walnut Tree Farm* (2008), the posthumous collection of Roger's notebooks.

SARAH BLUNT Radio producer with the BBC Natural History Unit who made Roger's three radio programmes for Radio 4: *The House*, *The Garden* and *Cigarette on the Waveney*.

RONALD BLYTHE Author of *Akenfield* (1969), the classic account of village life, Blythe has written novels, books of essays and many collections of his long-running *Church Times* column. Deeply rooted in Essex and Suffolk, Blythe is one of the most brilliant writers of English rural life. Roger greatly admired Ronnie and became friends with him in his final years. Ronnie died, aged 100, in 2023.

NIGEL BROWN A friend of Roger from Haberdashers', Nigel also went to Cambridge where he studied history. Was in touch with Roger later when his company, IBM, supported Roger's Common Ground charity.

JONATHAN BURNHAM Publishing director at Chatto who signed up Roger to write *Waterlog*. Left the company for a US publishing job before *Waterlog* was published.

ERICA BURT NÉE ROBERTON Roger's most serious girlfriend at Cambridge, Erica studied to become a teacher at Homerton College. They were in touch again after Roger wrote *Waterlog*.

MAY LING CADWALLADER The wife of Graham Cadwallader who was a friend of Roger from Cambridge and, like Roger, worked in advertising in the 1960s.

GEORGINA CAPEL A literary agent who became Roger's agent in 2001, and arranged the publishing deal with Hamish Hamilton for what became *Wildwood*.

REBECCA CARTER Editor of *Waterlog*, which was Carter's first major editorial job at Chatto & Windus. She later became a literary agent.

JULES CASHFORD Writer and thinker and teacher who trained as a Jungian analyst, Cashford is the author of *The Moon: Symbol of Transformation* (2003) and co-author of *The Myth of the Goddess: Evolution of an Image* (1993). She became friends with Roger when she was Dudley Young's partner at Cambridge in the 1960s. For many years, she was a source of sisterly advice for Roger, and helped him with Somerset swims in *Waterlog*.

CELIA Celia met Roger aged twenty while working as a secretary at advertising agency Leo Burnett, where Roger was a copywriter. She was his girlfriend from 1967 to 1968. She later married and had children and asked for her surname not to be used in this book.

MAVIS CHEEK Comic literary novelist with fifteen books to her name, including *Dog Days* (1990), *Mrs Fytton's Country Life* (2000) and *The Sex Life of My Aunt* (2002). Having met at Caroline Soper's fiftieth birthday party, she and Roger became good friends from 1996, going to book launches and meeting their mutual friend Terence Blacker at the Chelsea Arts Club. Mavis provided Roger with moral support during the writing of *Waterlog*.

SUE CLIFFORD Co-founder with her partner Angela King and Roger of the charity Common Ground. She and King met Roger in the 1970s through King's position as wildlife campaigner for Friends of the Earth. King and Clifford continued to run Common Ground until 2015 when they retired, with the charity passing to Adrian Cooper, the founder of Little Toller Books. Remained good friends with Roger, who stayed with them during his *Waterlog* swims.

CAROLINE CLIFTON-MOGG A journalist and author who was a friend of Roger in the 1960s and beyond. Caroline introduced Roger to Jenny Hind, who became his wife. Caroline later married Roger's Cambridge friend Charlie Levison, a lawyer who became a senior figure in the music business and died in the same year as Roger.

RICHARD COOK A copywriter hired by Roger in 1973 to join him at Interlink. Became friends with Roger and spent time with him at Walnut Tree Farm.

ANDREW CRACKNELL Copywriter and an extremely successful creative director and advertising executive in Britain and the United States. Andrew met and became friends with Roger when they worked at nearby agencies in Covent Garden in 1973 and stayed friends with Roger through later decades.

PIPPA CRACKNELL Former wife of Andrew Cracknell, who visited Walnut Tree Farm in the late 1970s, 1980s and 1990s.

ANNE CRAWFORD A girlfriend of Roger in the 1960s, Anne is a medieval historian, archivist and author of *The Yorkists: The History of a Dynasty* (2007).

SARAH CRAWFORD A pupil of Roger during his time at Diss Grammar School (1975–78), Sarah read English at Cambridge.

ANDREW CROOK The son of Ivy Crook, sister of Gwen Deakin. Andrew was eighteen months younger than Roger and the two cousins often played together as children.

IAN CROOK Andrew's younger brother. The Crooks' father, Frank Crook, took Roger and his boys hunting for fossils and, once, on an expedition to shoot a squirrel. Roger wrote an affectionate poem for Frank on his ninetieth birthday.

RUFUS DEAKIN Roger's son and only child, with Jenny, his wife. Rufus became a chef in London and later restored houses and ran a micro-bakery in Spain. Now lives in the United States with his jeweller wife, Emily.

SARAH DICKINSON A girlfriend of Roger in the 1960s, Sarah became a broadcaster, novelist and founder of Ladbroke Radio. Like many girlfriends, she stayed on good terms and in touch with Roger and she and her husband, John, would visit Walnut Tree Farm.

JOHN and JENNY FARLEY Neighbours and friends of Roger in Mellis.

BARRY GOATER Assistant biology master at Haberdashers' when Roger arrived at the school, Barry became Head of Department in 1958. He introduced the New Forest ecology camps which inspired Roger and many others. Barry continued to teach at Haberdashers' until 1988, clocking up 102 terms at the school. Later, he met Roger again when he was researching *Wildwood*. Barry died, aged ninety-one, in 2022.

RICHARD HANDFORD An English student at Peterhouse College, Cambridge, who became room-mates and friends with Roger from his second year. Richard became a successful TV producer and director working on series including *Emmerdale*, *The Bill* and *Casualty*, as well as *Stig of the Dump*.

BEN HARKER A design engineer and carpenter who came to work on Walnut Tree Farm as a young man and also helped Serena and Roger on their house in Chalk Farm. Also worked for Matt Marchbank.

ALISON HASTIE Roger's partner from 2002 until his death, Alison founded Green Shoes, an ethical footwear company based in Devon. She still lives in Devon and recently sold her business.

MICHAEL HOLLINGTON A professor of English at the University of East Anglia and later at the University of New South Wales, Sydney, Michael was a friend of Roger in his early years at Haberdashers'.

JOHN HUGGINS Friend of Roger from Haberdashers', John rowed with Roger and Tony Axon. He was a loyal writer to Roger at university and hitch-hiked with him through France one summer holiday. Roger was John's best man at his marriage to SUE REID.

SAM HUTT In one life, a paediatrician; in another, the country and western singer Hank Wangford. Sam Hutt was a fixture of the Barsham Fairs and the Waveney Valley scene in the seventies, and Roger made an ITV documentary about him in 1993. During the sixties, Hutt was a rock-and-roll doctor, treating stars such as Gram Parsons, who converted him to country music.

ANDREW 'ROON' HUTTON With his brother, Bullus, Roon lived in another flat on Queen's Gardens. Roon formed a band, Mushroon, with Roger's flatmate Tony Barrell. He has been a musician all his life. When I interviewed him in 2021, he still lived in a flat on Queen's Gardens.

BULLUS HUTTON A friend of Roger in the late sixties and early seventies. Bullus was a rock-and-roll accountant and emigrated with his wife, Marta, to Canada, where he lives today.

SERENA INSKIP Roger's partner from 1980 to 1990. Today Serena lives in Suffolk and continues to campaign for sustainable farming and against nuclear power. She has two children, with her first husband.

JAYNE IVIMEY A painter who is inspired by the natural world, Jayne got to know Roger with her first husband, Clive Davies, a potter, when they lived close to the River Waveney. She was good friends with Roger in his later years. She now lives on the north Norfolk coast and continues to paint and exhibit.

ROSIE JACKSON An author, poet and academic who taught English at the University of East Anglia in the 1970s and 1980s. Rosie was Roger's lover in early 1977. Her books include *Fantasy: The Literature of Subversion* (2002) and her memoir, *The Glass Mother* (2016). Extracts here are kindly reproduced with Rosie's permission.

BARRIE JUNIPER Reader in plant sciences at the University of Oxford and author of *The Extraordinary Story of the Apple* (2019). Angela King and Sue Clifford introduced Roger to Barrie, who advised him on his trip to Kazakhstan for *Wildwood*.

JENNY KEMBER NÉE HIND Met Roger in 1968; they fell in love and married in 1973, Jenny giving birth to their son, Rufus, in December 1974. Jenny and Roger split in 1976. Jenny later married Joe Kember and they had three daughters. Today they live in Kent close to their daughters and grandchildren.

HOLLY KERR A colleague of Caroline Soper at Chatham House who was given a characteristic tour of Walnut Tree Farm by Roger after meeting at Soper's fiftieth birthday party.

TOBY KIDD One of the three children of Helen Kidd, a teacher and poet who was Roger's cousin on his mother's side. Helen and Adrian were the children of Margaret Wood, Gwen's younger sister, and Roger probably felt closest to them of all his cousins in adulthood. Adrian, who features in Roger's Welsh adventures in *Waterlog*, died shortly before he was fifty, soon after *Waterlog* was published.

ANGELA KING Co-founder with Roger and her partner Sue Clifford of the charity Common Ground in 1983. King and Clifford met Roger in the 1970s through Friends of the Earth, where King was wildlife campaigner and ran the Save the Whale! campaign. King and Clifford continued to run Common Ground until 2015 when they retired, with the charity passing to Adrian Cooper, the founder of Little Toller Books. Remained good friends with Roger, who stayed with them during his *Waterlog* swims.

ANNETTE KOBAK Writer, painter, biographer, literary critic and broadcaster, Annette first met Roger through mutual friends shortly after they both studied at Cambridge in 1961–64. They met again in 2000 and fell in love. Annette inspired Roger to travel to Poland and Ukraine, and they both wrote about their travels together – Annette in her memoir about her father, *Joe's War* (2004), and Roger in *Wildwood*. They parted in 2002.

RAMONA KOVAL The Australian writer and broadcaster Romana Koval met Roger at the Edinburgh Festival in 1999 and gave him great help during his two trips to Australia. Her many books include *Jewish Cooking, Jewish Cooks* (2000) and *A Letter to Layla* (2020).

EDDIE and CHRISTINE LANCHESTER Neighbours of Roger. Eddie helped Roger rebuild Walnut Tree Farm in the early 1970s.

RICHARD MABEY The pre-eminent British nature writer for many decades, Richard was a friend of Roger from Common Ground days through to his writing life. Richard moved to the Waveney Valley near Roger in 2002 and wrote about this change of landscape – and Roger – in *Nature Cure* (2005).

ROBERT MACFARLANE Internationally acclaimed writer and fellow of Emmanuel College, Cambridge, Robert was an important friend for Roger from 2003 until his death in 2006. They met after Roger read and loved Macfarlane's first book, *Mountains of the Mind* (2003). Robert later became Roger's literary executor.

MATT MARCHBANK A skilled carpenter and craftsman, Matt was friends with Serena and then Roger in the 1980s and 1990s. As well as building some of London's most fashionable watering holes, Matt also did some work for Roger.

BOB MARSHALL-ANDREWS A barrister who later became a Labour MP under the Blair administration, Marshall-Andrews got to know Roger in the 1960s and became a good friend and flatmate of Roger at 23 Queen's Gardens. In 1981, he helped Roger in his legal battle to protect Cowpasture Lane.

SIR CHRISTOPHER MEYER Diplomat and former Ambassador to the United States who was friends with Roger at Cambridge University and for several years afterwards.

JOHN MILLS Roger's eldest cousin, John, is the son of Doris, the eldest of the five Wood sisters of whom Roger's mum, Gwen, was the second oldest.

VICKY MINET First got to know Roger in the 1970s through her then boyfriend, Dudley Young. Vicky later became a sheep farmer and good friends with Roger and Serena. She was an important confidante for Roger in his later life and the woods on her small farm in Essex were a source of inspiration for Roger and feature in *Wildwood*.

ALISON MITCHELL An artist and weaver who lived near Roger in south Norfolk and had a brief relationship with him in 1979.

CLAIRE MORTIMER Pupil in Roger's 3Z form at Diss Grammar School who, like a number of former pupils, became a teacher, in part inspired by Roger.

LUCY MOY-THOMAS Keen swimmer and friend of Roger in the late 1990s; teacher in further education, poet and painter.

JANE NORRIS The wife of Tony Barrell, and an architect and film production designer.

ROSEMARY PALMER A teacher at Diss Grammar School during Roger's time (1975–78), she was deputy head when he left in 1978 and became head teacher as the school was merged with the town's secondary modern to become Diss High School.

ROB PARFITT AND CHRISTINE SMITH Rob Parfitt became friends with Roger in the 1970s through the *Waveney Chronicle* and the Barsham Fairs scene. A teacher who also ran a small farm and restored a derelict house, Rob taught Roger's son, Rufus, when he briefly attended a primary school in Harleston.

JASPER PARROTT Became friends with Roger during the 1960s and moved into Roger's flat at 23 Queen's Gardens for a short period at the end of the decade. In 1969, in Queen's Gardens, Parrott set up HarrisonParrott, an international classical music management agency.

BRIAN PERMAN Husband of Roger's first literary agent, Jane Turnbull, Brian was a schoolfriend of Roger who lived in nearby Pinner and hung out with Roger as a young teenager. Met Roger again when they both worked in advertising and later became a managing director in publishing and chief executive of the Book Trust charity. He was sought out again by Roger for his literary connections in 1995 when Roger first considered writing a book.

GEORGE PETERKEN A renowned woodland ecologist and author, Peterken studied at Haberdashers' several years ahead of Roger, and attended the same New Forest ecology camps with their inspirational teacher, Barry Goater. Roger interviewed Peterken in *Wildwood*.

SIMON POULTER An artist, curator and art consultant who was a pupil of Roger at Diss Grammar School.

SIMON PROSSER Publisher of Hamish Hamilton. In 2001, Simon signed a deal with Roger for *Wildwood*, which was originally called 'Touching Wood'. He helped Roger finish his book, which was published in 2007, the year after Roger's death. He also published *Notes from Walnut Tree Farm*, a collection of Roger's notebooks edited by Alison Hastie and Terence Blacker.

TIM RAYNER First husband of Meg Amsden and a TV director, he knew Roger in the 1970s and in 1990 hired him to help make the ITV environmental series *A Beetle Called Derek*.

GILBERT REID A Canadian who became part of Roger's Cambridge friendship group in the mid to late 1960s, coalesced around Dudley Young. Gilbert is now a novelist based in Canada but for thirty years worked as a diplomat in Ottawa, London and Rome. He has worked as an economist, in public relations, for film festivals and taught English literature in Italy.

SUE REID John Huggins's first wife, Sue knew Roger as a teenager.

SUE ROE Roger was friends with two Sue Roes. Sue Roe the biographer and poet is the author of *Gwen John: A Life* (2001) and *The Private Lives of the Impressionists* (2006). She was a friend in the 1990s and advised Roger on *Waterlog*. Later, Roger also became friends with another Sue Roe who worked for the Woodland Trust for twenty years (and isn't quoted in this biography).

JO ROLFE A pupil of Roger at Diss Grammar School, Jo was part of his sixth-form group who were later given extra tuition by Roger at Walnut Tree Farm. She stayed friends with Roger throughout his life.

GARY and VIVA ROWLAND   An advertising art director, Gary Rowland began working with Roger on environmental campaigns in the 1970s. Became a particularly close friend after moving to Norfolk with Viva in the latter years of Roger's life.

TITUS and JASMIN ROWLANDSON   Childhood friends of Rufus, the couple bought Walnut Tree Farm from him in 2007 – and inherited Roger's precious cats, Millie and Alphonse. Titus and Jasmin still live there today. Titus restores old Alfa Romeos and Jasmin is a painter and jeweller. She created the endpapers in this book.

ANDREW SANDERS   A film production designer who has worked with Merchant Ivory and many leading directors including Martin Scorsese, Bernardo Bertolucci, Nic Roeg, Stephen Frears and Ang Lee. Films include *The White Countess*, *The Golden Bowl* and *Spider*. Became good friends with Roger in the late 1990s after buying a house in Eye, Suffolk.

BILL SEAMAN   A pupil of Roger at Diss Grammar School from 1975 to 1976. Like many former pupils, Bill was in touch with Roger during much of his later life.

TRACY SHARP   A pupil of Roger at Diss Grammar School from 1975 to 1978, Tracy was part of his sixth-form group who were later given extra tuition by Roger at Walnut Tree Farm. She stayed friends with Roger throughout his life.

PETER and JOAO SMITH   Friends of Roger who lived in south Norfolk. Peter is a photographer who photographed Jimi Hendrix, the Rolling Stones and others. Joao bakes exceedingly good Portuguese cakes.

CAROLINE SOPER   Became friends with Roger through a friendship with Serena in the 1980s. Caroline worked at Chatham House for many years and is the former wife of Terence Blacker.

JO SOUTHON   Worked at Interlink with Roger in 1973–74 where she and Roger began an affair. Jo later retrained to become an English teacher.

MIKE SOUTHON   A renowned cinematographer, Mike met Roger in the 1970s and they later collaborated on big-budget advertising campaigns. In the 1980s and 1990s, Mike also filmed many movies and major rock videos for international stars including Guns N' Roses ('November Rain'), George Michael and U2.

ANGELA SYKES Partner of Terence Blacker and programme manager for Diss Corn Hall.

ANN THWAITE The acclaimed biographer of A. A. Milne and Frances Hodgson Burnett and wife of the poet and editor Anthony Thwaite, whom Roger met in 1976 and greatly admired. The Thwaites lived in south Norfolk, not far from Roger.

LUCY THWAITE Daughter of Ann and Anthony Thwaite. Roger taught Lucy French at Diss Grammar School (1975–78). Her mother was so despairing of her progress that she hired Rosie Jackson (who by coincidence was one of Roger's lovers) as a private tutor.

MARY TODD A pupil of Roger at Diss Grammar School from 1975 to 1978, Mary was another member of his sixth-form group who were later given extra tuition by Roger at Walnut Tree Farm. She became a head teacher in London during her career.

JANE TURNBULL A literary agent and the wife of Roger's schoolfriend Brian Perman, Jane represented Roger. In 1996 she obtained his first book deal, with Chatto, to publish *Waterlog*.

ANNA WADDELL Daughter of Margot Waddell and Bob Young (1935–2019). Bob Young was an American-born historian and philosopher of science who taught at Cambridge.

MARGOT WADDELL A psychoanalyst and psychotherapist, author and editor who worked for many years in the Tavistock Clinic's Adolescent Department. Roger fell in love with Margot in the 1960s, they became good friends and then partners from 1990 to 1995. She is the author of books including *Inside Lives* (1998) and *On Adolescence* (2018).

NICHOLAS WADDELL Son of Margot Waddell and Bob Young.

ERROLLYN WALLEN Belize-born British composer who was the first black woman to have a piece performed at the Proms (with Roger and Errollyn in the audience). They met through Roger's friends Laurence Aston and John L. Walters, and Errollyn introduced him to the Gogmagogs, for whom Roger became a trustee. He and

Errollyn were partners from 1997 to 1999. Her music featured in the opening of the 2012 Paralympic Games and has been played in space.

HANK WANGFORD See Sam Hutt.

MIKE and KATE WESTBROOK Mike Westbrook is a legendary jazz musician and composer; his wife, Kate, is a musician and painter. They met Roger when he invited them to perform at Snape Maltings in 1983, with Roger leading the Aldeburgh Foundation to commission a unique new piece of work, *A Young Person's Guide to the Jazz Orchestra*. The Westbrooks became friends with Roger who accompanied them on a musical tour of Prague. They also feature in *Waterlog*.

BUNDLE WESTON Bundle is the wife of Tony Weston (1941–2020), a friend of Roger from Haberdashers'. Bundle and Tony were the first of Roger's generation to move to the country and do up a ruined house, and provided Roger with continued inspiration over the years about how to escape the rat race. Bundle was a teacher; Tony was an accomplished potter and poet. Their daughter, Sophie Weston, has also contributed memories of Roger and his friends.

JULES WILKINSON A BBC radio journalist who became friends with Roger shortly before *Waterlog* was published and first got him on BBC Radio 4 programmes.

DUDLEY YOUNG (1941–2021) American-born author and lecturer in literature at Essex University (1968–2005), Dudley was an important influence and friend for Roger after they met in his final year at Peterhouse College, Cambridge, where Dudley embarked upon a PhD on Yeats. Roger sought Dudley's advice over *Waterlog* but they fell out soon afterwards. When I spoke to Dudley in 2021, he was sure they would've been close again.

ACKNOWLEDGEMENTS

In 2019, Lisa, my wife, spotted on an open-water swimming website that people could now stay at Roger Deakin's old place and swim in his moat. Knowing my fondness for Roger's books, and being a proper swimmer herself, Lisa booked us a night in Roger's railway wagon at Walnut Tree Farm. By coincidence, around the same time, I was emailed about a new book, *Life at Walnut Tree Farm*. Roger's son, Rufus Deakin, and Rufus's childhood friend Titus Rowlandson had published an excellent short history of the farm, with evocative old photographs of Roger's restoration. With my knack for turning fun into work, I persuaded the *Guardian*'s travel editor to let me write about our stay.

Ever since reading *Waterlog*, I had pictured Roger's frog's-eye view of his world, and its magic only deepened on reading Robert Macfarlane's *Wild Places* (2007) and *Landmarks* (2015). Even so, the reality of Walnut Tree Farm eclipsed my romantic imaginings. Titus and his wife, Jasmin, had resisted any temptation to gentrify Walnut Tree Farm, and the old house and fields still sang with what I imagined was the spirit of Roger.

I wondered why no one had written about his life and whether I could, and so I asked his literary executor, Robert Macfarlane, about it. First of all, deep thanks to Rob for considering me fit for the task, for his inspiring support and for helping this biography take root and later for his excellent creative suggestions to improve the book.

My next step was to travel to Spain to meet Roger's son, Rufus. Thanks to Rufus and his wife, Emily, for their hospitality and for being open to this idea. Rufus said he didn't want a hagiography, which stuck in my mind, and gave me a long list of his dad's many friends alongside a pithily perceptive assessment of each one. Over the coming months, he answered many more questions and kindly gave me access to a box of old notebooks and photographs that provided a great trove of insights. Thank you, Rufus.

The biography was offered to Simon Prosser at Hamish Hamilton who published *Wildwood* and *Notes from Walnut Tree Farm*, and enjoyed an excellent working relationship with Roger. I thank Simon for making another Roger book happen; for his wisdom, enthusiasm and acute editorial judgement, from the big picture to the line edit.

Roger's friends lived and thrived through collaboration and I took a collaborative approach to this biography which was both exhausting and rewarding, checking sections and the most sensitive passages with many people, particularly his lovers.

The global pandemic struck as I began my research but I beat the lockdown to meet Tony Axon, Roger's oldest friend, and enjoyed the first of many conversations. Exactly as Roger wrote, Tony is a wonderful storyteller. Over three years, I bombarded Tony with more 'Rog' emails and questions than anyone else, and I can't thank him enough really for his excellent answers, his sense of proportion and good humour.

My next interviewees were Titus and Jasmin Rowlandson, who have known Roger since they were teenagers, being childhood friends of Rufus. From the first moment, the Rowlandsons generously opened up their home, writing space, and their fields as a place for interviews. Titus's discovery of Roger's old iMac and overlooked school magazines in the loft provided me with a hugely important additional archive of his writing and he also helped me retrieve old photographs. Jazzy designed the brilliant endpapers to this book and was a source of uncanny emotional wisdom and knowledge. Thank you, Jazzy and Titus.

I first interviewed Serena Inskip at Walnut Tree Farm. Its pastures provided a tranquil space to discuss some of the difficulties she experienced with Roger. I'm extremely grateful to Serena for her courage, for her willingness to revisit traumatic experiences, for many hours of discussions over her contribution, and for trusting in my biographical process.

I would also particularly like to thank the following for discussing the joy and pain of sharing a life with Roger, and for sharing some of Roger's letters and photographs: Jenny Kember, Alison Hastie, Jo Southon, Annette Kobak and Margot Waddell. Between my first visit to Margot and my second, she was diagnosed with Alzheimer's, which is a particularly cruel fate for someone possessed of such a magnificent mind. As Margot's memory retreats, I am indebted to her children, Nicholas and Anna Waddell, for helping me navigate the past. Thank you.

Thanks to Terence Blacker, who read a draft of the biography and provided me with much astute guidance as well as a robust critique.

All the above join a long list of Roger's friends and family who have spent hours being interviewed by me, sometimes on multiple occasions, over three years. In the order that I first spoke to them, thanks so much to the following for their memories, honesty, time and hospitality (a trip to meet one of Roger's friends usually involves departing laden with cake or apples or runner beans or home-made chutney or some other undeserved gift from the garden):

Rufus Deakin

Tony Axon

Jasmin and Titus Rowlandson

Serena Inskip

Richard Mabey

Gary and Viva Rowland

Terence Blacker and Angela Sykes

Jayne Ivimey

Alison Hastie

Ronnie Blythe

Margot Waddell

Peter and Joao Smith

Ramona Koval

Jenny Kember

Julia Blackburn

John and Jenny Farley

Eddie and Christine Lanchester

Meg Amsden and Tim Hunkin

Lucy Bailey

Andrew Sanders

Rob Parfitt and Christine Smith

Rosie Jackson

Bob Marshall-Andrews

Bundle Weston and Sophie Weston

Mike and Kate Westbrook

Sue Clifford and Angela King

Lucy Thwaite

Andrew Cracknell

Pippa Cracknell

Anne Crawford

Mike Southon

Laurence Aston

Sir Christopher Meyer

Sam Hutt

Emma Bernard

Steve Ashley

Charles Anson

Caroline Soper

Holly Kerr

Simon Poulter

Graham 'Ben' Barker-Benfield

Bullus Hutton

Tracy Sharp

Michael Hollington

Vicky Minet

Jo Rolfe

Peter Berglund

Dudley Young

Richard Handford

Sue Roe

Robert Macfarlane

Erica Burt

Mike Brearley

Annette Kobak

Mike Dibb

Jules Cashford

Toby Kidd

Bill Seaman

Mary Todd

Jasper Parrott

Debbie Bartlett

Andrew 'Roon' Hutton

Andrew Crook

Ian Crook

Matt Marchbank

George Peterken

Barry Goater

Caroline Clifton-Mogg

Sarah Dickinson

Nigel Brown

Ken Barrell
Rosemary Palmer
Sarah Crawford
Ian Baker
John Huggins
Sue Reid
Mavis Cheek
Tim Rayner
Anna Waddell
Jo Southon
May Ling Cadwallader
Jules Wilkinson
Gilbert Reid
John Mills
Jane Turnbull
Brian Perman
Jonathan Burnham
Sarah Blunt
Rebecca Carter
Simon Prosser
Richard Cook
John Bayley
Andrea Arnold
Jane Norris
Alison Mitchell
Nicholas Waddell
Ben Harker
Georgina Capel
Celia
Lucy Moy-Thomas
Claire Mortimer

*

Of Roger's many friends, Andrew Cracknell has been tremendously funny and helped lift the veil on Roger's rather mysterious advertising career. Gary and Viva Rowland have been extremely helpful and perspicacious; thank you, Gary, for the cover shot. I am indebted to Michael Hollington for his insights and also for digging into his annals of Haberdashers' magazine, *Skylark*, on my behalf. I would also like to particularly thank some of Roger's female friends for their wisdom – Bundle Weston, Jules Cashford, Jayne Ivimey, Julia Blackburn and Vicky Minet, thank you.

Thanks to Bundle for permission to reproduce Tony Weston's poems, and Jane Norris for permission to quote from Tony Barrell's unpublished memoirs.

Thanks also to Errollyn Wallen, Joe Gibbs, Peter Smith (for sharing his superb photographs), Polly Lavender, Clare Crick, Paul Willetts, Lesley Ward, John Blagden, Rodney Jakeman, Kevin Tierney, Hugh Thomson, Simon Hattenstone, Joe Minihane and Brian Guthrie for their help and information.

Under Robert Macfarlane's guidance, Roger's barn-load of notebooks, diaries and papers were lodged in an archive at the University of East Anglia. The archivists Justine Mann and Bridget Gillies have been fantastically help-ful, and I thank them for giving me access to this fabulous trove in a time of coronavirus, for retrieving so much, and for making the UEA library a pleas-ure to work within.

Another blessing was to discover that the History of Advertising Trust has its unique archive tucked away in the Norfolk countryside not far from my home – thanks to archivist Eve Read and her colleagues for their invaluable help.

Many thanks to the East Anglian Film Archive for providing digital ver-sions of Roger's fabulous documentaries. Sincere thanks to Haberdashers' archivist Carmel du Parc Braham for the superb gift of Roger's report card (what a gem!) and to Haberdashers' old-boys liaison officer Roger Llewellyn for his help in locating old boys who provided some excellent insights. Thanks to Peterhouse College, Cambridge, for spreading the word among alumni who also provided some nice insights into college life between 1961 and 1964.

Thanks to my *Guardian* editor Natalie Hanman and managing editor Sheila Pulham for granting me unpaid leave to finish this book, and thanks to my *Guardian* colleagues for their comradeship.

When I began writing, I somehow obtained a residential retreat at the Jan Michalski Foundation in Switzerland. Thanks to Vera Michalski-Hoffmann, Chantal Buffet and Guillaume Dollmann and the wonderful writers and translators I shared time with there: my three weeks writing were a dream of focused intensity and brief refreshment in the forests, where I bumped into a lynx for the first and probably only time.

Thanks to the editorial team at Hamish Hamilton who worked so tirelessly on this complicated book, including editor Hannah Chukwu, editorial assistant Ruby Fatimilehin and copyeditor Sarah-Jane Forder, who saved me from more than a few blushes, as well as a few hundred repetitions. Thanks to managing editorial director Emma Brown, Jon Gray for his cover design, and associate publisher Anna Ridley and Hayley Cox for masterminding publicity.

And finally, thank you to my family: Suzanne Barkham, John Barkham (my first reader), Henrietta Barkham, Carla and Amelie Barkham, Jan and Rob Palmer, Andrew, Jess, Imogen and Ella Walpole, Kevin and Eve Walpole, and especially Lisa Walpole (who guided me towards the title) and our children, Milly, Esme and Ted. 'Roger, Roger, Roger. All you talk about is Roger. Can you stop now?' I've been touched by him but yes, I can stop now.